The Best Of
Alex
2014

Russell Taylor

Charles Peattie

Charles Peattie & Russell Taylor

Masterley Publishing

The Best Of

Alex

2014

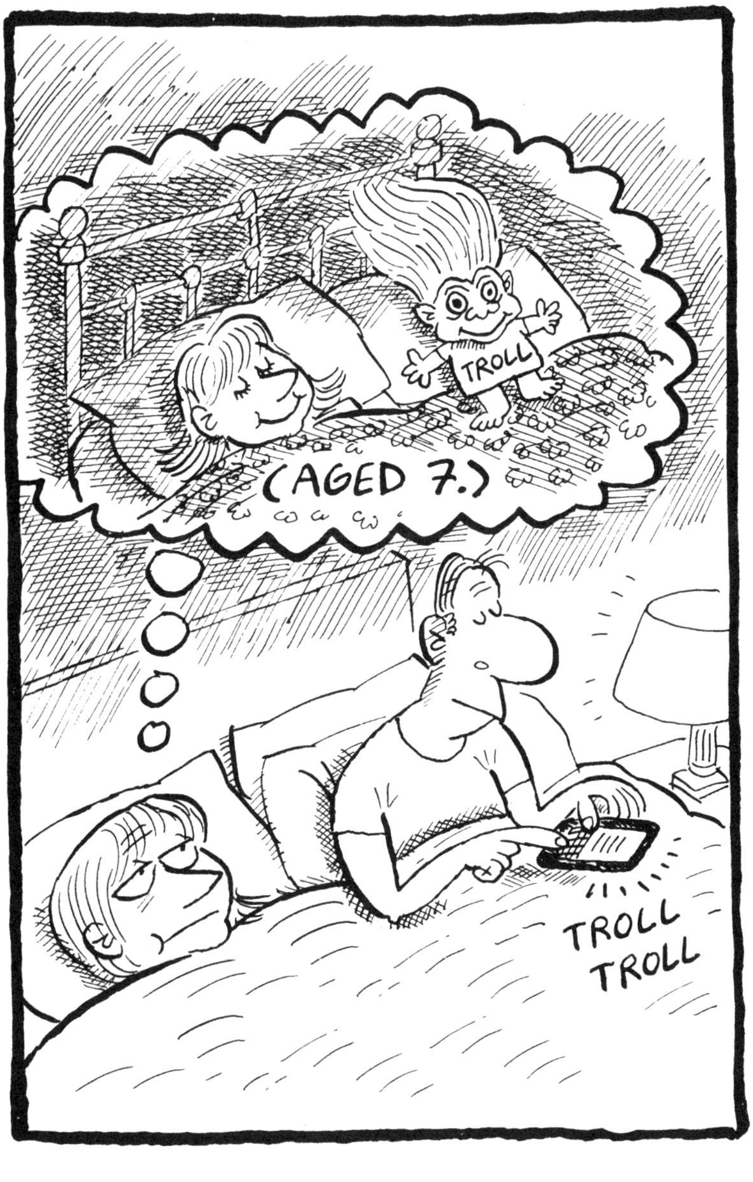
TROLL
(AGED 7.)
TROLL
TROLL

First Published in 2014 by MASTERLEY PUBLISHING

Layout and Artwork: Suzette Field and Louise Newton

ISBN: 978-1853759161

Printed in the UK by CPI William Clowes Beccles NR34 7TL

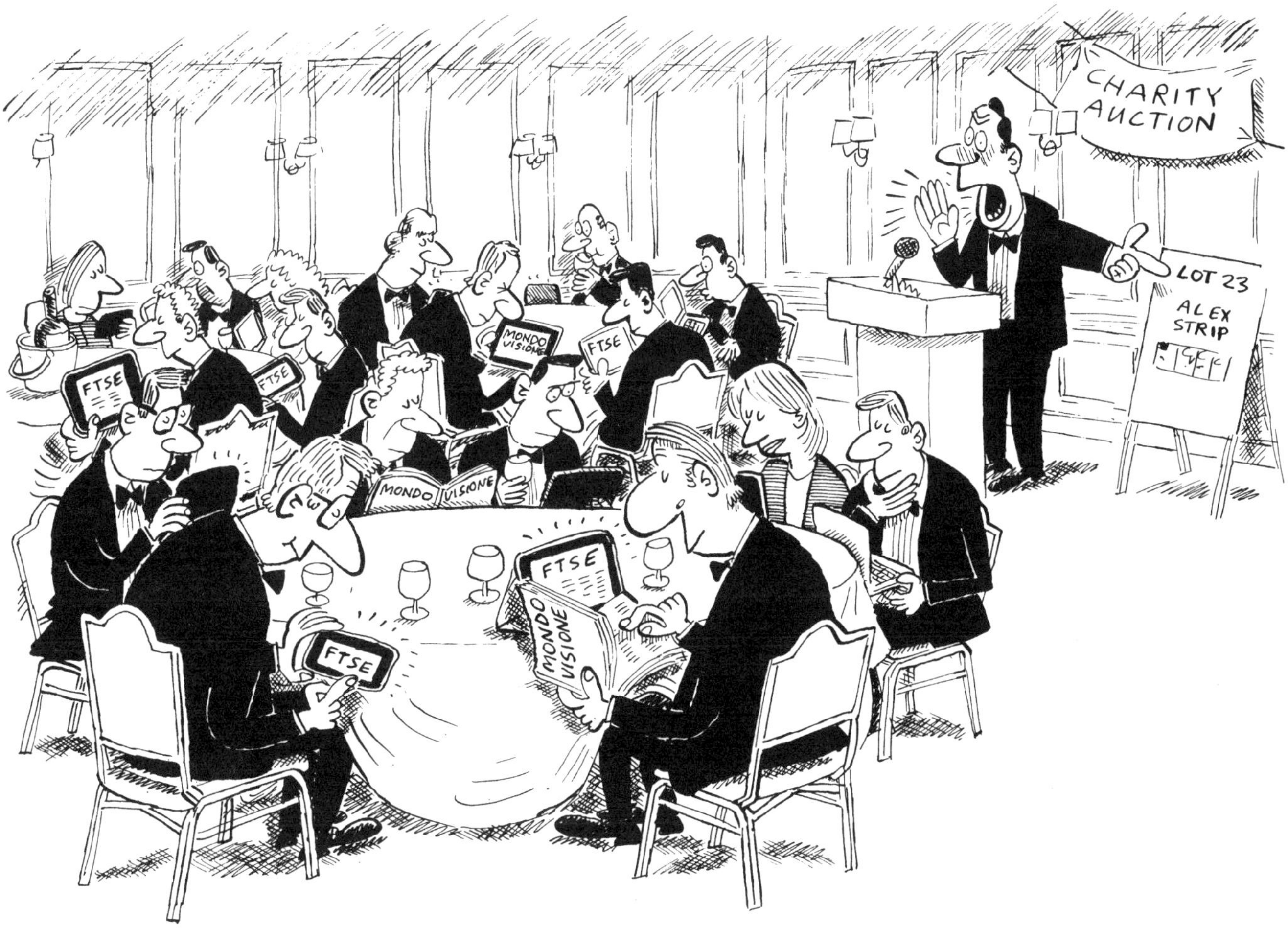
CHARITY AUCTION
LOT 23
ALEX STRIP
FTSE
MONDO VISIONE
FTSE
FTSE
MONDO VISIONE
FTSE
FTSE
MONDO VISIONE
FTSE

Our usual gratitude goes to our generous sponsors.

FTSE Group (FTSE) is the world-leader in the creation and management of index solutions.

Mondo Visione provides vital knowledge about the world's exchanges and trading venues.

FOREWORD

If you've received this book in your Christmas stocking you might want to think before reading any further. Should you not declare it to compliance? It is after all a gift, so might it represent an inducement? Perhaps it is a present from a contact in the professional world who is angling for your business. Or maybe just from a relative with the intention of instilling in you some Yuletide good cheer. In either case this would constitute a gross breach of regulations. If your family hear any sounds of mirth emanating from your smallest room on Boxing Day they may have to turn you in.

But if you do decide to declare this book to compliance, just consider all the tedious and time-consuming forms you will have to fill out. All that box-ticking for an item worth £9.99 (or whatever scandalous price Amazon has discounted it to). Frankly it might be easier just to fob this tainted freebie off on a niece or nephew and go out and buy your own copy.

Luckily cartooning is not yet a regulated industry, so that fact that the advice we are here offering you is totally self-serving and will directly lead to our own financial advancement by doubling the amount we earn in royalties is quite immaterial.

While on this subject we should also warn you to be vigilant about the giving or receipt of hospitality over the festive season. For example any instance of carol singers visiting houses and singing songs in exchange for mince pies and mulled wine should be escalated to compliance immediately. You should also report it if you find a silver sixpence in your slice of the Christmas pudding, which would clearly be in contravention of the Bribery Act, not to mention Health and Safety.

May we take this opportunity to wish you a very merry and fully compliant Christmas.

Charles Peattie and Russell Taylor

Alex - Investment banker

Penny - Alex's wife

Christopher - their son

Clive - Alex's colleague

Bridget - Clive's wife

Rupert - Senior banker

Cyrus - Alex's boss

Nigel & Philip - gay bankers

Hardcastle - Alex's client

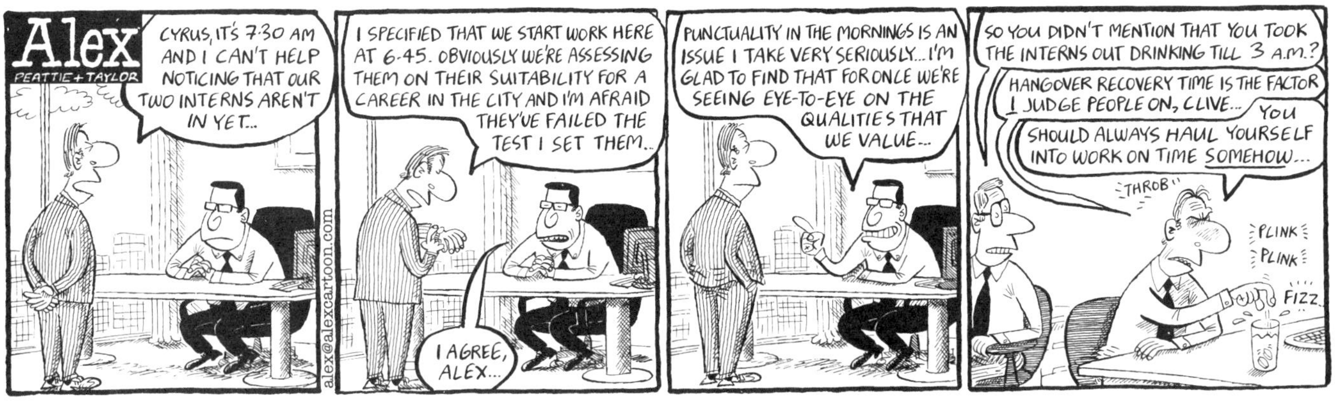
Alex
PEATTIE + TAYLOR
CYRUS, IT'S 7:30 AM AND I CAN'T HELP NOTICING THAT OUR TWO INTERNS AREN'T IN YET...
alex@alexcartoon.com
I SPECIFIED THAT WE START WORK HERE AT 6.45. OBVIOUSLY WE'RE ASSESSING THEM ON THEIR SUITABILITY FOR A CAREER IN THE CITY AND I'M AFRAID THEY'VE FAILED THE TEST I SET THEM...
I AGREE, ALEX...
PUNCTUALITY IN THE MORNINGS IS AN ISSUE I TAKE VERY SERIOUSLY... I'M GLAD TO FIND THAT FOR ONCE WE'RE SEEING EYE-TO-EYE ON THE QUALITIES THAT WE VALUE...
SO YOU DIDN'T MENTION THAT YOU TOOK THE INTERNS OUT DRINKING TILL 3 A.M.?
HANGOVER RECOVERY TIME IS THE FACTOR I JUDGE PEOPLE ON, CLIVE... YOU SHOULD ALWAYS HAUL YOURSELF INTO WORK ON TIME SOMEHOW...
THROB
PLINK
PLINK
FIZZ

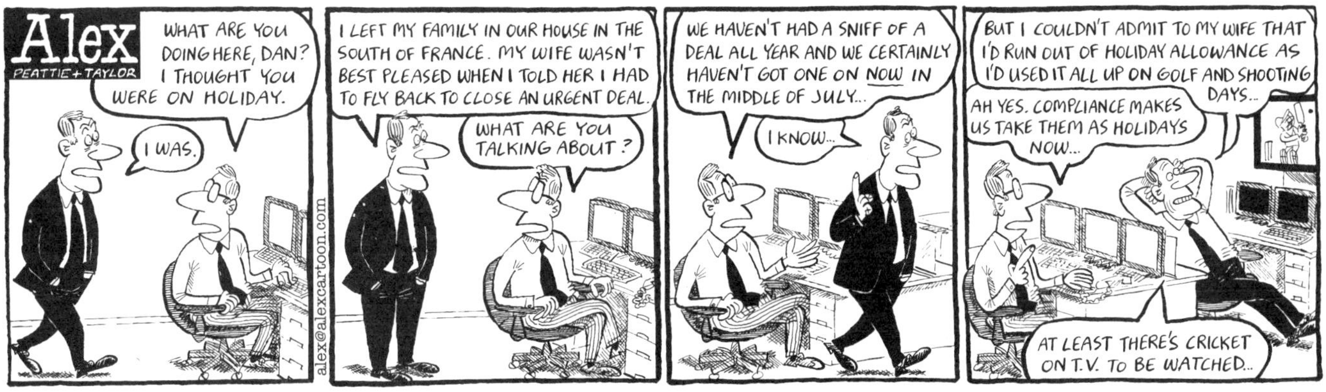
Alex
PEATTIE + TAYLOR
WHAT ARE YOU DOING HERE, DAN? I THOUGHT YOU WERE ON HOLIDAY.
I WAS.
alex@alexcartoon.com
I LEFT MY FAMILY IN OUR HOUSE IN THE SOUTH OF FRANCE. MY WIFE WASN'T BEST PLEASED WHEN I TOLD HER I HAD TO FLY BACK TO CLOSE AN URGENT DEAL.
WHAT ARE YOU TALKING ABOUT?
WE HAVEN'T HAD A SNIFF OF A DEAL ALL YEAR AND WE CERTAINLY HAVEN'T GOT ONE ON NOW IN THE MIDDLE OF JULY...
I KNOW...
BUT I COULDN'T ADMIT TO MY WIFE THAT I'D RUN OUT OF HOLIDAY ALLOWANCE AS I'D USED IT ALL UP ON GOLF AND SHOOTING DAYS...
AH YES. COMPLIANCE MAKES US TAKE THEM AS HOLIDAYS NOW...
AT LEAST THERE'S CRICKET ON T.V. TO BE WATCHED...

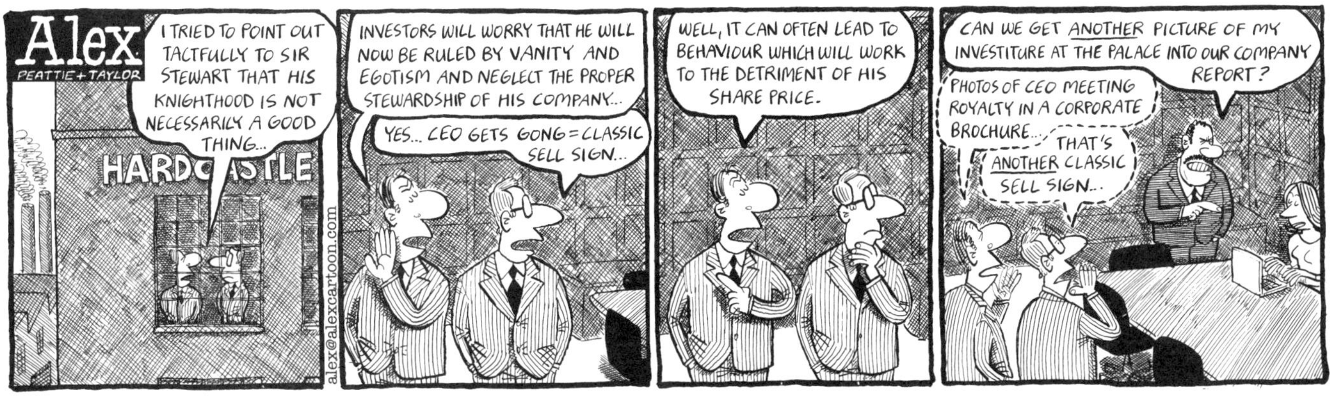
Alex
PEATTIE + TAYLOR
I TRIED TO POINT OUT TACTFULLY TO SIR STEWART THAT HIS KNIGHTHOOD IS NOT NECESSARILY A GOOD THING...
HARDCASTLE
alex@alexcartoon.com
INVESTORS WILL WORRY THAT HE WILL NOW BE RULED BY VANITY AND EGOTISM AND NEGLECT THE PROPER STEWARDSHIP OF HIS COMPANY...
YES... CEO GETS GONG = CLASSIC SELL SIGN...
WELL, IT CAN OFTEN LEAD TO BEHAVIOUR WHICH WILL WORK TO THE DETRIMENT OF HIS SHARE PRICE.
CAN WE GET ANOTHER PICTURE OF MY INVESTITURE AT THE PALACE INTO OUR COMPANY REPORT?
PHOTOS OF CEO MEETING ROYALTY IN A CORPORATE BROCHURE...
THAT'S ANOTHER CLASSIC SELL SIGN...

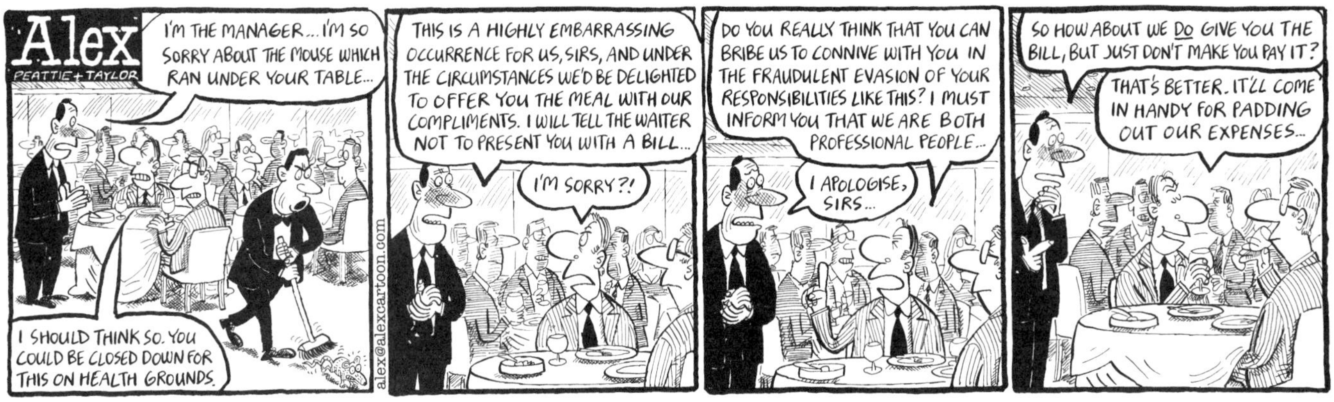
Alex
PEATTIE + TAYLOR
I'M THE MANAGER... I'M SO SORRY ABOUT THE MOUSE WHICH RAN UNDER YOUR TABLE...
I SHOULD THINK SO. YOU COULD BE CLOSED DOWN FOR THIS ON HEALTH GROUNDS.
alex@alexcartoon.com
THIS IS A HIGHLY EMBARRASSING OCCURRENCE FOR US, SIRS, AND UNDER THE CIRCUMSTANCES WE'D BE DELIGHTED TO OFFER YOU THE MEAL WITH OUR COMPLIMENTS. I WILL TELL THE WAITER NOT TO PRESENT YOU WITH A BILL...
I'M SORRY?!
DO YOU REALLY THINK THAT YOU CAN BRIBE US TO CONNIVE WITH YOU IN THE FRAUDULENT EVASION OF YOUR RESPONSIBILITIES LIKE THIS? I MUST INFORM YOU THAT WE ARE BOTH PROFESSIONAL PEOPLE...
I APOLOGISE, SIRS...
SO HOW ABOUT WE DO GIVE YOU THE BILL, BUT JUST DON'T MAKE YOU PAY IT?
THAT'S BETTER. IT'LL COME IN HANDY FOR PADDING OUT OUR EXPENSES...

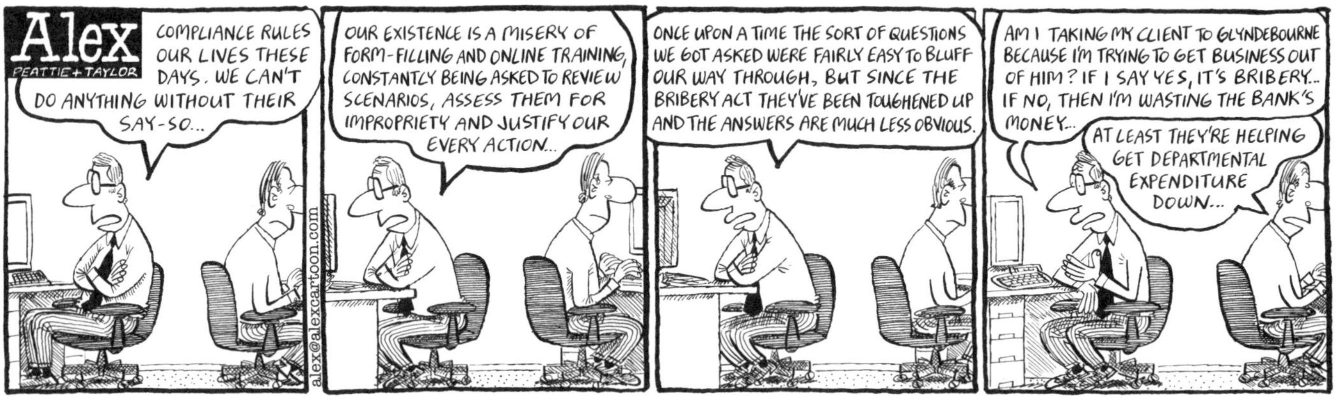
Alex
PEATTIE+TAYLOR
COMPLIANCE RULES OUR LIVES THESE DAYS. WE CAN'T DO ANYTHING WITHOUT THEIR SAY-SO...
alex@alexcartoon.com
OUR EXISTENCE IS A MISERY OF FORM-FILLING AND ONLINE TRAINING, CONSTANTLY BEING ASKED TO REVIEW SCENARIOS, ASSESS THEM FOR IMPROPRIETY AND JUSTIFY OUR EVERY ACTION...
ONCE UPON A TIME THE SORT OF QUESTIONS WE GOT ASKED WERE FAIRLY EASY TO BLUFF OUR WAY THROUGH, BUT SINCE THE BRIBERY ACT THEY'VE BEEN TOUGHENED UP AND THE ANSWERS ARE MUCH LESS OBVIOUS.
AM I TAKING MY CLIENT TO GLYNDEBOURNE BECAUSE I'M TRYING TO GET BUSINESS OUT OF HIM? IF I SAY YES, IT'S BRIBERY... IF NO, THEN I'M WASTING THE BANK'S MONEY...
AT LEAST THEY'RE HELPING GET DEPARTMENTAL EXPENDITURE DOWN...

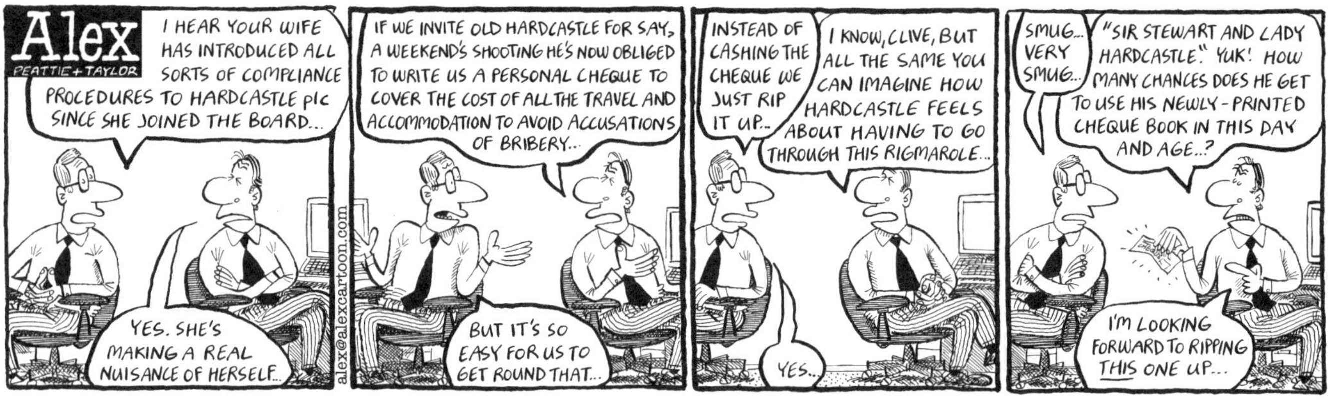
Alex
PEATTIE+TAYLOR
I HEAR YOUR WIFE HAS INTRODUCED ALL SORTS OF COMPLIANCE PROCEDURES TO HARDCASTLE plc SINCE SHE JOINED THE BOARD...
YES. SHE'S MAKING A REAL NUISANCE OF HERSELF...
alex@alexcartoon.com
IF WE INVITE OLD HARDCASTLE FOR SAY, A WEEKEND'S SHOOTING HE'S NOW OBLIGED TO WRITE US A PERSONAL CHEQUE TO COVER THE COST OF ALL THE TRAVEL AND ACCOMMODATION TO AVOID ACCUSATIONS OF BRIBERY...
BUT IT'S SO EASY FOR US TO GET ROUND THAT...
INSTEAD OF CASHING THE CHEQUE WE JUST RIP IT UP...
I KNOW, CLIVE, BUT ALL THE SAME YOU CAN IMAGINE HOW HARDCASTLE FEELS ABOUT HAVING TO GO THROUGH THIS RIGMAROLE...
YES...
SMUG... VERY SMUG...
"SIR STEWART AND LADY HARDCASTLE." YUK! HOW MANY CHANCES DOES HE GET TO USE HIS NEWLY-PRINTED CHEQUE BOOK IN THIS DAY AND AGE...?
I'M LOOKING FORWARD TO RIPPING THIS ONE UP...

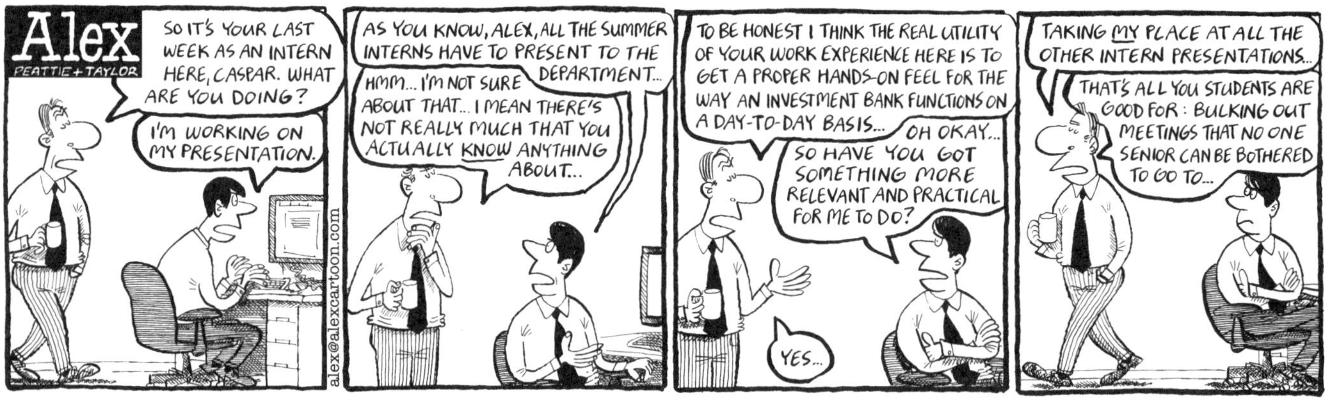
Alex
PEATTIE+TAYLOR
SO IT'S YOUR LAST WEEK AS AN INTERN HERE, CASPAR. WHAT ARE YOU DOING?
I'M WORKING ON MY PRESENTATION.
alex@alexcartoon.com
AS YOU KNOW, ALEX, ALL THE SUMMER INTERNS HAVE TO PRESENT TO THE DEPARTMENT...
HMM... I'M NOT SURE ABOUT THAT... I MEAN THERE'S NOT REALLY MUCH THAT YOU ACTUALLY KNOW ANYTHING ABOUT...
TO BE HONEST I THINK THE REAL UTILITY OF YOUR WORK EXPERIENCE HERE IS TO GET A PROPER HANDS-ON FEEL FOR THE WAY AN INVESTMENT BANK FUNCTIONS ON A DAY-TO-DAY BASIS...
OH OKAY... SO HAVE YOU GOT SOMETHING MORE RELEVANT AND PRACTICAL FOR ME TO DO?
YES...
TAKING MY PLACE AT ALL THE OTHER INTERN PRESENTATIONS...
THAT'S ALL YOU STUDENTS ARE GOOD FOR: BULKING OUT MEETINGS THAT NO ONE SENIOR CAN BE BOTHERED TO GO TO...

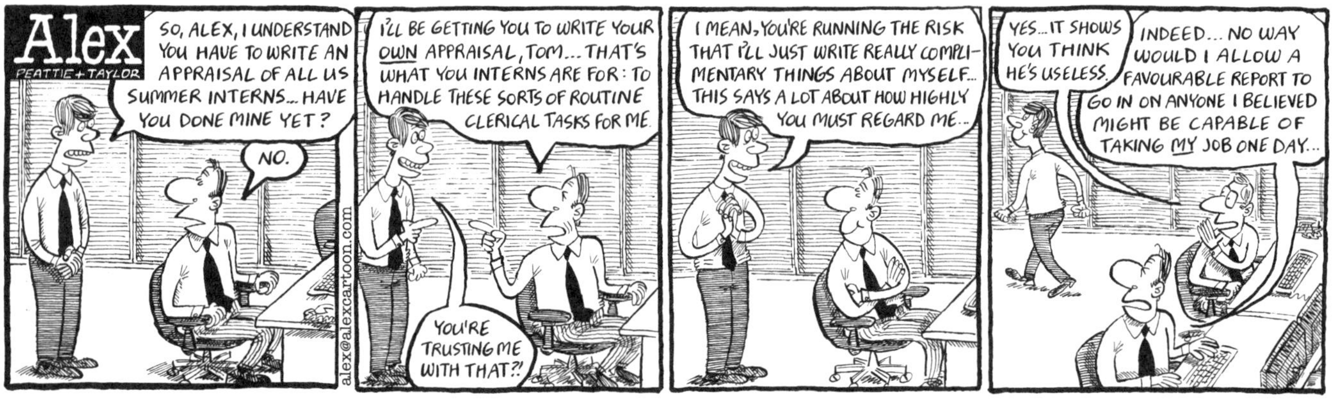
Alex
PEATTIE+TAYLOR
SO, ALEX, I UNDERSTAND YOU HAVE TO WRITE AN APPRAISAL OF ALL US SUMMER INTERNS... HAVE YOU DONE MINE YET?
NO.
alex@alexcartoon.com
I'LL BE GETTING YOU TO WRITE YOUR OWN APPRAISAL, TOM... THAT'S WHAT YOU INTERNS ARE FOR: TO HANDLE THESE SORTS OF ROUTINE CLERICAL TASKS FOR ME.
YOU'RE TRUSTING ME WITH THAT?!
I MEAN, YOU'RE RUNNING THE RISK THAT I'LL JUST WRITE REALLY COMPLIMENTARY THINGS ABOUT MYSELF... THIS SAYS A LOT ABOUT HOW HIGHLY YOU MUST REGARD ME...
YES... IT SHOWS YOU THINK HE'S USELESS.
INDEED... NO WAY WOULD I ALLOW A FAVOURABLE REPORT TO GO IN ON ANYONE I BELIEVED MIGHT BE CAPABLE OF TAKING MY JOB ONE DAY...

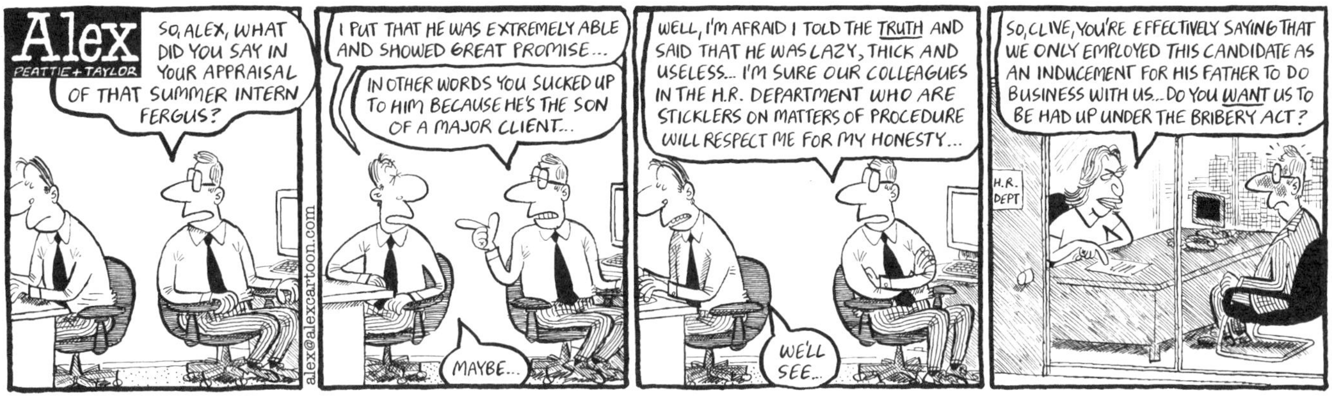
Alex
PEATTIE + TAYLOR
SO, ALEX, WHAT DID YOU SAY IN YOUR APPRAISAL OF THAT SUMMER INTERN FERGUS?
I PUT THAT HE WAS EXTREMELY ABLE AND SHOWED GREAT PROMISE...
IN OTHER WORDS YOU SUCKED UP TO HIM BECAUSE HE'S THE SON OF A MAJOR CLIENT...
MAYBE...
alex@alexcartoon.com
WELL, I'M AFRAID I TOLD THE TRUTH AND SAID THAT HE WAS LAZY, THICK AND USELESS... I'M SURE OUR COLLEAGUES IN THE H.R. DEPARTMENT WHO ARE STICKLERS ON MATTERS OF PROCEDURE WILL RESPECT ME FOR MY HONESTY...
WE'LL SEE...
SO, CLIVE, YOU'RE EFFECTIVELY SAYING THAT WE ONLY EMPLOYED THIS CANDIDATE AS AN INDUCEMENT FOR HIS FATHER TO DO BUSINESS WITH US... DO YOU WANT US TO BE HAD UP UNDER THE BRIBERY ACT?
H.R. DEPT

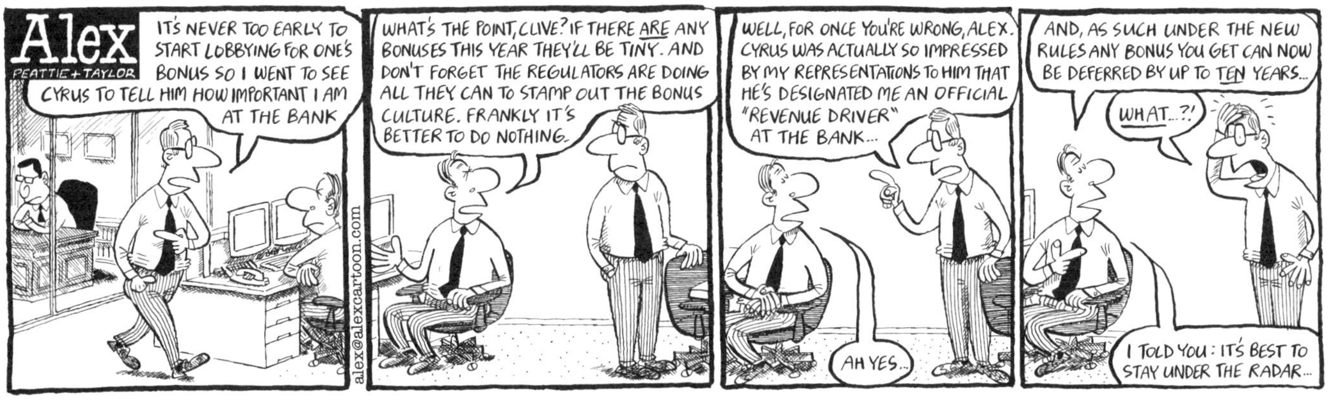
Alex
PEATTIE + TAYLOR
IT'S NEVER TOO EARLY TO START LOBBYING FOR ONE'S BONUS SO I WENT TO SEE CYRUS TO TELL HIM HOW IMPORTANT I AM AT THE BANK
alex@alexcartoon.com
WHAT'S THE POINT, CLIVE? IF THERE ARE ANY BONUSES THIS YEAR THEY'LL BE TINY. AND DON'T FORGET THE REGULATORS ARE DOING ALL THEY CAN TO STAMP OUT THE BONUS CULTURE. FRANKLY IT'S BETTER TO DO NOTHING.
WELL, FOR ONCE YOU'RE WRONG, ALEX. CYRUS WAS ACTUALLY SO IMPRESSED BY MY REPRESENTATIONS TO HIM THAT HE'S DESIGNATED ME AN OFFICIAL "REVENUE DRIVER" AT THE BANK...
AH YES...
AND, AS SUCH UNDER THE NEW RULES ANY BONUS YOU GET CAN NOW BE DEFERRED BY UP TO TEN YEARS...
WHAT...?!
I TOLD YOU: IT'S BEST TO STAY UNDER THE RADAR...

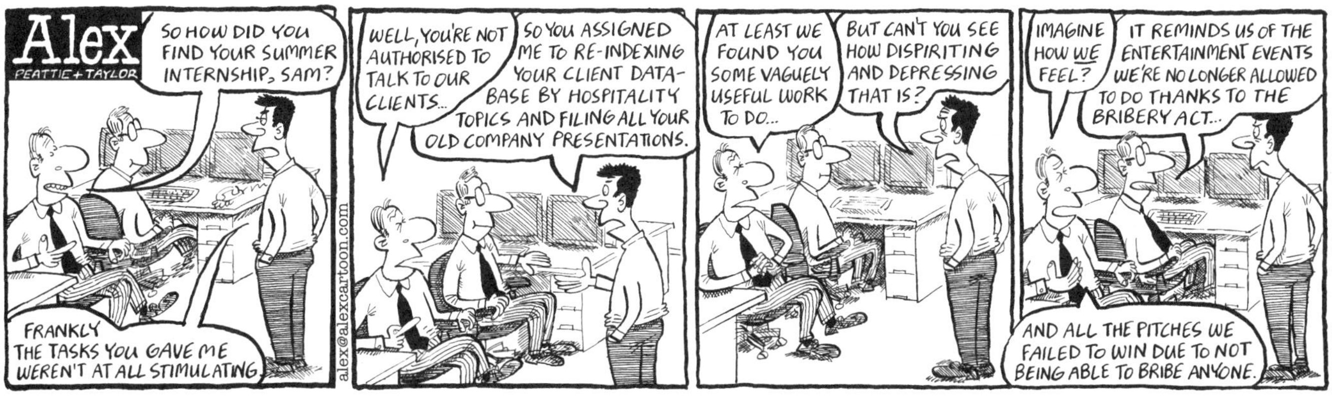
Alex
PEATTIE + TAYLOR
SO HOW DID YOU FIND YOUR SUMMER INTERNSHIP, SAM?
FRANKLY THE TASKS YOU GAVE ME WEREN'T AT ALL STIMULATING.
alex@alexcartoon.com
SO YOU ASSIGNED ME TO RE-INDEXING YOUR CLIENT DATA-BASE BY HOSPITALITY TOPICS AND FILING ALL YOUR OLD COMPANY PRESENTATIONS.
WELL, YOU'RE NOT AUTHORISED TO TALK TO OUR CLIENTS...
BUT CAN'T YOU SEE HOW DISPIRITING AND DEPRESSING THAT IS?
AT LEAST WE FOUND YOU SOME VAGUELY USEFUL WORK TO DO...
IMAGINE HOW WE FEEL?
IT REMINDS US OF THE ENTERTAINMENT EVENTS WE'RE NO LONGER ALLOWED TO DO THANKS TO THE BRIBERY ACT...
AND ALL THE PITCHES WE FAILED TO WIN DUE TO NOT BEING ABLE TO BRIBE ANYONE.

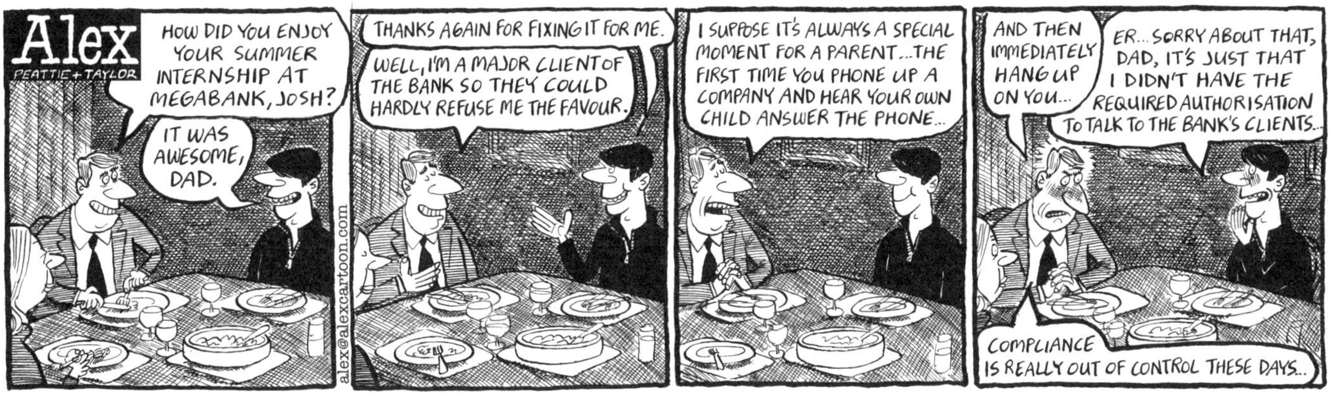
Alex
PEATTIE + TAYLOR
HOW DID YOU ENJOY YOUR SUMMER INTERNSHIP AT MEGABANK, JOSH?
IT WAS AWESOME, DAD.
alex@alexcartoon.com
THANKS AGAIN FOR FIXING IT FOR ME.
WELL, I'M A MAJOR CLIENT OF THE BANK SO THEY COULD HARDLY REFUSE ME THE FAVOUR.
I SUPPOSE IT'S ALWAYS A SPECIAL MOMENT FOR A PARENT... THE FIRST TIME YOU PHONE UP A COMPANY AND HEAR YOUR OWN CHILD ANSWER THE PHONE...
AND THEN IMMEDIATELY HANG UP ON YOU...
ER... SORRY ABOUT THAT, DAD, IT'S JUST THAT I DIDN'T HAVE THE REQUIRED AUTHORISATION TO TALK TO THE BANK'S CLIENTS...
COMPLIANCE IS REALLY OUT OF CONTROL THESE DAYS...

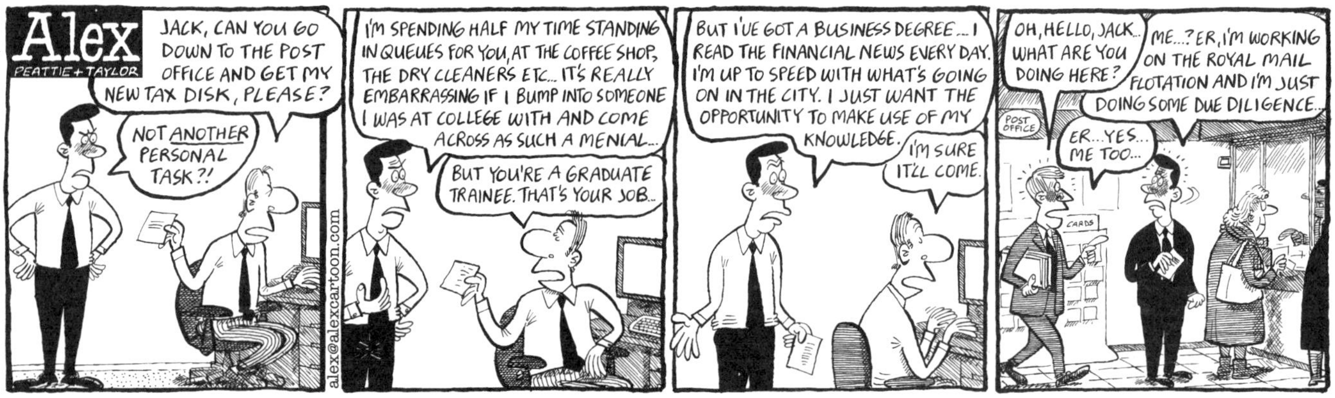
Alex
PEATTIE+TAYLOR
JACK, CAN YOU GO DOWN TO THE POST OFFICE AND GET MY NEW TAX DISK, PLEASE?
NOT ANOTHER PERSONAL TASK?!
alex@alexcartoon.com
I'M SPENDING HALF MY TIME STANDING IN QUEUES FOR YOU, AT THE COFFEE SHOP, THE DRY CLEANERS ETC... IT'S REALLY EMBARRASSING IF I BUMP INTO SOMEONE I WAS AT COLLEGE WITH AND COME ACROSS AS SUCH A MENIAL...
BUT YOU'RE A GRADUATE TRAINEE. THAT'S YOUR JOB...
BUT I'VE GOT A BUSINESS DEGREE... I READ THE FINANCIAL NEWS EVERY DAY. I'M UP TO SPEED WITH WHAT'S GOING ON IN THE CITY. I JUST WANT THE OPPORTUNITY TO MAKE USE OF MY KNOWLEDGE.
I'M SURE IT'LL COME.
OH, HELLO, JACK... WHAT ARE YOU DOING HERE?
ME...? ER, I'M WORKING ON THE ROYAL MAIL FLOTATION AND I'M JUST DOING SOME DUE DILIGENCE...
ER... YES... ME TOO...
POST OFFICE
CARDS

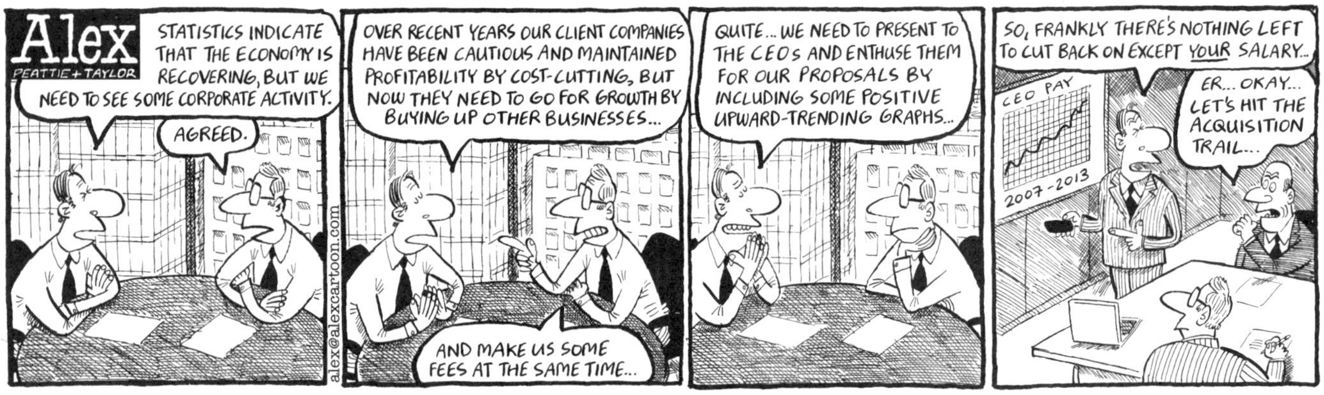
Alex
PEATTIE+TAYLOR
STATISTICS INDICATE THAT THE ECONOMY IS RECOVERING, BUT WE NEED TO SEE SOME CORPORATE ACTIVITY.
AGREED.
alex@alexcartoon.com
OVER RECENT YEARS OUR CLIENT COMPANIES HAVE BEEN CAUTIOUS AND MAINTAINED PROFITABILITY BY COST-CUTTING, BUT NOW THEY NEED TO GO FOR GROWTH BY BUYING UP OTHER BUSINESSES...
AND MAKE US SOME FEES AT THE SAME TIME...
QUITE... WE NEED TO PRESENT TO THE CEOs AND ENTHUSE THEM FOR OUR PROPOSALS BY INCLUDING SOME POSITIVE UPWARD-TRENDING GRAPHS...
SO, FRANKLY THERE'S NOTHING LEFT TO CUT BACK ON EXCEPT YOUR SALARY...
CEO PAY
2007-2013
ER... OKAY... LET'S HIT THE ACQUISITION TRAIL...

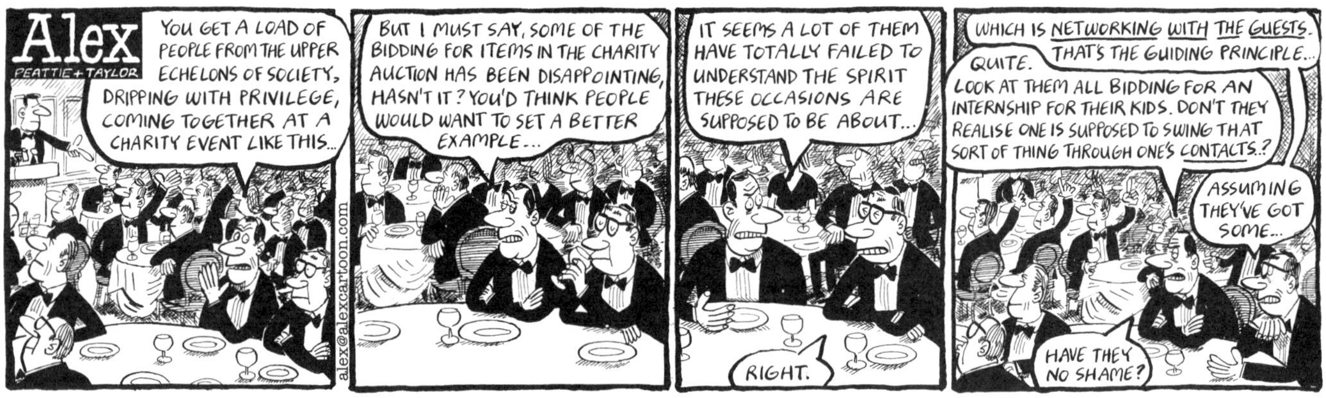
Alex
PEATTIE+TAYLOR
YOU GET A LOAD OF PEOPLE FROM THE UPPER ECHELONS OF SOCIETY, DRIPPING WITH PRIVILEGE, COMING TOGETHER AT A CHARITY EVENT LIKE THIS...
alex@alexcartoon.com
BUT I MUST SAY, SOME OF THE BIDDING FOR ITEMS IN THE CHARITY AUCTION HAS BEEN DISAPPOINTING, HASN'T IT? YOU'D THINK PEOPLE WOULD WANT TO SET A BETTER EXAMPLE...
IT SEEMS A LOT OF THEM HAVE TOTALLY FAILED TO UNDERSTAND THE SPIRIT THESE OCCASIONS ARE SUPPOSED TO BE ABOUT...
RIGHT.
WHICH IS NETWORKING WITH THE GUESTS. THAT'S THE GUIDING PRINCIPLE...
QUITE.
LOOK AT THEM ALL BIDDING FOR AN INTERNSHIP FOR THEIR KIDS. DON'T THEY REALISE ONE IS SUPPOSED TO SWING THAT SORT OF THING THROUGH ONE'S CONTACTS.?
ASSUMING THEY'VE GOT SOME...
HAVE THEY NO SHAME?

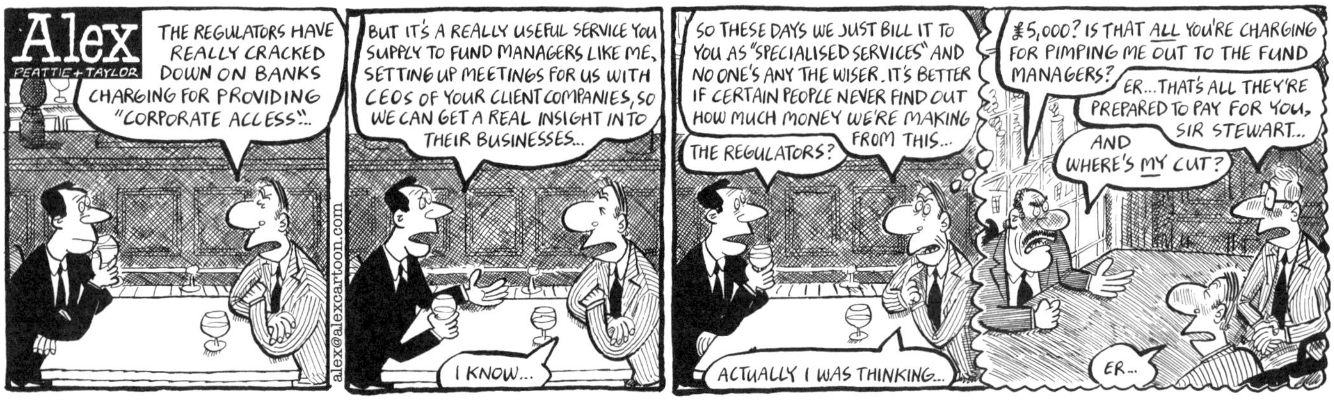
Alex
PEATTIE+TAYLOR
THE REGULATORS HAVE REALLY CRACKED DOWN ON BANKS CHARGING FOR PROVIDING "CORPORATE ACCESS"...
alex@alexcartoon.com
BUT IT'S A REALLY USEFUL SERVICE YOU SUPPLY TO FUND MANAGERS LIKE ME, SETTING UP MEETINGS FOR US WITH CEOS OF YOUR CLIENT COMPANIES, SO WE CAN GET A REAL INSIGHT INTO THEIR BUSINESSES...
I KNOW...
SO THESE DAYS WE JUST BILL IT TO YOU AS "SPECIALISED SERVICES" AND NO ONE'S ANY THE WISER. IT'S BETTER IF CERTAIN PEOPLE NEVER FIND OUT HOW MUCH MONEY WE'RE MAKING FROM THIS...
THE REGULATORS?
ACTUALLY I WAS THINKING...
£5,000? IS THAT ALL YOU'RE CHARGING FOR PIMPING ME OUT TO THE FUND MANAGERS?
ER... THAT'S ALL THEY'RE PREPARED TO PAY FOR YOU, SIR STEWART...
AND WHERE'S MY CUT?
ER...

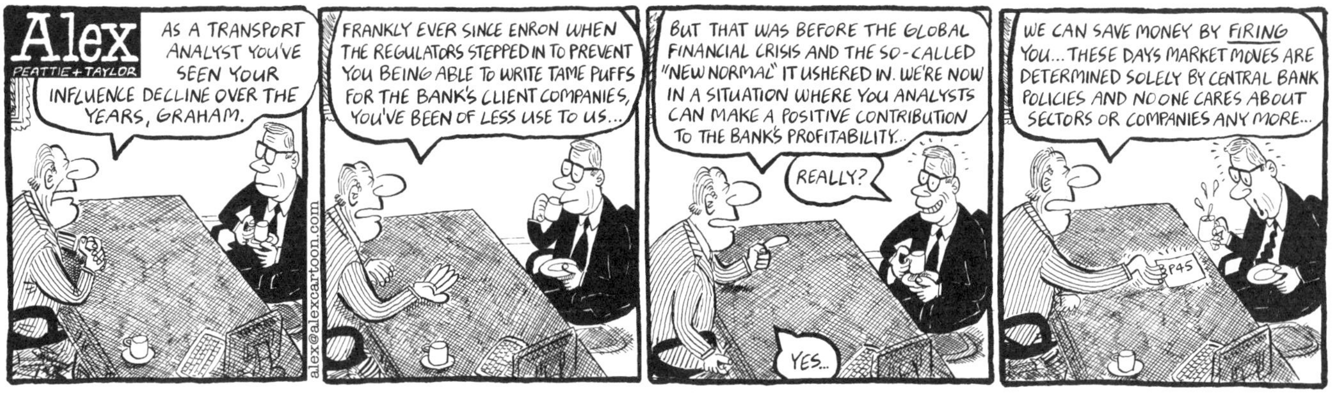
Alex
PEATTIE + TAYLOR
AS A TRANSPORT ANALYST YOU'VE SEEN YOUR INFLUENCE DECLINE OVER THE YEARS, GRAHAM.
FRANKLY EVER SINCE ENRON WHEN THE REGULATORS STEPPED IN TO PREVENT YOU BEING ABLE TO WRITE TAME PUFFS FOR THE BANK'S CLIENT COMPANIES, YOU'VE BEEN OF LESS USE TO US...
alex@alexcartoon.com
BUT THAT WAS BEFORE THE GLOBAL FINANCIAL CRISIS AND THE SO-CALLED "NEW NORMAL" IT USHERED IN. WE'RE NOW IN A SITUATION WHERE YOU ANALYSTS CAN MAKE A POSITIVE CONTRIBUTION TO THE BANK'S PROFITABILITY...
REALLY?
YES...
WE CAN SAVE MONEY BY FIRING YOU... THESE DAYS MARKET MOVES ARE DETERMINED SOLELY BY CENTRAL BANK POLICIES AND NO ONE CARES ABOUT SECTORS OR COMPANIES ANY MORE...
P45

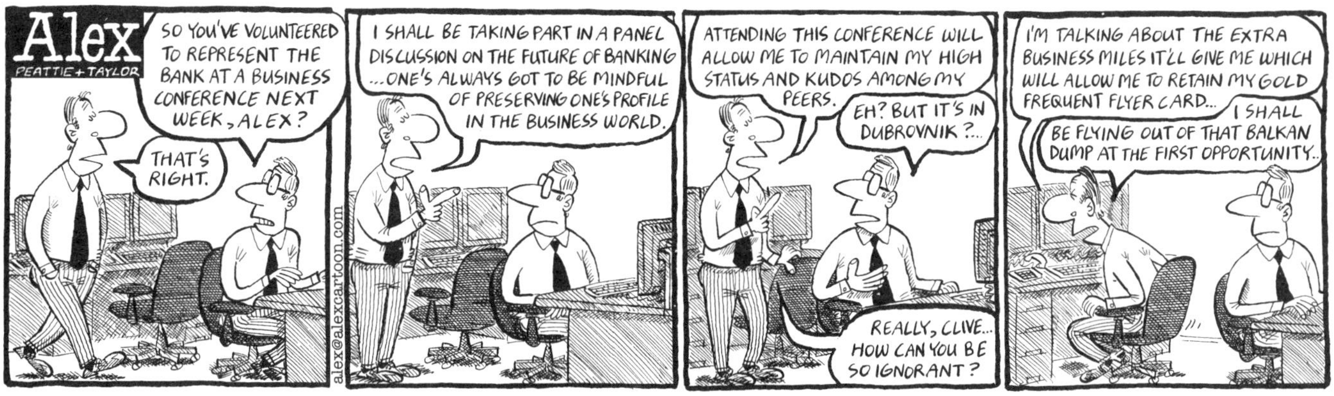
Alex
PEATTIE + TAYLOR
SO YOU'VE VOLUNTEERED TO REPRESENT THE BANK AT A BUSINESS CONFERENCE NEXT WEEK, ALEX?
THAT'S RIGHT.
I SHALL BE TAKING PART IN A PANEL DISCUSSION ON THE FUTURE OF BANKING ...ONE'S ALWAYS GOT TO BE MINDFUL OF PRESERVING ONE'S PROFILE IN THE BUSINESS WORLD.
alex@alexcartoon.com
ATTENDING THIS CONFERENCE WILL ALLOW ME TO MAINTAIN MY HIGH STATUS AND KUDOS AMONG MY PEERS.
EH? BUT IT'S IN DUBROVNIK?...
REALLY, CLIVE... HOW CAN YOU BE SO IGNORANT?
I'M TALKING ABOUT THE EXTRA BUSINESS MILES IT'LL GIVE ME WHICH WILL ALLOW ME TO RETAIN MY GOLD FREQUENT FLYER CARD...
I SHALL BE FLYING OUT OF THAT BALKAN DUMP AT THE FIRST OPPORTUNITY...

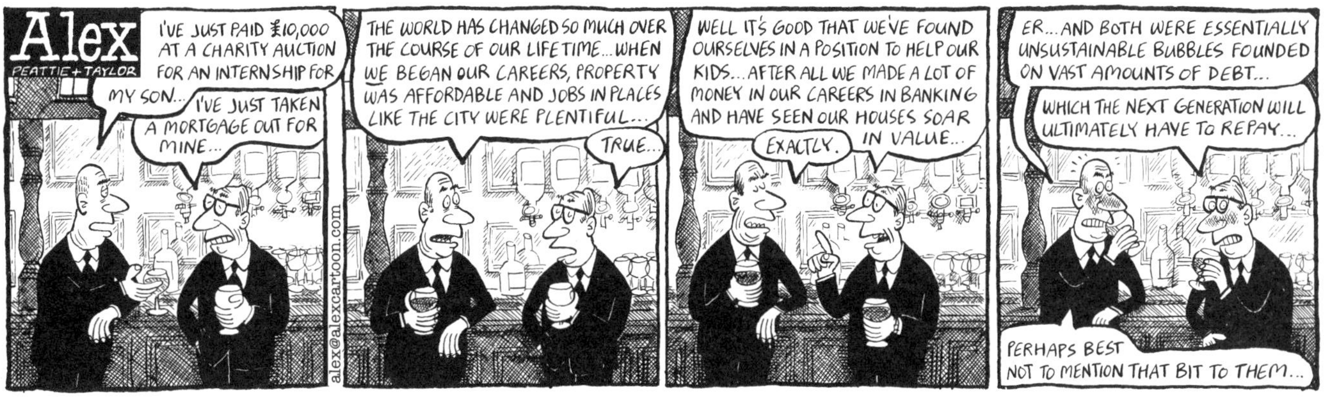
Alex
PEATTIE + TAYLOR
I'VE JUST PAID £10,000 AT A CHARITY AUCTION FOR AN INTERNSHIP FOR MY SON...
I'VE JUST TAKEN A MORTGAGE OUT FOR MINE...
THE WORLD HAS CHANGED SO MUCH OVER THE COURSE OF OUR LIFETIME... WHEN WE BEGAN OUR CAREERS, PROPERTY WAS AFFORDABLE AND JOBS IN PLACES LIKE THE CITY WERE PLENTIFUL...
TRUE...
alex@alexcartoon.com
WELL IT'S GOOD THAT WE'VE FOUND OURSELVES IN A POSITION TO HELP OUR KIDS... AFTER ALL WE MADE A LOT OF MONEY IN OUR CAREERS IN BANKING AND HAVE SEEN OUR HOUSES SOAR IN VALUE...
EXACTLY.
ER... AND BOTH WERE ESSENTIALLY UNSUSTAINABLE BUBBLES FOUNDED ON VAST AMOUNTS OF DEBT...
WHICH THE NEXT GENERATION WILL ULTIMATELY HAVE TO REPAY...
PERHAPS BEST NOT TO MENTION THAT BIT TO THEM...

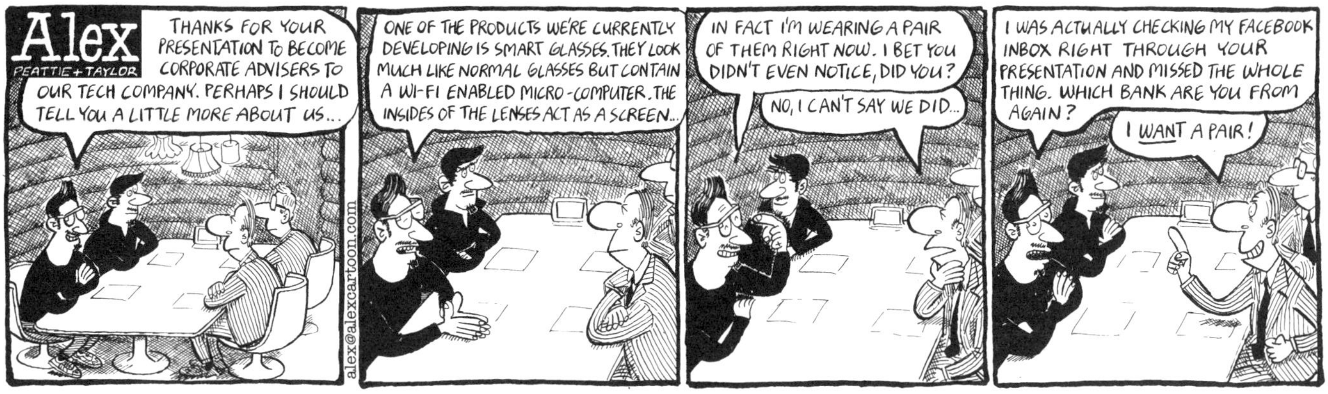
Alex
PEATTIE + TAYLOR
THANKS FOR YOUR PRESENTATION TO BECOME CORPORATE ADVISERS TO OUR TECH COMPANY. PERHAPS I SHOULD TELL YOU A LITTLE MORE ABOUT US...
ONE OF THE PRODUCTS WE'RE CURRENTLY DEVELOPING IS SMART GLASSES. THEY LOOK MUCH LIKE NORMAL GLASSES BUT CONTAIN A WI-FI ENABLED MICRO-COMPUTER. THE INSIDES OF THE LENSES ACT AS A SCREEN...
alex@alexcartoon.com
IN FACT I'M WEARING A PAIR OF THEM RIGHT NOW. I BET YOU DIDN'T EVEN NOTICE, DID YOU?
NO, I CAN'T SAY WE DID...
I WAS ACTUALLY CHECKING MY FACEBOOK INBOX RIGHT THROUGH YOUR PRESENTATION AND MISSED THE WHOLE THING. WHICH BANK ARE YOU FROM AGAIN?
I WANT A PAIR!

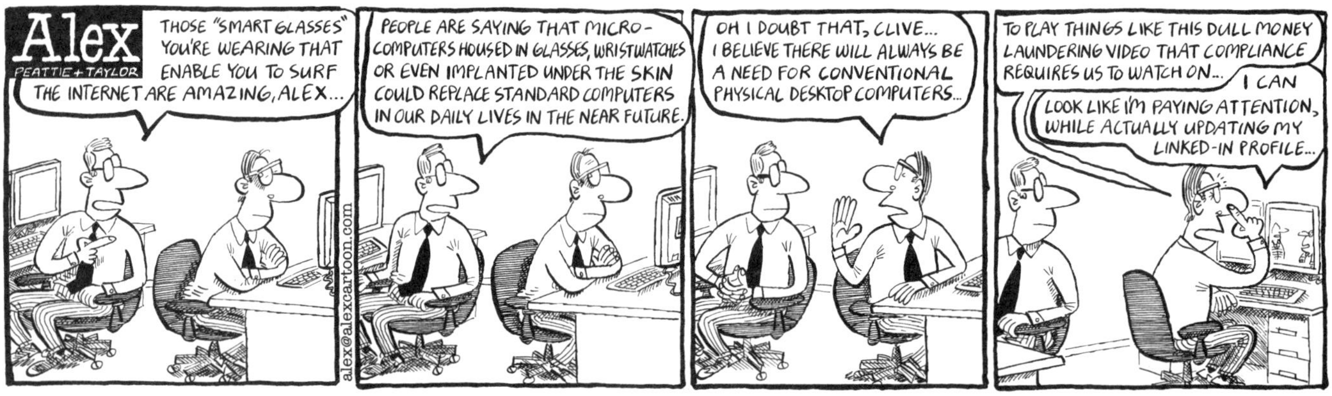
Alex
PEATTIE + TAYLOR
THOSE "SMART GLASSES" YOU'RE WEARING THAT ENABLE YOU TO SURF THE INTERNET ARE AMAZING, ALEX...
alex@alexcartoon.com
PEOPLE ARE SAYING THAT MICRO-COMPUTERS HOUSED IN GLASSES, WRISTWATCHES OR EVEN IMPLANTED UNDER THE SKIN COULD REPLACE STANDARD COMPUTERS IN OUR DAILY LIVES IN THE NEAR FUTURE.
OH I DOUBT THAT, CLIVE... I BELIEVE THERE WILL ALWAYS BE A NEED FOR CONVENTIONAL PHYSICAL DESKTOP COMPUTERS...
TO PLAY THINGS LIKE THIS DULL MONEY LAUNDERING VIDEO THAT COMPLIANCE REQUIRES US TO WATCH ON...
I CAN LOOK LIKE I'M PAYING ATTENTION, WHILE ACTUALLY UPDATING MY LINKED-IN PROFILE...

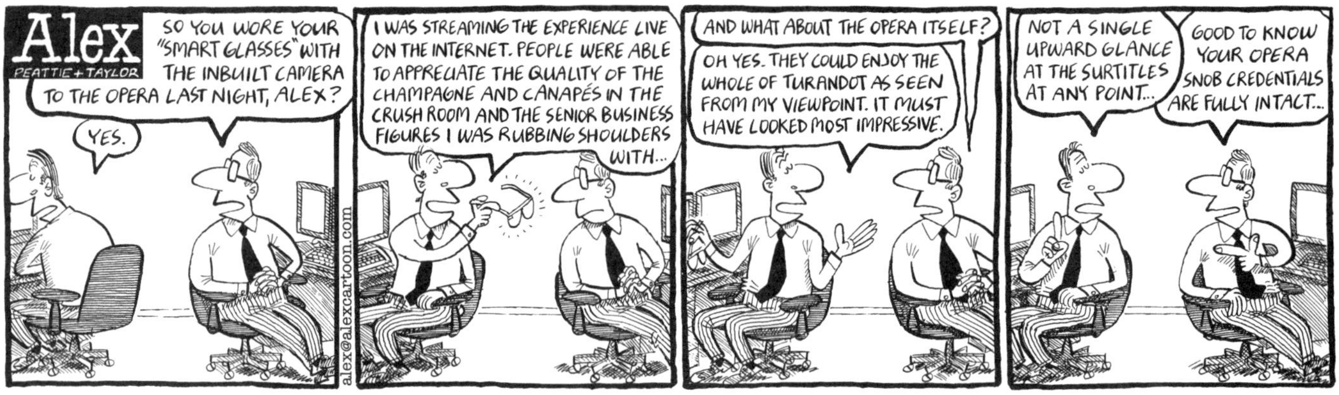
Alex
PEATTIE + TAYLOR
SO YOU WORE YOUR "SMART GLASSES" WITH THE INBUILT CAMERA TO THE OPERA LAST NIGHT, ALEX?
YES.
alex@alexcartoon.com
I WAS STREAMING THE EXPERIENCE LIVE ON THE INTERNET. PEOPLE WERE ABLE TO APPRECIATE THE QUALITY OF THE CHAMPAGNE AND CANAPÉS IN THE CRUSH ROOM AND THE SENIOR BUSINESS FIGURES I WAS RUBBING SHOULDERS WITH...
AND WHAT ABOUT THE OPERA ITSELF?
OH YES. THEY COULD ENJOY THE WHOLE OF TURANDOT AS SEEN FROM MY VIEWPOINT. IT MUST HAVE LOOKED MOST IMPRESSIVE.
NOT A SINGLE UPWARD GLANCE AT THE SURTITLES AT ANY POINT...
GOOD TO KNOW YOUR OPERA SNOB CREDENTIALS ARE FULLY INTACT...

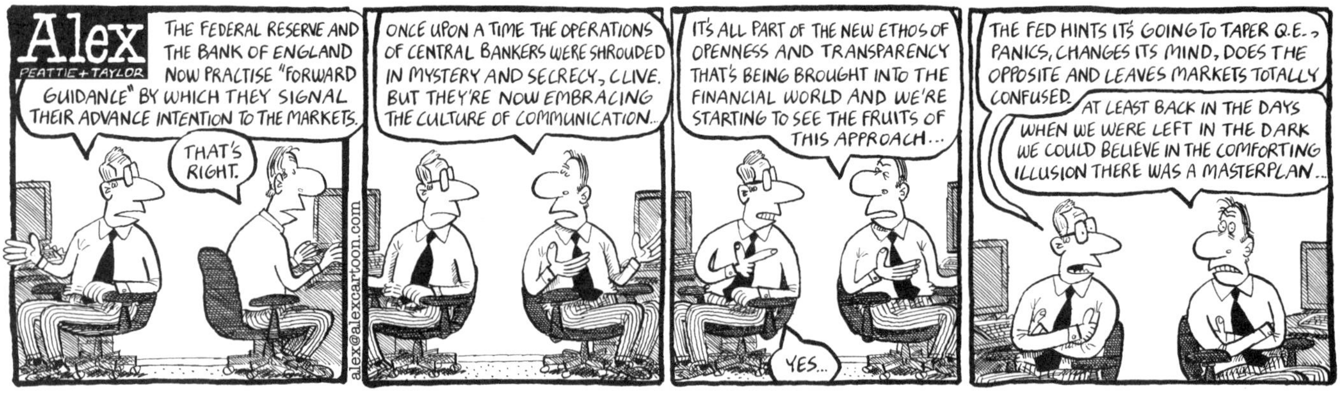
Alex
PEATTIE + TAYLOR
THE FEDERAL RESERVE AND THE BANK OF ENGLAND NOW PRACTISE "FORWARD GUIDANCE" BY WHICH THEY SIGNAL THEIR ADVANCE INTENTION TO THE MARKETS.
THAT'S RIGHT.
alex@alexcartoon.com
ONCE UPON A TIME THE OPERATIONS OF CENTRAL BANKERS WERE SHROUDED IN MYSTERY AND SECRECY, CLIVE. BUT THEY'RE NOW EMBRACING THE CULTURE OF COMMUNICATION...
IT'S ALL PART OF THE NEW ETHOS OF OPENNESS AND TRANSPARENCY THAT'S BEING BROUGHT INTO THE FINANCIAL WORLD AND WE'RE STARTING TO SEE THE FRUITS OF THIS APPROACH...
YES...
THE FED HINTS IT'S GOING TO TAPER Q.E., PANICS, CHANGES ITS MIND, DOES THE OPPOSITE AND LEAVES MARKETS TOTALLY CONFUSED.
AT LEAST BACK IN THE DAYS WHEN WE WERE LEFT IN THE DARK WE COULD BELIEVE IN THE COMFORTING ILLUSION THERE WAS A MASTERPLAN...

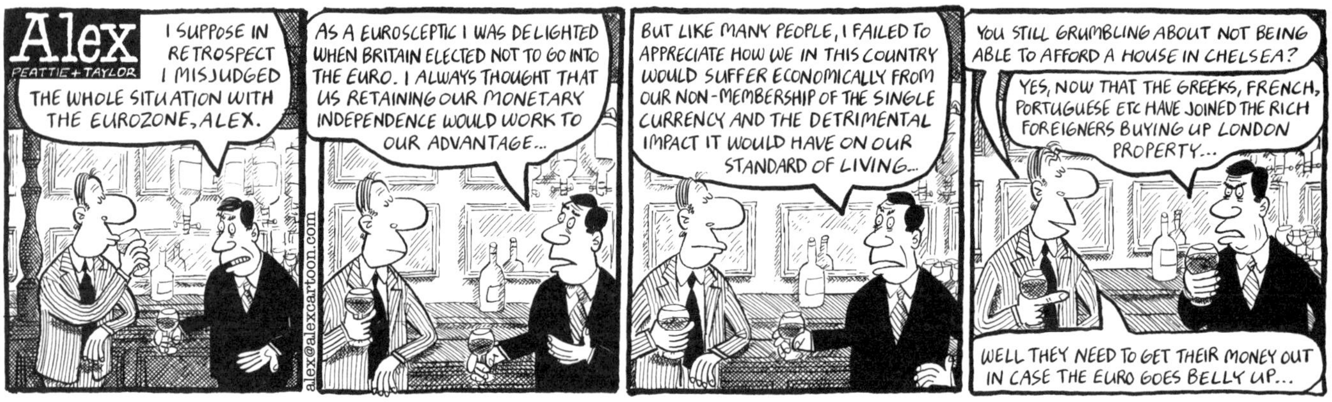
Alex
PEATTIE + TAYLOR
I SUPPOSE IN RETROSPECT I MISJUDGED THE WHOLE SITUATION WITH THE EUROZONE, ALEX.
alex@alexcartoon.com
AS A EUROSCEPTIC I WAS DELIGHTED WHEN BRITAIN ELECTED NOT TO GO INTO THE EURO. I ALWAYS THOUGHT THAT US RETAINING OUR MONETARY INDEPENDENCE WOULD WORK TO OUR ADVANTAGE...
BUT LIKE MANY PEOPLE, I FAILED TO APPRECIATE HOW WE IN THIS COUNTRY WOULD SUFFER ECONOMICALLY FROM OUR NON-MEMBERSHIP OF THE SINGLE CURRENCY AND THE DETRIMENTAL IMPACT IT WOULD HAVE ON OUR STANDARD OF LIVING...
YOU STILL GRUMBLING ABOUT NOT BEING ABLE TO AFFORD A HOUSE IN CHELSEA?
YES, NOW THAT THE GREEKS, FRENCH, PORTUGUESE ETC HAVE JOINED THE RICH FOREIGNERS BUYING UP LONDON PROPERTY...
WELL THEY NEED TO GET THEIR MONEY OUT IN CASE THE EURO GOES BELLY UP...

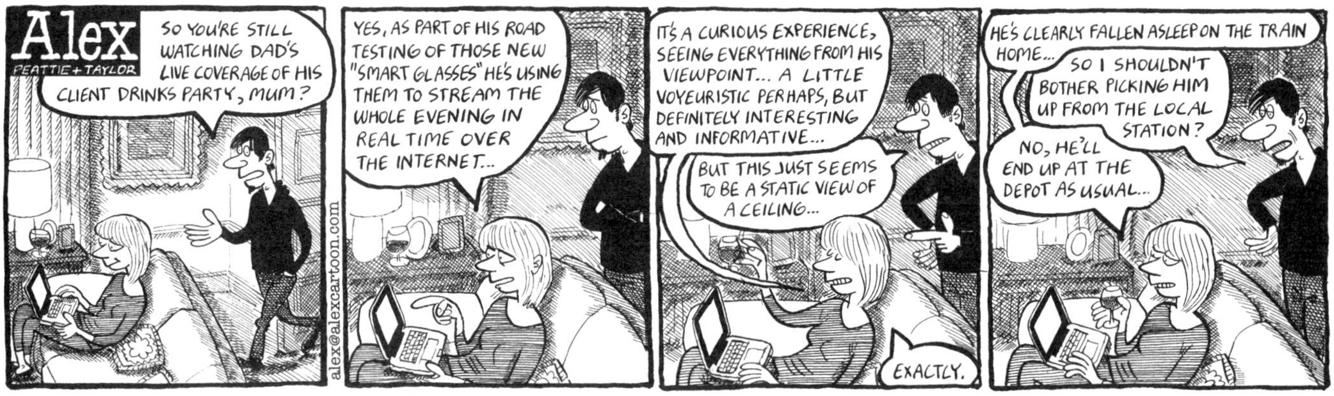
Alex
PEATTIE + TAYLOR
SO YOU'RE STILL WATCHING DAD'S LIVE COVERAGE OF HIS CLIENT DRINKS PARTY, MUM?
alex@alexcartoon.com
YES, AS PART OF HIS ROAD TESTING OF THOSE NEW "SMART GLASSES" HE'S USING THEM TO STREAM THE WHOLE EVENING IN REAL TIME OVER THE INTERNET...
IT'S A CURIOUS EXPERIENCE, SEEING EVERYTHING FROM HIS VIEWPOINT... A LITTLE VOYEURISTIC PERHAPS, BUT DEFINITELY INTERESTING AND INFORMATIVE...
BUT THIS JUST SEEMS TO BE A STATIC VIEW OF A CEILING...
EXACTLY.
HE'S CLEARLY FALLEN ASLEEP ON THE TRAIN HOME...
SO I SHOULDN'T BOTHER PICKING HIM UP FROM THE LOCAL STATION?
NO, HE'LL END UP AT THE DEPOT AS USUAL...

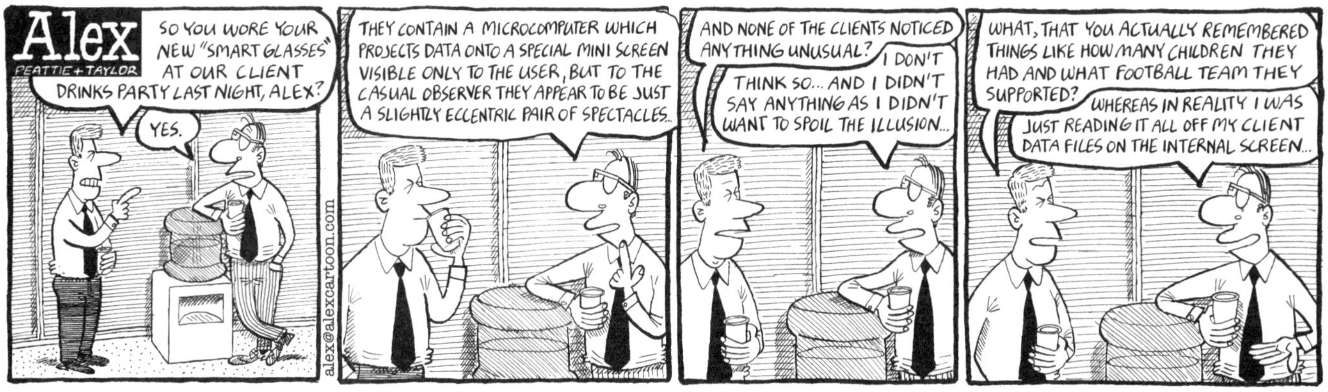
Alex
PEATTIE + TAYLOR
SO YOU WORE YOUR NEW "SMART GLASSES" AT OUR CLIENT DRINKS PARTY LAST NIGHT, ALEX?
YES.
alex@alexcartoon.com
THEY CONTAIN A MICROCOMPUTER WHICH PROJECTS DATA ONTO A SPECIAL MINI SCREEN VISIBLE ONLY TO THE USER, BUT TO THE CASUAL OBSERVER THEY APPEAR TO BE JUST A SLIGHTLY ECCENTRIC PAIR OF SPECTACLES...
AND NONE OF THE CLIENTS NOTICED ANYTHING UNUSUAL?
I DON'T THINK SO... AND I DIDN'T SAY ANYTHING AS I DIDN'T WANT TO SPOIL THE ILLUSION...
WHAT, THAT YOU ACTUALLY REMEMBERED THINGS LIKE HOW MANY CHILDREN THEY HAD AND WHAT FOOTBALL TEAM THEY SUPPORTED?
WHEREAS IN REALITY I WAS JUST READING IT ALL OFF MY CLIENT DATA FILES ON THE INTERNAL SCREEN...

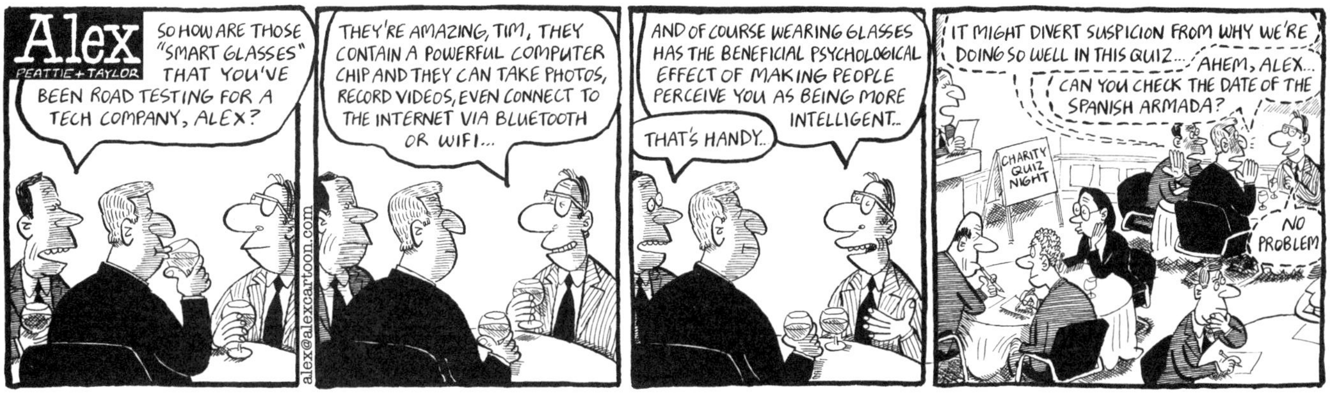
Alex
PEATTIE + TAYLOR
SO HOW ARE THOSE "SMART GLASSES" THAT YOU'VE BEEN ROAD TESTING FOR A TECH COMPANY, ALEX?
alex@alexcartoon.com
THEY'RE AMAZING, TIM, THEY CONTAIN A POWERFUL COMPUTER CHIP AND THEY CAN TAKE PHOTOS, RECORD VIDEOS, EVEN CONNECT TO THE INTERNET VIA BLUETOOTH OR WIFI...
AND OF COURSE WEARING GLASSES HAS THE BENEFICIAL PSYCHOLOGICAL EFFECT OF MAKING PEOPLE PERCEIVE YOU AS BEING MORE INTELLIGENT...
THAT'S HANDY...
IT MIGHT DIVERT SUSPICION FROM WHY WE'RE DOING SO WELL IN THIS QUIZ...
AHEM, ALEX... CAN YOU CHECK THE DATE OF THE SPANISH ARMADA?
CHARITY QUIZ NIGHT
NO PROBLEM

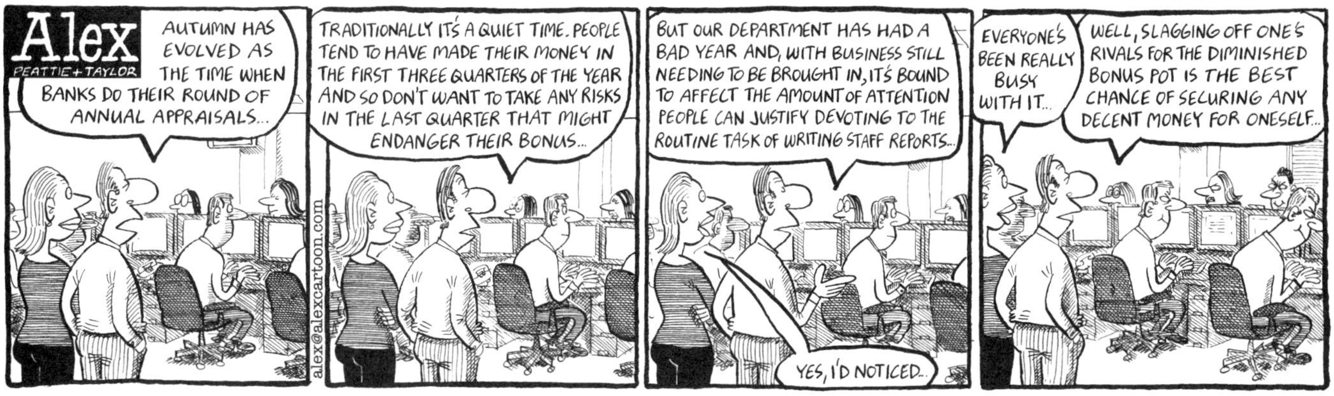
Alex
PEATTIE + TAYLOR
AUTUMN HAS EVOLVED AS THE TIME WHEN BANKS DO THEIR ROUND OF ANNUAL APPRAISALS...
alex@alexcartoon.com
TRADITIONALLY IT'S A QUIET TIME. PEOPLE TEND TO HAVE MADE THEIR MONEY IN THE FIRST THREE QUARTERS OF THE YEAR AND SO DON'T WANT TO TAKE ANY RISKS IN THE LAST QUARTER THAT MIGHT ENDANGER THEIR BONUS...
BUT OUR DEPARTMENT HAS HAD A BAD YEAR AND, WITH BUSINESS STILL NEEDING TO BE BROUGHT IN, IT'S BOUND TO AFFECT THE AMOUNT OF ATTENTION PEOPLE CAN JUSTIFY DEVOTING TO THE ROUTINE TASK OF WRITING STAFF REPORTS...
YES, I'D NOTICED...
EVERYONE'S BEEN REALLY BUSY WITH IT...
WELL, SLAGGING OFF ONE'S RIVALS FOR THE DIMINISHED BONUS POT IS THE BEST CHANCE OF SECURING ANY DECENT MONEY FOR ONESELF...

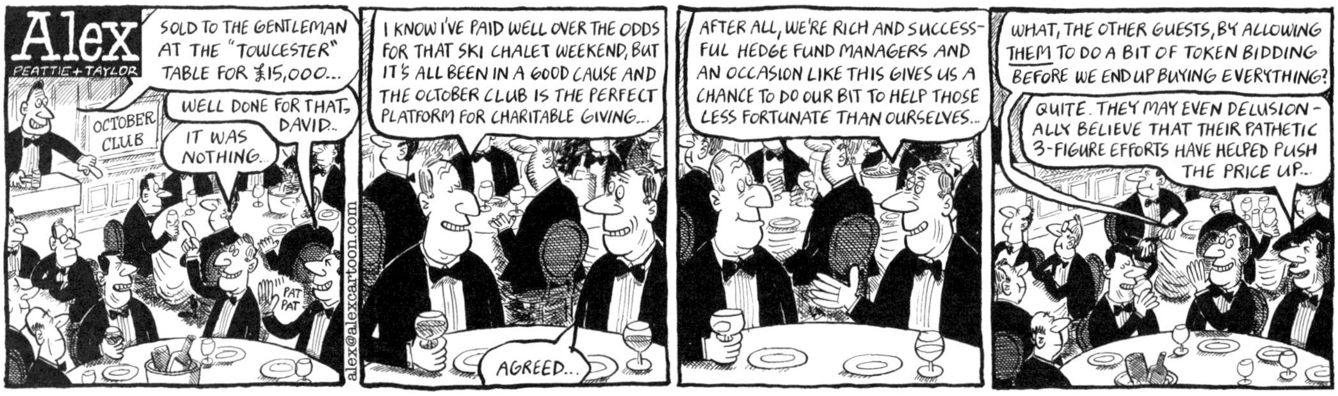
Alex
PEATTIE + TAYLOR
SOLD TO THE GENTLEMAN AT THE "TOWCESTER" TABLE FOR £15,000...
WELL DONE FOR THAT, DAVID..
IT WAS NOTHING..
OCTOBER CLUB
PAT PAT
alex@alexcartoon.com
I KNOW I'VE PAID WELL OVER THE ODDS FOR THAT SKI CHALET WEEKEND, BUT IT'S ALL BEEN IN A GOOD CAUSE AND THE OCTOBER CLUB IS THE PERFECT PLATFORM FOR CHARITABLE GIVING...
AGREED...
AFTER ALL, WE'RE RICH AND SUCCESSFUL HEDGE FUND MANAGERS AND AN OCCASION LIKE THIS GIVES US A CHANCE TO DO OUR BIT TO HELP THOSE LESS FORTUNATE THAN OURSELVES...
WHAT, THE OTHER GUESTS, BY ALLOWING THEM TO DO A BIT OF TOKEN BIDDING BEFORE WE END UP BUYING EVERYTHING?
QUITE. THEY MAY EVEN DELUSIONALLY BELIEVE THAT THEIR PATHETIC 3-FIGURE EFFORTS HAVE HELPED PUSH THE PRICE UP..

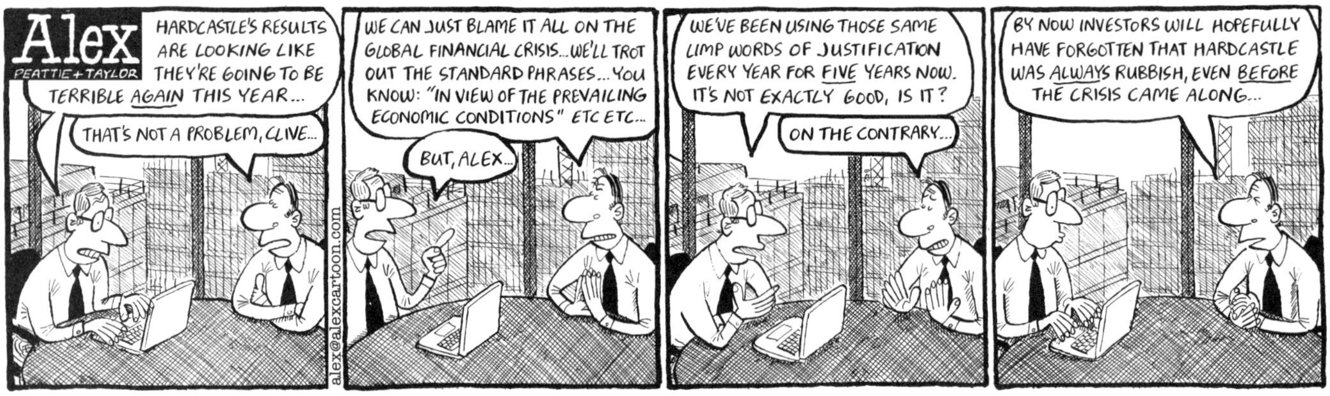
Alex
PEATTIE + TAYLOR
HARDCASTLE'S RESULTS ARE LOOKING LIKE THEY'RE GOING TO BE TERRIBLE AGAIN THIS YEAR...
THAT'S NOT A PROBLEM, CLIVE...
alex@alexcartoon.com
WE CAN JUST BLAME IT ALL ON THE GLOBAL FINANCIAL CRISIS...WE'LL TROT OUT THE STANDARD PHRASES... YOU KNOW: "IN VIEW OF THE PREVAILING ECONOMIC CONDITIONS" ETC ETC...
BUT, ALEX...
WE'VE BEEN USING THOSE SAME LIMP WORDS OF JUSTIFICATION EVERY YEAR FOR FIVE YEARS NOW. IT'S NOT EXACTLY GOOD, IS IT?
ON THE CONTRARY...
BY NOW INVESTORS WILL HOPEFULLY HAVE FORGOTTEN THAT HARDCASTLE WAS ALWAYS RUBBISH, EVEN BEFORE THE CRISIS CAME ALONG...

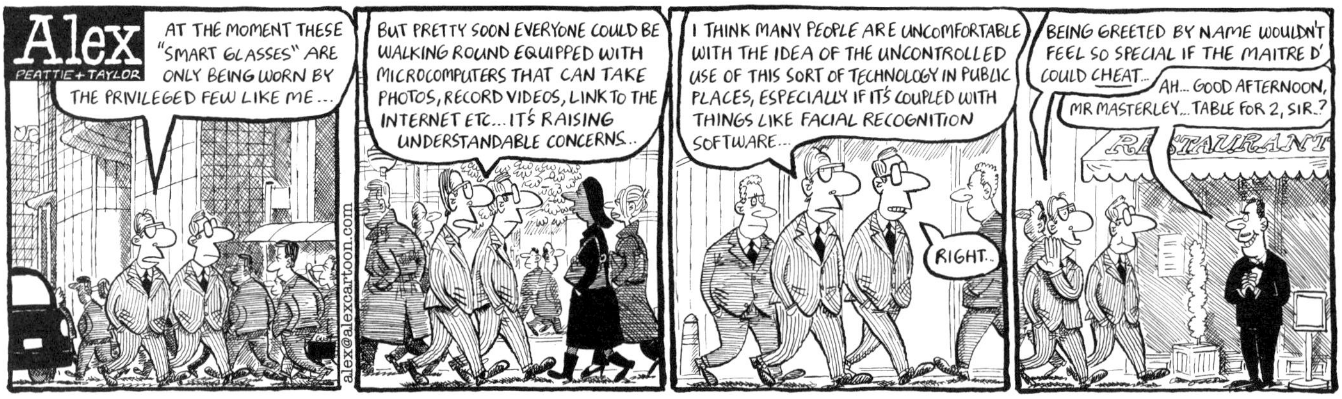
Alex
PEATTIE + TAYLOR
AT THE MOMENT THESE "SMART GLASSES" ARE ONLY BEING WORN BY THE PRIVILEGED FEW LIKE ME...
alex@alexcartoon.com
BUT PRETTY SOON EVERYONE COULD BE WALKING ROUND EQUIPPED WITH MICROCOMPUTERS THAT CAN TAKE PHOTOS, RECORD VIDEOS, LINK TO THE INTERNET ETC... IT'S RAISING UNDERSTANDABLE CONCERNS...
I THINK MANY PEOPLE ARE UNCOMFORTABLE WITH THE IDEA OF THE UNCONTROLLED USE OF THIS SORT OF TECHNOLOGY IN PUBLIC PLACES, ESPECIALLY IF IT'S COUPLED WITH THINGS LIKE FACIAL RECOGNITION SOFTWARE...
RIGHT..
BEING GREETED BY NAME WOULDN'T FEEL SO SPECIAL IF THE MAITRE D' COULD CHEAT...
AH... GOOD AFTERNOON, MR MASTERLEY... TABLE FOR 2, SIR..?
RESTAURANT

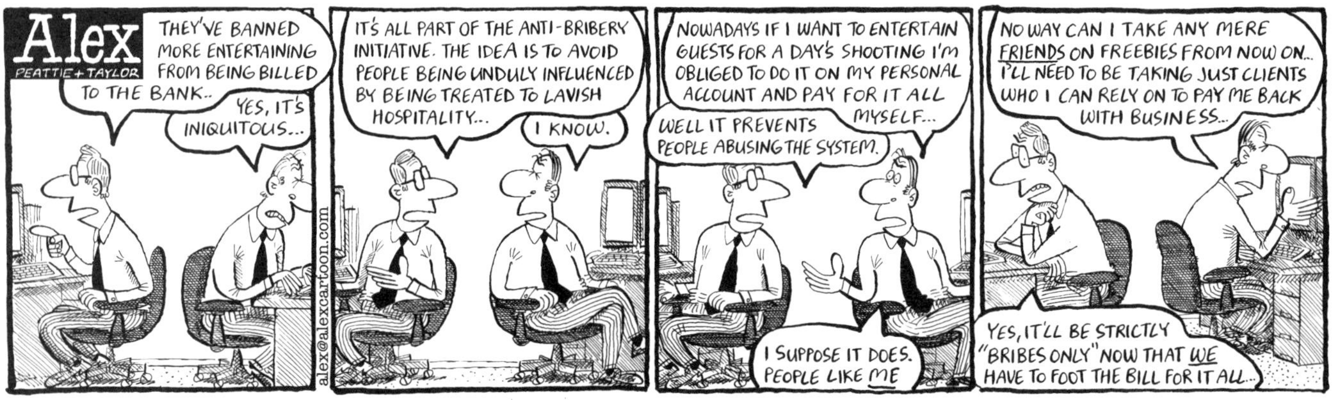
Alex
PEATTIE + TAYLOR
THEY'VE BANNED MORE ENTERTAINING FROM BEING BILLED TO THE BANK..
YES, IT'S INIQUITOUS...
alex@alexcartoon.com
IT'S ALL PART OF THE ANTI-BRIBERY INITIATIVE. THE IDEA IS TO AVOID PEOPLE BEING UNDULY INFLUENCED BY BEING TREATED TO LAVISH HOSPITALITY...
I KNOW.
NOWADAYS IF I WANT TO ENTERTAIN GUESTS FOR A DAY'S SHOOTING I'M OBLIGED TO DO IT ON MY PERSONAL ACCOUNT AND PAY FOR IT ALL MYSELF...
WELL IT PREVENTS PEOPLE ABUSING THE SYSTEM.
I SUPPOSE IT DOES. PEOPLE LIKE ME
NO WAY CAN I TAKE ANY MERE FRIENDS ON FREEBIES FROM NOW ON... I'LL NEED TO BE TAKING JUST CLIENTS WHO I CAN RELY ON TO PAY ME BACK WITH BUSINESS...
YES, IT'LL BE STRICTLY "BRIBES ONLY" NOW THAT WE HAVE TO FOOT THE BILL FOR IT ALL...

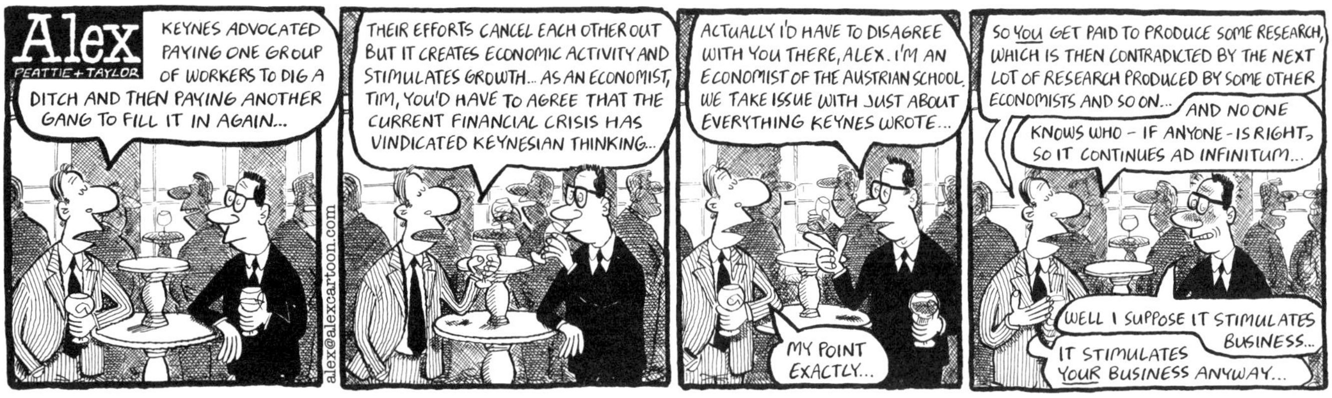
Alex
PEATTIE+TAYLOR
KEYNES ADVOCATED PAYING ONE GROUP OF WORKERS TO DIG A DITCH AND THEN PAYING ANOTHER GANG TO FILL IT IN AGAIN...
alex@alexcartoon.com
THEIR EFFORTS CANCEL EACH OTHER OUT BUT IT CREATES ECONOMIC ACTIVITY AND STIMULATES GROWTH... AS AN ECONOMIST, TIM, YOU'D HAVE TO AGREE THAT THE CURRENT FINANCIAL CRISIS HAS VINDICATED KEYNESIAN THINKING...
ACTUALLY I'D HAVE TO DISAGREE WITH YOU THERE, ALEX. I'M AN ECONOMIST OF THE AUSTRIAN SCHOOL. WE TAKE ISSUE WITH JUST ABOUT EVERYTHING KEYNES WROTE...
MY POINT EXACTLY...
SO YOU GET PAID TO PRODUCE SOME RESEARCH, WHICH IS THEN CONTRADICTED BY THE NEXT LOT OF RESEARCH PRODUCED BY SOME OTHER ECONOMISTS AND SO ON...
AND NO ONE KNOWS WHO - IF ANYONE - IS RIGHT, SO IT CONTINUES AD INFINITUM...
WELL I SUPPOSE IT STIMULATES BUSINESS...
IT STIMULATES YOUR BUSINESS ANYWAY...

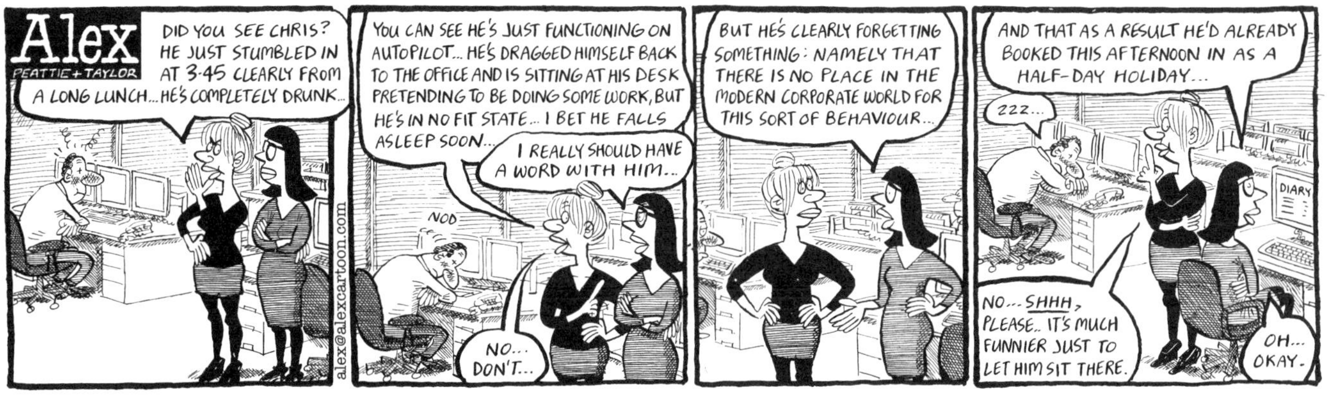
Alex
PEATTIE+TAYLOR
DID YOU SEE CHRIS? HE JUST STUMBLED IN AT 3.45 CLEARLY FROM A LONG LUNCH... HE'S COMPLETELY DRUNK...
alex@alexcartoon.com
YOU CAN SEE HE'S JUST FUNCTIONING ON AUTOPILOT... HE'S DRAGGED HIMSELF BACK TO THE OFFICE AND IS SITTING AT HIS DESK PRETENDING TO BE DOING SOME WORK, BUT HE'S IN NO FIT STATE... I BET HE FALLS ASLEEP SOON...
I REALLY SHOULD HAVE A WORD WITH HIM...
NOD
NO... DON'T...
BUT HE'S CLEARLY FORGETTING SOMETHING: NAMELY THAT THERE IS NO PLACE IN THE MODERN CORPORATE WORLD FOR THIS SORT OF BEHAVIOUR...
AND THAT AS A RESULT HE'D ALREADY BOOKED THIS AFTERNOON IN AS A HALF-DAY HOLIDAY...
ZZZ...
DIARY
NO... SHHH, PLEASE.. IT'S MUCH FUNNIER JUST TO LET HIM SIT THERE.
OH... OKAY.

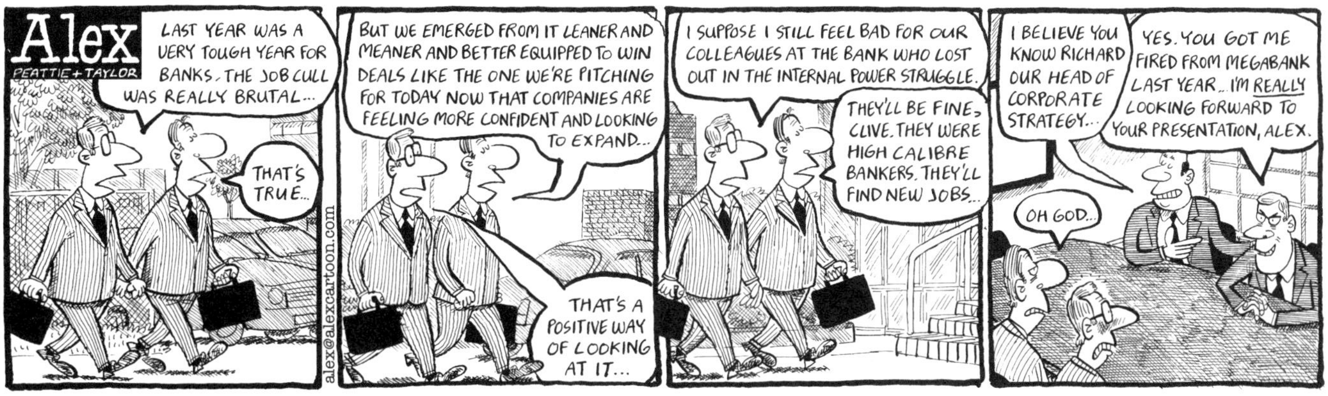
Alex
PEATTIE+TAYLOR
LAST YEAR WAS A VERY TOUGH YEAR FOR BANKS. THE JOB CULL WAS REALLY BRUTAL...
THAT'S TRUE...
alex@alexcartoon.com
BUT WE EMERGED FROM IT LEANER AND MEANER AND BETTER EQUIPPED TO WIN DEALS LIKE THE ONE WE'RE PITCHING FOR TODAY NOW THAT COMPANIES ARE FEELING MORE CONFIDENT AND LOOKING TO EXPAND...
THAT'S A POSITIVE WAY OF LOOKING AT IT...
I SUPPOSE I STILL FEEL BAD FOR OUR COLLEAGUES AT THE BANK WHO LOST OUT IN THE INTERNAL POWER STRUGGLE.
THEY'LL BE FINE, CLIVE. THEY WERE HIGH CALIBRE BANKERS. THEY'LL FIND NEW JOBS...
I BELIEVE YOU KNOW RICHARD OUR HEAD OF CORPORATE STRATEGY...
YES. YOU GOT ME FIRED FROM MEGABANK LAST YEAR... I'M REALLY LOOKING FORWARD TO YOUR PRESENTATION, ALEX.
OH GOD...

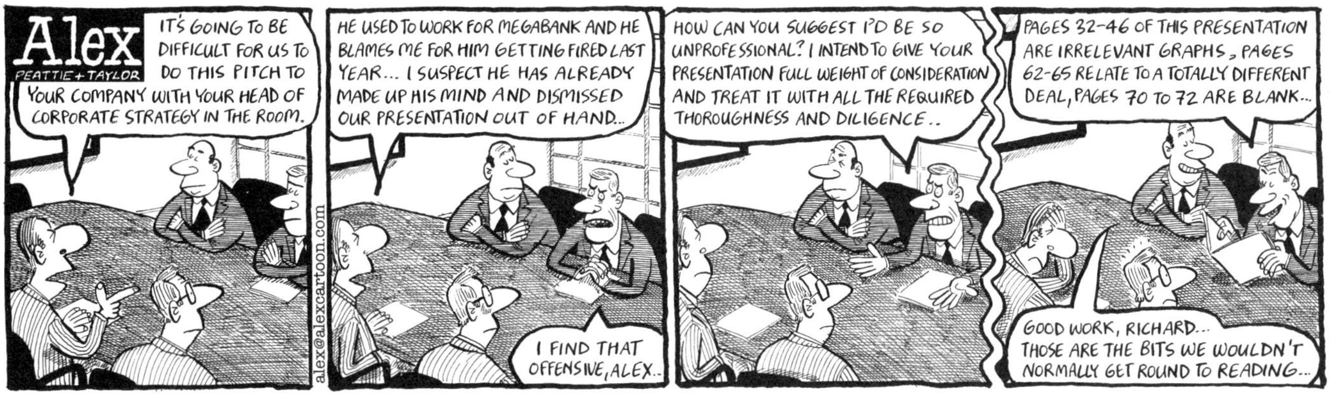
Alex
PEATTIE+TAYLOR
IT'S GOING TO BE DIFFICULT FOR US TO DO THIS PITCH TO YOUR COMPANY WITH YOUR HEAD OF CORPORATE STRATEGY IN THE ROOM.
alex@alexcartoon.com
HE USED TO WORK FOR MEGABANK AND HE BLAMES ME FOR HIM GETTING FIRED LAST YEAR... I SUSPECT HE HAS ALREADY MADE UP HIS MIND AND DISMISSED OUR PRESENTATION OUT OF HAND...
I FIND THAT OFFENSIVE, ALEX..
HOW CAN YOU SUGGEST I'D BE SO UNPROFESSIONAL? I INTEND TO GIVE YOUR PRESENTATION FULL WEIGHT OF CONSIDERATION AND TREAT IT WITH ALL THE REQUIRED THOROUGHNESS AND DILIGENCE..
PAGES 32-46 OF THIS PRESENTATION ARE IRRELEVANT GRAPHS, PAGES 62-65 RELATE TO A TOTALLY DIFFERENT DEAL, PAGES 70 TO 72 ARE BLANK...
GOOD WORK, RICHARD... THOSE ARE THE BITS WE WOULDN'T NORMALLY GET ROUND TO READING...

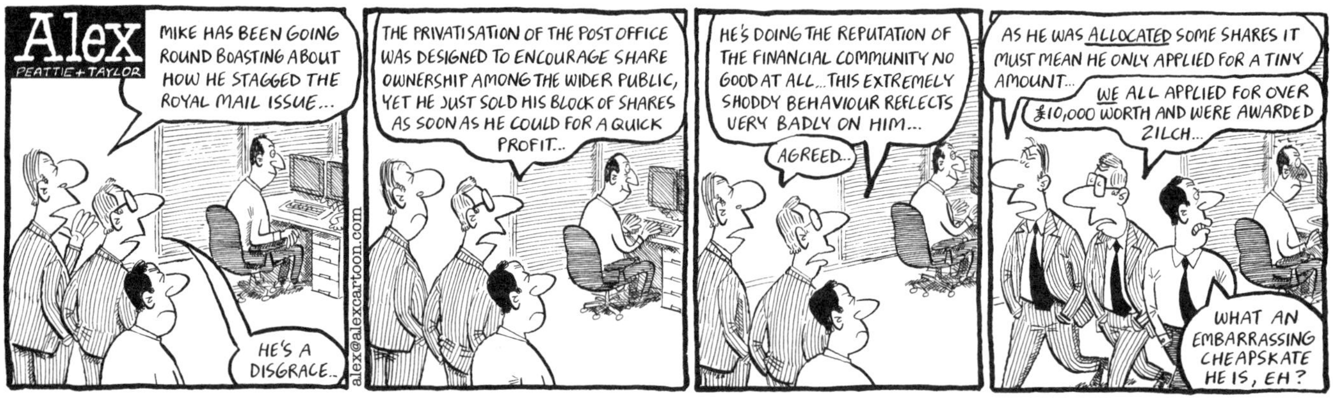
Alex
PEATTIE + TAYLOR
MIKE HAS BEEN GOING ROUND BOASTING ABOUT HOW HE STAGGED THE ROYAL MAIL ISSUE...
HE'S A DISGRACE...
alex@alexcartoon.com
THE PRIVATISATION OF THE POST OFFICE WAS DESIGNED TO ENCOURAGE SHARE OWNERSHIP AMONG THE WIDER PUBLIC, YET HE JUST SOLD HIS BLOCK OF SHARES AS SOON AS HE COULD FOR A QUICK PROFIT...
HE'S DOING THE REPUTATION OF THE FINANCIAL COMMUNITY NO GOOD AT ALL... THIS EXTREMELY SHODDY BEHAVIOUR REFLECTS VERY BADLY ON HIM...
AGREED...
AS HE WAS ALLOCATED SOME SHARES IT MUST MEAN HE ONLY APPLIED FOR A TINY AMOUNT...
WE ALL APPLIED FOR OVER £10,000 WORTH AND WERE AWARDED ZILCH...
WHAT AN EMBARRASSING CHEAPSKATE HE IS, EH?

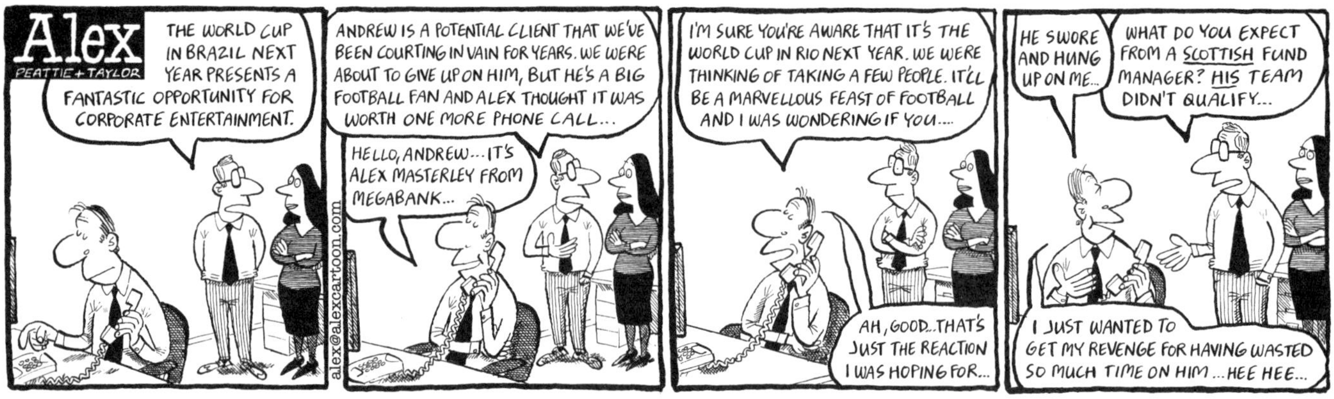
Alex
PEATTIE + TAYLOR
THE WORLD CUP IN BRAZIL NEXT YEAR PRESENTS A FANTASTIC OPPORTUNITY FOR CORPORATE ENTERTAINMENT.
alex@alexcartoon.com
ANDREW IS A POTENTIAL CLIENT THAT WE'VE BEEN COURTING IN VAIN FOR YEARS. WE WERE ABOUT TO GIVE UP ON HIM, BUT HE'S A BIG FOOTBALL FAN AND ALEX THOUGHT IT WAS WORTH ONE MORE PHONE CALL...
HELLO, ANDREW... IT'S ALEX MASTERLEY FROM MEGABANK...
I'M SURE YOU'RE AWARE THAT IT'S THE WORLD CUP IN RIO NEXT YEAR. WE WERE THINKING OF TAKING A FEW PEOPLE. IT'LL BE A MARVELLOUS FEAST OF FOOTBALL AND I WAS WONDERING IF YOU....
AH, GOOD... THAT'S JUST THE REACTION I WAS HOPING FOR...
HE SWORE AND HUNG UP ON ME...
WHAT DO YOU EXPECT FROM A SCOTTISH FUND MANAGER? HIS TEAM DIDN'T QUALIFY...
I JUST WANTED TO GET MY REVENGE FOR HAVING WASTED SO MUCH TIME ON HIM ... HEE HEE...

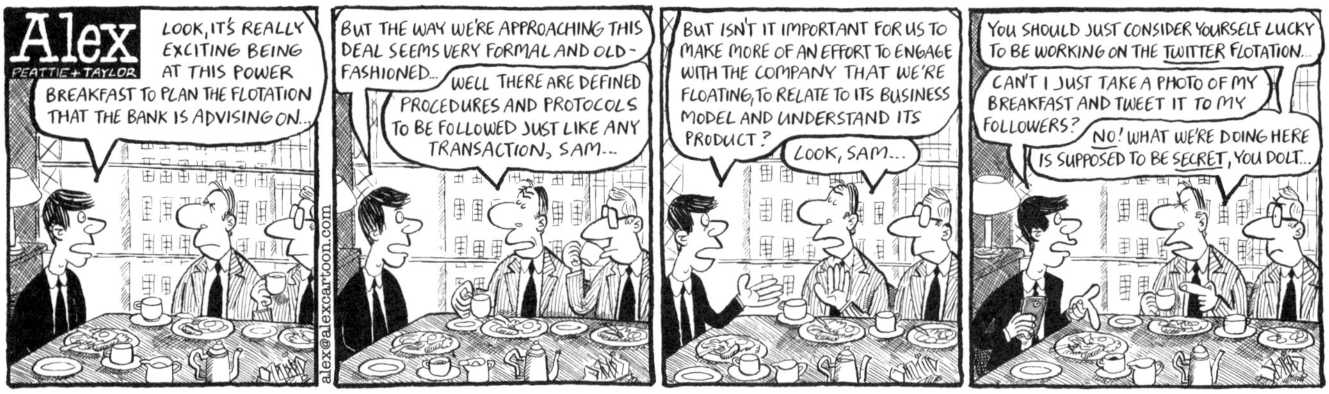
Alex
PEATTIE + TAYLOR
LOOK, IT'S REALLY EXCITING BEING AT THIS POWER BREAKFAST TO PLAN THE FLOTATION THAT THE BANK IS ADVISING ON...
alex@alexcartoon.com
BUT THE WAY WE'RE APPROACHING THIS DEAL SEEMS VERY FORMAL AND OLD-FASHIONED...
WELL THERE ARE DEFINED PROCEDURES AND PROTOCOLS TO BE FOLLOWED JUST LIKE ANY TRANSACTION, SAM...
BUT ISN'T IT IMPORTANT FOR US TO MAKE MORE OF AN EFFORT TO ENGAGE WITH THE COMPANY THAT WE'RE FLOATING, TO RELATE TO ITS BUSINESS MODEL AND UNDERSTAND ITS PRODUCT?
LOOK, SAM...
YOU SHOULD JUST CONSIDER YOURSELF LUCKY TO BE WORKING ON THE TWITTER FLOTATION...
CAN'T I JUST TAKE A PHOTO OF MY BREAKFAST AND TWEET IT TO MY FOLLOWERS?
NO! WHAT WE'RE DOING HERE IS SUPPOSED TO BE SECRET, YOU DOLT...

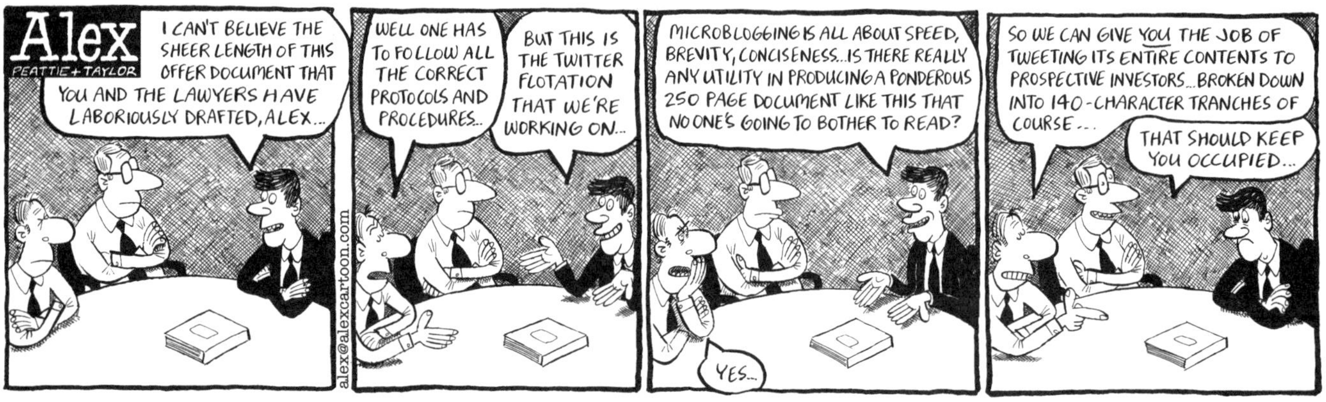
Alex
PEATTIE + TAYLOR
I CAN'T BELIEVE THE SHEER LENGTH OF THIS OFFER DOCUMENT THAT YOU AND THE LAWYERS HAVE LABORIOUSLY DRAFTED, ALEX...
alex@alexcartoon.com
WELL ONE HAS TO FOLLOW ALL THE CORRECT PROTOCOLS AND PROCEDURES...
BUT THIS IS THE TWITTER FLOTATION THAT WE'RE WORKING ON...
MICROBLOGGING IS ALL ABOUT SPEED, BREVITY, CONCISENESS... IS THERE REALLY ANY UTILITY IN PRODUCING A PONDEROUS 250 PAGE DOCUMENT LIKE THIS THAT NO ONE'S GOING TO BOTHER TO READ?
YES...
SO WE CAN GIVE YOU THE JOB OF TWEETING ITS ENTIRE CONTENTS TO PROSPECTIVE INVESTORS... BROKEN DOWN INTO 140-CHARACTER TRANCHES OF COURSE...
THAT SHOULD KEEP YOU OCCUPIED...

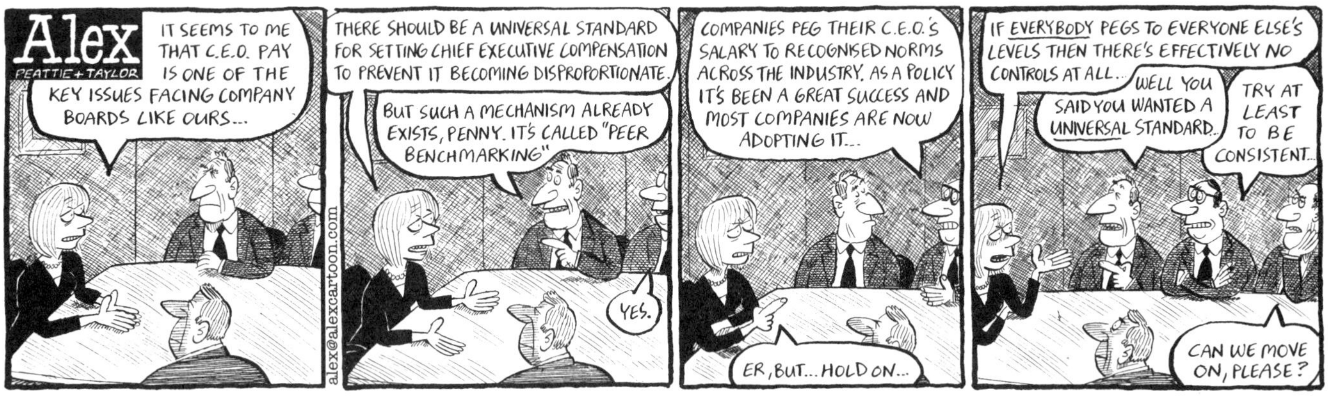
Alex
PEATTIE+TAYLOR
IT SEEMS TO ME THAT C.E.O. PAY IS ONE OF THE KEY ISSUES FACING COMPANY BOARDS LIKE OURS...
THERE SHOULD BE A UNIVERSAL STANDARD FOR SETTING CHIEF EXECUTIVE COMPENSATION TO PREVENT IT BECOMING DISPROPORTIONATE.
BUT SUCH A MECHANISM ALREADY EXISTS, PENNY. IT'S CALLED "PEER BENCHMARKING"
YES.
alex@alexcartoon.com
COMPANIES PEG THEIR C.E.O.'S SALARY TO RECOGNISED NORMS ACROSS THE INDUSTRY. AS A POLICY IT'S BEEN A GREAT SUCCESS AND MOST COMPANIES ARE NOW ADOPTING IT...
ER, BUT... HOLD ON...
IF EVERYBODY PEGS TO EVERYONE ELSE'S LEVELS THEN THERE'S EFFECTIVELY NO CONTROLS AT ALL...
WELL YOU SAID YOU WANTED A UNIVERSAL STANDARD.
TRY AT LEAST TO BE CONSISTENT...
CAN WE MOVE ON, PLEASE?

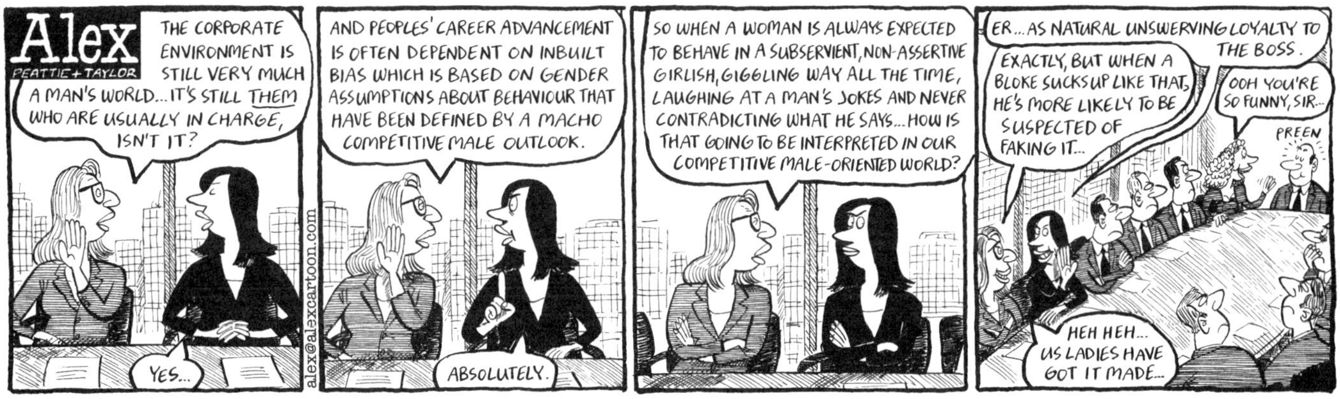
Alex
PEATTIE+TAYLOR
THE CORPORATE ENVIRONMENT IS STILL VERY MUCH A MAN'S WORLD... IT'S STILL THEM WHO ARE USUALLY IN CHARGE, ISN'T IT?
YES...
alex@alexcartoon.com
AND PEOPLES' CAREER ADVANCEMENT IS OFTEN DEPENDENT ON INBUILT BIAS WHICH IS BASED ON GENDER ASSUMPTIONS ABOUT BEHAVIOUR THAT HAVE BEEN DEFINED BY A MACHO COMPETITIVE MALE OUTLOOK.
ABSOLUTELY.
SO WHEN A WOMAN IS ALWAYS EXPECTED TO BEHAVE IN A SUBSERVIENT, NON-ASSERTIVE GIRLISH, GIGGLING WAY ALL THE TIME, LAUGHING AT A MAN'S JOKES AND NEVER CONTRADICTING WHAT HE SAYS... HOW IS THAT GOING TO BE INTERPRETED IN OUR COMPETITIVE MALE-ORIENTED WORLD?
ER... AS NATURAL UNSWERVING LOYALTY TO THE BOSS.
EXACTLY, BUT WHEN A BLOKE SUCKS UP LIKE THAT, HE'S MORE LIKELY TO BE SUSPECTED OF FAKING IT...
OOH YOU'RE SO FUNNY, SIR...
PREEN
HEH HEH... US LADIES HAVE GOT IT MADE...

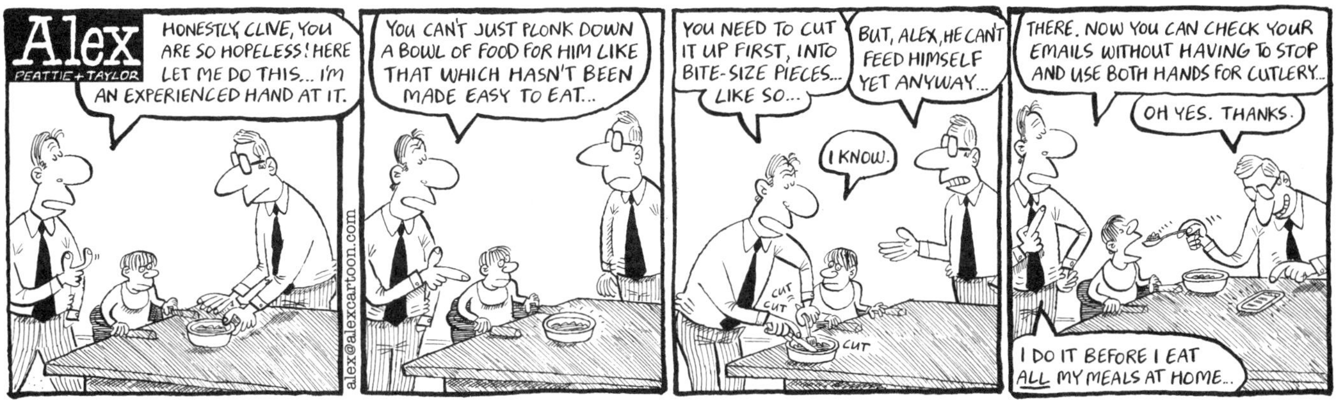
Alex
PEATTIE+TAYLOR
HONESTLY, CLIVE, YOU ARE SO HOPELESS! HERE LET ME DO THIS... I'M AN EXPERIENCED HAND AT IT.
YOU CAN'T JUST PLONK DOWN A BOWL OF FOOD FOR HIM LIKE THAT WHICH HASN'T BEEN MADE EASY TO EAT...
alex@alexcartoon.com
YOU NEED TO CUT IT UP FIRST, INTO BITE-SIZE PIECES... LIKE SO...
BUT, ALEX, HE CAN'T FEED HIMSELF YET ANYWAY...
I KNOW.
CUT
CUT
CUT
THERE. NOW YOU CAN CHECK YOUR EMAILS WITHOUT HAVING TO STOP AND USE BOTH HANDS FOR CUTLERY...
OH YES. THANKS.
I DO IT BEFORE I EAT ALL MY MEALS AT HOME...

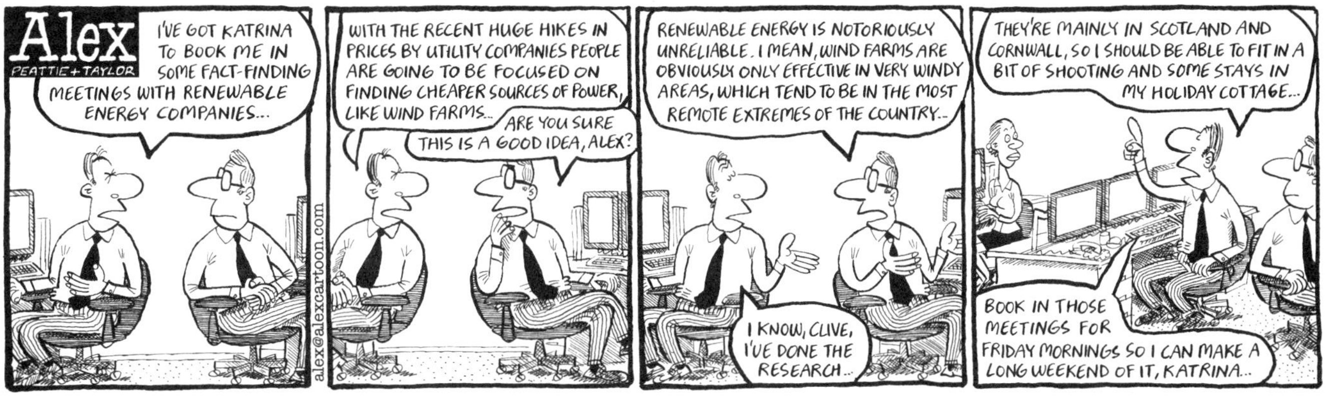
Alex
PEATTIE+TAYLOR
I'VE GOT KATRINA TO BOOK ME IN SOME FACT-FINDING MEETINGS WITH RENEWABLE ENERGY COMPANIES...
alex@alexcartoon.com
WITH THE RECENT HUGE HIKES IN PRICES BY UTILITY COMPANIES PEOPLE ARE GOING TO BE FOCUSED ON FINDING CHEAPER SOURCES OF POWER, LIKE WIND FARMS...
ARE YOU SURE THIS IS A GOOD IDEA, ALEX?
RENEWABLE ENERGY IS NOTORIOUSLY UNRELIABLE. I MEAN, WIND FARMS ARE OBVIOUSLY ONLY EFFECTIVE IN VERY WINDY AREAS, WHICH TEND TO BE IN THE MOST REMOTE EXTREMES OF THE COUNTRY...
I KNOW, CLIVE, I'VE DONE THE RESEARCH...
THEY'RE MAINLY IN SCOTLAND AND CORNWALL, SO I SHOULD BE ABLE TO FIT IN A BIT OF SHOOTING AND SOME STAYS IN MY HOLIDAY COTTAGE...
BOOK IN THOSE MEETINGS FOR FRIDAY MORNINGS SO I CAN MAKE A LONG WEEKEND OF IT, KATRINA...

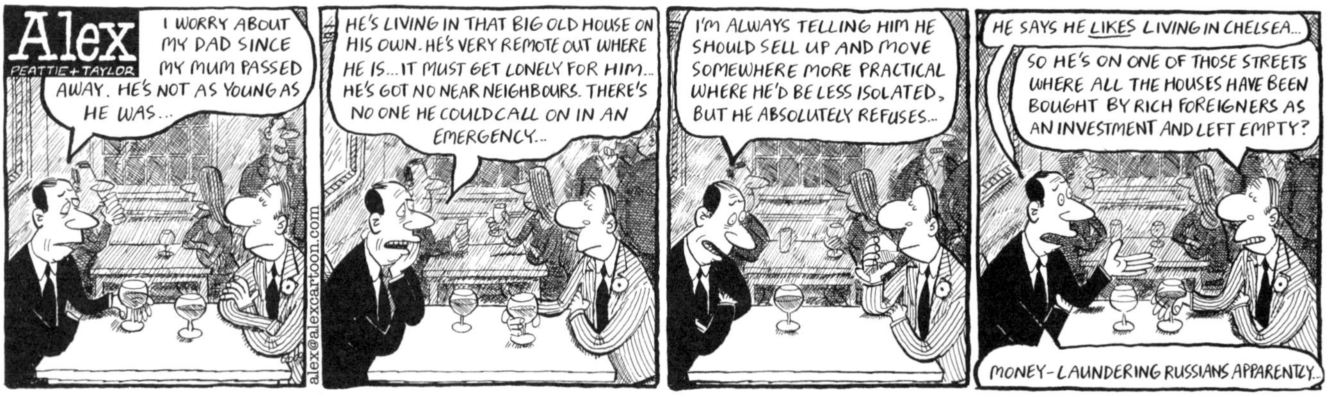
Alex
PEATTIE+TAYLOR
I WORRY ABOUT MY DAD SINCE MY MUM PASSED AWAY. HE'S NOT AS YOUNG AS HE WAS...
HE'S LIVING IN THAT BIG OLD HOUSE ON HIS OWN. HE'S VERY REMOTE OUT WHERE HE IS... IT MUST GET LONELY FOR HIM... HE'S GOT NO NEAR NEIGHBOURS. THERE'S NO ONE HE COULD CALL ON IN AN EMERGENCY...
alex@alexcartoon.com
I'M ALWAYS TELLING HIM HE SHOULD SELL UP AND MOVE SOMEWHERE MORE PRACTICAL WHERE HE'D BE LESS ISOLATED, BUT HE ABSOLUTELY REFUSES...
HE SAYS HE LIKES LIVING IN CHELSEA...
SO HE'S ON ONE OF THOSE STREETS WHERE ALL THE HOUSES HAVE BEEN BOUGHT BY RICH FOREIGNERS AS AN INVESTMENT AND LEFT EMPTY?
MONEY-LAUNDERING RUSSIANS APPARENTLY...

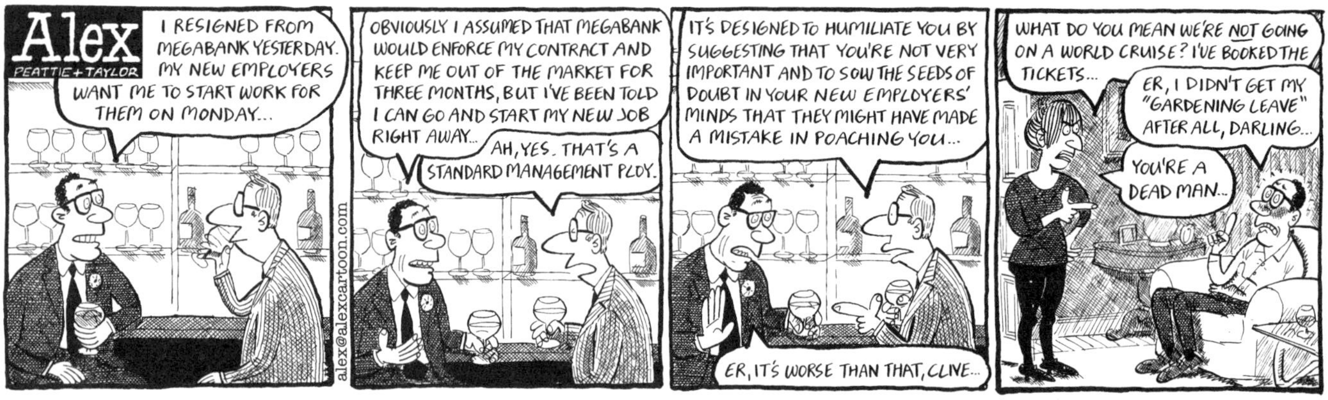
Alex
PEATTIE+TAYLOR
I RESIGNED FROM MEGABANK YESTERDAY. MY NEW EMPLOYERS WANT ME TO START WORK FOR THEM ON MONDAY...
OBVIOUSLY I ASSUMED THAT MEGABANK WOULD ENFORCE MY CONTRACT AND KEEP ME OUT OF THE MARKET FOR THREE MONTHS, BUT I'VE BEEN TOLD I CAN GO AND START MY NEW JOB RIGHT AWAY...
AH, YES. THAT'S A STANDARD MANAGEMENT PLOY.
alex@alexcartoon.com
IT'S DESIGNED TO HUMILIATE YOU BY SUGGESTING THAT YOU'RE NOT VERY IMPORTANT AND TO SOW THE SEEDS OF DOUBT IN YOUR NEW EMPLOYERS' MINDS THAT THEY MIGHT HAVE MADE A MISTAKE IN POACHING YOU...
ER, IT'S WORSE THAN THAT, CLIVE...
WHAT DO YOU MEAN WE'RE NOT GOING ON A WORLD CRUISE? I'VE BOOKED THE TICKETS...
ER, I DIDN'T GET MY "GARDENING LEAVE" AFTER ALL, DARLING...
YOU'RE A DEAD MAN...

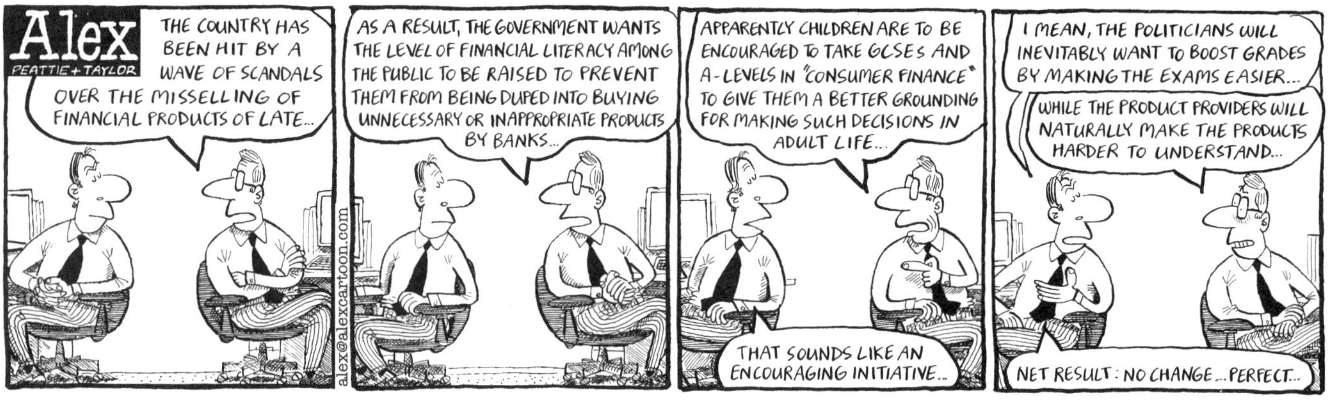
Alex
PEATTIE+TAYLOR
THE COUNTRY HAS BEEN HIT BY A WAVE OF SCANDALS OVER THE MISSELLING OF FINANCIAL PRODUCTS OF LATE...
AS A RESULT, THE GOVERNMENT WANTS THE LEVEL OF FINANCIAL LITERACY AMONG THE PUBLIC TO BE RAISED TO PREVENT THEM FROM BEING DUPED INTO BUYING UNNECESSARY OR INAPPROPRIATE PRODUCTS BY BANKS...
alex@alexcartoon.com
APPARENTLY CHILDREN ARE TO BE ENCOURAGED TO TAKE GCSEs AND A-LEVELS IN "CONSUMER FINANCE" TO GIVE THEM A BETTER GROUNDING FOR MAKING SUCH DECISIONS IN ADULT LIFE...
THAT SOUNDS LIKE AN ENCOURAGING INITIATIVE...
I MEAN, THE POLITICIANS WILL INEVITABLY WANT TO BOOST GRADES BY MAKING THE EXAMS EASIER...
WHILE THE PRODUCT PROVIDERS WILL NATURALLY MAKE THE PRODUCTS HARDER TO UNDERSTAND...
NET RESULT: NO CHANGE... PERFECT...

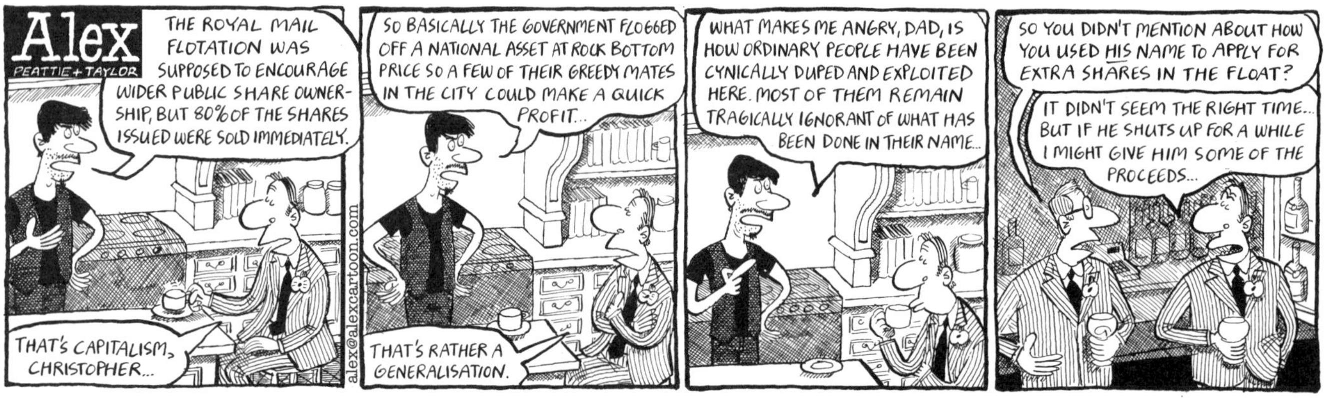
Alex
PEATTIE+TAYLOR
THE ROYAL MAIL FLOTATION WAS SUPPOSED TO ENCOURAGE WIDER PUBLIC SHARE OWNERSHIP, BUT 80% OF THE SHARES ISSUED WERE SOLD IMMEDIATELY.
THAT'S CAPITALISM, CHRISTOPHER...
SO BASICALLY THE GOVERNMENT FLOGGED OFF A NATIONAL ASSET AT ROCK BOTTOM PRICE SO A FEW OF THEIR GREEDY MATES IN THE CITY COULD MAKE A QUICK PROFIT...
THAT'S RATHER A GENERALISATION.
alex@alexcartoon.com
WHAT MAKES ME ANGRY, DAD, IS HOW ORDINARY PEOPLE HAVE BEEN CYNICALLY DUPED AND EXPLOITED HERE. MOST OF THEM REMAIN TRAGICALLY IGNORANT OF WHAT HAS BEEN DONE IN THEIR NAME...
SO YOU DIDN'T MENTION ABOUT HOW YOU USED HIS NAME TO APPLY FOR EXTRA SHARES IN THE FLOAT?
IT DIDN'T SEEM THE RIGHT TIME... BUT IF HE SHUTS UP FOR A WHILE I MIGHT GIVE HIM SOME OF THE PROCEEDS...

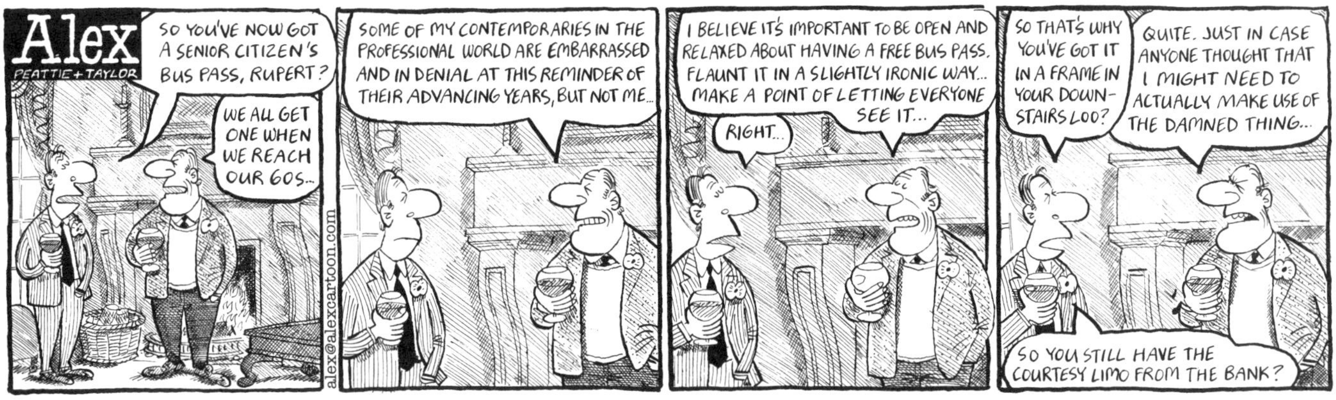
Alex
PEATTIE + TAYLOR
SO YOU'VE NOW GOT A SENIOR CITIZEN'S BUS PASS, RUPERT?
WE ALL GET ONE WHEN WE REACH OUR 60S...
alex@alexcartoon.com
SOME OF MY CONTEMPORARIES IN THE PROFESSIONAL WORLD ARE EMBARRASSED AND IN DENIAL AT THIS REMINDER OF THEIR ADVANCING YEARS, BUT NOT ME...
I BELIEVE IT'S IMPORTANT TO BE OPEN AND RELAXED ABOUT HAVING A FREE BUS PASS. FLAUNT IT IN A SLIGHTLY IRONIC WAY... MAKE A POINT OF LETTING EVERYONE SEE IT...
RIGHT...
SO THAT'S WHY YOU'VE GOT IT IN A FRAME IN YOUR DOWNSTAIRS LOO?
QUITE. JUST IN CASE ANYONE THOUGHT THAT I MIGHT NEED TO ACTUALLY MAKE USE OF THE DAMNED THING...
SO YOU STILL HAVE THE COURTESY LIMO FROM THE BANK?

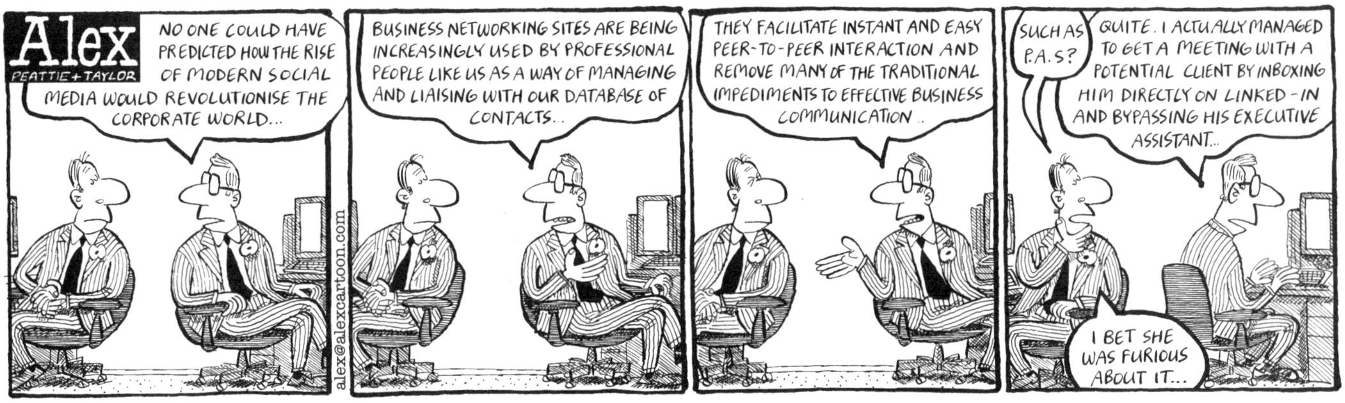
Alex
PEATTIE + TAYLOR
NO ONE COULD HAVE PREDICTED HOW THE RISE OF MODERN SOCIAL MEDIA WOULD REVOLUTIONISE THE CORPORATE WORLD...
alex@alexcartoon.com
BUSINESS NETWORKING SITES ARE BEING INCREASINGLY USED BY PROFESSIONAL PEOPLE LIKE US AS A WAY OF MANAGING AND LIAISING WITH OUR DATABASE OF CONTACTS...
THEY FACILITATE INSTANT AND EASY PEER-TO-PEER INTERACTION AND REMOVE MANY OF THE TRADITIONAL IMPEDIMENTS TO EFFECTIVE BUSINESS COMMUNICATION...
SUCH AS P.A.S?
QUITE. I ACTUALLY MANAGED TO GET A MEETING WITH A POTENTIAL CLIENT BY INBOXING HIM DIRECTLY ON LINKED-IN AND BYPASSING HIS EXECUTIVE ASSISTANT...
I BET SHE WAS FURIOUS ABOUT IT...

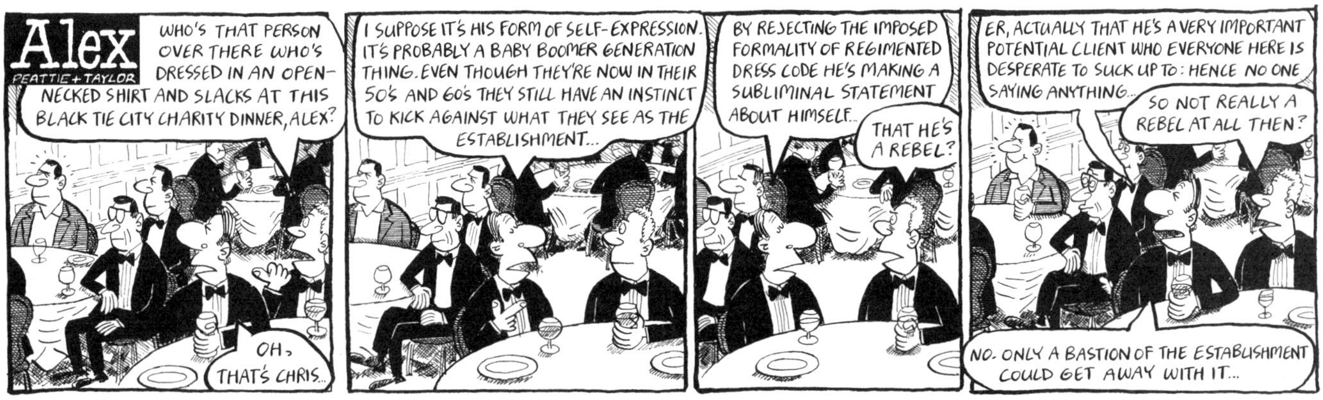
Alex
PEATTIE + TAYLOR
WHO'S THAT PERSON OVER THERE WHO'S DRESSED IN AN OPEN-NECKED SHIRT AND SLACKS AT THIS BLACK TIE CITY CHARITY DINNER, ALEX?
OH, THAT'S CHRIS...
I SUPPOSE IT'S HIS FORM OF SELF-EXPRESSION. IT'S PROBABLY A BABY BOOMER GENERATION THING. EVEN THOUGH THEY'RE NOW IN THEIR 50'S AND 60'S THEY STILL HAVE AN INSTINCT TO KICK AGAINST WHAT THEY SEE AS THE ESTABLISHMENT...
BY REJECTING THE IMPOSED FORMALITY OF REGIMENTED DRESS CODE HE'S MAKING A SUBLIMINAL STATEMENT ABOUT HIMSELF...
THAT HE'S A REBEL?
ER, ACTUALLY THAT HE'S A VERY IMPORTANT POTENTIAL CLIENT WHO EVERYONE HERE IS DESPERATE TO SUCK UP TO: HENCE NO ONE SAYING ANYTHING...
SO NOT REALLY A REBEL AT ALL THEN?
NO. ONLY A BASTION OF THE ESTABLISHMENT COULD GET AWAY WITH IT...

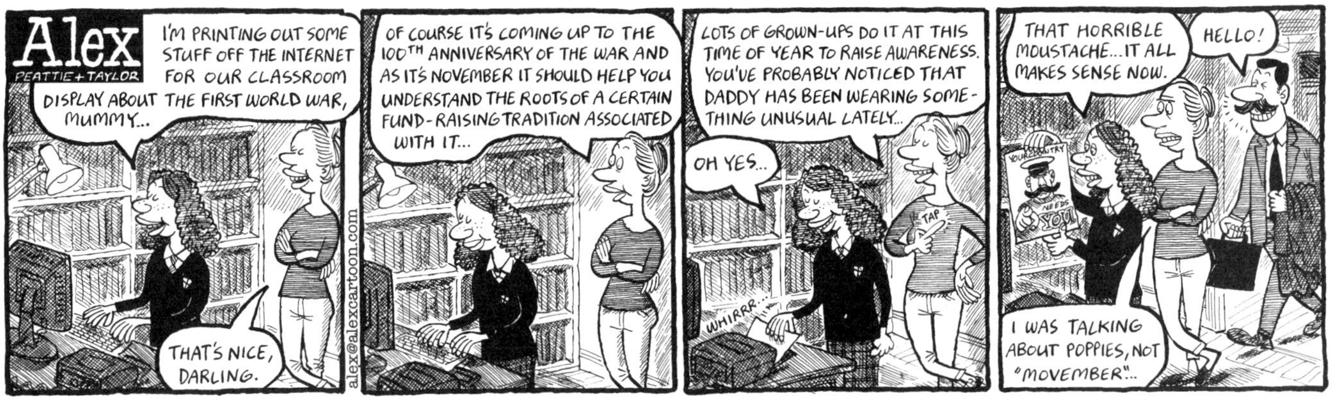
Alex
PEATTIE + TAYLOR
I'M PRINTING OUT SOME STUFF OFF THE INTERNET FOR OUR CLASSROOM DISPLAY ABOUT THE FIRST WORLD WAR, MUMMY...
THAT'S NICE, DARLING.
alex@alexcartoon.com
OF COURSE IT'S COMING UP TO THE 100TH ANNIVERSARY OF THE WAR AND AS IT'S NOVEMBER IT SHOULD HELP YOU UNDERSTAND THE ROOTS OF A CERTAIN FUND-RAISING TRADITION ASSOCIATED WITH IT...
LOTS OF GROWN-UPS DO IT AT THIS TIME OF YEAR TO RAISE AWARENESS. YOU'VE PROBABLY NOTICED THAT DADDY HAS BEEN WEARING SOMETHING UNUSUAL LATELY...
OH YES...
TAP
WHIRRR...
THAT HORRIBLE MOUSTACHE... IT ALL MAKES SENSE NOW.
HELLO!
YOU
I WAS TALKING ABOUT POPPIES, NOT "MOVEMBER"...

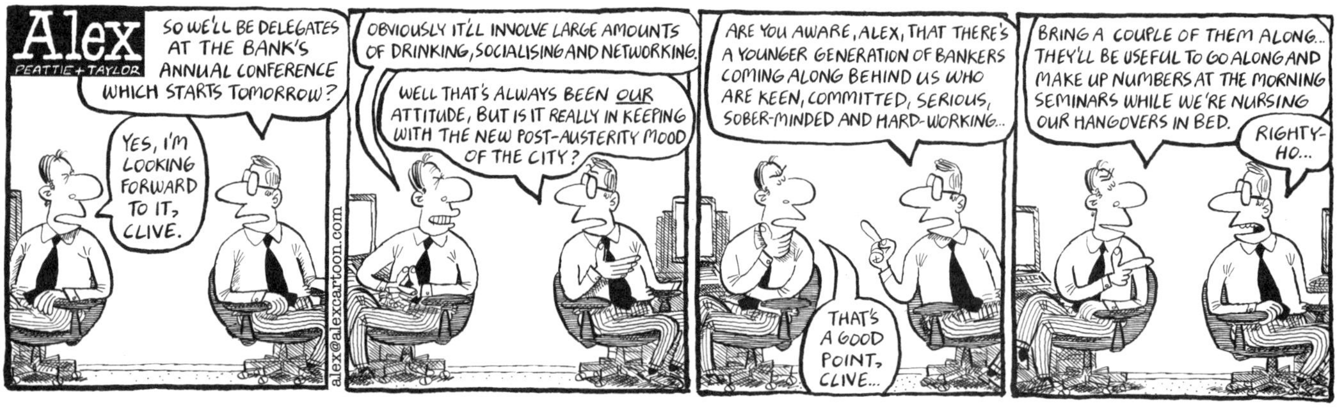
Alex
PEATTIE+TAYLOR
SO WE'LL BE DELEGATES AT THE BANK'S ANNUAL CONFERENCE WHICH STARTS TOMORROW?
YES, I'M LOOKING FORWARD TO IT, CLIVE.
OBVIOUSLY IT'LL INVOLVE LARGE AMOUNTS OF DRINKING, SOCIALISING AND NETWORKING.
WELL THAT'S ALWAYS BEEN OUR ATTITUDE, BUT IS IT REALLY IN KEEPING WITH THE NEW POST-AUSTERITY MOOD OF THE CITY?
ARE YOU AWARE, ALEX, THAT THERE'S A YOUNGER GENERATION OF BANKERS COMING ALONG BEHIND US WHO ARE KEEN, COMMITTED, SERIOUS, SOBER-MINDED AND HARD-WORKING...
THAT'S A GOOD POINT, CLIVE...
BRING A COUPLE OF THEM ALONG... THEY'LL BE USEFUL TO GO ALONG AND MAKE UP NUMBERS AT THE MORNING SEMINARS WHILE WE'RE NURSING OUR HANGOVERS IN BED.
RIGHTY-HO...
alex@alexcartoon.com

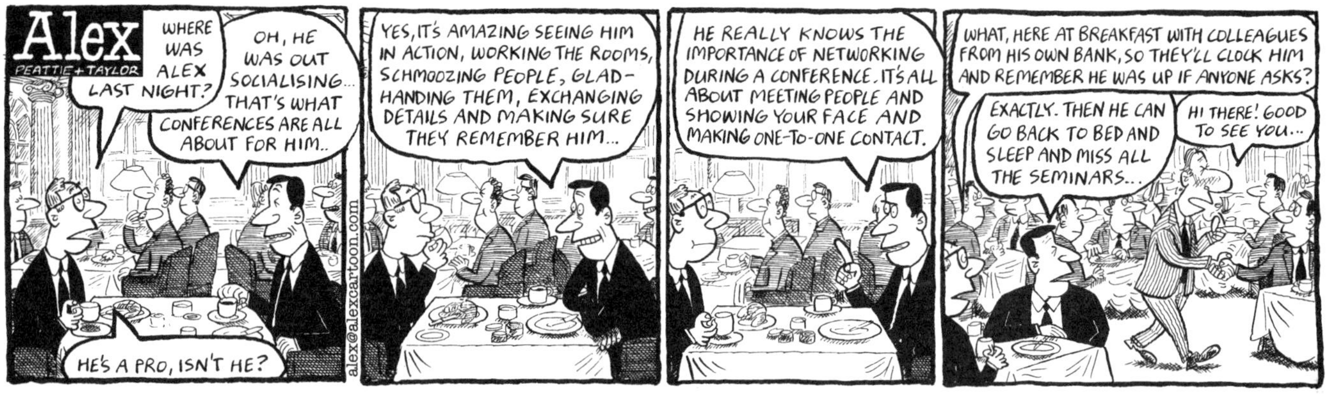
Alex
PEATTIE+TAYLOR
WHERE WAS ALEX LAST NIGHT?
OH, HE WAS OUT SOCIALISING... THAT'S WHAT CONFERENCES ARE ALL ABOUT FOR HIM..
HE'S A PRO, ISN'T HE?
YES, IT'S AMAZING SEEING HIM IN ACTION, WORKING THE ROOMS, SCHMOOZING PEOPLE, GLAD-HANDING THEM, EXCHANGING DETAILS AND MAKING SURE THEY REMEMBER HIM...
HE REALLY KNOWS THE IMPORTANCE OF NETWORKING DURING A CONFERENCE. IT'S ALL ABOUT MEETING PEOPLE AND SHOWING YOUR FACE AND MAKING ONE-TO-ONE CONTACT.
WHAT, HERE AT BREAKFAST WITH COLLEAGUES FROM HIS OWN BANK, SO THEY'LL CLOCK HIM AND REMEMBER HE WAS UP IF ANYONE ASKS?
EXACTLY. THEN HE CAN GO BACK TO BED AND SLEEP AND MISS ALL THE SEMINARS...
HI THERE! GOOD TO SEE YOU...
alex@alexcartoon.com

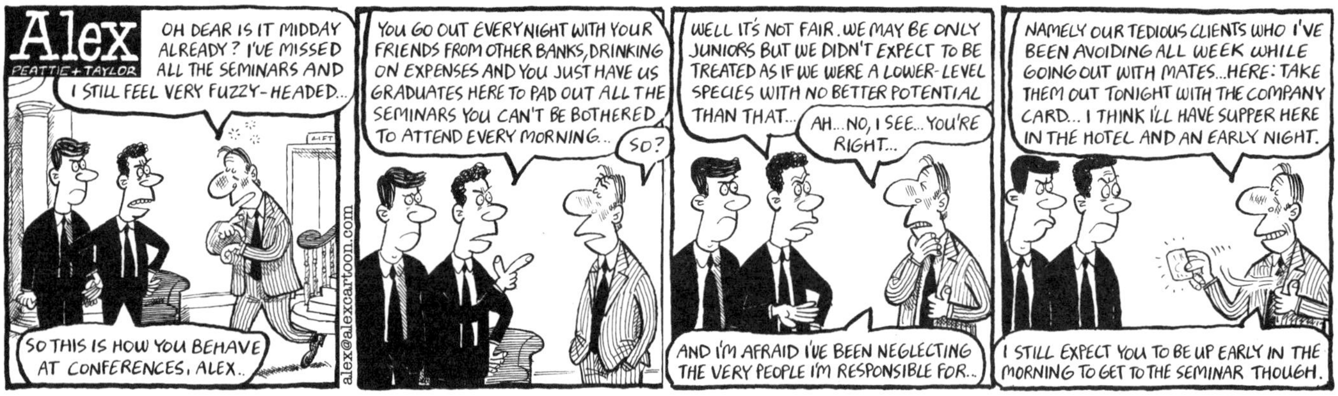
Alex
PEATTIE+TAYLOR
OH DEAR IS IT MIDDAY ALREADY? I'VE MISSED ALL THE SEMINARS AND I STILL FEEL VERY FUZZY-HEADED...
SO THIS IS HOW YOU BEHAVE AT CONFERENCES, ALEX..
YOU GO OUT EVERY NIGHT WITH YOUR FRIENDS FROM OTHER BANKS, DRINKING ON EXPENSES AND YOU JUST HAVE US GRADUATES HERE TO PAD OUT ALL THE SEMINARS YOU CAN'T BE BOTHERED TO ATTEND EVERY MORNING...
SO?
WELL IT'S NOT FAIR. WE MAY BE ONLY JUNIORS BUT WE DIDN'T EXPECT TO BE TREATED AS IF WE WERE A LOWER-LEVEL SPECIES WITH NO BETTER POTENTIAL THAN THAT...
AH... NO, I SEE... YOU'RE RIGHT...
AND I'M AFRAID I'VE BEEN NEGLECTING THE VERY PEOPLE I'M RESPONSIBLE FOR...
NAMELY OUR TEDIOUS CLIENTS WHO I'VE BEEN AVOIDING ALL WEEK WHILE GOING OUT WITH MATES... HERE: TAKE THEM OUT TONIGHT WITH THE COMPANY CARD... I THINK I'LL HAVE SUPPER HERE IN THE HOTEL AND AN EARLY NIGHT.
I STILL EXPECT YOU TO BE UP EARLY IN THE MORNING TO GET TO THE SEMINAR THOUGH.
alex@alexcartoon.com

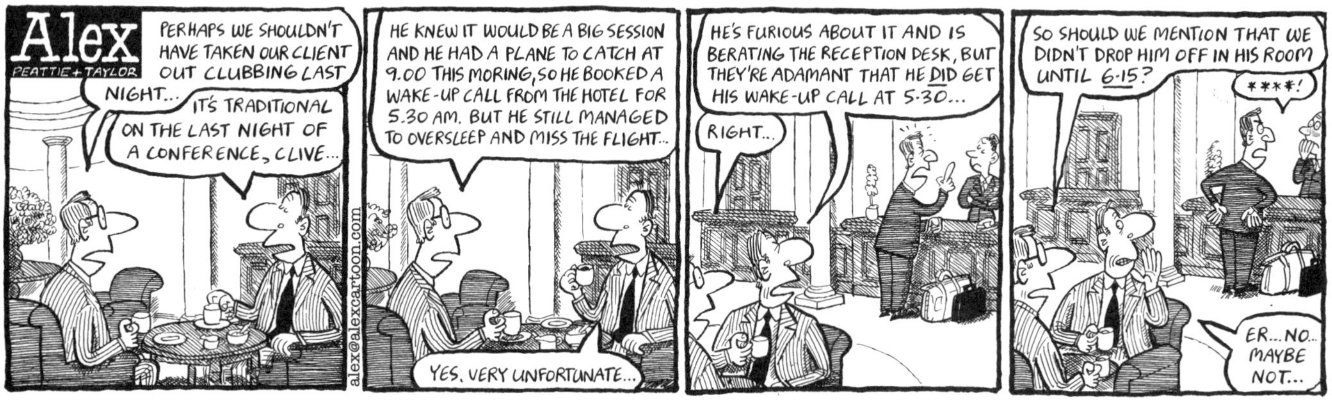
Alex
PEATTIE+TAYLOR
PERHAPS WE SHOULDN'T HAVE TAKEN OUR CLIENT OUT CLUBBING LAST NIGHT...
IT'S TRADITIONAL ON THE LAST NIGHT OF A CONFERENCE, CLIVE...
HE KNEW IT WOULD BE A BIG SESSION AND HE HAD A PLANE TO CATCH AT 9.00 THIS MORING, SO HE BOOKED A WAKE-UP CALL FROM THE HOTEL FOR 5.30 AM. BUT HE STILL MANAGED TO OVERSLEEP AND MISS THE FLIGHT...
YES, VERY UNFORTUNATE...
HE'S FURIOUS ABOUT IT AND IS BERATING THE RECEPTION DESK, BUT THEY'RE ADAMANT THAT HE DID GET HIS WAKE-UP CALL AT 5.30...
RIGHT..
SO SHOULD WE MENTION THAT WE DIDN'T DROP HIM OFF IN HIS ROOM UNTIL 6.15?
****!
ER... NO... MAYBE NOT...
alex@alexcartoon.com

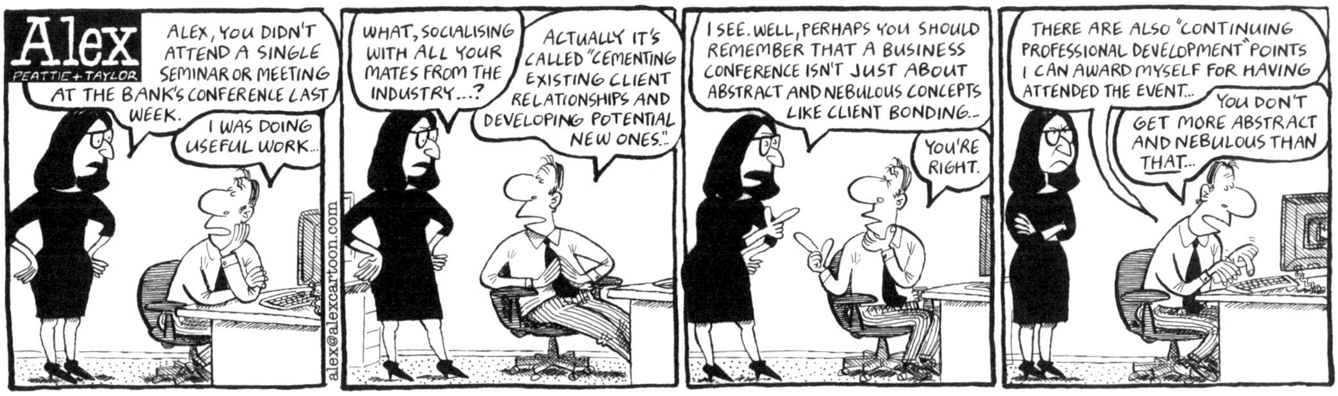
Alex
PEATTIE + TAYLOR
ALEX, YOU DIDN'T ATTEND A SINGLE SEMINAR OR MEETING AT THE BANK'S CONFERENCE LAST WEEK.
I WAS DOING USEFUL WORK...
WHAT, SOCIALISING WITH ALL YOUR MATES FROM THE INDUSTRY...?
ACTUALLY IT'S CALLED "CEMENTING EXISTING CLIENT RELATIONSHIPS AND DEVELOPING POTENTIAL NEW ONES."
I SEE. WELL, PERHAPS YOU SHOULD REMEMBER THAT A BUSINESS CONFERENCE ISN'T JUST ABOUT ABSTRACT AND NEBULOUS CONCEPTS LIKE CLIENT BONDING...
YOU'RE RIGHT.
THERE ARE ALSO "CONTINUING PROFESSIONAL DEVELOPMENT" POINTS I CAN AWARD MYSELF FOR HAVING ATTENDED THE EVENT...
YOU DON'T GET MORE ABSTRACT AND NEBULOUS THAN THAT...
alex@alexcartoon.com

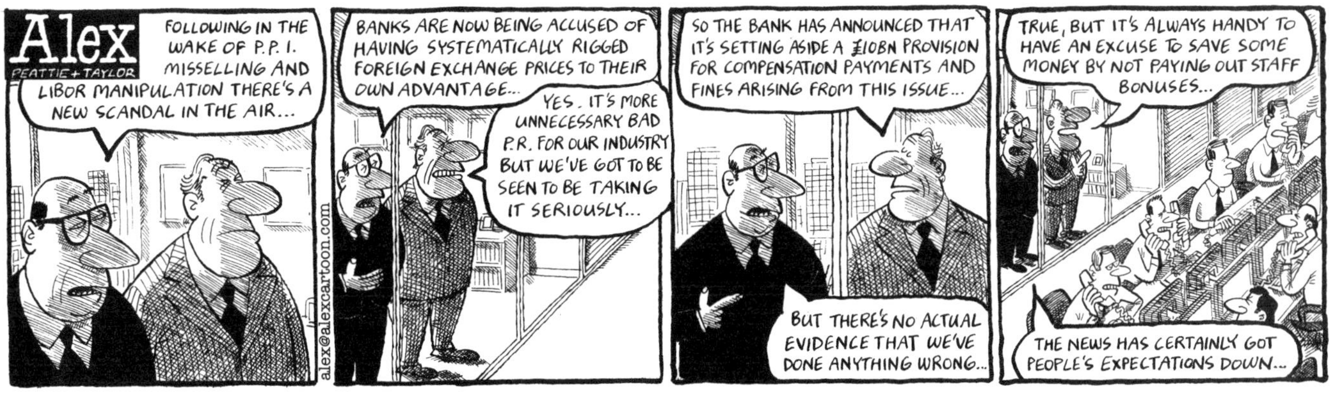
Alex
PEATTIE + TAYLOR
FOLLOWING IN THE WAKE OF P.P.I. MISSELLING AND LIBOR MANIPULATION THERE'S A NEW SCANDAL IN THE AIR...
BANKS ARE NOW BEING ACCUSED OF HAVING SYSTEMATICALLY RIGGED FOREIGN EXCHANGE PRICES TO THEIR OWN ADVANTAGE...
YES. IT'S MORE UNNECESSARY BAD P.R. FOR OUR INDUSTRY BUT WE'VE GOT TO BE SEEN TO BE TAKING IT SERIOUSLY...
SO THE BANK HAS ANNOUNCED THAT IT'S SETTING ASIDE A £10BN PROVISION FOR COMPENSATION PAYMENTS AND FINES ARISING FROM THIS ISSUE...
BUT THERE'S NO ACTUAL EVIDENCE THAT WE'VE DONE ANYTHING WRONG...
TRUE, BUT IT'S ALWAYS HANDY TO HAVE AN EXCUSE TO SAVE SOME MONEY BY NOT PAYING OUT STAFF BONUSES...
THE NEWS HAS CERTAINLY GOT PEOPLE'S EXPECTATIONS DOWN...
alex@alexcartoon.com

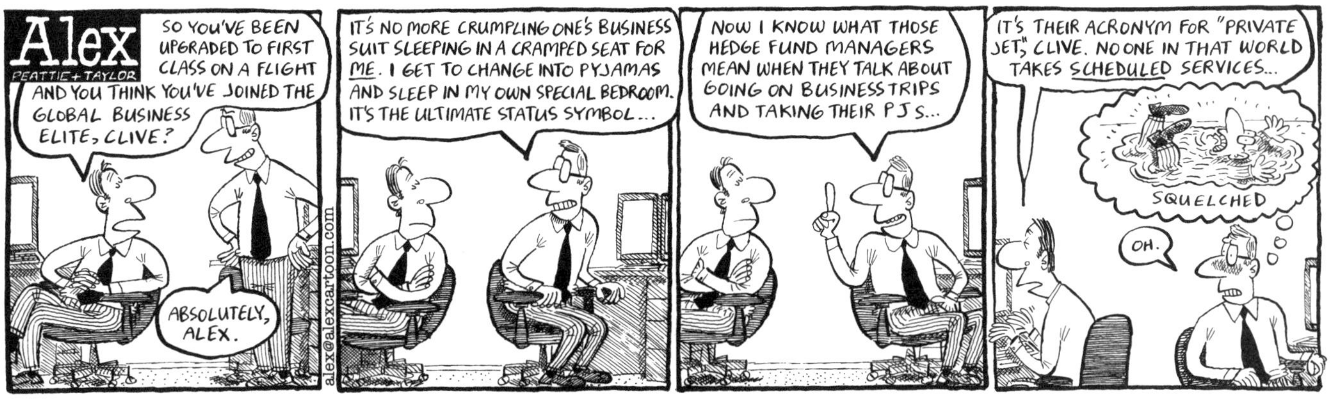
Alex
PEATTIE + TAYLOR
SO YOU'VE BEEN UPGRADED TO FIRST CLASS ON A FLIGHT AND YOU THINK YOU'VE JOINED THE GLOBAL BUSINESS ELITE, CLIVE?
ABSOLUTELY, ALEX.
IT'S NO MORE CRUMPLING ONE'S BUSINESS SUIT SLEEPING IN A CRAMPED SEAT FOR ME. I GET TO CHANGE INTO PYJAMAS AND SLEEP IN MY OWN SPECIAL BEDROOM. IT'S THE ULTIMATE STATUS SYMBOL...
NOW I KNOW WHAT THOSE HEDGE FUND MANAGERS MEAN WHEN THEY TALK ABOUT GOING ON BUSINESS TRIPS AND TAKING THEIR PJS...
IT'S THEIR ACRONYM FOR "PRIVATE JET," CLIVE. NO ONE IN THAT WORLD TAKES SCHEDULED SERVICES...
SQUELCHED
OH.
alex@alexcartoon.com

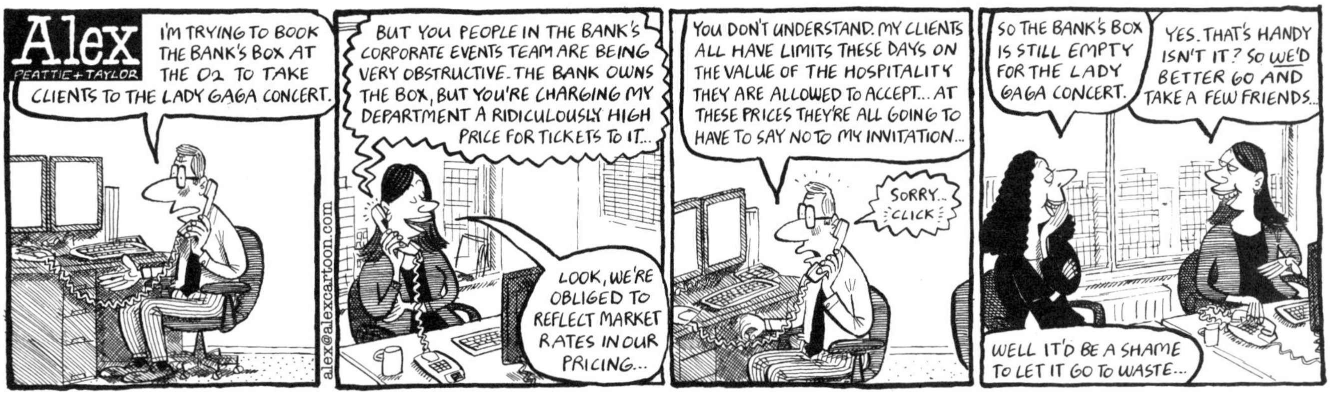
Alex
PEATTIE + TAYLOR
I'M TRYING TO BOOK THE BANK'S BOX AT THE O2 TO TAKE CLIENTS TO THE LADY GAGA CONCERT.
BUT YOU PEOPLE IN THE BANK'S CORPORATE EVENTS TEAM ARE BEING VERY OBSTRUCTIVE. THE BANK OWNS THE BOX, BUT YOU'RE CHARGING MY DEPARTMENT A RIDICULOUSLY HIGH PRICE FOR TICKETS TO IT...
LOOK, WE'RE OBLIGED TO REFLECT MARKET RATES IN OUR PRICING...
YOU DON'T UNDERSTAND. MY CLIENTS ALL HAVE LIMITS THESE DAYS ON THE VALUE OF THE HOSPITALITY THEY ARE ALLOWED TO ACCEPT... AT THESE PRICES THEY'RE ALL GOING TO HAVE TO SAY NO TO MY INVITATION...
SORRY... CLICK
SO THE BANK'S BOX IS STILL EMPTY FOR THE LADY GAGA CONCERT.
YES. THAT'S HANDY ISN'T IT? SO WE'D BETTER GO AND TAKE A FEW FRIENDS...
WELL IT'D BE A SHAME TO LET IT GO TO WASTE...
alex@alexcartoon.com

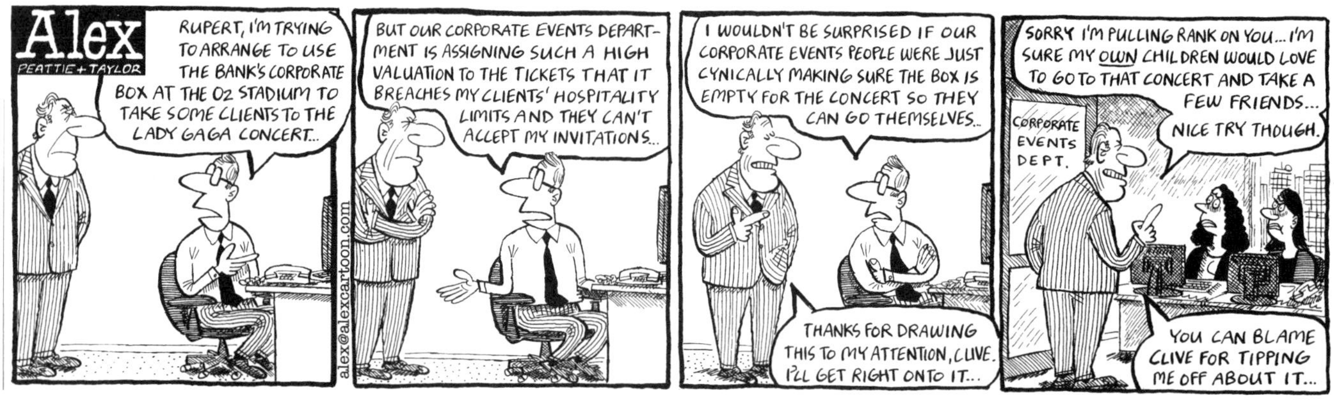
Alex
PEATTIE+TAYLOR
RUPERT, I'M TRYING TO ARRANGE TO USE THE BANK'S CORPORATE BOX AT THE O2 STADIUM TO TAKE SOME CLIENTS TO THE LADY GAGA CONCERT...
alex@alexcartoon.com
BUT OUR CORPORATE EVENTS DEPARTMENT IS ASSIGNING SUCH A HIGH VALUATION TO THE TICKETS THAT IT BREACHES MY CLIENTS' HOSPITALITY LIMITS AND THEY CAN'T ACCEPT MY INVITATIONS...
I WOULDN'T BE SURPRISED IF OUR CORPORATE EVENTS PEOPLE WERE JUST CYNICALLY MAKING SURE THE BOX IS EMPTY FOR THE CONCERT SO THEY CAN GO THEMSELVES...
THANKS FOR DRAWING THIS TO MY ATTENTION, CLIVE. I'LL GET RIGHT ONTO IT...
CORPORATE EVENTS DEPT.
SORRY I'M PULLING RANK ON YOU... I'M SURE MY OWN CHILDREN WOULD LOVE TO GO TO THAT CONCERT AND TAKE A FEW FRIENDS...
NICE TRY THOUGH.
YOU CAN BLAME CLIVE FOR TIPPING ME OFF ABOUT IT...

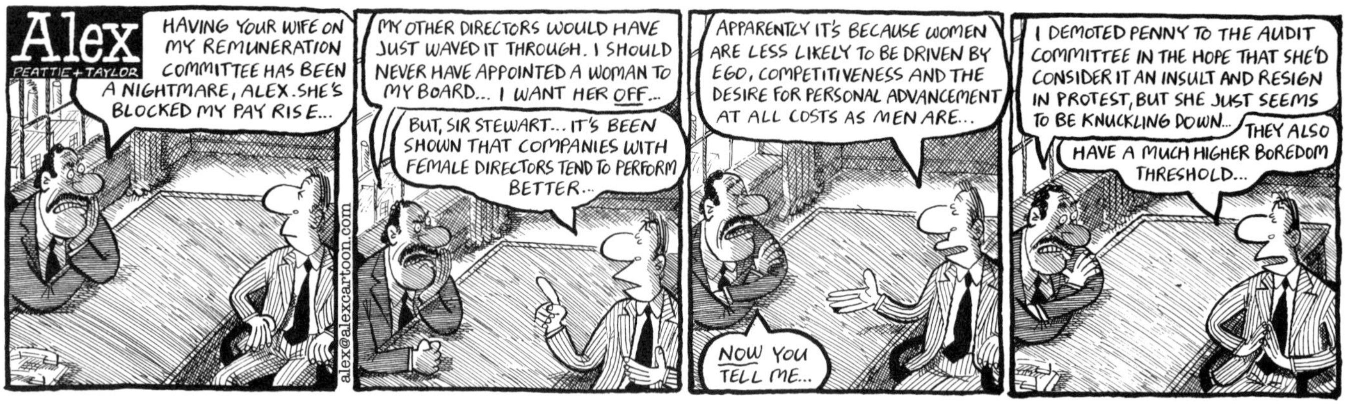
Alex
PEATTIE+TAYLOR
HAVING YOUR WIFE ON MY REMUNERATION COMMITTEE HAS BEEN A NIGHTMARE, ALEX. SHE'S BLOCKED MY PAY RISE...
alex@alexcartoon.com
MY OTHER DIRECTORS WOULD HAVE JUST WAVED IT THROUGH. I SHOULD NEVER HAVE APPOINTED A WOMAN TO MY BOARD... I WANT HER OFF...
BUT, SIR STEWART... IT'S BEEN SHOWN THAT COMPANIES WITH FEMALE DIRECTORS TEND TO PERFORM BETTER...
APPARENTLY IT'S BECAUSE WOMEN ARE LESS LIKELY TO BE DRIVEN BY EGO, COMPETITIVENESS AND THE DESIRE FOR PERSONAL ADVANCEMENT AT ALL COSTS AS MEN ARE...
NOW YOU TELL ME...
I DEMOTED PENNY TO THE AUDIT COMMITTEE IN THE HOPE THAT SHE'D CONSIDER IT AN INSULT AND RESIGN IN PROTEST, BUT SHE JUST SEEMS TO BE KNUCKLING DOWN...
THEY ALSO HAVE A MUCH HIGHER BOREDOM THRESHOLD...

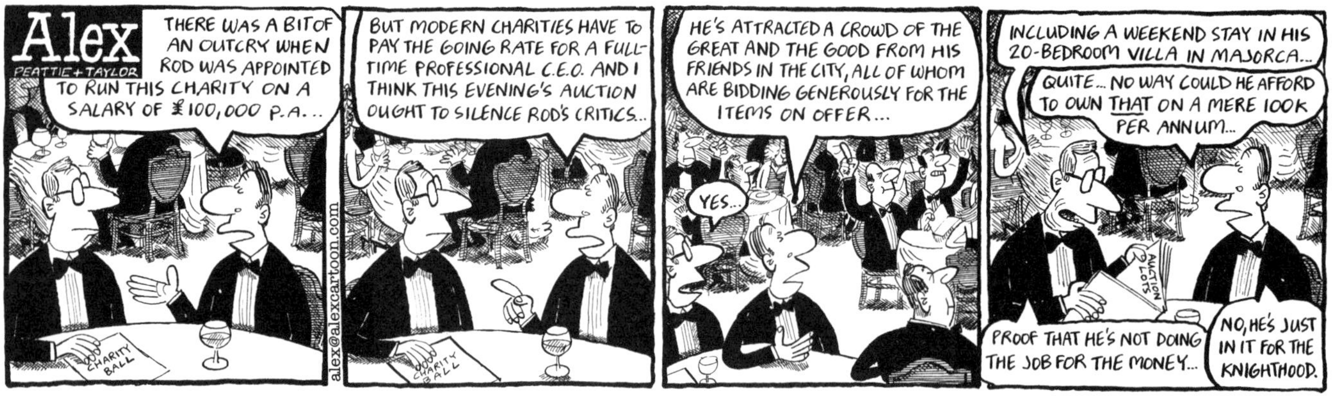
Alex
PEATTIE+TAYLOR
THERE WAS A BIT OF AN OUTCRY WHEN ROD WAS APPOINTED TO RUN THIS CHARITY ON A SALARY OF £100,000 P.A...
CHARITY BALL
alex@alexcartoon.com
BUT MODERN CHARITIES HAVE TO PAY THE GOING RATE FOR A FULL-TIME PROFESSIONAL C.E.O. AND I THINK THIS EVENING'S AUCTION OUGHT TO SILENCE ROD'S CRITICS...
CHARITY BALL
HE'S ATTRACTED A CROWD OF THE GREAT AND THE GOOD FROM HIS FRIENDS IN THE CITY, ALL OF WHOM ARE BIDDING GENEROUSLY FOR THE ITEMS ON OFFER...
YES...
INCLUDING A WEEKEND STAY IN HIS 20-BEDROOM VILLA IN MAJORCA...
QUITE... NO WAY COULD HE AFFORD TO OWN THAT ON A MERE 100K PER ANNUM...
AUCTION LOTS
PROOF THAT HE'S NOT DOING THE JOB FOR THE MONEY...
NO, HE'S JUST IN IT FOR THE KNIGHTHOOD.

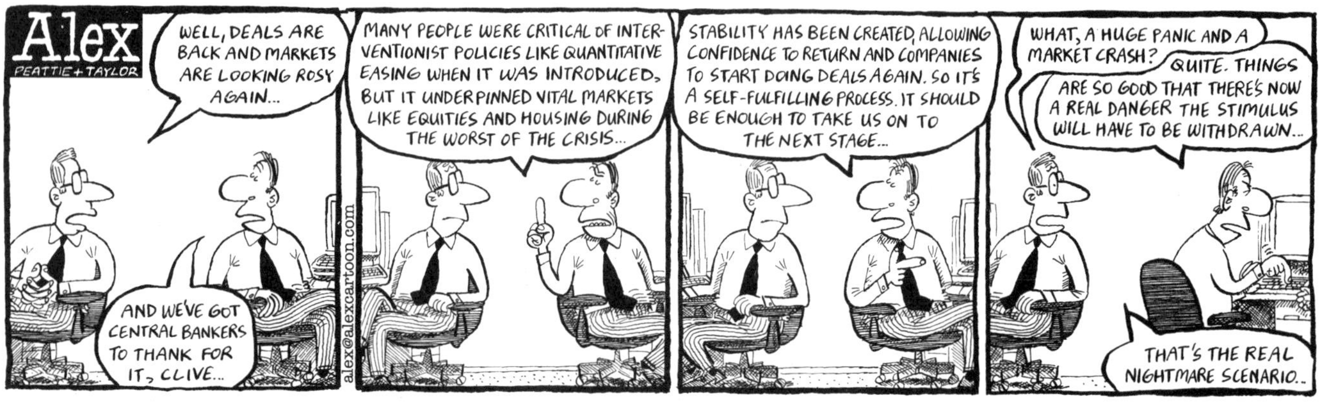
Alex
PEATTIE+TAYLOR
WELL, DEALS ARE BACK AND MARKETS ARE LOOKING ROSY AGAIN...
AND WE'VE GOT CENTRAL BANKERS TO THANK FOR IT, CLIVE...
alex@alexcartoon.com
MANY PEOPLE WERE CRITICAL OF INTERVENTIONIST POLICIES LIKE QUANTITATIVE EASING WHEN IT WAS INTRODUCED, BUT IT UNDERPINNED VITAL MARKETS LIKE EQUITIES AND HOUSING DURING THE WORST OF THE CRISIS...
STABILITY HAS BEEN CREATED, ALLOWING CONFIDENCE TO RETURN AND COMPANIES TO START DOING DEALS AGAIN. SO IT'S A SELF-FULFILLING PROCESS. IT SHOULD BE ENOUGH TO TAKE US ON TO THE NEXT STAGE...
WHAT, A HUGE PANIC AND A MARKET CRASH?
QUITE. THINGS ARE SO GOOD THAT THERE'S NOW A REAL DANGER THE STIMULUS WILL HAVE TO BE WITHDRAWN...
THAT'S THE REAL NIGHTMARE SCENARIO...

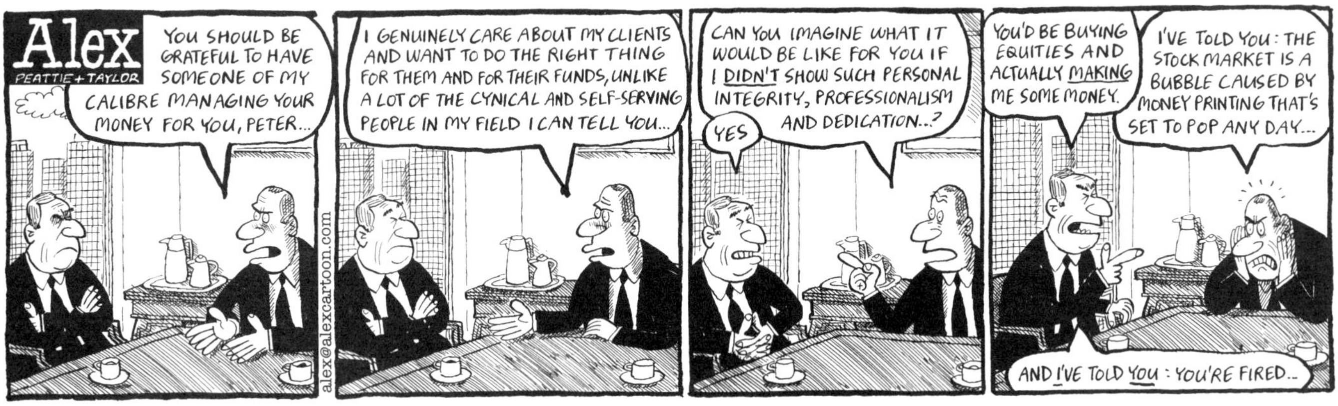
Alex
PEATTIE + TAYLOR
YOU SHOULD BE GRATEFUL TO HAVE SOMEONE OF MY CALIBRE MANAGING YOUR MONEY FOR YOU, PETER...
alex@alexcartoon.com
I GENUINELY CARE ABOUT MY CLIENTS AND WANT TO DO THE RIGHT THING FOR THEM AND FOR THEIR FUNDS, UNLIKE A LOT OF THE CYNICAL AND SELF-SERVING PEOPLE IN MY FIELD I CAN TELL YOU...
CAN YOU IMAGINE WHAT IT WOULD BE LIKE FOR YOU IF I DIDN'T SHOW SUCH PERSONAL INTEGRITY, PROFESSIONALISM AND DEDICATION..?
YES
YOU'D BE BUYING EQUITIES AND ACTUALLY MAKING ME SOME MONEY.
I'VE TOLD YOU: THE STOCK MARKET IS A BUBBLE CAUSED BY MONEY PRINTING THAT'S SET TO POP ANY DAY...
AND I'VE TOLD YOU: YOU'RE FIRED...

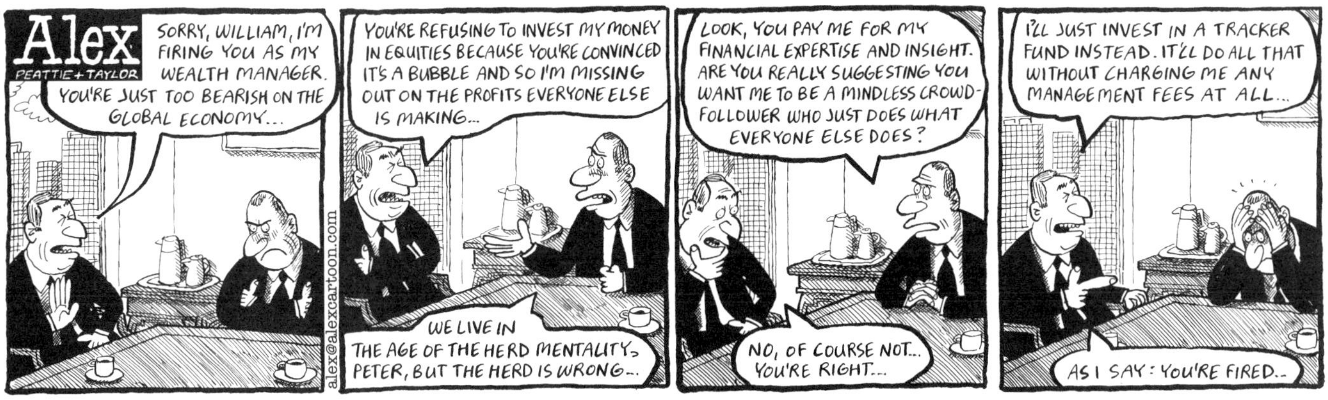
Alex
PEATTIE + TAYLOR
SORRY, WILLIAM, I'M FIRING YOU AS MY WEALTH MANAGER.
YOU'RE JUST TOO BEARISH ON THE GLOBAL ECONOMY...
alex@alexcartoon.com
YOU'RE REFUSING TO INVEST MY MONEY IN EQUITIES BECAUSE YOU'RE CONVINCED IT'S A BUBBLE AND SO I'M MISSING OUT ON THE PROFITS EVERYONE ELSE IS MAKING...
WE LIVE IN THE AGE OF THE HERD MENTALITY, PETER, BUT THE HERD IS WRONG...
LOOK, YOU PAY ME FOR MY FINANCIAL EXPERTISE AND INSIGHT. ARE YOU REALLY SUGGESTING YOU WANT ME TO BE A MINDLESS CROWD-FOLLOWER WHO JUST DOES WHAT EVERYONE ELSE DOES?
NO, OF COURSE NOT... YOU'RE RIGHT...
I'LL JUST INVEST IN A TRACKER FUND INSTEAD. IT'LL DO ALL THAT WITHOUT CHARGING ME ANY MANAGEMENT FEES AT ALL...
AS I SAY: YOU'RE FIRED...

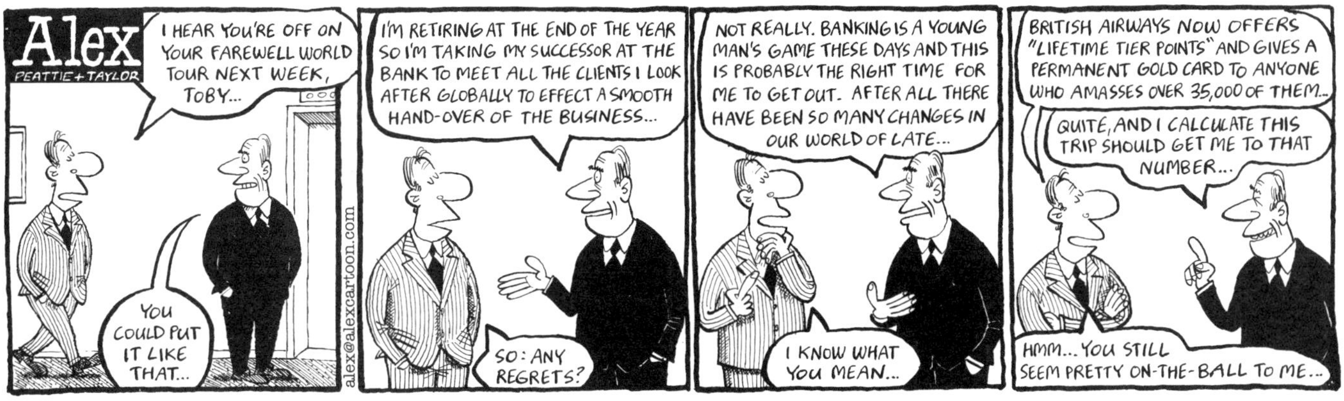
Alex
PEATTIE + TAYLOR
I HEAR YOU'RE OFF ON YOUR FAREWELL WORLD TOUR NEXT WEEK, TOBY...
YOU COULD PUT IT LIKE THAT...
alex@alexcartoon.com
I'M RETIRING AT THE END OF THE YEAR SO I'M TAKING MY SUCCESSOR AT THE BANK TO MEET ALL THE CLIENTS I LOOK AFTER GLOBALLY TO EFFECT A SMOOTH HAND-OVER OF THE BUSINESS...
SO: ANY REGRETS?
NOT REALLY. BANKING IS A YOUNG MAN'S GAME THESE DAYS AND THIS IS PROBABLY THE RIGHT TIME FOR ME TO GET OUT. AFTER ALL THERE HAVE BEEN SO MANY CHANGES IN OUR WORLD OF LATE...
I KNOW WHAT YOU MEAN...
BRITISH AIRWAYS NOW OFFERS "LIFETIME TIER POINTS" AND GIVES A PERMANENT GOLD CARD TO ANYONE WHO AMASSES OVER 35,000 OF THEM...
QUITE, AND I CALCULATE THIS TRIP SHOULD GET ME TO THAT NUMBER...
HMM... YOU STILL SEEM PRETTY ON-THE-BALL TO ME...

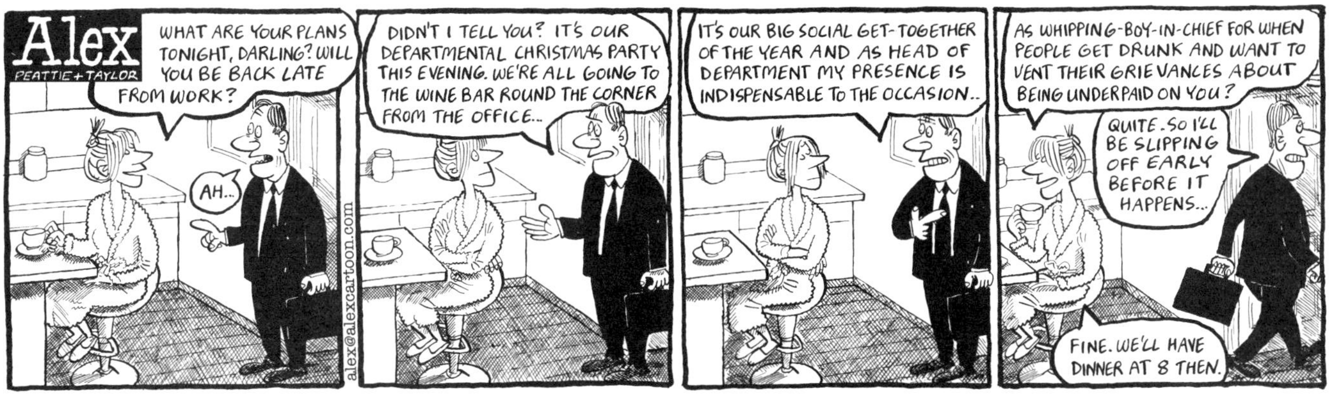
Alex
PEATTIE + TAYLOR
WHAT ARE YOUR PLANS TONIGHT, DARLING? WILL YOU BE BACK LATE FROM WORK?
AH...
alex@alexcartoon.com
DIDN'T I TELL YOU? IT'S OUR DEPARTMENTAL CHRISTMAS PARTY THIS EVENING. WE'RE ALL GOING TO THE WINE BAR ROUND THE CORNER FROM THE OFFICE...
IT'S OUR BIG SOCIAL GET-TOGETHER OF THE YEAR AND AS HEAD OF DEPARTMENT MY PRESENCE IS INDISPENSABLE TO THE OCCASION...
AS WHIPPING-BOY-IN-CHIEF FOR WHEN PEOPLE GET DRUNK AND WANT TO VENT THEIR GRIEVANCES ABOUT BEING UNDERPAID ON YOU?
QUITE. SO I'LL BE SLIPPING OFF EARLY BEFORE IT HAPPENS...
FINE. WE'LL HAVE DINNER AT 8 THEN.

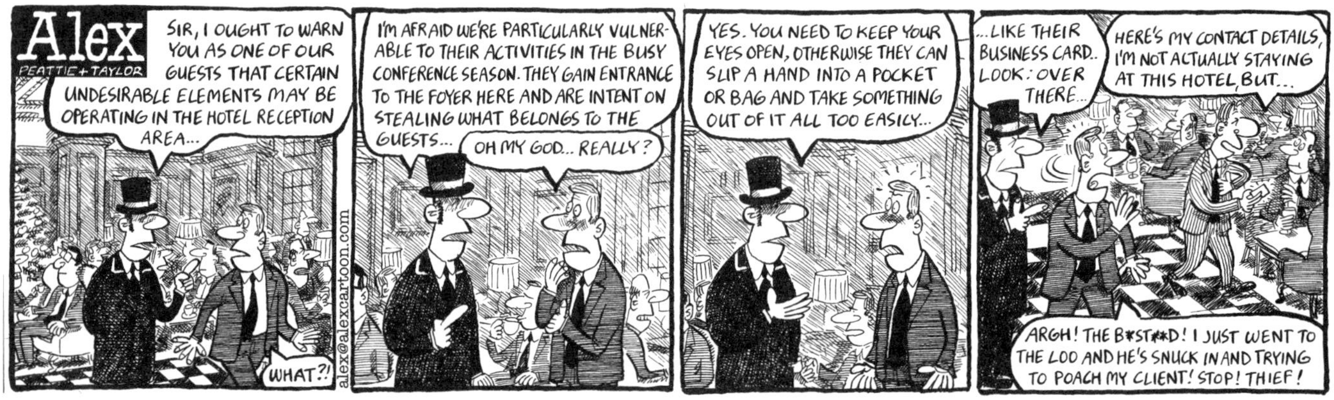
Alex
PEATTIE+TAYLOR
SIR, I OUGHT TO WARN YOU AS ONE OF OUR GUESTS THAT CERTAIN UNDESIRABLE ELEMENTS MAY BE OPERATING IN THE HOTEL RECEPTION AREA...
WHAT?!
I'M AFRAID WE'RE PARTICULARLY VULNERABLE TO THEIR ACTIVITIES IN THE BUSY CONFERENCE SEASON. THEY GAIN ENTRANCE TO THE FOYER HERE AND ARE INTENT ON STEALING WHAT BELONGS TO THE GUESTS...
OH MY GOD... REALLY?
alex@alexcartoon.com
YES. YOU NEED TO KEEP YOUR EYES OPEN, OTHERWISE THEY CAN SLIP A HAND INTO A POCKET OR BAG AND TAKE SOMETHING OUT OF IT ALL TOO EASILY...
...LIKE THEIR BUSINESS CARD.. LOOK: OVER THERE...
HERE'S MY CONTACT DETAILS, I'M NOT ACTUALLY STAYING AT THIS HOTEL, BUT...
ARGH! THE B*ST**D! I JUST WENT TO THE LOO AND HE'S SNUCK IN AND TRYING TO POACH MY CLIENT! STOP! THIEF!

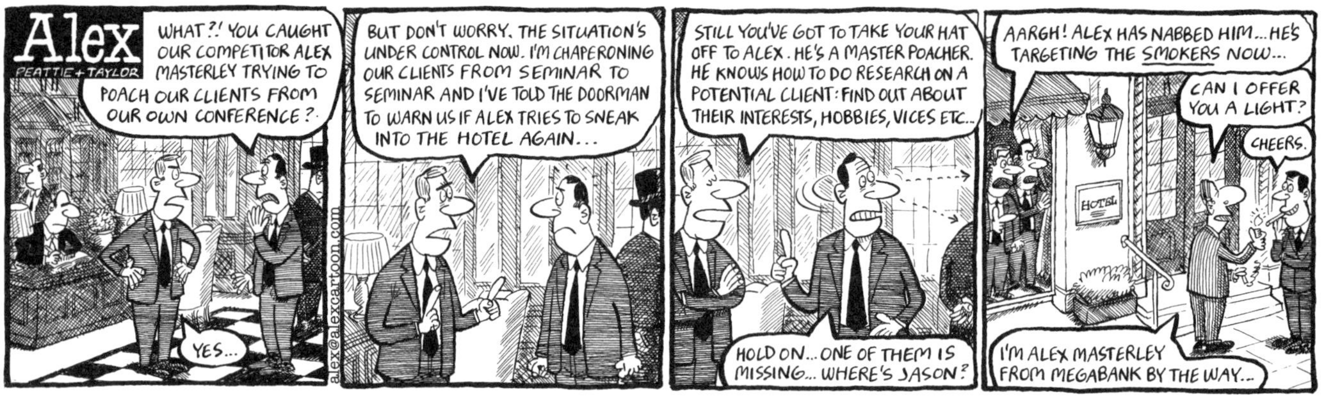
Alex
PEATTIE+TAYLOR
WHAT?! YOU CAUGHT OUR COMPETITOR ALEX MASTERLEY TRYING TO POACH OUR CLIENTS FROM OUR OWN CONFERENCE?
YES...
alex@alexcartoon.com
BUT DON'T WORRY. THE SITUATION'S UNDER CONTROL NOW. I'M CHAPERONING OUR CLIENTS FROM SEMINAR TO SEMINAR AND I'VE TOLD THE DOORMAN TO WARN US IF ALEX TRIES TO SNEAK INTO THE HOTEL AGAIN...
STILL YOU'VE GOT TO TAKE YOUR HAT OFF TO ALEX. HE'S A MASTER POACHER. HE KNOWS HOW TO DO RESEARCH ON A POTENTIAL CLIENT: FIND OUT ABOUT THEIR INTERESTS, HOBBIES, VICES ETC...
HOLD ON... ONE OF THEM IS MISSING... WHERE'S JASON?
AARGH! ALEX HAS NABBED HIM... HE'S TARGETING THE SMOKERS NOW...
CAN I OFFER YOU A LIGHT?
CHEERS.
HOTEL
I'M ALEX MASTERLEY FROM MEGABANK BY THE WAY...

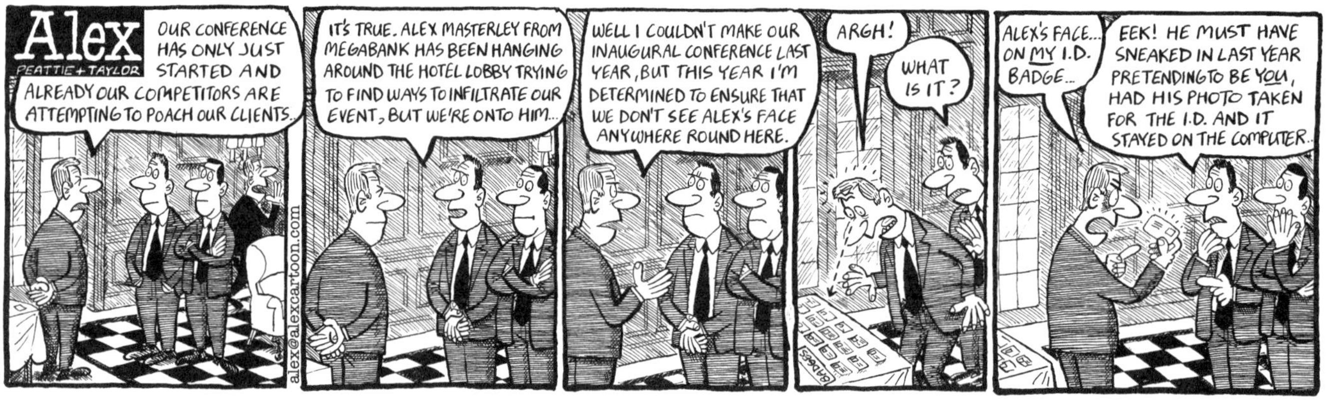
Alex
PEATTIE+TAYLOR
OUR CONFERENCE HAS ONLY JUST STARTED AND ALREADY OUR COMPETITORS ARE ATTEMPTING TO POACH OUR CLIENTS..
alex@alexcartoon.com
IT'S TRUE. ALEX MASTERLEY FROM MEGABANK HAS BEEN HANGING AROUND THE HOTEL LOBBY TRYING TO FIND WAYS TO INFILTRATE OUR EVENT, BUT WE'RE ONTO HIM...
WELL I COULDN'T MAKE OUR INAUGURAL CONFERENCE LAST YEAR, BUT THIS YEAR I'M DETERMINED TO ENSURE THAT WE DON'T SEE ALEX'S FACE ANYWHERE ROUND HERE.
ARGH!
WHAT IS IT?
ALEX'S FACE... ON MY I.D. BADGE...
EEK! HE MUST HAVE SNEAKED IN LAST YEAR PRETENDING TO BE YOU, HAD HIS PHOTO TAKEN FOR THE I.D. AND IT STAYED ON THE COMPUTER..

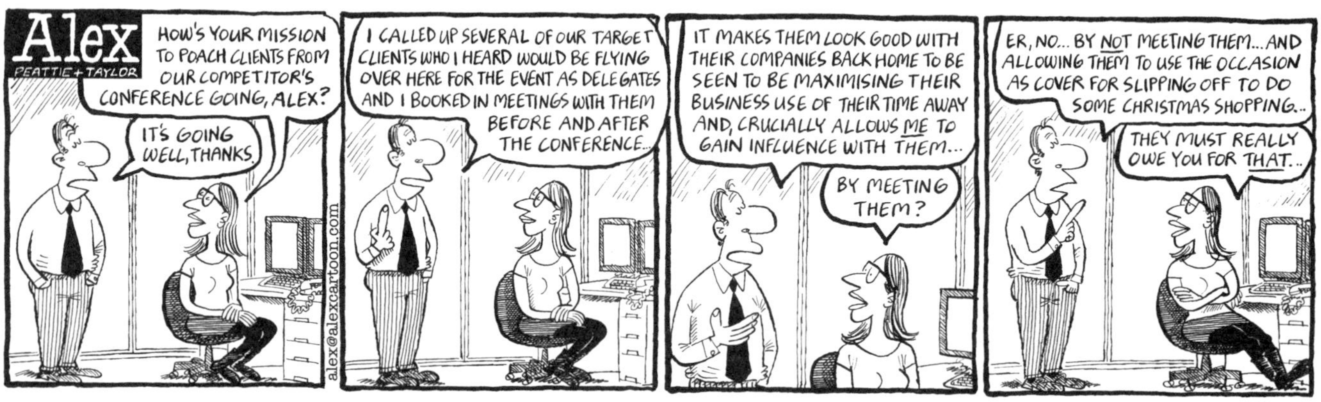
Alex
PEATTIE+TAYLOR
HOW'S YOUR MISSION TO POACH CLIENTS FROM OUR COMPETITOR'S CONFERENCE GOING, ALEX?
IT'S GOING WELL, THANKS.
alex@alexcartoon.com
I CALLED UP SEVERAL OF OUR TARGET CLIENTS WHO I HEARD WOULD BE FLYING OVER HERE FOR THE EVENT AS DELEGATES AND I BOOKED IN MEETINGS WITH THEM BEFORE AND AFTER THE CONFERENCE..
IT MAKES THEM LOOK GOOD WITH THEIR COMPANIES BACK HOME TO BE SEEN TO BE MAXIMISING THEIR BUSINESS USE OF THEIR TIME AWAY AND, CRUCIALLY ALLOWS ME TO GAIN INFLUENCE WITH THEM...
BY MEETING THEM?
ER, NO... BY NOT MEETING THEM... AND ALLOWING THEM TO USE THE OCCASION AS COVER FOR SLIPPING OFF TO DO SOME CHRISTMAS SHOPPING..
THEY MUST REALLY OWE YOU FOR THAT...

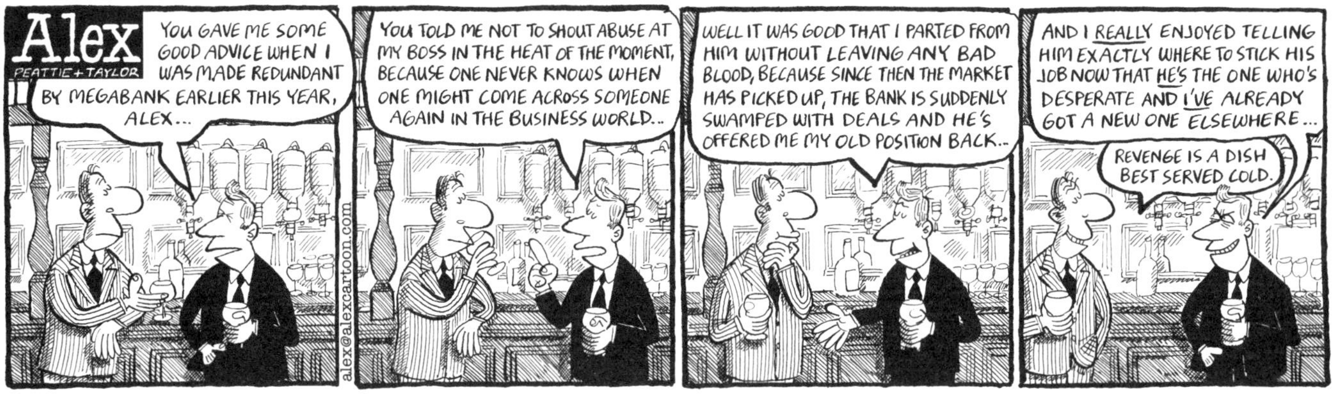
Alex
PEATTIE + TAYLOR
YOU GAVE ME SOME GOOD ADVICE WHEN I WAS MADE REDUNDANT BY MEGABANK EARLIER THIS YEAR, ALEX...
YOU TOLD ME NOT TO SHOUT ABUSE AT MY BOSS IN THE HEAT OF THE MOMENT, BECAUSE ONE NEVER KNOWS WHEN ONE MIGHT COME ACROSS SOMEONE AGAIN IN THE BUSINESS WORLD...
WELL IT WAS GOOD THAT I PARTED FROM HIM WITHOUT LEAVING ANY BAD BLOOD, BECAUSE SINCE THEN THE MARKET HAS PICKED UP, THE BANK IS SUDDENLY SWAMPED WITH DEALS AND HE'S OFFERED ME MY OLD POSITION BACK...
AND I REALLY ENJOYED TELLING HIM EXACTLY WHERE TO STICK HIS JOB NOW THAT HE'S THE ONE WHO'S DESPERATE AND I'VE ALREADY GOT A NEW ONE ELSEWHERE...
REVENGE IS A DISH BEST SERVED COLD.
alex@alexcartoon.com

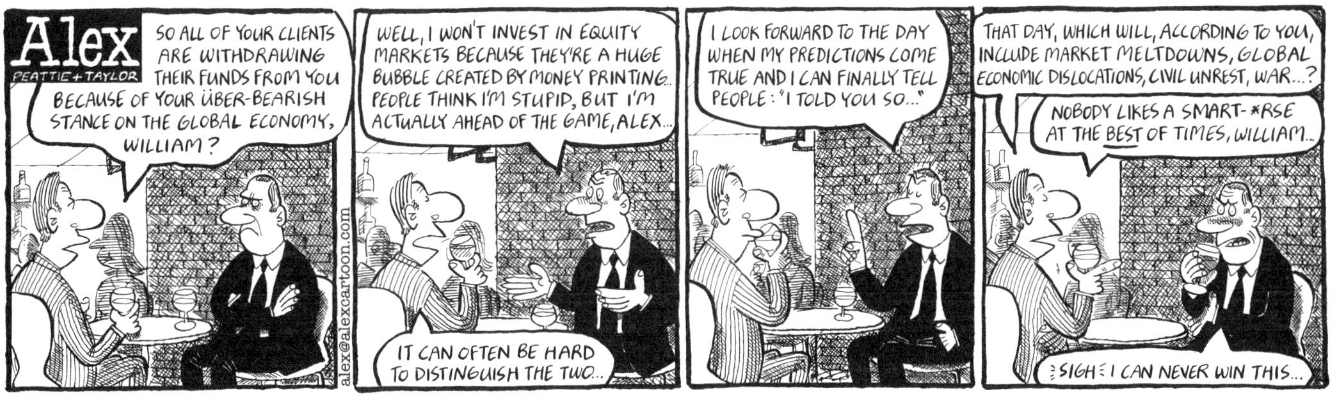
Alex
PEATTIE + TAYLOR
SO ALL OF YOUR CLIENTS ARE WITHDRAWING THEIR FUNDS FROM YOU BECAUSE OF YOUR ÜBER-BEARISH STANCE ON THE GLOBAL ECONOMY, WILLIAM?
WELL, I WON'T INVEST IN EQUITY MARKETS BECAUSE THEY'RE A HUGE BUBBLE CREATED BY MONEY PRINTING... PEOPLE THINK I'M STUPID, BUT I'M ACTUALLY AHEAD OF THE GAME, ALEX...
IT CAN OFTEN BE HARD TO DISTINGUISH THE TWO...
I LOOK FORWARD TO THE DAY WHEN MY PREDICTIONS COME TRUE AND I CAN FINALLY TELL PEOPLE: "I TOLD YOU SO..."
THAT DAY, WHICH WILL, ACCORDING TO YOU, INCLUDE MARKET MELTDOWNS, GLOBAL ECONOMIC DISLOCATIONS, CIVIL UNREST, WAR...?
NOBODY LIKES A SMART-*RSE AT THE BEST OF TIMES, WILLIAM...
SIGH I CAN NEVER WIN THIS...
alex@alexcartoon.com

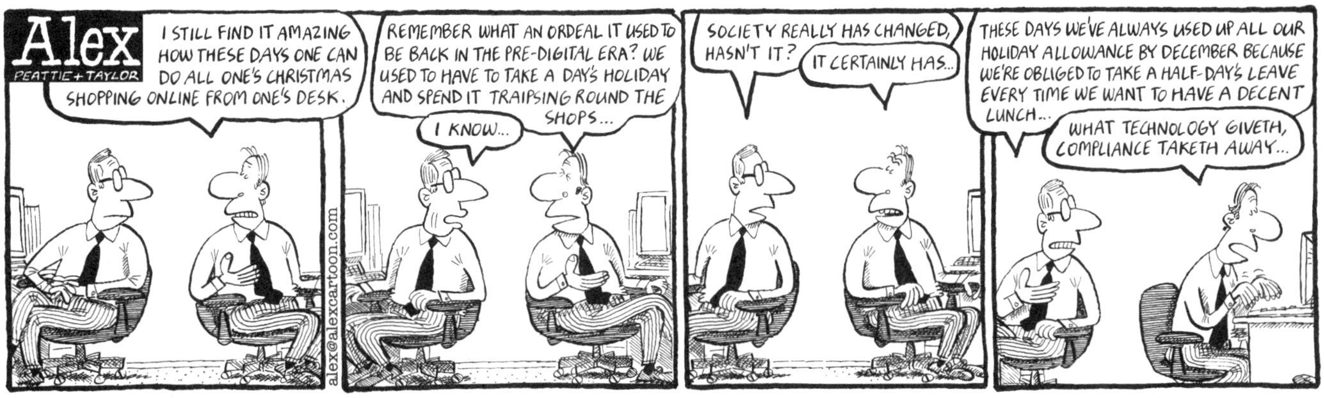
Alex
PEATTIE + TAYLOR
I STILL FIND IT AMAZING HOW THESE DAYS ONE CAN DO ALL ONE'S CHRISTMAS SHOPPING ONLINE FROM ONE'S DESK.
REMEMBER WHAT AN ORDEAL IT USED TO BE BACK IN THE PRE-DIGITAL ERA? WE USED TO HAVE TO TAKE A DAY'S HOLIDAY AND SPEND IT TRAIPSING ROUND THE SHOPS...
I KNOW...
SOCIETY REALLY HAS CHANGED, HASN'T IT?
IT CERTAINLY HAS...
THESE DAYS WE'VE ALWAYS USED UP ALL OUR HOLIDAY ALLOWANCE BY DECEMBER BECAUSE WE'RE OBLIGED TO TAKE A HALF-DAY'S LEAVE EVERY TIME WE WANT TO HAVE A DECENT LUNCH...
WHAT TECHNOLOGY GIVETH, COMPLIANCE TAKETH AWAY...
alex@alexcartoon.com

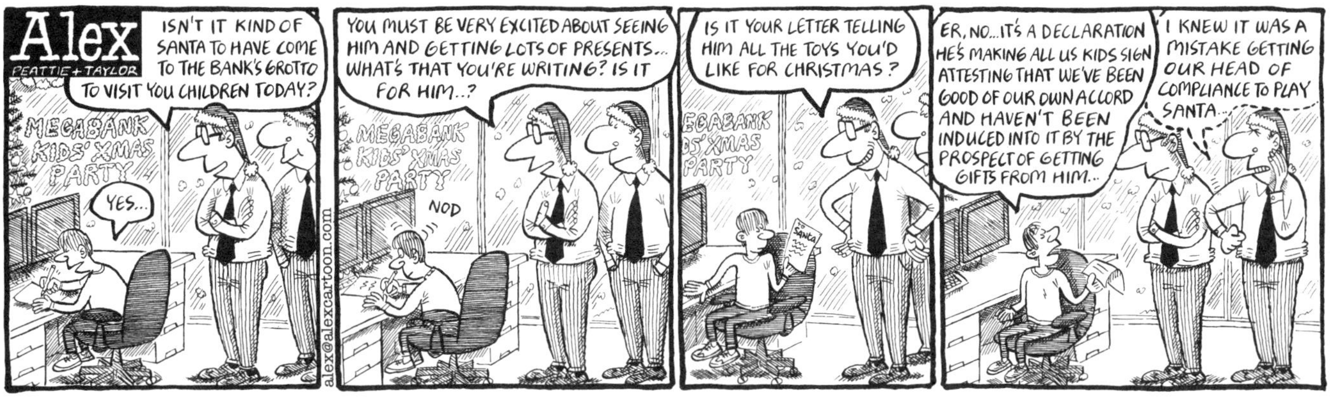
Alex
PEATTIE + TAYLOR
ISN'T IT KIND OF SANTA TO HAVE COME TO THE BANK'S GROTTO TO VISIT YOU CHILDREN TODAY?
MEGABANK KIDS' XMAS PARTY
YES...
YOU MUST BE VERY EXCITED ABOUT SEEING HIM AND GETTING LOTS OF PRESENTS... WHAT'S THAT YOU'RE WRITING? IS IT FOR HIM...?
NOD
IS IT YOUR LETTER TELLING HIM ALL THE TOYS YOU'D LIKE FOR CHRISTMAS?
ER, NO... IT'S A DECLARATION HE'S MAKING ALL US KIDS SIGN ATTESTING THAT WE'VE BEEN GOOD OF OUR OWN ACCORD AND HAVEN'T BEEN INDUCED INTO IT BY THE PROSPECT OF GETTING GIFTS FROM HIM...
I KNEW IT WAS A MISTAKE GETTING OUR HEAD OF COMPLIANCE TO PLAY SANTA...
alex@alexcartoon.com

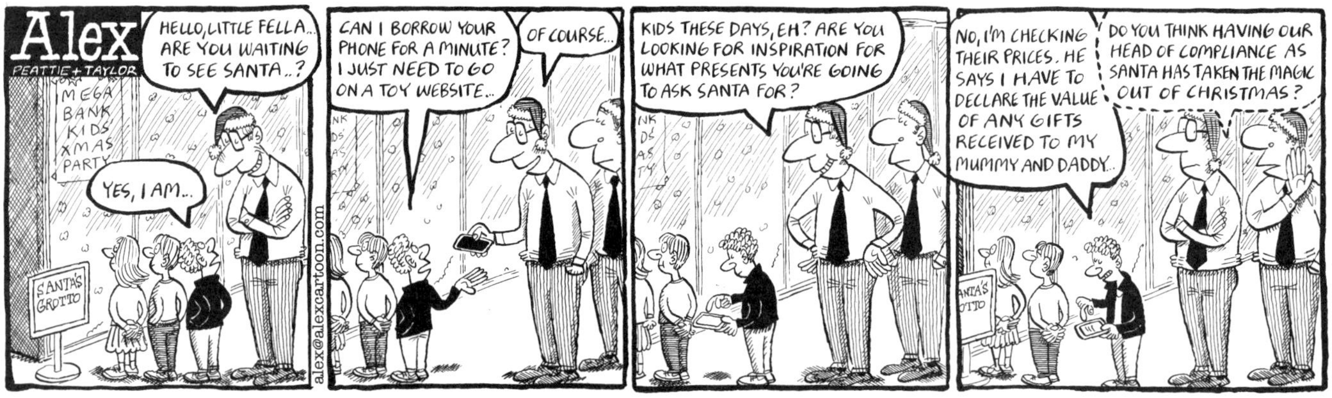
Alex
PEATTIE + TAYLOR
HELLO, LITTLE FELLA... ARE YOU WAITING TO SEE SANTA..?
MEGA BANK KIDS' XMAS PARTY
YES, I AM...
SANTA'S GROTTO
alex@alexcartoon.com
CAN I BORROW YOUR PHONE FOR A MINUTE? I JUST NEED TO GO ON A TOY WEBSITE...
OF COURSE...
KIDS THESE DAYS, EH? ARE YOU LOOKING FOR INSPIRATION FOR WHAT PRESENTS YOU'RE GOING TO ASK SANTA FOR?
NO, I'M CHECKING THEIR PRICES. HE SAYS I HAVE TO DECLARE THE VALUE OF ANY GIFTS RECEIVED TO MY MUMMY AND DADDY...
DO YOU THINK HAVING OUR HEAD OF COMPLIANCE AS SANTA HAS TAKEN THE MAGIC OUT OF CHRISTMAS?

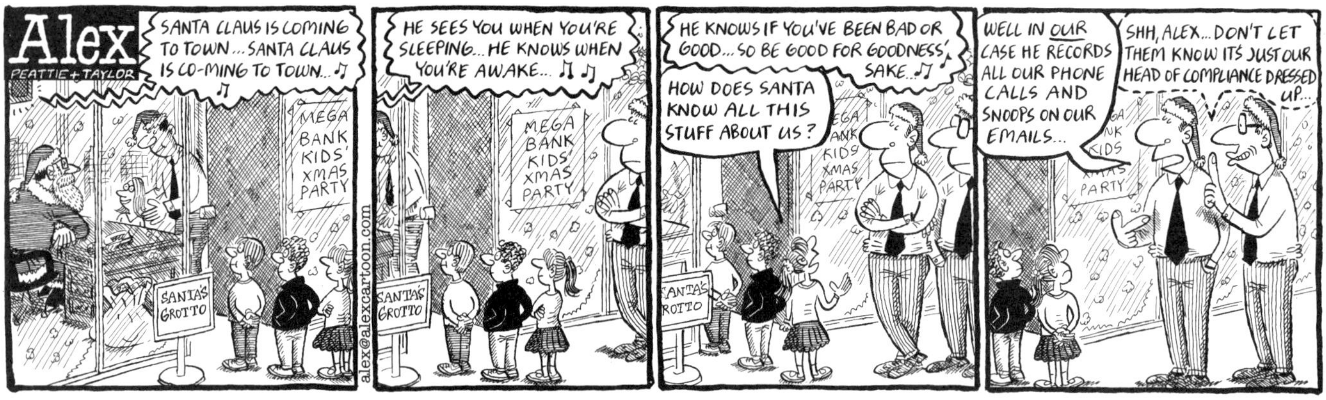
Alex
PEATTIE + TAYLOR
SANTA CLAUS IS COMING TO TOWN... SANTA CLAUS IS CO-MING TO TOWN... ♫ ♫
MEGA BANK KIDS' XMAS PARTY
SANTA'S GROTTO
alex@alexcartoon.com
HE SEES YOU WHEN YOU'RE SLEEPING... HE KNOWS WHEN YOU'RE AWAKE... ♫ ♫
HE KNOWS IF YOU'VE BEEN BAD OR GOOD... SO BE GOOD FOR GOODNESS' SAKE... ♫ ♫
HOW DOES SANTA KNOW ALL THIS STUFF ABOUT US?
WELL IN OUR CASE HE RECORDS ALL OUR PHONE CALLS AND SNOOPS ON OUR EMAILS...
SHH, ALEX... DON'T LET THEM KNOW IT'S JUST OUR HEAD OF COMPLIANCE DRESSED UP...

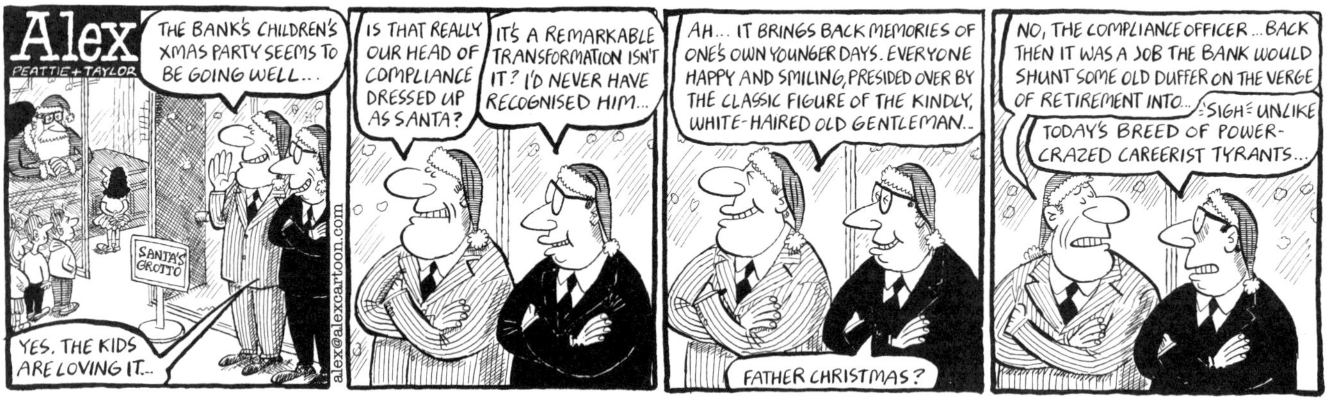
Alex
PEATTIE + TAYLOR
THE BANK'S CHILDREN'S XMAS PARTY SEEMS TO BE GOING WELL...
SANTA'S GROTTO
YES. THE KIDS ARE LOVING IT...
alex@alexcartoon.com
IS THAT REALLY OUR HEAD OF COMPLIANCE DRESSED UP AS SANTA?
IT'S A REMARKABLE TRANSFORMATION ISN'T IT? I'D NEVER HAVE RECOGNISED HIM...
AH... IT BRINGS BACK MEMORIES OF ONE'S OWN YOUNGER DAYS. EVERYONE HAPPY AND SMILING, PRESIDED OVER BY THE CLASSIC FIGURE OF THE KINDLY, WHITE-HAIRED OLD GENTLEMAN...
FATHER CHRISTMAS?
NO, THE COMPLIANCE OFFICER... BACK THEN IT WAS A JOB THE BANK WOULD SHUNT SOME OLD DUFFER ON THE VERGE OF RETIREMENT INTO...
SIGH UNLIKE TODAY'S BREED OF POWER-CRAZED CAREERIST TYRANTS...

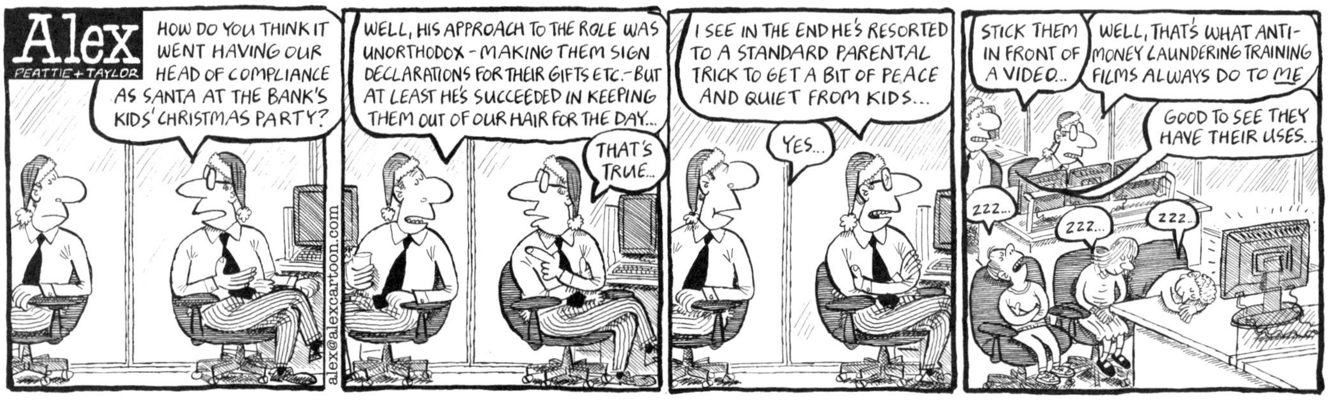
Alex
PEATTIE + TAYLOR
HOW DO YOU THINK IT WENT HAVING OUR HEAD OF COMPLIANCE AS SANTA AT THE BANK'S KIDS' CHRISTMAS PARTY?
alex@alexcartoon.com
WELL, HIS APPROACH TO THE ROLE WAS UNORTHODOX - MAKING THEM SIGN DECLARATIONS FOR THEIR GIFTS ETC. - BUT AT LEAST HE'S SUCCEEDED IN KEEPING THEM OUT OF OUR HAIR FOR THE DAY...
THAT'S TRUE...
I SEE IN THE END HE'S RESORTED TO A STANDARD PARENTAL TRICK TO GET A BIT OF PEACE AND QUIET FROM KIDS...
YES...
STICK THEM IN FRONT OF A VIDEO...
WELL, THAT'S WHAT ANTI-MONEY LAUNDERING TRAINING FILMS ALWAYS DO TO ME
GOOD TO SEE THEY HAVE THEIR USES...
ZZZ...
ZZZ...
ZZZ...

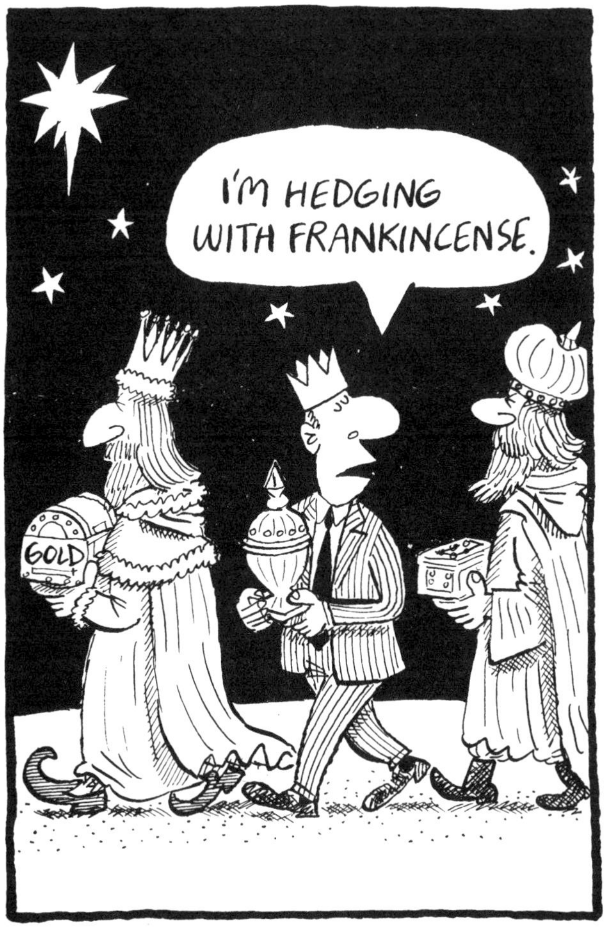
I'M HEDGING
WITH FRANKINCENSE.
GOLD

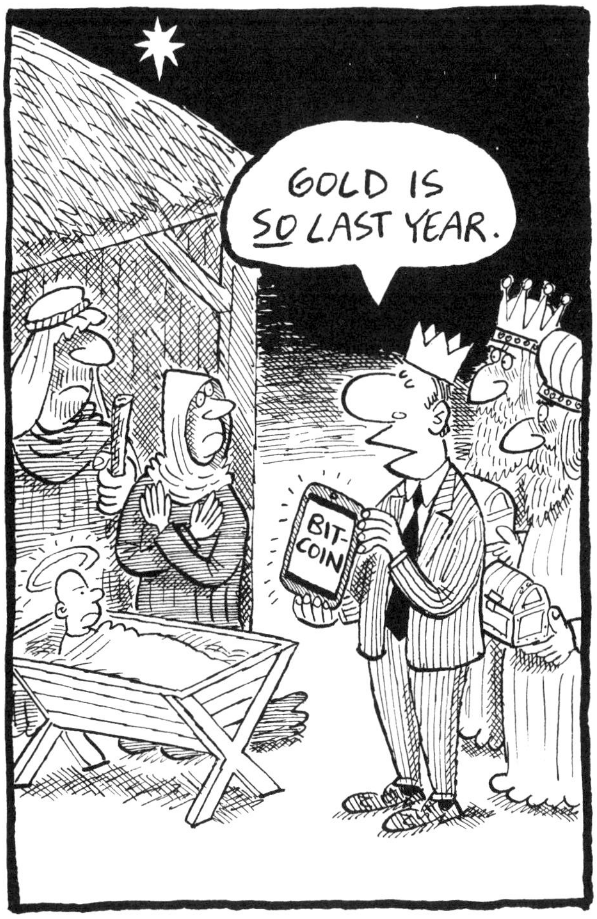
GOLD IS
SO LAST YEAR.
BIT-
COIN

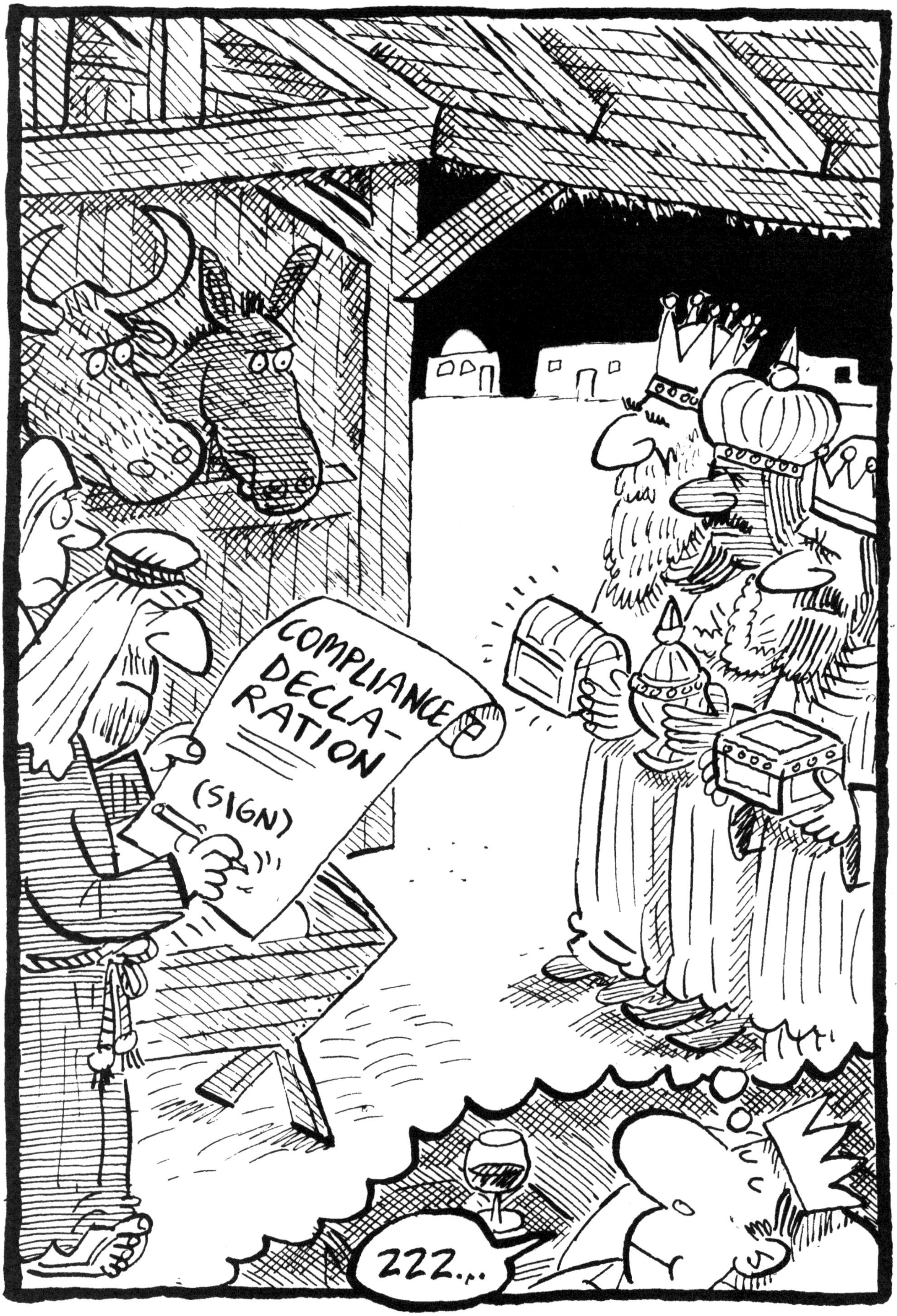
COMPLIANCE DECLA-RATION
(SIGN)
ZZZ...

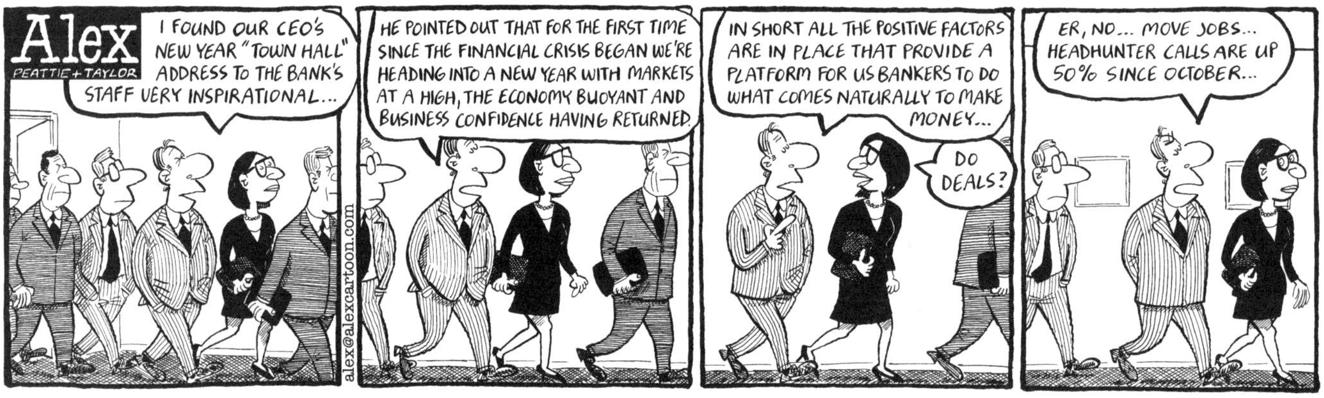
Alex
PEATTIE + TAYLOR
I FOUND OUR CEO'S NEW YEAR "TOWN HALL" ADDRESS TO THE BANK'S STAFF VERY INSPIRATIONAL...
alex@alexcartoon.com
HE POINTED OUT THAT FOR THE FIRST TIME SINCE THE FINANCIAL CRISIS BEGAN WE'RE HEADING INTO A NEW YEAR WITH MARKETS AT A HIGH, THE ECONOMY BUOYANT AND BUSINESS CONFIDENCE HAVING RETURNED.
IN SHORT ALL THE POSITIVE FACTORS ARE IN PLACE THAT PROVIDE A PLATFORM FOR US BANKERS TO DO WHAT COMES NATURALLY TO MAKE MONEY...
DO DEALS?
ER, NO... MOVE JOBS... HEADHUNTER CALLS ARE UP 50% SINCE OCTOBER...

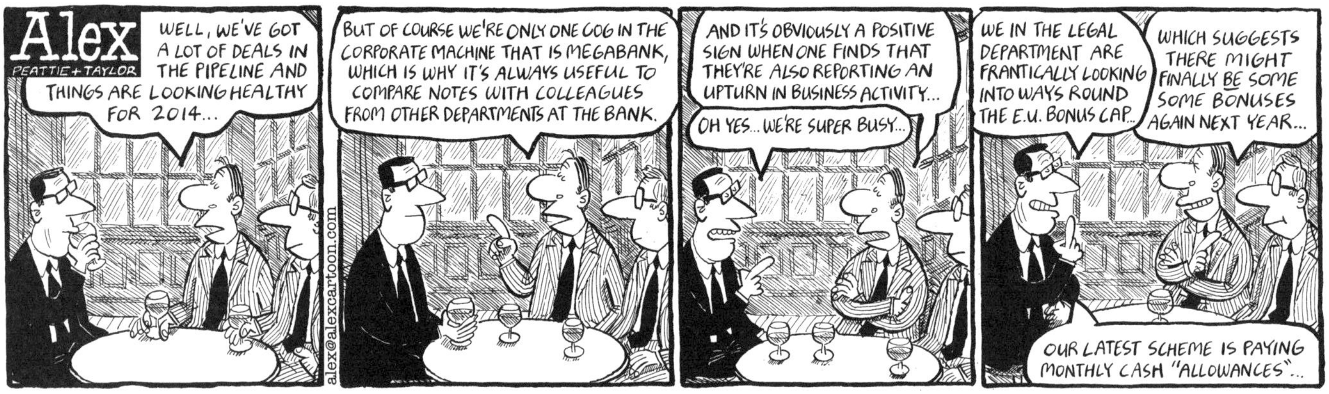
Alex
PEATTIE + TAYLOR
WELL, WE'VE GOT A LOT OF DEALS IN THE PIPELINE AND THINGS ARE LOOKING HEALTHY FOR 2014...
alex@alexcartoon.com
BUT OF COURSE WE'RE ONLY ONE COG IN THE CORPORATE MACHINE THAT IS MEGABANK, WHICH IS WHY IT'S ALWAYS USEFUL TO COMPARE NOTES WITH COLLEAGUES FROM OTHER DEPARTMENTS AT THE BANK.
AND IT'S OBVIOUSLY A POSITIVE SIGN WHEN ONE FINDS THAT THEY'RE ALSO REPORTING AN UPTURN IN BUSINESS ACTIVITY...
OH YES... WE'RE SUPER BUSY...
WE IN THE LEGAL DEPARTMENT ARE FRANTICALLY LOOKING INTO WAYS ROUND THE E.U. BONUS CAP...
WHICH SUGGESTS THERE MIGHT FINALLY BE SOME SOME BONUSES AGAIN NEXT YEAR...
OUR LATEST SCHEME IS PAYING MONTHLY CASH "ALLOWANCES"...

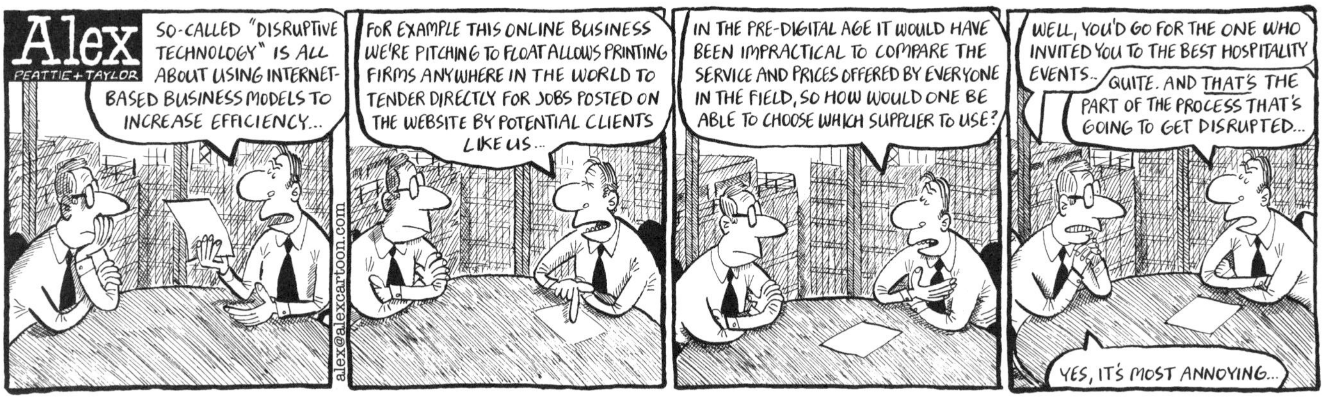
Alex
PEATTIE + TAYLOR
SO-CALLED "DISRUPTIVE TECHNOLOGY" IS ALL ABOUT USING INTERNET-BASED BUSINESS MODELS TO INCREASE EFFICIENCY...
alex@alexcartoon.com
FOR EXAMPLE THIS ONLINE BUSINESS WE'RE PITCHING TO FLOAT ALLOWS PRINTING FIRMS ANYWHERE IN THE WORLD TO TENDER DIRECTLY FOR JOBS POSTED ON THE WEBSITE BY POTENTIAL CLIENTS LIKE US...
IN THE PRE-DIGITAL AGE IT WOULD HAVE BEEN IMPRACTICAL TO COMPARE THE SERVICE AND PRICES OFFERED BY EVERYONE IN THE FIELD, SO HOW WOULD ONE BE ABLE TO CHOOSE WHICH SUPPLIER TO USE?
WELL, YOU'D GO FOR THE ONE WHO INVITED YOU TO THE BEST HOSPITALITY EVENTS...
QUITE. AND THAT'S THE PART OF THE PROCESS THAT'S GOING TO GET DISRUPTED...
YES, IT'S MOST ANNOYING...

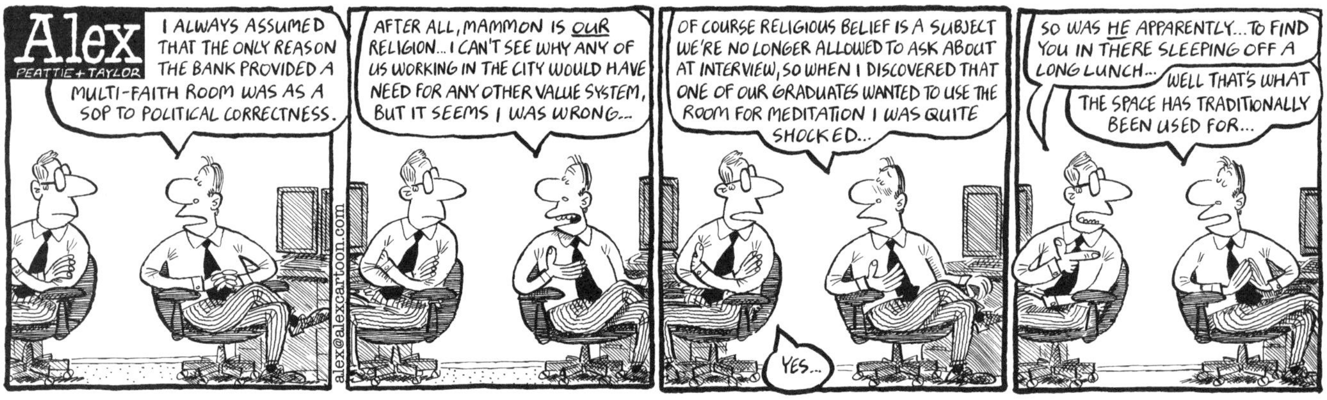
Alex
PEATTIE + TAYLOR
I ALWAYS ASSUMED THAT THE ONLY REASON THE BANK PROVIDED A MULTI-FAITH ROOM WAS AS A SOP TO POLITICAL CORRECTNESS.
alex@alexcartoon.com
AFTER ALL, MAMMON IS OUR RELIGION... I CAN'T SEE WHY ANY OF US WORKING IN THE CITY WOULD HAVE NEED FOR ANY OTHER VALUE SYSTEM, BUT IT SEEMS I WAS WRONG...
OF COURSE RELIGIOUS BELIEF IS A SUBJECT WE'RE NO LONGER ALLOWED TO ASK ABOUT AT INTERVIEW, SO WHEN I DISCOVERED THAT ONE OF OUR GRADUATES WANTED TO USE THE ROOM FOR MEDITATION I WAS QUITE SHOCKED...
YES...
SO WAS HE APPARENTLY... TO FIND YOU IN THERE SLEEPING OFF A LONG LUNCH...
WELL THAT'S WHAT THE SPACE HAS TRADITIONALLY BEEN USED FOR...

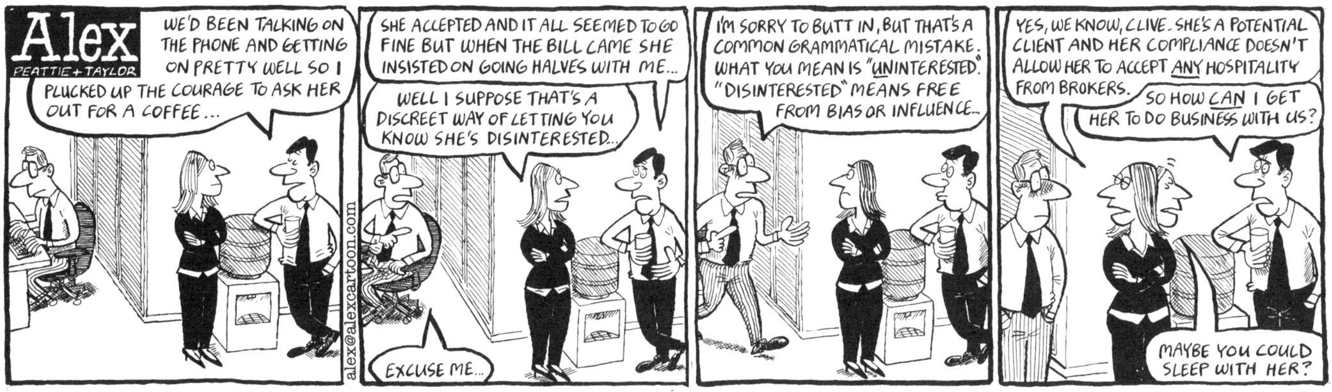
Alex
PEATTIE+TAYLOR
WE'D BEEN TALKING ON THE PHONE AND GETTING ON PRETTY WELL SO I PLUCKED UP THE COURAGE TO ASK HER OUT FOR A COFFEE...
alex@alexcartoon.com
SHE ACCEPTED AND IT ALL SEEMED TO GO FINE BUT WHEN THE BILL CAME SHE INSISTED ON GOING HALVES WITH ME...
WELL I SUPPOSE THAT'S A DISCREET WAY OF LETTING YOU KNOW SHE'S DISINTERESTED...
EXCUSE ME...
I'M SORRY TO BUTT IN, BUT THAT'S A COMMON GRAMMATICAL MISTAKE. WHAT YOU MEAN IS "UNINTERESTED". "DISINTERESTED" MEANS FREE FROM BIAS OR INFLUENCE...
YES, WE KNOW, CLIVE. SHE'S A POTENTIAL CLIENT AND HER COMPLIANCE DOESN'T ALLOW HER TO ACCEPT ANY HOSPITALITY FROM BROKERS.
SO HOW CAN I GET HER TO DO BUSINESS WITH US?
MAYBE YOU COULD SLEEP WITH HER?

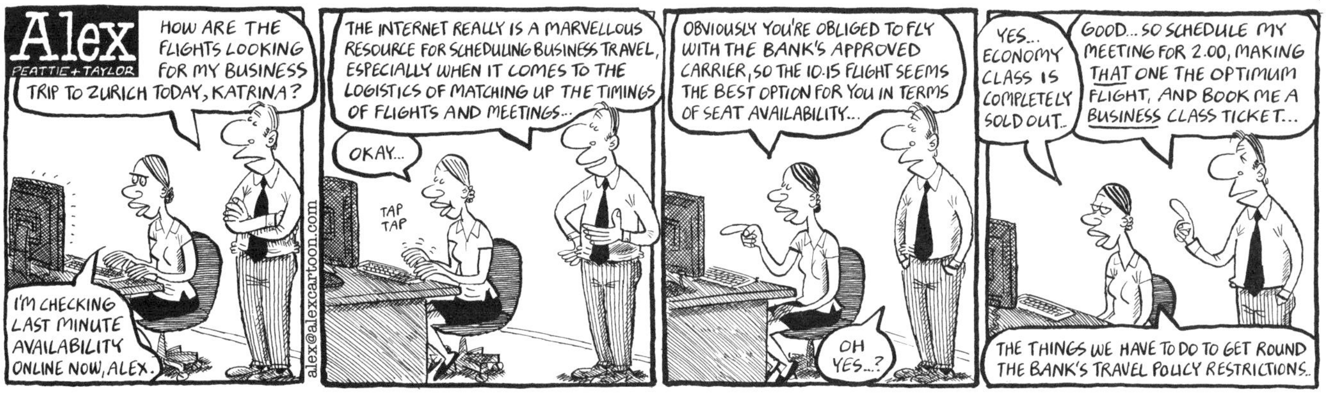
Alex
PEATTIE+TAYLOR
HOW ARE THE FLIGHTS LOOKING FOR MY BUSINESS TRIP TO ZURICH TODAY, KATRINA?
I'M CHECKING LAST MINUTE AVAILABILITY ONLINE NOW, ALEX.
alex@alexcartoon.com
THE INTERNET REALLY IS A MARVELLOUS RESOURCE FOR SCHEDULING BUSINESS TRAVEL, ESPECIALLY WHEN IT COMES TO THE LOGISTICS OF MATCHING UP THE TIMINGS OF FLIGHTS AND MEETINGS...
OKAY...
TAP TAP
OBVIOUSLY YOU'RE OBLIGED TO FLY WITH THE BANK'S APPROVED CARRIER, SO THE 10.15 FLIGHT SEEMS THE BEST OPTION FOR YOU IN TERMS OF SEAT AVAILABILITY...
OH YES...?
YES... ECONOMY CLASS IS COMPLETELY SOLD OUT...
GOOD... SO SCHEDULE MY MEETING FOR 2.00, MAKING THAT ONE THE OPTIMUM FLIGHT, AND BOOK ME A BUSINESS CLASS TICKET...
THE THINGS WE HAVE TO DO TO GET ROUND THE BANK'S TRAVEL POLICY RESTRICTIONS...

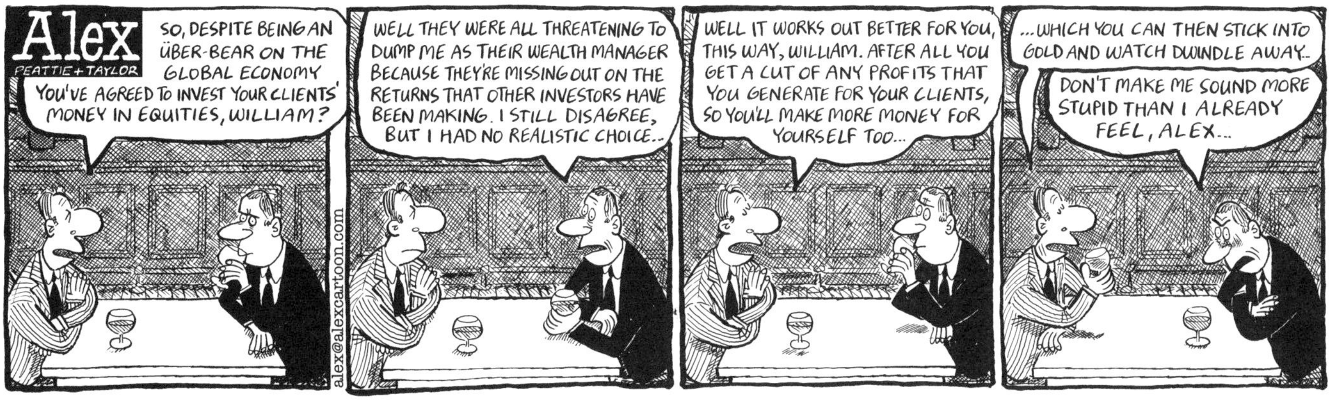
Alex
PEATTIE+TAYLOR
SO, DESPITE BEING AN ÜBER-BEAR ON THE GLOBAL ECONOMY YOU'VE AGREED TO INVEST YOUR CLIENTS' MONEY IN EQUITIES, WILLIAM?
alex@alexcartoon.com
WELL THEY WERE ALL THREATENING TO DUMP ME AS THEIR WEALTH MANAGER BECAUSE THEY'RE MISSING OUT ON THE RETURNS THAT OTHER INVESTORS HAVE BEEN MAKING. I STILL DISAGREE, BUT I HAD NO REALISTIC CHOICE...
WELL IT WORKS OUT BETTER FOR YOU, THIS WAY, WILLIAM. AFTER ALL YOU GET A CUT OF ANY PROFITS THAT YOU GENERATE FOR YOUR CLIENTS, SO YOU'LL MAKE MORE MONEY FOR YOURSELF TOO...
...WHICH YOU CAN THEN STICK INTO GOLD AND WATCH DWINDLE AWAY...
DON'T MAKE ME SOUND MORE STUPID THAN I ALREADY FEEL, ALEX...

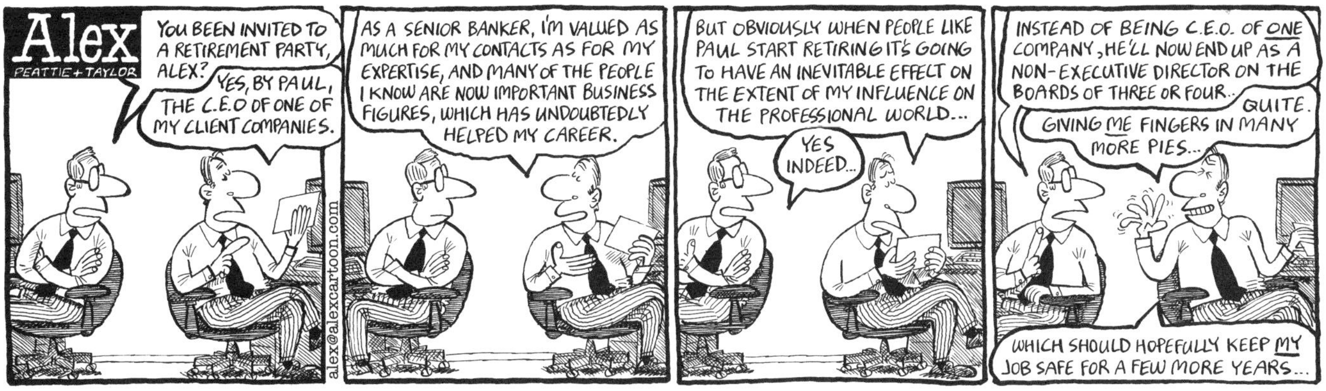
Alex
PEATTIE+TAYLOR
YOU BEEN INVITED TO A RETIREMENT PARTY, ALEX?
YES, BY PAUL, THE C.E.O OF ONE OF MY CLIENT COMPANIES.
alex@alexcartoon.com
AS A SENIOR BANKER, I'M VALUED AS MUCH FOR MY CONTACTS AS FOR MY EXPERTISE, AND MANY OF THE PEOPLE I KNOW ARE NOW IMPORTANT BUSINESS FIGURES, WHICH HAS UNDOUBTEDLY HELPED MY CAREER.
BUT OBVIOUSLY WHEN PEOPLE LIKE PAUL START RETIRING IT'S GOING TO HAVE AN INEVITABLE EFFECT ON THE EXTENT OF MY INFLUENCE ON THE PROFESSIONAL WORLD...
YES INDEED...
INSTEAD OF BEING C.E.O. OF ONE COMPANY, HE'LL NOW END UP AS A NON-EXECUTIVE DIRECTOR ON THE BOARDS OF THREE OR FOUR...
QUITE. GIVING ME FINGERS IN MANY MORE PIES...
WHICH SHOULD HOPEFULLY KEEP MY JOB SAFE FOR A FEW MORE YEARS...

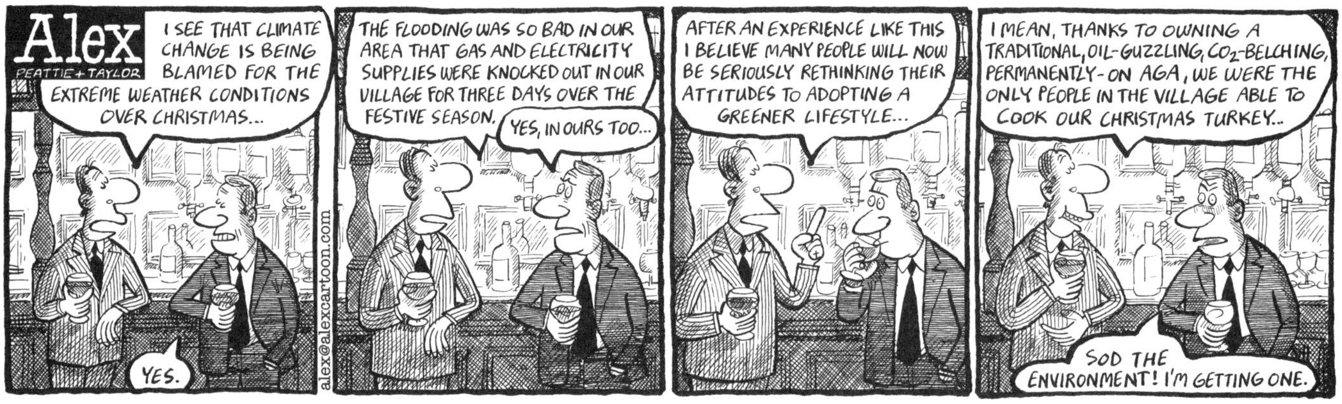
Alex
PEATTIE + TAYLOR
I SEE THAT CLIMATE CHANGE IS BEING BLAMED FOR THE EXTREME WEATHER CONDITIONS OVER CHRISTMAS...
YES.
alex@alexcartoon.com
THE FLOODING WAS SO BAD IN OUR AREA THAT GAS AND ELECTRICITY SUPPLIES WERE KNOCKED OUT IN OUR VILLAGE FOR THREE DAYS OVER THE FESTIVE SEASON.
YES, IN OURS TOO...
AFTER AN EXPERIENCE LIKE THIS I BELIEVE MANY PEOPLE WILL NOW BE SERIOUSLY RETHINKING THEIR ATTITUDES TO ADOPTING A GREENER LIFESTYLE...
I MEAN, THANKS TO OWNING A TRADITIONAL, OIL-GUZZLING, CO2-BELCHING, PERMANENTLY-ON AGA, WE WERE THE ONLY PEOPLE IN THE VILLAGE ABLE TO COOK OUR CHRISTMAS TURKEY...
SOD THE ENVIRONMENT! I'M GETTING ONE.

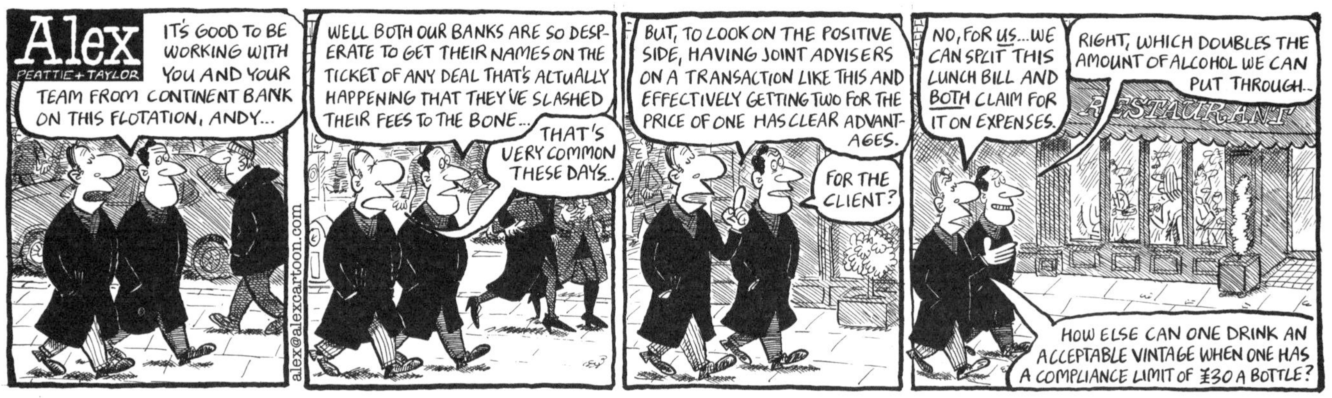
Alex
PEATTIE + TAYLOR
IT'S GOOD TO BE WORKING WITH YOU AND YOUR TEAM FROM CONTINENT BANK ON THIS FLOTATION, ANDY...
alex@alexcartoon.com
WELL BOTH OUR BANKS ARE SO DESPERATE TO GET THEIR NAMES ON THE TICKET OF ANY DEAL THAT'S ACTUALLY HAPPENING THAT THEY'VE SLASHED THEIR FEES TO THE BONE...
THAT'S VERY COMMON THESE DAYS...
BUT, TO LOOK ON THE POSITIVE SIDE, HAVING JOINT ADVISERS ON A TRANSACTION LIKE THIS AND EFFECTIVELY GETTING TWO FOR THE PRICE OF ONE HAS CLEAR ADVANTAGES.
FOR THE CLIENT?
NO, FOR US... WE CAN SPLIT THIS LUNCH BILL AND BOTH CLAIM FOR IT ON EXPENSES.
RIGHT, WHICH DOUBLES THE AMOUNT OF ALCOHOL WE CAN PUT THROUGH...
RESTAURANT
HOW ELSE CAN ONE DRINK AN ACCEPTABLE VINTAGE WHEN ONE HAS A COMPLIANCE LIMIT OF £30 A BOTTLE?

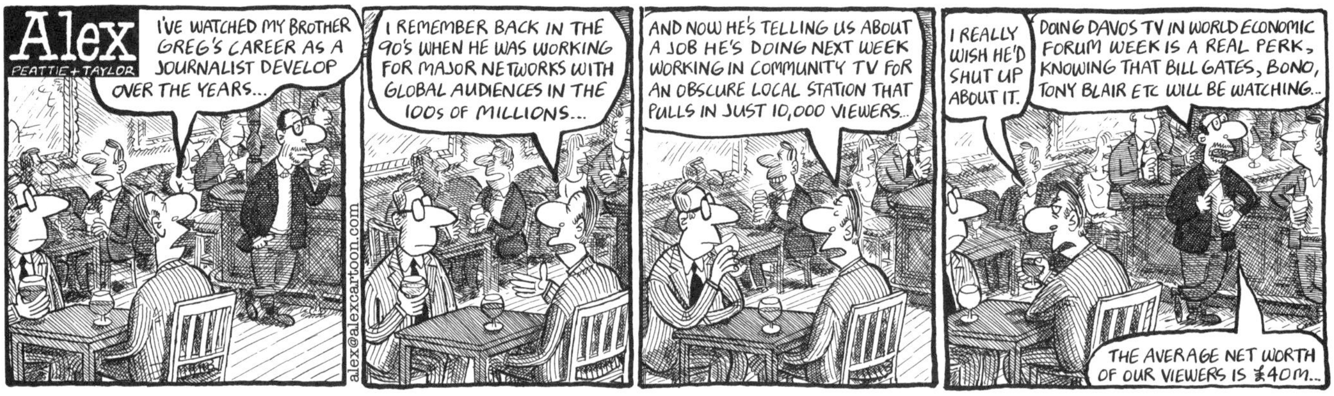
Alex
PEATTIE + TAYLOR
I'VE WATCHED MY BROTHER GREG'S CAREER AS A JOURNALIST DEVELOP OVER THE YEARS...
alex@alexcartoon.com
I REMEMBER BACK IN THE 90'S WHEN HE WAS WORKING FOR MAJOR NETWORKS WITH GLOBAL AUDIENCES IN THE 100S OF MILLIONS...
AND NOW HE'S TELLING US ABOUT A JOB HE'S DOING NEXT WEEK WORKING IN COMMUNITY TV FOR AN OBSCURE LOCAL STATION THAT PULLS IN JUST 10,000 VIEWERS...
I REALLY WISH HE'D SHUT UP ABOUT IT.
DOING DAVOS TV IN WORLD ECONOMIC FORUM WEEK IS A REAL PERK, KNOWING THAT BILL GATES, BONO, TONY BLAIR ETC WILL BE WATCHING...
THE AVERAGE NET WORTH OF OUR VIEWERS IS £40M...

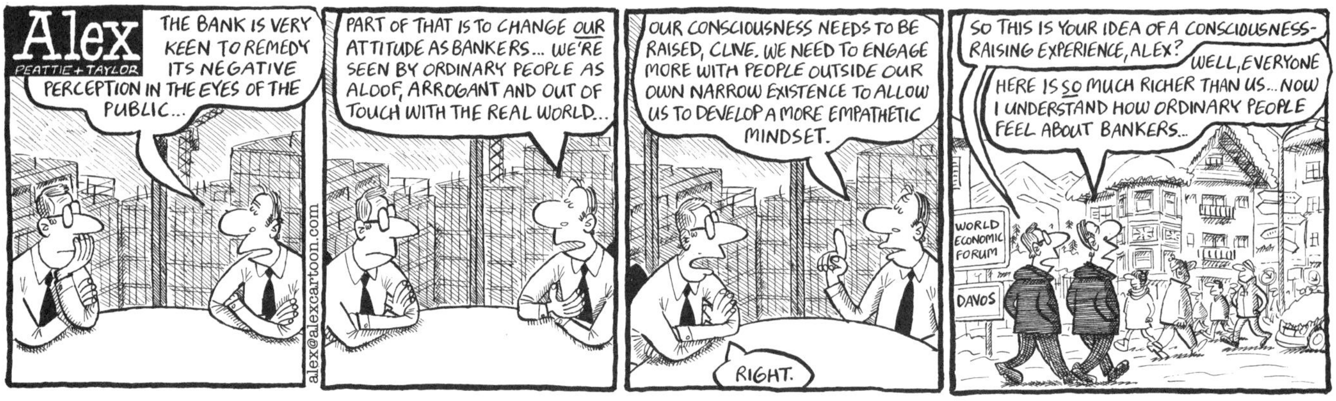
Alex
PEATTIE + TAYLOR
THE BANK IS VERY KEEN TO REMEDY ITS NEGATIVE PERCEPTION IN THE EYES OF THE PUBLIC...
alex@alexcartoon.com
PART OF THAT IS TO CHANGE OUR ATTITUDE AS BANKERS... WE'RE SEEN BY ORDINARY PEOPLE AS ALOOF, ARROGANT AND OUT OF TOUCH WITH THE REAL WORLD...
OUR CONSCIOUSNESS NEEDS TO BE RAISED, CLIVE. WE NEED TO ENGAGE MORE WITH PEOPLE OUTSIDE OUR OWN NARROW EXISTENCE TO ALLOW US TO DEVELOP A MORE EMPATHETIC MINDSET.
RIGHT.
SO THIS IS YOUR IDEA OF A CONSCIOUSNESS-RAISING EXPERIENCE, ALEX?
WELL, EVERYONE HERE IS SO MUCH RICHER THAN US... NOW I UNDERSTAND HOW ORDINARY PEOPLE FEEL ABOUT BANKERS...
WORLD ECONOMIC FORUM
DAVOS

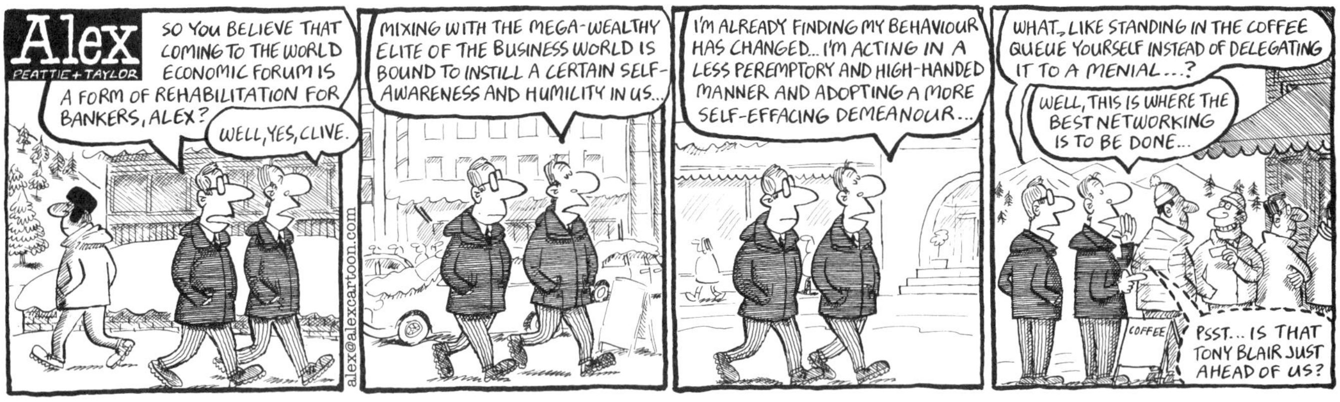
Alex
PEATTIE + TAYLOR
SO YOU BELIEVE THAT COMING TO THE WORLD ECONOMIC FORUM IS A FORM OF REHABILITATION FOR BANKERS, ALEX?
WELL, YES, CLIVE.
alex@alexcartoon.com
MIXING WITH THE MEGA-WEALTHY ELITE OF THE BUSINESS WORLD IS BOUND TO INSTILL A CERTAIN SELF-AWARENESS AND HUMILITY IN US...
I'M ALREADY FINDING MY BEHAVIOUR HAS CHANGED... I'M ACTING IN A LESS PEREMPTORY AND HIGH-HANDED MANNER AND ADOPTING A MORE SELF-EFFACING DEMEANOUR...
WHAT... LIKE STANDING IN THE COFFEE QUEUE YOURSELF INSTEAD OF DELEGATING IT TO A MENIAL...?
WELL, THIS IS WHERE THE BEST NETWORKING IS TO BE DONE...
COFFEE
PSST... IS THAT TONY BLAIR JUST AHEAD OF US?

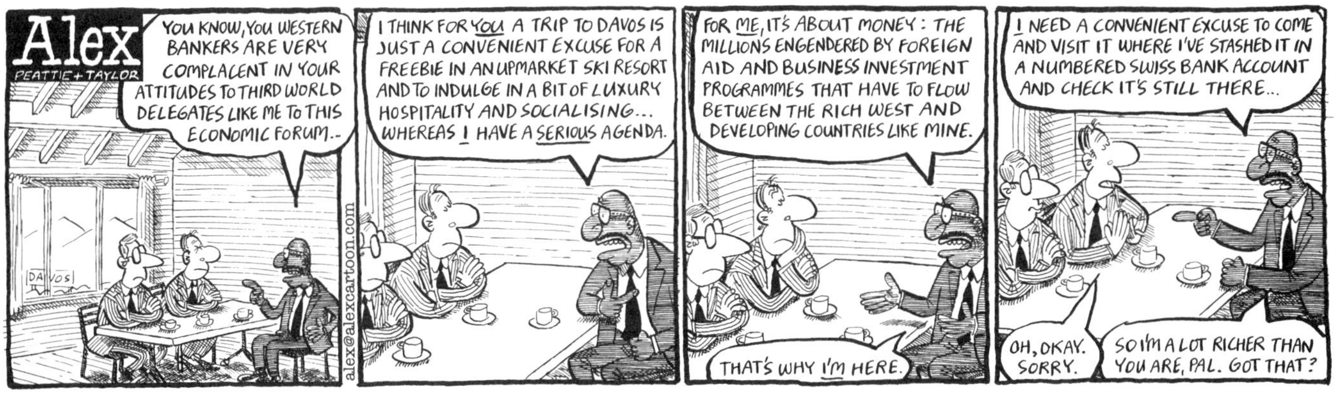
Alex
PEATTIE + TAYLOR
YOU KNOW, YOU WESTERN BANKERS ARE VERY COMPLACENT IN YOUR ATTITUDES TO THIRD WORLD DELEGATES LIKE ME TO THIS ECONOMIC FORUM...
DAVOS
alex@alexcartoon.com
I THINK FOR YOU A TRIP TO DAVOS IS JUST A CONVENIENT EXCUSE FOR A FREEBIE IN AN UPMARKET SKI RESORT AND TO INDULGE IN A BIT OF LUXURY HOSPITALITY AND SOCIALISING... WHEREAS I HAVE A SERIOUS AGENDA.
FOR ME, IT'S ABOUT MONEY: THE MILLIONS ENGENDERED BY FOREIGN AID AND BUSINESS INVESTMENT PROGRAMMES THAT HAVE TO FLOW BETWEEN THE RICH WEST AND DEVELOPING COUNTRIES LIKE MINE.
THAT'S WHY I'M HERE.
I NEED A CONVENIENT EXCUSE TO COME AND VISIT IT WHERE I'VE STASHED IT IN A NUMBERED SWISS BANK ACCOUNT AND CHECK IT'S STILL THERE...
OH, OKAY. SORRY.
SO I'M A LOT RICHER THAN YOU ARE, PAL. GOT THAT?

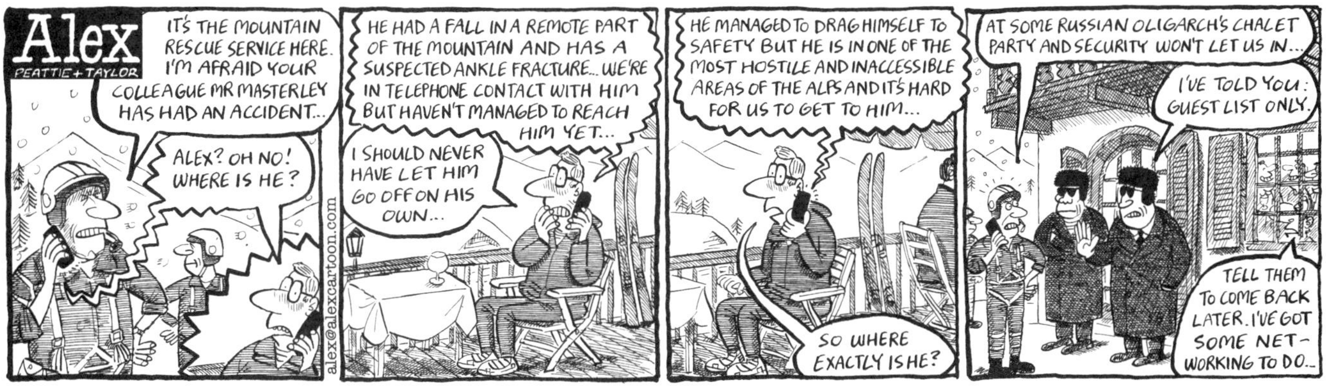
Alex
PEATTIE + TAYLOR
IT'S THE MOUNTAIN RESCUE SERVICE HERE. I'M AFRAID YOUR COLLEAGUE MR MASTERLEY HAS HAD AN ACCIDENT...
ALEX? OH NO! WHERE IS HE?
alex@alexcartoon.com
HE HAD A FALL IN A REMOTE PART OF THE MOUNTAIN AND HAS A SUSPECTED ANKLE FRACTURE... WE'RE IN TELEPHONE CONTACT WITH HIM BUT HAVEN'T MANAGED TO REACH HIM YET...
I SHOULD NEVER HAVE LET HIM GO OFF ON HIS OWN...
HE MANAGED TO DRAG HIMSELF TO SAFETY BUT HE IS IN ONE OF THE MOST HOSTILE AND INACCESSIBLE AREAS OF THE ALPS AND IT'S HARD FOR US TO GET TO HIM...
SO WHERE EXACTLY IS HE?
AT SOME RUSSIAN OLIGARCH'S CHALET PARTY AND SECURITY WON'T LET US IN...
I'VE TOLD YOU: GUEST LIST ONLY.
TELL THEM TO COME BACK LATER. I'VE GOT SOME NET-WORKING TO DO...

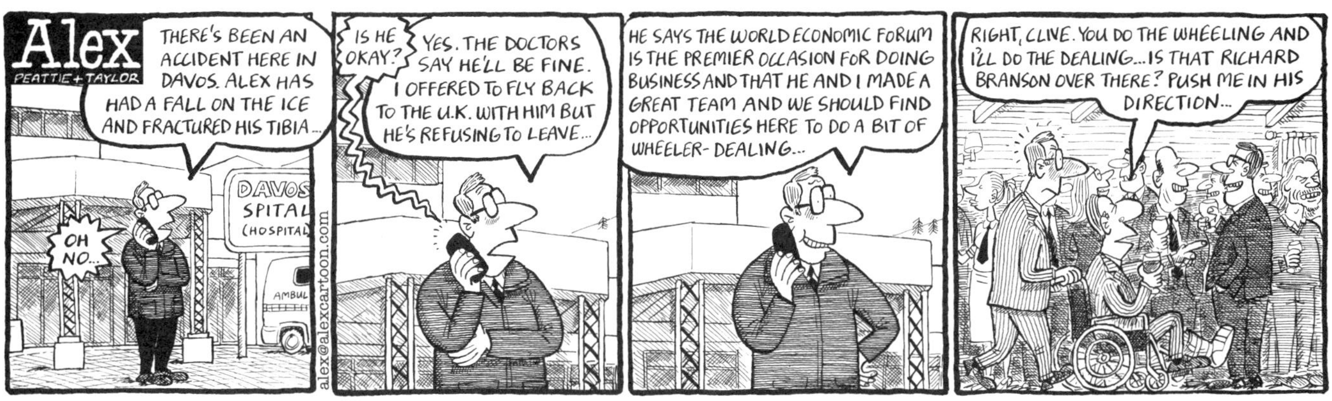
Alex
PEATTIE + TAYLOR
THERE'S BEEN AN ACCIDENT HERE IN DAVOS. ALEX HAS HAD A FALL ON THE ICE AND FRACTURED HIS TIBIA...
OH NO...
DAVOS SPITAL (HOSPITAL)
AMBUL
alex@alexcartoon.com
IS HE OKAY?
YES. THE DOCTORS SAY HE'LL BE FINE. I OFFERED TO FLY BACK TO THE U.K. WITH HIM BUT HE'S REFUSING TO LEAVE...
HE SAYS THE WORLD ECONOMIC FORUM IS THE PREMIER OCCASION FOR DOING BUSINESS AND THAT HE AND I MADE A GREAT TEAM AND WE SHOULD FIND OPPORTUNITIES HERE TO DO A BIT OF WHEELER-DEALING...
RIGHT, CLIVE. YOU DO THE WHEELING AND I'LL DO THE DEALING... IS THAT RICHARD BRANSON OVER THERE? PUSH ME IN HIS DIRECTION...

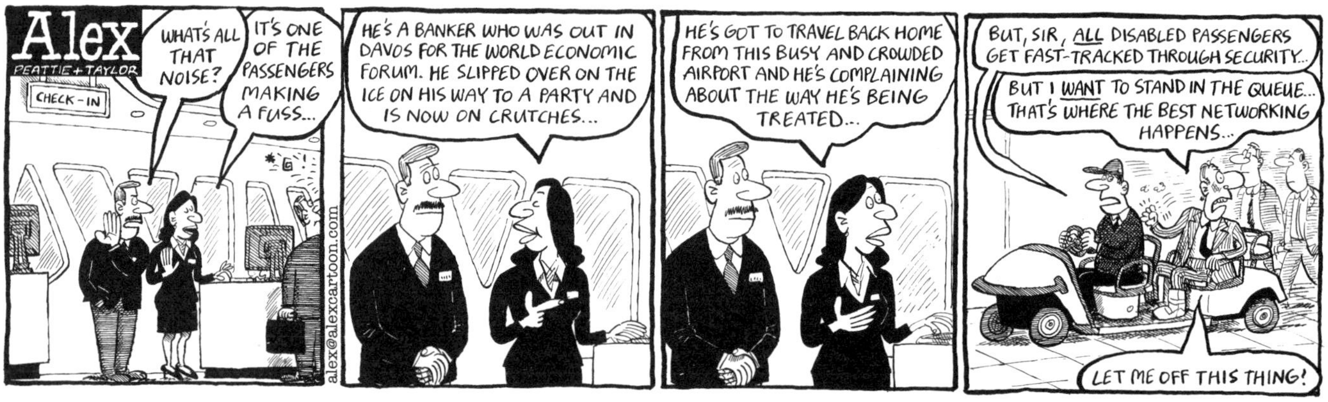
Alex
PEATTIE+TAYLOR
CHECK-IN
WHAT'S ALL THAT NOISE?
IT'S ONE OF THE PASSENGERS MAKING A FUSS...
alex@alexcartoon.com
HE'S A BANKER WHO WAS OUT IN DAVOS FOR THE WORLD ECONOMIC FORUM. HE SLIPPED OVER ON THE ICE ON HIS WAY TO A PARTY AND IS NOW ON CRUTCHES...
HE'S GOT TO TRAVEL BACK HOME FROM THIS BUSY AND CROWDED AIRPORT AND HE'S COMPLAINING ABOUT THE WAY HE'S BEING TREATED...
BUT, SIR, ALL DISABLED PASSENGERS GET FAST-TRACKED THROUGH SECURITY...
BUT I WANT TO STAND IN THE QUEUE... THAT'S WHERE THE BEST NETWORKING HAPPENS...
LET ME OFF THIS THING!

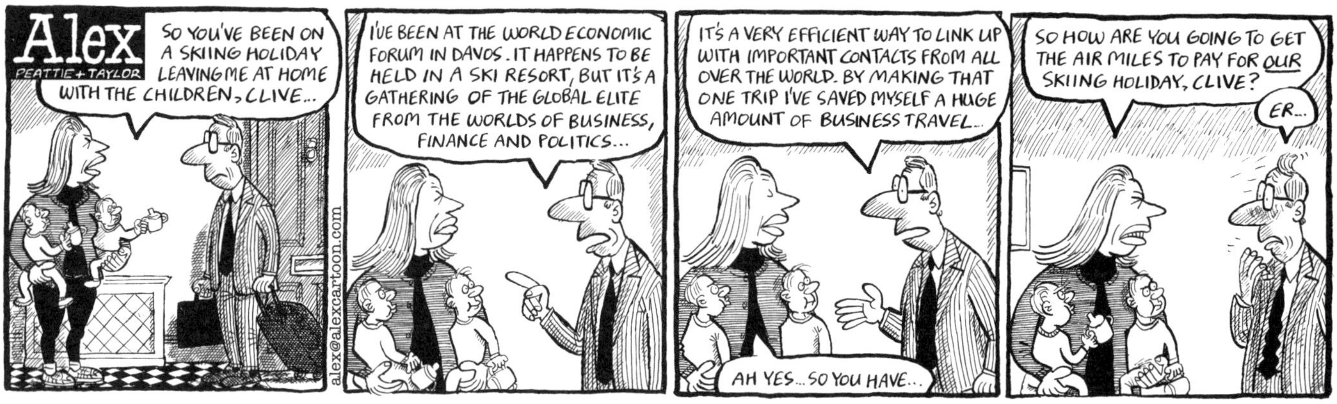
Alex
PEATTIE+TAYLOR
SO YOU'VE BEEN ON A SKIING HOLIDAY LEAVING ME AT HOME WITH THE CHILDREN, CLIVE...
alex@alexcartoon.com
I'VE BEEN AT THE WORLD ECONOMIC FORUM IN DAVOS. IT HAPPENS TO BE HELD IN A SKI RESORT, BUT IT'S A GATHERING OF THE GLOBAL ELITE FROM THE WORLDS OF BUSINESS, FINANCE AND POLITICS...
IT'S A VERY EFFICIENT WAY TO LINK UP WITH IMPORTANT CONTACTS FROM ALL OVER THE WORLD. BY MAKING THAT ONE TRIP I'VE SAVED MYSELF A HUGE AMOUNT OF BUSINESS TRAVEL...
AH YES... SO YOU HAVE...
SO HOW ARE YOU GOING TO GET THE AIR MILES TO PAY FOR OUR SKIING HOLIDAY, CLIVE?
ER...

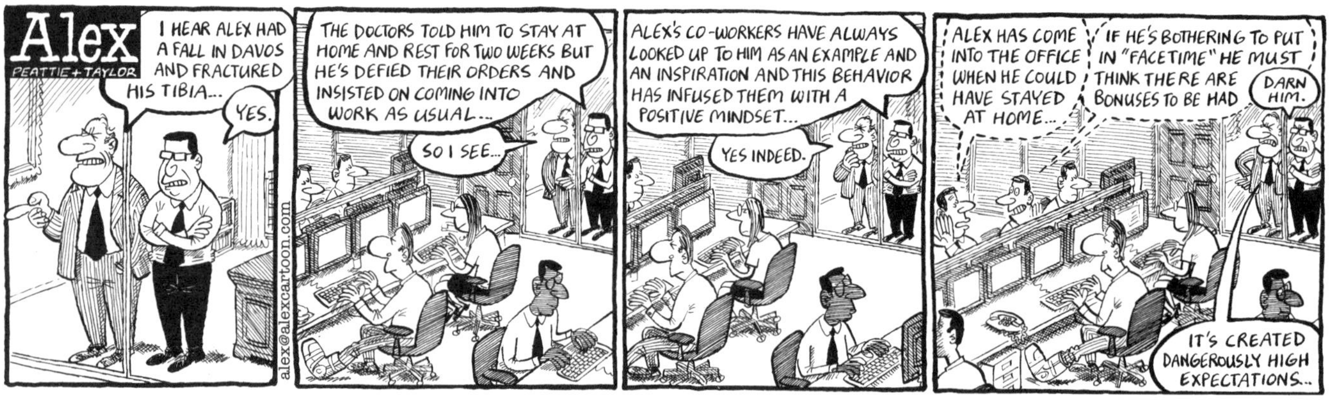
Alex
PEATTIE+TAYLOR
I HEAR ALEX HAD A FALL IN DAVOS AND FRACTURED HIS TIBIA...
YES.
alex@alexcartoon.com
THE DOCTORS TOLD HIM TO STAY AT HOME AND REST FOR TWO WEEKS BUT HE'S DEFIED THEIR ORDERS AND INSISTED ON COMING INTO WORK AS USUAL...
SO I SEE...
ALEX'S CO-WORKERS HAVE ALWAYS LOOKED UP TO HIM AS AN EXAMPLE AND AN INSPIRATION AND THIS BEHAVIOR HAS INFUSED THEM WITH A POSITIVE MINDSET...
YES INDEED.
ALEX HAS COME INTO THE OFFICE WHEN HE COULD HAVE STAYED AT HOME...
IF HE'S BOTHERING TO PUT IN "FACETIME" HE MUST THINK THERE ARE BONUSES TO BE HAD
DARN HIM.
IT'S CREATED DANGEROUSLY HIGH EXPECTATIONS...

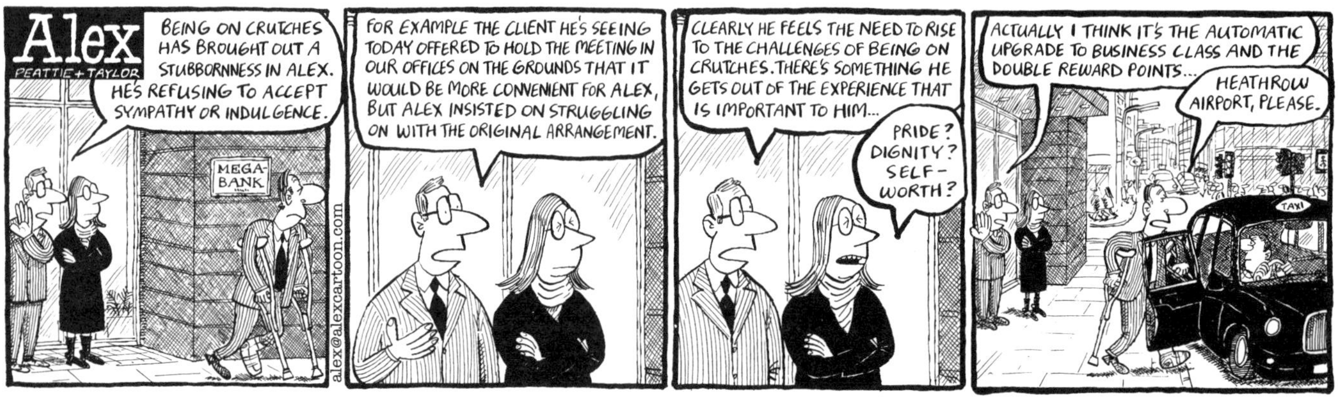
Alex
PEATTIE+TAYLOR
BEING ON CRUTCHES HAS BROUGHT OUT A STUBBORNNESS IN ALEX. HE'S REFUSING TO ACCEPT SYMPATHY OR INDULGENCE.
MEGA-BANK
alex@alexcartoon.com
FOR EXAMPLE THE CLIENT HE'S SEEING TODAY OFFERED TO HOLD THE MEETING IN OUR OFFICES ON THE GROUNDS THAT IT WOULD BE MORE CONVENIENT FOR ALEX, BUT ALEX INSISTED ON STRUGGLING ON WITH THE ORIGINAL ARRANGEMENT.
CLEARLY HE FEELS THE NEED TO RISE TO THE CHALLENGES OF BEING ON CRUTCHES. THERE'S SOMETHING HE GETS OUT OF THE EXPERIENCE THAT IS IMPORTANT TO HIM...
PRIDE? DIGNITY? SELF-WORTH?
ACTUALLY I THINK IT'S THE AUTOMATIC UPGRADE TO BUSINESS CLASS AND THE DOUBLE REWARD POINTS...
HEATHROW AIRPORT, PLEASE.
TAXI

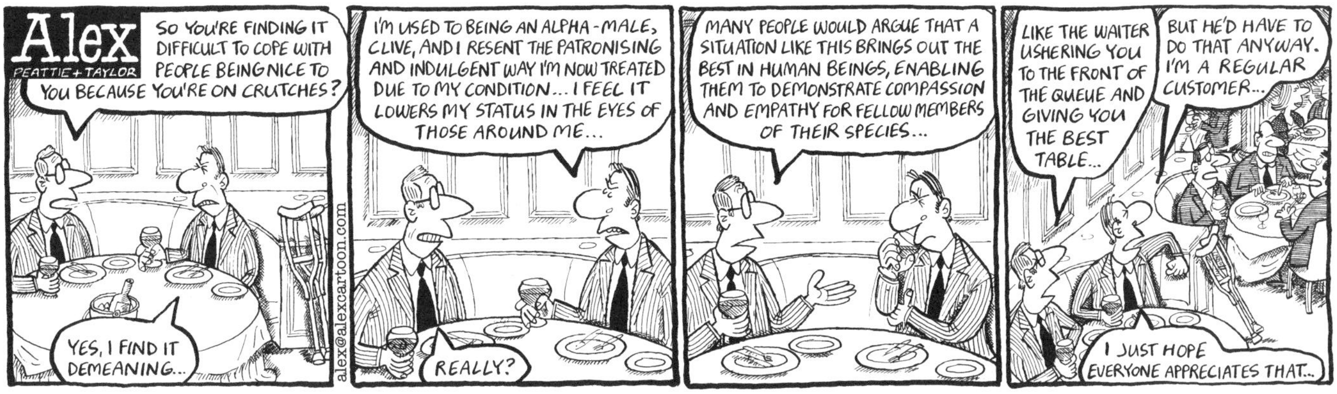
Alex
PEATTIE + TAYLOR
SO YOU'RE FINDING IT DIFFICULT TO COPE WITH PEOPLE BEING NICE TO YOU BECAUSE YOU'RE ON CRUTCHES?
YES, I FIND IT DEMEANING...
alex@alexcartoon.com
I'M USED TO BEING AN ALPHA-MALE, CLIVE, AND I RESENT THE PATRONISING AND INDULGENT WAY I'M NOW TREATED DUE TO MY CONDITION... I FEEL IT LOWERS MY STATUS IN THE EYES OF THOSE AROUND ME...
REALLY?
MANY PEOPLE WOULD ARGUE THAT A SITUATION LIKE THIS BRINGS OUT THE BEST IN HUMAN BEINGS, ENABLING THEM TO DEMONSTRATE COMPASSION AND EMPATHY FOR FELLOW MEMBERS OF THEIR SPECIES...
LIKE THE WAITER USHERING YOU TO THE FRONT OF THE QUEUE AND GIVING YOU THE BEST TABLE...
BUT HE'D HAVE TO DO THAT ANYWAY. I'M A REGULAR CUSTOMER...
I JUST HOPE EVERYONE APPRECIATES THAT...

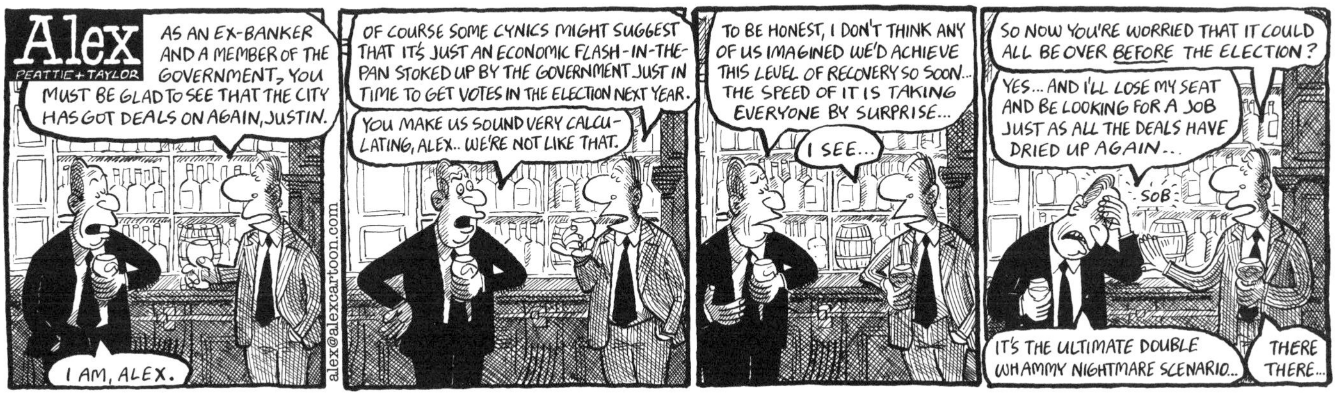
Alex
PEATTIE + TAYLOR
AS AN EX-BANKER AND A MEMBER OF THE GOVERNMENT, YOU MUST BE GLAD TO SEE THAT THE CITY HAS GOT DEALS ON AGAIN, JUSTIN.
I AM, ALEX.
alex@alexcartoon.com
OF COURSE SOME CYNICS MIGHT SUGGEST THAT IT'S JUST AN ECONOMIC FLASH-IN-THE-PAN STOKED UP BY THE GOVERNMENT JUST IN TIME TO GET VOTES IN THE ELECTION NEXT YEAR.
YOU MAKE US SOUND VERY CALCULATING, ALEX.. WE'RE NOT LIKE THAT.
TO BE HONEST, I DON'T THINK ANY OF US IMAGINED WE'D ACHIEVE THIS LEVEL OF RECOVERY SO SOON... THE SPEED OF IT IS TAKING EVERYONE BY SURPRISE...
I SEE...
SO NOW YOU'RE WORRIED THAT IT COULD ALL BE OVER BEFORE THE ELECTION?
YES... AND I'LL LOSE MY SEAT AND BE LOOKING FOR A JOB JUST AS ALL THE DEALS HAVE DRIED UP AGAIN...
SOB
IT'S THE ULTIMATE DOUBLE WHAMMY NIGHTMARE SCENARIO...
THERE THERE...

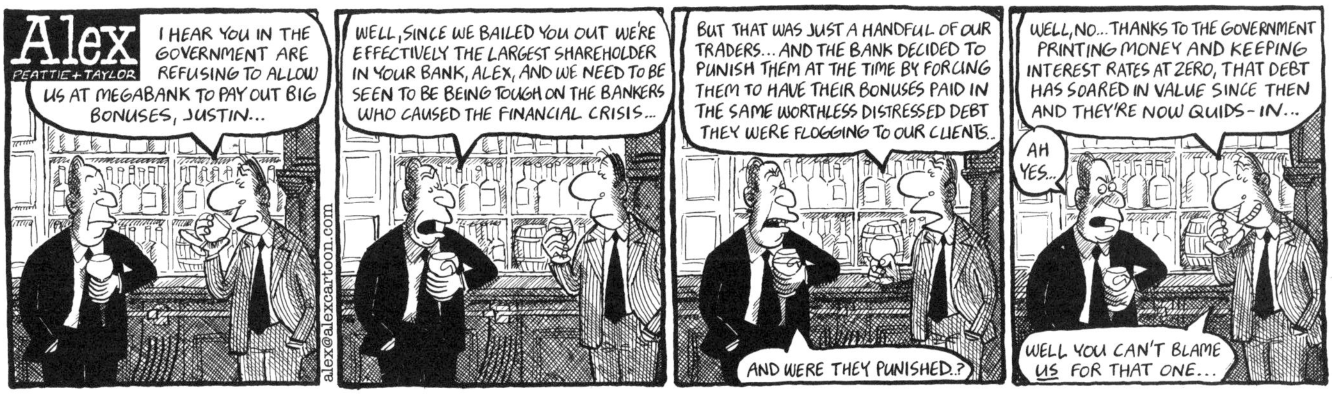
Alex
PEATTIE + TAYLOR
I HEAR YOU IN THE GOVERNMENT ARE REFUSING TO ALLOW US AT MEGABANK TO PAY OUT BIG BONUSES, JUSTIN...
alex@alexcartoon.com
WELL, SINCE WE BAILED YOU OUT WE'RE EFFECTIVELY THE LARGEST SHAREHOLDER IN YOUR BANK, ALEX, AND WE NEED TO BE SEEN TO BE BEING TOUGH ON THE BANKERS WHO CAUSED THE FINANCIAL CRISIS...
BUT THAT WAS JUST A HANDFUL OF OUR TRADERS... AND THE BANK DECIDED TO PUNISH THEM AT THE TIME BY FORCING THEM TO HAVE THEIR BONUSES PAID IN THE SAME WORTHLESS DISTRESSED DEBT THEY WERE FLOGGING TO OUR CLIENTS..
AND WERE THEY PUNISHED..?
WELL, NO... THANKS TO THE GOVERNMENT PRINTING MONEY AND KEEPING INTEREST RATES AT ZERO, THAT DEBT HAS SOARED IN VALUE SINCE THEN AND THEY'RE NOW QUIDS-IN...
AH YES...
WELL YOU CAN'T BLAME US FOR THAT ONE...

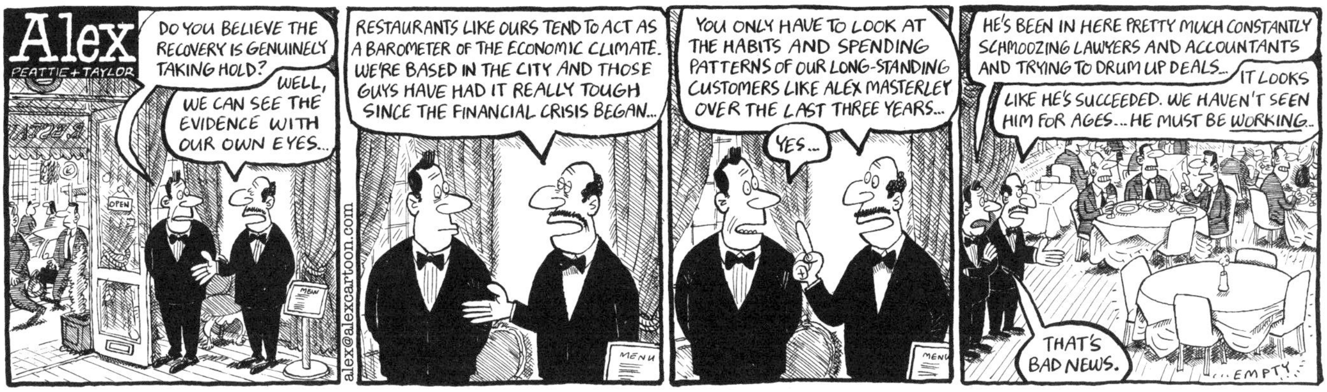
Alex
PEATTIE + TAYLOR
DO YOU BELIEVE THE RECOVERY IS GENUINELY TAKING HOLD?
WELL, WE CAN SEE THE EVIDENCE WITH OUR OWN EYES...
OPEN
MENU
alex@alexcartoon.com
RESTAURANTS LIKE OURS TEND TO ACT AS A BAROMETER OF THE ECONOMIC CLIMATE. WE'RE BASED IN THE CITY AND THOSE GUYS HAVE HAD IT REALLY TOUGH SINCE THE FINANCIAL CRISIS BEGAN...
MENU
YOU ONLY HAVE TO LOOK AT THE HABITS AND SPENDING PATTERNS OF OUR LONG-STANDING CUSTOMERS LIKE ALEX MASTERLEY OVER THE LAST THREE YEARS...
YES...
MENU
HE'S BEEN IN HERE PRETTY MUCH CONSTANTLY SCHMOOZING LAWYERS AND ACCOUNTANTS AND TRYING TO DRUM UP DEALS...
IT LOOKS LIKE HE'S SUCCEEDED. WE HAVEN'T SEEN HIM FOR AGES... HE MUST BE WORKING...
THAT'S BAD NEWS.
...EMPTY...

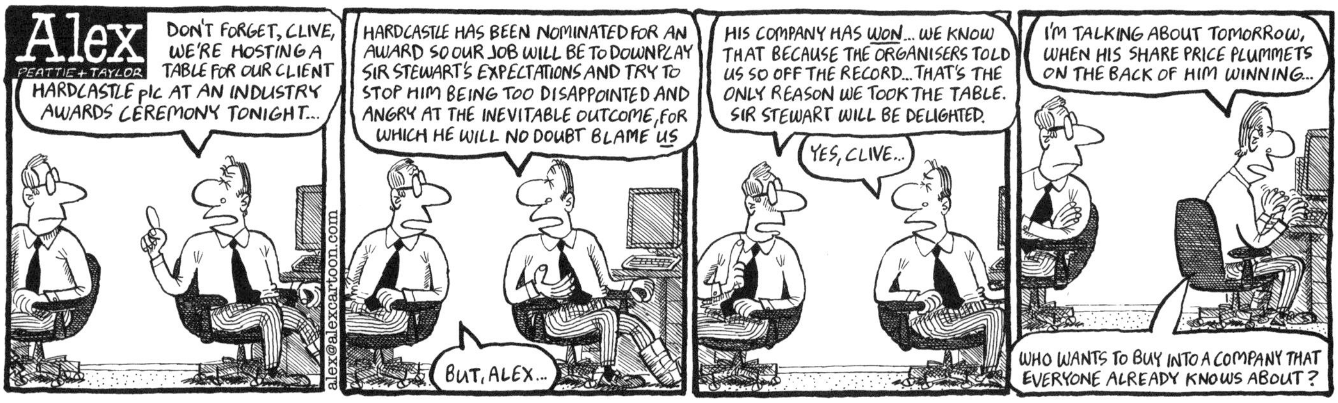
Alex
PEATTIE + TAYLOR
DON'T FORGET, CLIVE, WE'RE HOSTING A TABLE FOR OUR CLIENT HARDCASTLE plc AT AN INDUSTRY AWARDS CEREMONY TONIGHT...
alex@alexcartoon.com
HARDCASTLE HAS BEEN NOMINATED FOR AN AWARD SO OUR JOB WILL BE TO DOWNPLAY SIR STEWART'S EXPECTATIONS AND TRY TO STOP HIM BEING TOO DISAPPOINTED AND ANGRY AT THE INEVITABLE OUTCOME, FOR WHICH HE WILL NO DOUBT BLAME US
BUT, ALEX...
HIS COMPANY HAS WON... WE KNOW THAT BECAUSE THE ORGANISERS TOLD US SO OFF THE RECORD... THAT'S THE ONLY REASON WE TOOK THE TABLE. SIR STEWART WILL BE DELIGHTED.
YES, CLIVE...
I'M TALKING ABOUT TOMORROW, WHEN HIS SHARE PRICE PLUMMETS ON THE BACK OF HIM WINNING...
WHO WANTS TO BUY INTO A COMPANY THAT EVERYONE ALREADY KNOWS ABOUT?

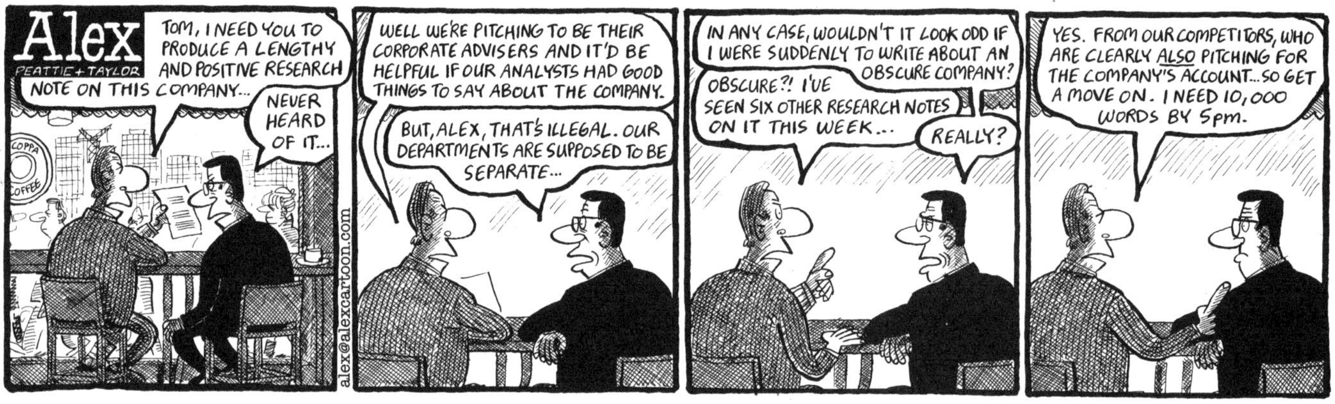
Alex
PEATTIE + TAYLOR
TOM, I NEED YOU TO PRODUCE A LENGTHY AND POSITIVE RESEARCH NOTE ON THIS COMPANY...
NEVER HEARD OF IT...
alex@alexcartoon.com
WELL WE'RE PITCHING TO BE THEIR CORPORATE ADVISERS AND IT'D BE HELPFUL IF OUR ANALYSTS HAD GOOD THINGS TO SAY ABOUT THE COMPANY.
BUT, ALEX, THAT'S ILLEGAL. OUR DEPARTMENTS ARE SUPPOSED TO BE SEPARATE...
IN ANY CASE, WOULDN'T IT LOOK ODD IF I WERE SUDDENLY TO WRITE ABOUT AN OBSCURE COMPANY?
OBSCURE?! I'VE SEEN SIX OTHER RESEARCH NOTES ON IT THIS WEEK...
REALLY?
YES. FROM OUR COMPETITORS, WHO ARE CLEARLY ALSO PITCHING FOR THE COMPANY'S ACCOUNT... SO GET A MOVE ON. I NEED 10,000 WORDS BY 5pm.

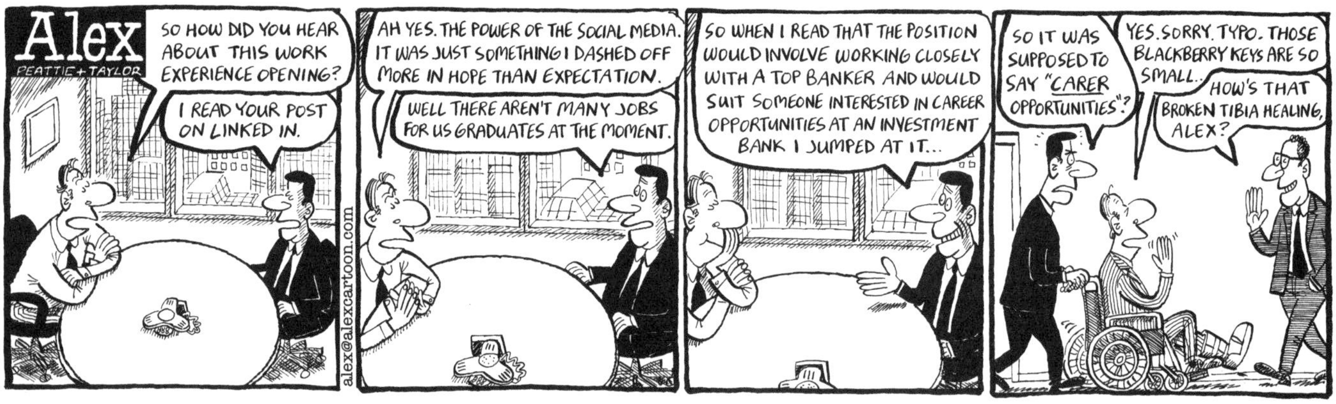
Alex
PEATTIE + TAYLOR
SO HOW DID YOU HEAR ABOUT THIS WORK EXPERIENCE OPENING?
I READ YOUR POST ON LINKED IN.
alex@alexcartoon.com
AH YES. THE POWER OF THE SOCIAL MEDIA. IT WAS JUST SOMETHING I DASHED OFF MORE IN HOPE THAN EXPECTATION.
WELL THERE AREN'T MANY JOBS FOR US GRADUATES AT THE MOMENT.
SO WHEN I READ THAT THE POSITION WOULD INVOLVE WORKING CLOSELY WITH A TOP BANKER AND WOULD SUIT SOMEONE INTERESTED IN CAREER OPPORTUNITIES AT AN INVESTMENT BANK I JUMPED AT IT...
SO IT WAS SUPPOSED TO SAY "CARER OPPORTUNITIES"?
YES. SORRY. TYPO. THOSE BLACKBERRY KEYS ARE SO SMALL...
HOW'S THAT BROKEN TIBIA HEALING, ALEX?

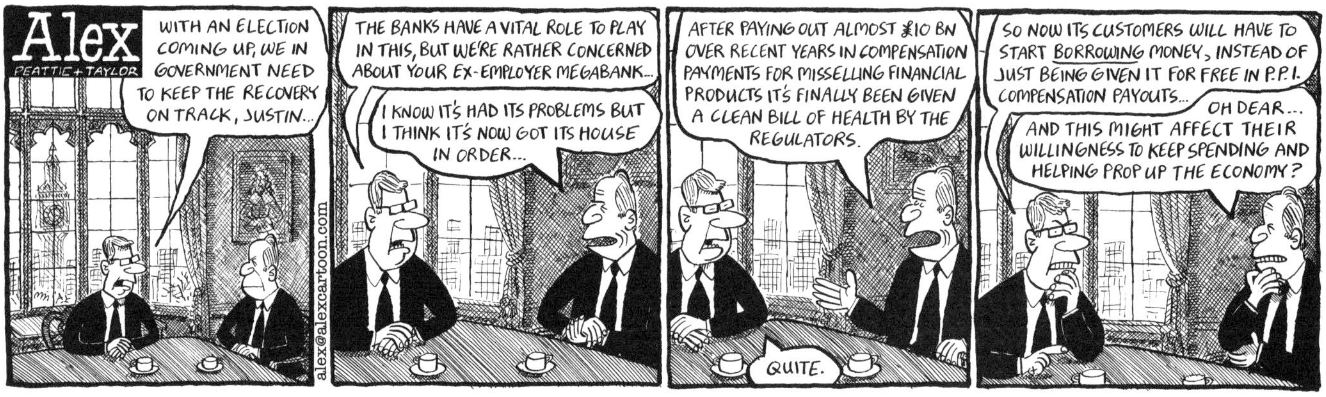
Alex
PEATTIE + TAYLOR
WITH AN ELECTION COMING UP, WE IN GOVERNMENT NEED TO KEEP THE RECOVERY ON TRACK, JUSTIN...
alex@alexcartoon.com
THE BANKS HAVE A VITAL ROLE TO PLAY IN THIS, BUT WE'RE RATHER CONCERNED ABOUT YOUR EX-EMPLOYER MEGABANK...
I KNOW IT'S HAD ITS PROBLEMS BUT I THINK IT'S NOW GOT ITS HOUSE IN ORDER...
AFTER PAYING OUT ALMOST £10 BN OVER RECENT YEARS IN COMPENSATION PAYMENTS FOR MISSELLING FINANCIAL PRODUCTS IT'S FINALLY BEEN GIVEN A CLEAN BILL OF HEALTH BY THE REGULATORS.
QUITE.
SO NOW ITS CUSTOMERS WILL HAVE TO START BORROWING MONEY, INSTEAD OF JUST BEING GIVEN IT FOR FREE IN P.P.I. COMPENSATION PAYOUTS...
OH DEAR...
AND THIS MIGHT AFFECT THEIR WILLINGNESS TO KEEP SPENDING AND HELPING PROP UP THE ECONOMY?

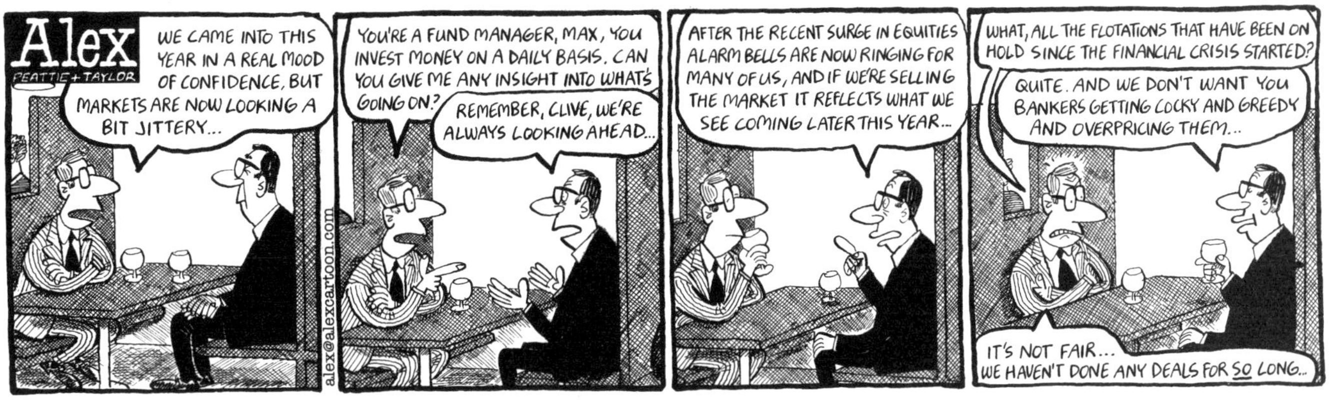
Alex
PEATTIE + TAYLOR
WE CAME INTO THIS YEAR IN A REAL MOOD OF CONFIDENCE, BUT MARKETS ARE NOW LOOKING A BIT JITTERY...
YOU'RE A FUND MANAGER, MAX, YOU INVEST MONEY ON A DAILY BASIS. CAN YOU GIVE ME ANY INSIGHT INTO WHAT'S GOING ON?
REMEMBER, CLIVE, WE'RE ALWAYS LOOKING AHEAD...
alex@alexcartoon.com
AFTER THE RECENT SURGE IN EQUITIES ALARM BELLS ARE NOW RINGING FOR MANY OF US, AND IF WE'RE SELLING THE MARKET IT REFLECTS WHAT WE SEE COMING LATER THIS YEAR...
WHAT, ALL THE FLOTATIONS THAT HAVE BEEN ON HOLD SINCE THE FINANCIAL CRISIS STARTED?
QUITE. AND WE DON'T WANT YOU BANKERS GETTING COCKY AND GREEDY AND OVERPRICING THEM...
IT'S NOT FAIR... WE HAVEN'T DONE ANY DEALS FOR SO LONG...

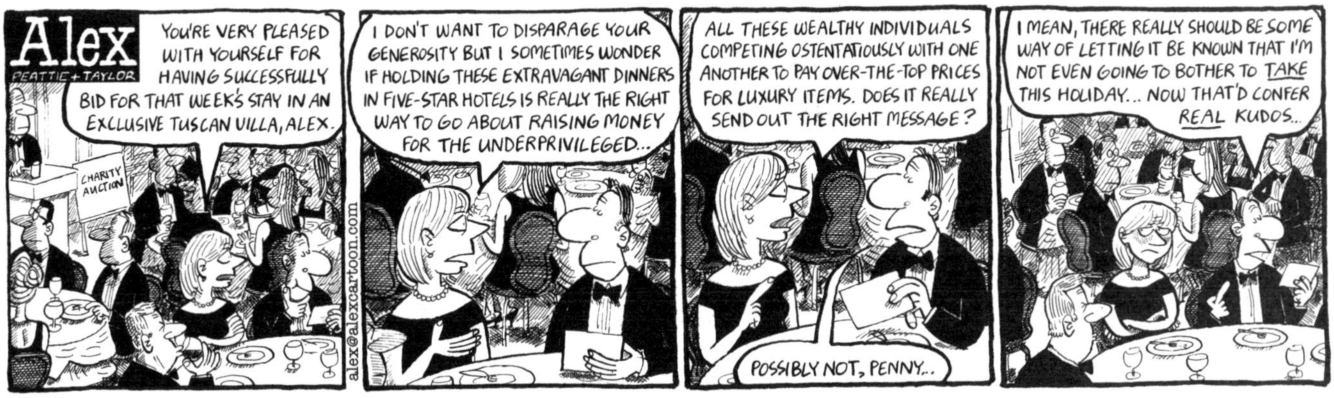
Alex
PEATTIE + TAYLOR
YOU'RE VERY PLEASED WITH YOURSELF FOR HAVING SUCCESSFULLY BID FOR THAT WEEK'S STAY IN AN EXCLUSIVE TUSCAN VILLA, ALEX.
CHARITY AUCTION
I DON'T WANT TO DISPARAGE YOUR GENEROSITY BUT I SOMETIMES WONDER IF HOLDING THESE EXTRAVAGANT DINNERS IN FIVE-STAR HOTELS IS REALLY THE RIGHT WAY TO GO ABOUT RAISING MONEY FOR THE UNDERPRIVILEGED...
alex@alexcartoon.com
ALL THESE WEALTHY INDIVIDUALS COMPETING OSTENTATIOUSLY WITH ONE ANOTHER TO PAY OVER-THE-TOP PRICES FOR LUXURY ITEMS. DOES IT REALLY SEND OUT THE RIGHT MESSAGE?
POSSIBLY NOT, PENNY...
I MEAN, THERE REALLY SHOULD BE SOME WAY OF LETTING IT BE KNOWN THAT I'M NOT EVEN GOING TO BOTHER TO TAKE THIS HOLIDAY... NOW THAT'D CONFER REAL KUDOS...

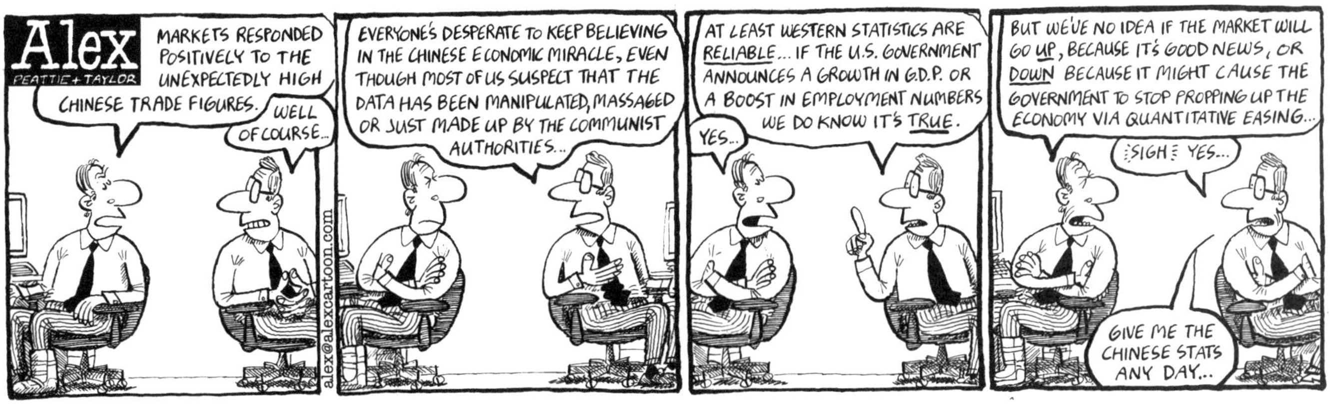
Alex
PEATTIE + TAYLOR
MARKETS RESPONDED POSITIVELY TO THE UNEXPECTEDLY HIGH CHINESE TRADE FIGURES.
WELL OF COURSE...
alex@alexcartoon.com
EVERYONE'S DESPERATE TO KEEP BELIEVING IN THE CHINESE ECONOMIC MIRACLE, EVEN THOUGH MOST OF US SUSPECT THAT THE DATA HAS BEEN MANIPULATED, MASSAGED OR JUST MADE UP BY THE COMMUNIST AUTHORITIES...
AT LEAST WESTERN STATISTICS ARE RELIABLE... IF THE U.S. GOVERNMENT ANNOUNCES A GROWTH IN G.D.P. OR A BOOST IN EMPLOYMENT NUMBERS WE DO KNOW IT'S TRUE.
YES...
BUT WE'VE NO IDEA IF THE MARKET WILL GO UP, BECAUSE IT'S GOOD NEWS, OR DOWN BECAUSE IT MIGHT CAUSE THE GOVERNMENT TO STOP PROPPING UP THE ECONOMY VIA QUANTITATIVE EASING...
SIGH YES...
GIVE ME THE CHINESE STATS ANY DAY...

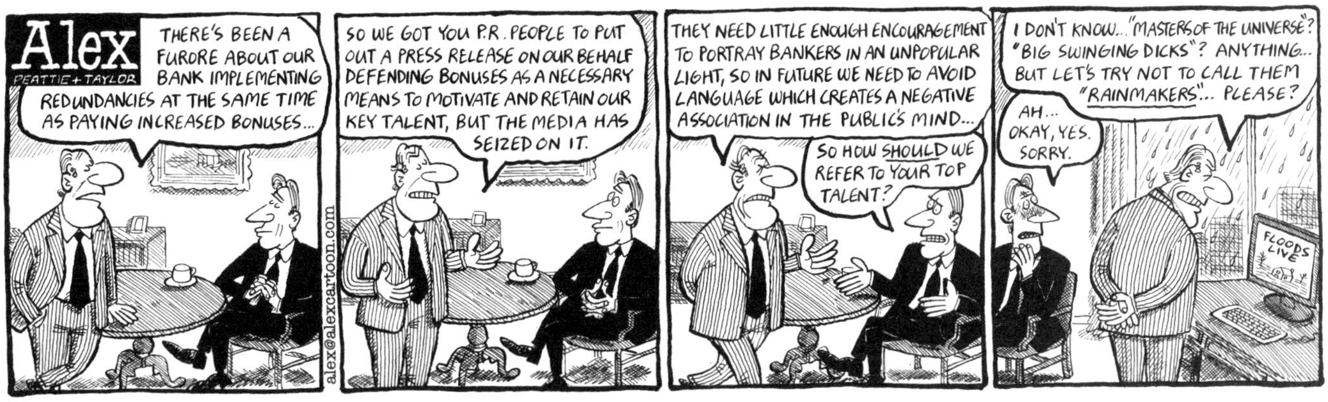
Alex
PEATTIE + TAYLOR
THERE'S BEEN A FURORE ABOUT OUR BANK IMPLEMENTING REDUNDANCIES AT THE SAME TIME AS PAYING INCREASED BONUSES...
alex@alexcartoon.com
SO WE GOT YOU P.R. PEOPLE TO PUT OUT A PRESS RELEASE ON OUR BEHALF DEFENDING BONUSES AS A NECESSARY MEANS TO MOTIVATE AND RETAIN OUR KEY TALENT, BUT THE MEDIA HAS SEIZED ON IT.
THEY NEED LITTLE ENOUGH ENCOURAGEMENT TO PORTRAY BANKERS IN AN UNPOPULAR LIGHT, SO IN FUTURE WE NEED TO AVOID LANGUAGE WHICH CREATES A NEGATIVE ASSOCIATION IN THE PUBLIC'S MIND...
SO HOW SHOULD WE REFER TO YOUR TOP TALENT?
I DON'T KNOW... "MASTERS OF THE UNIVERSE"? "BIG SWINGING DICKS"? ANYTHING... BUT LET'S TRY NOT TO CALL THEM "RAINMAKERS"... PLEASE?
AH... OKAY, YES. SORRY.
FLOODS LIVE

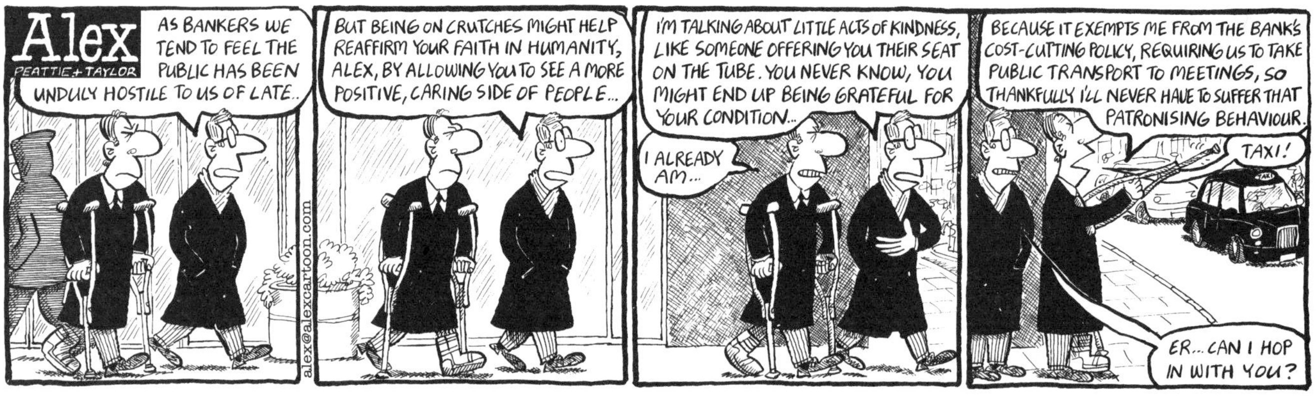
Alex
PEATTIE + TAYLOR
AS BANKERS WE TEND TO FEEL THE PUBLIC HAS BEEN UNDULY HOSTILE TO US OF LATE..
BUT BEING ON CRUTCHES MIGHT HELP REAFFIRM YOUR FAITH IN HUMANITY, ALEX, BY ALLOWING YOU TO SEE A MORE POSITIVE, CARING SIDE OF PEOPLE...
I'M TALKING ABOUT LITTLE ACTS OF KINDNESS, LIKE SOMEONE OFFERING YOU THEIR SEAT ON THE TUBE. YOU NEVER KNOW, YOU MIGHT END UP BEING GRATEFUL FOR YOUR CONDITION...
I ALREADY AM...
BECAUSE IT EXEMPTS ME FROM THE BANK'S COST-CUTTING POLICY, REQUIRING US TO TAKE PUBLIC TRANSPORT TO MEETINGS, SO THANKFULLY I'LL NEVER HAVE TO SUFFER THAT PATRONISING BEHAVIOUR.
TAXI!
ER... CAN I HOP IN WITH YOU?
alex@alexcartoon.com

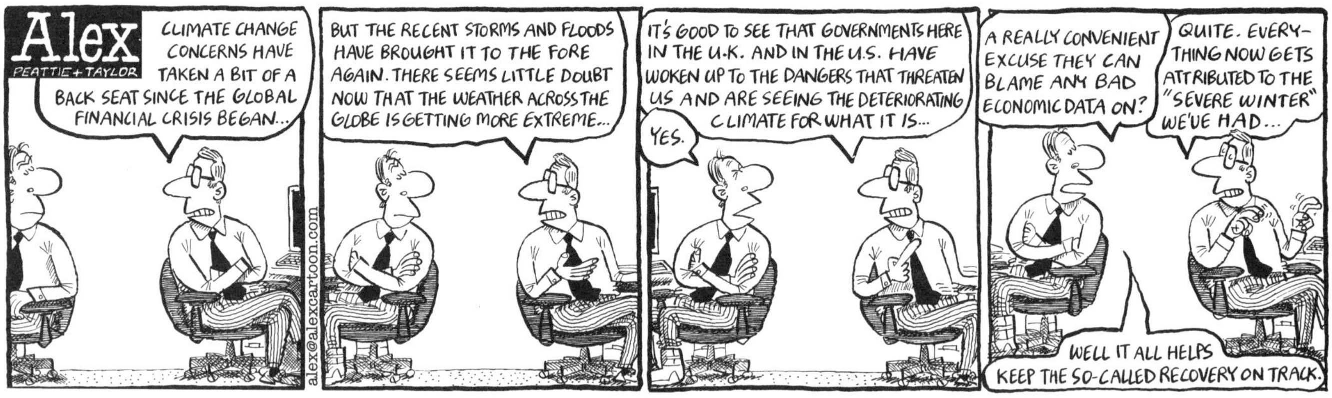
Alex
PEATTIE + TAYLOR
CLIMATE CHANGE CONCERNS HAVE TAKEN A BIT OF A BACK SEAT SINCE THE GLOBAL FINANCIAL CRISIS BEGAN...
BUT THE RECENT STORMS AND FLOODS HAVE BROUGHT IT TO THE FORE AGAIN. THERE SEEMS LITTLE DOUBT NOW THAT THE WEATHER ACROSS THE GLOBE IS GETTING MORE EXTREME...
IT'S GOOD TO SEE THAT GOVERNMENTS HERE IN THE U.K. AND IN THE U.S. HAVE WOKEN UP TO THE DANGERS THAT THREATEN US AND ARE SEEING THE DETERIORATING CLIMATE FOR WHAT IT IS...
YES.
A REALLY CONVENIENT EXCUSE THEY CAN BLAME ANY BAD ECONOMIC DATA ON?
QUITE. EVERYTHING NOW GETS ATTRIBUTED TO THE "SEVERE WINTER" WE'VE HAD...
WELL IT ALL HELPS KEEP THE SO-CALLED RECOVERY ON TRACK.
alex@alexcartoon.com

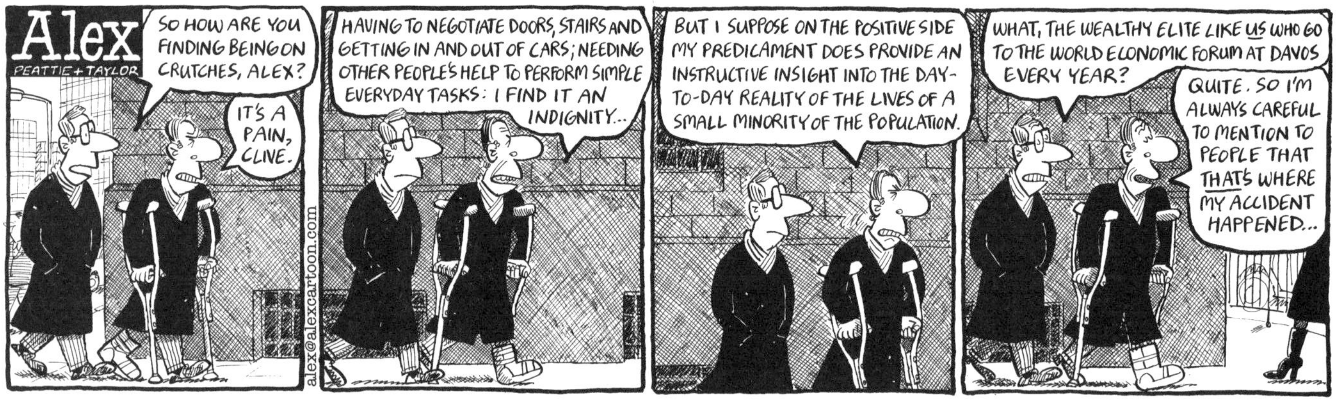
Alex
PEATTIE + TAYLOR
SO HOW ARE YOU FINDING BEING ON CRUTCHES, ALEX?
IT'S A PAIN, CLIVE.
HAVING TO NEGOTIATE DOORS, STAIRS AND GETTING IN AND OUT OF CARS; NEEDING OTHER PEOPLE'S HELP TO PERFORM SIMPLE EVERYDAY TASKS: I FIND IT AN INDIGNITY...
BUT I SUPPOSE ON THE POSITIVE SIDE MY PREDICAMENT DOES PROVIDE AN INSTRUCTIVE INSIGHT INTO THE DAY-TO-DAY REALITY OF THE LIVES OF A SMALL MINORITY OF THE POPULATION.
WHAT, THE WEALTHY ELITE LIKE US WHO GO TO THE WORLD ECONOMIC FORUM AT DAVOS EVERY YEAR?
QUITE. SO I'M ALWAYS CAREFUL TO MENTION TO PEOPLE THAT THAT'S WHERE MY ACCIDENT HAPPENED...
alex@alexcartoon.com

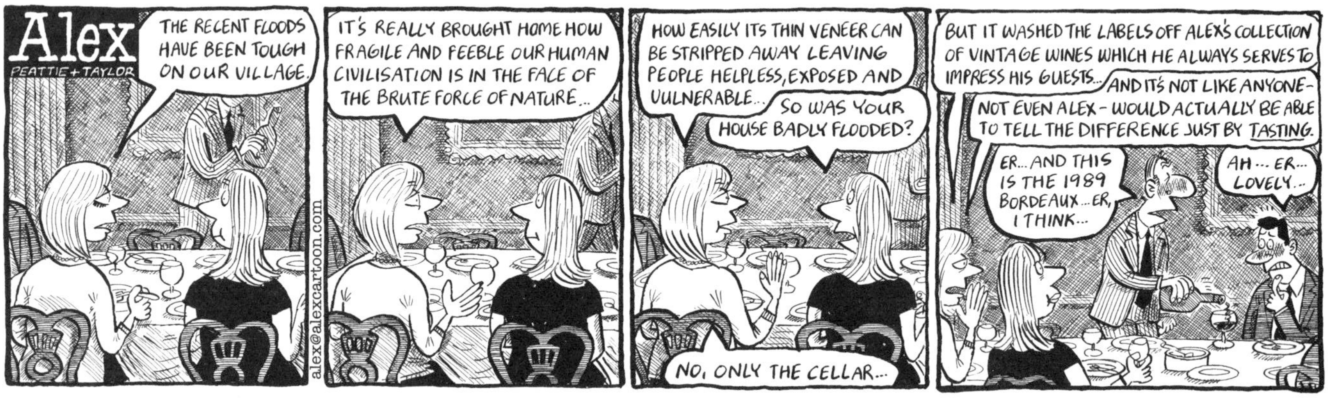
Alex
PEATTIE + TAYLOR
THE RECENT FLOODS HAVE BEEN TOUGH ON OUR VILLAGE.
IT'S REALLY BROUGHT HOME HOW FRAGILE AND FEEBLE OUR HUMAN CIVILISATION IS IN THE FACE OF THE BRUTE FORCE OF NATURE...
HOW EASILY ITS THIN VENEER CAN BE STRIPPED AWAY LEAVING PEOPLE HELPLESS, EXPOSED AND VULNERABLE...
SO WAS YOUR HOUSE BADLY FLOODED?
NO, ONLY THE CELLAR...
BUT IT WASHED THE LABELS OFF ALEX'S COLLECTION OF VINTAGE WINES WHICH HE ALWAYS SERVES TO IMPRESS HIS GUESTS...
AND IT'S NOT LIKE ANYONE - NOT EVEN ALEX - WOULD ACTUALLY BE ABLE TO TELL THE DIFFERENCE JUST BY TASTING.
ER... AND THIS IS THE 1989 BORDEAUX... ER, I THINK...
AH... ER... LOVELY...
alex@alexcartoon.com

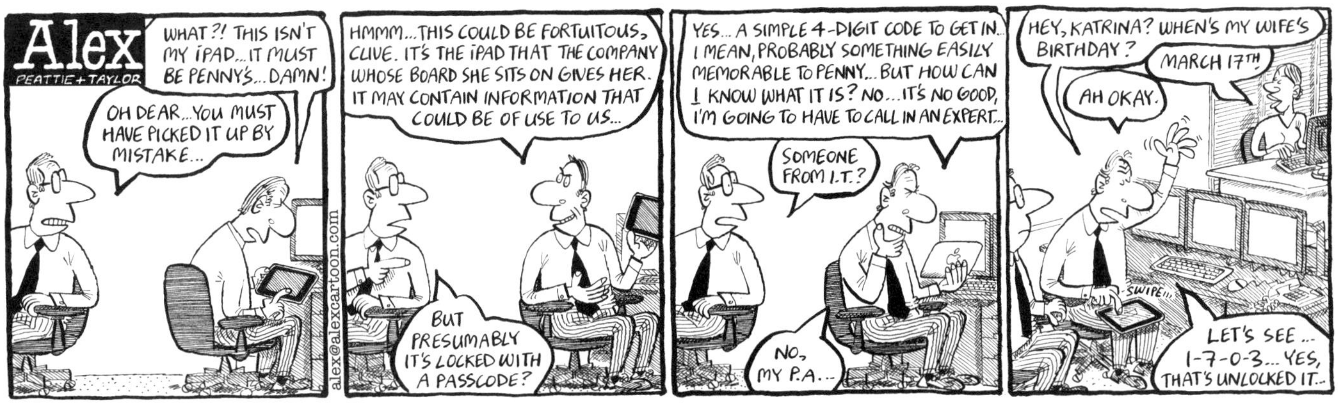
Alex
PEATTIE + TAYLOR
WHAT?! THIS ISN'T MY iPAD... IT MUST BE PENNY'S... DAMN!
OH DEAR... YOU MUST HAVE PICKED IT UP BY MISTAKE...
alex@alexcartoon.com
HMMM... THIS COULD BE FORTUITOUS, CLIVE. IT'S THE iPAD THAT THE COMPANY WHOSE BOARD SHE SITS ON GIVES HER. IT MAY CONTAIN INFORMATION THAT COULD BE OF USE TO US...
BUT PRESUMABLY IT'S LOCKED WITH A PASSCODE?
YES... A SIMPLE 4-DIGIT CODE TO GET IN... I MEAN, PROBABLY SOMETHING EASILY MEMORABLE TO PENNY... BUT HOW CAN I KNOW WHAT IT IS? NO... IT'S NO GOOD, I'M GOING TO HAVE TO CALL IN AN EXPERT...
SOMEONE FROM I.T.?
NO, MY P.A. ...
HEY, KATRINA? WHEN'S MY WIFE'S BIRTHDAY?
MARCH 17TH
AH OKAY.
SWIPE...
LET'S SEE... 1-7-0-3... YES, THAT'S UNLOCKED IT...

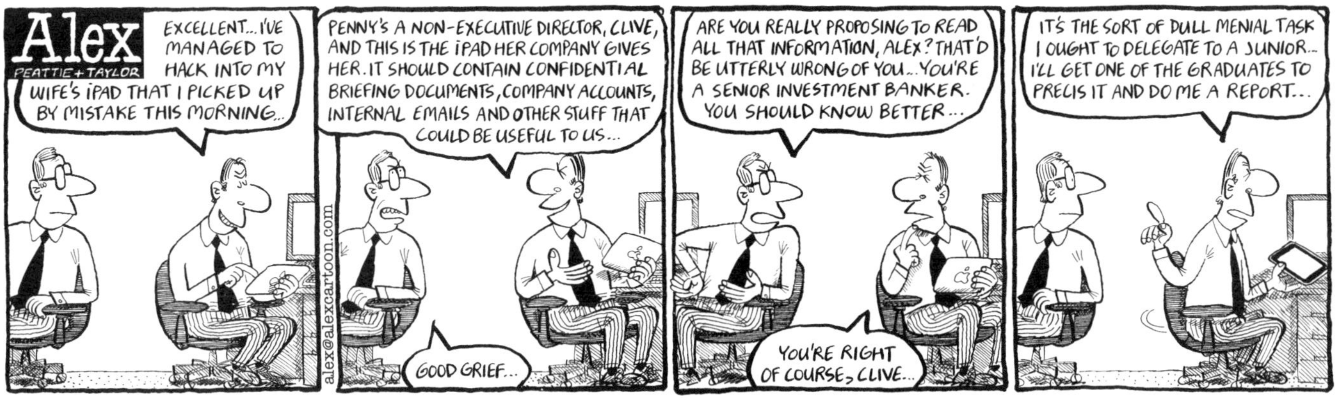
Alex
PEATTIE + TAYLOR
EXCELLENT... I'VE MANAGED TO HACK INTO MY WIFE'S iPAD THAT I PICKED UP BY MISTAKE THIS MORNING...
alex@alexcartoon.com
PENNY'S A NON-EXECUTIVE DIRECTOR, CLIVE, AND THIS IS THE iPAD HER COMPANY GIVES HER. IT SHOULD CONTAIN CONFIDENTIAL BRIEFING DOCUMENTS, COMPANY ACCOUNTS, INTERNAL EMAILS AND OTHER STUFF THAT COULD BE USEFUL TO US...
GOOD GRIEF...
ARE YOU REALLY PROPOSING TO READ ALL THAT INFORMATION, ALEX? THAT'D BE UTTERLY WRONG OF YOU... YOU'RE A SENIOR INVESTMENT BANKER. YOU SHOULD KNOW BETTER...
YOU'RE RIGHT OF COURSE, CLIVE...
IT'S THE SORT OF DULL MENIAL TASK I OUGHT TO DELEGATE TO A JUNIOR... I'LL GET ONE OF THE GRADUATES TO PRECIS IT AND DO ME A REPORT...

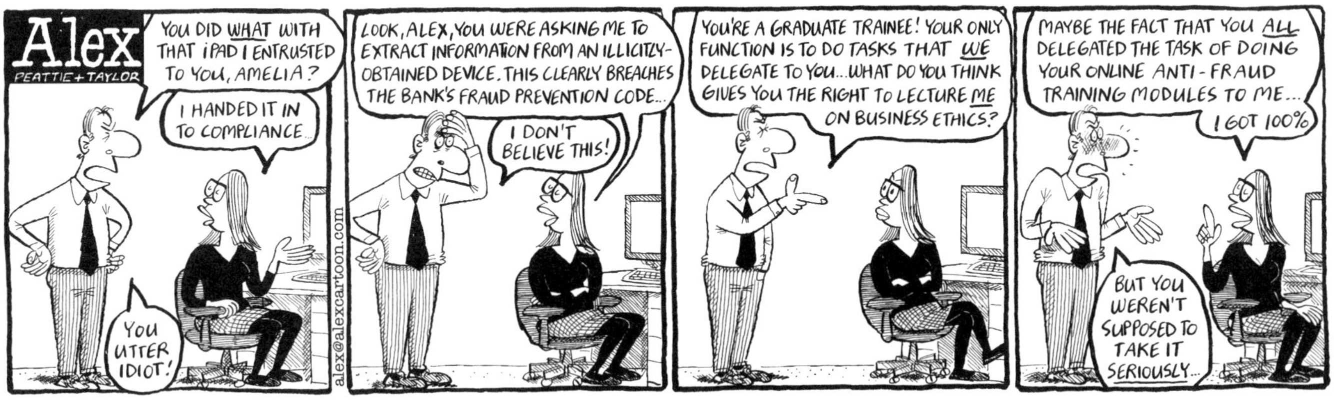
Alex
PEATTIE + TAYLOR
YOU DID WHAT WITH THAT iPAD I ENTRUSTED TO YOU, AMELIA?
I HANDED IT IN TO COMPLIANCE.
YOU UTTER IDIOT!
alex@alexcartoon.com
LOOK, ALEX, YOU WERE ASKING ME TO EXTRACT INFORMATION FROM AN ILLICITLY-OBTAINED DEVICE. THIS CLEARLY BREACHES THE BANK'S FRAUD PREVENTION CODE...
I DON'T BELIEVE THIS!
YOU'RE A GRADUATE TRAINEE! YOUR ONLY FUNCTION IS TO DO TASKS THAT WE DELEGATE TO YOU... WHAT DO YOU THINK GIVES YOU THE RIGHT TO LECTURE ME ON BUSINESS ETHICS?
MAYBE THE FACT THAT YOU ALL DELEGATED THE TASK OF DOING YOUR ONLINE ANTI-FRAUD TRAINING MODULES TO ME...
I GOT 100%
BUT YOU WEREN'T SUPPOSED TO TAKE IT SERIOUSLY...

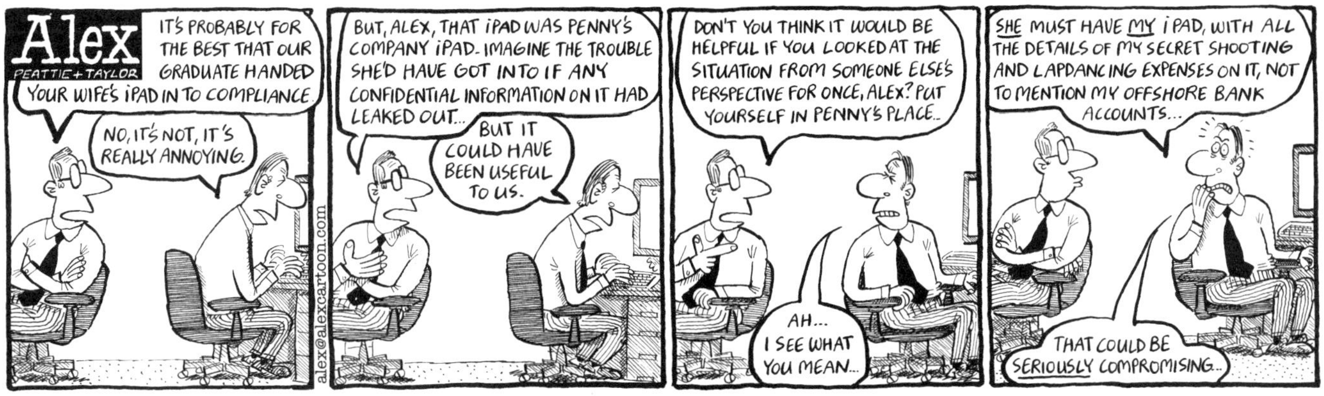
Alex
PEATTIE + TAYLOR
IT'S PROBABLY FOR THE BEST THAT OUR GRADUATE HANDED YOUR WIFE'S iPAD IN TO COMPLIANCE.
NO, IT'S NOT, IT'S REALLY ANNOYING.
alex@alexcartoon.com
BUT, ALEX, THAT iPAD WAS PENNY'S COMPANY iPAD. IMAGINE THE TROUBLE SHE'D HAVE GOT INTO IF ANY CONFIDENTIAL INFORMATION ON IT HAD LEAKED OUT...
BUT IT COULD HAVE BEEN USEFUL TO US.
DON'T YOU THINK IT WOULD BE HELPFUL IF YOU LOOKED AT THE SITUATION FROM SOMEONE ELSE'S PERSPECTIVE FOR ONCE, ALEX? PUT YOURSELF IN PENNY'S PLACE...
AH... I SEE WHAT YOU MEAN...
SHE MUST HAVE MY iPAD, WITH ALL THE DETAILS OF MY SECRET SHOOTING AND LAPDANCING EXPENSES ON IT, NOT TO MENTION MY OFFSHORE BANK ACCOUNTS...
THAT COULD BE SERIOUSLY COMPROMISING...

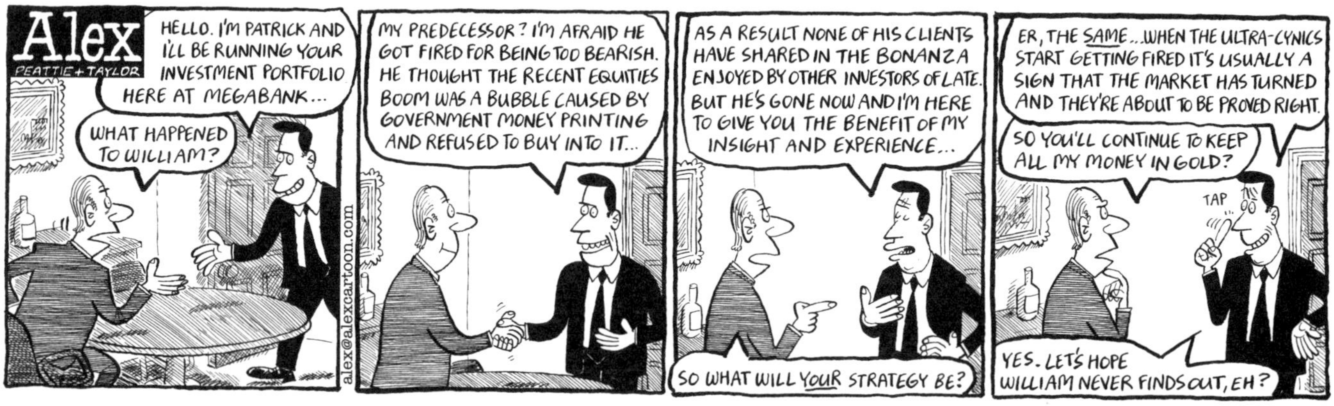
Alex
PEATTIE + TAYLOR
HELLO. I'M PATRICK AND I'LL BE RUNNING YOUR INVESTMENT PORTFOLIO HERE AT MEGABANK...
WHAT HAPPENED TO WILLIAM?
MY PREDECESSOR? I'M AFRAID HE GOT FIRED FOR BEING TOO BEARISH. HE THOUGHT THE RECENT EQUITIES BOOM WAS A BUBBLE CAUSED BY GOVERNMENT MONEY PRINTING AND REFUSED TO BUY INTO IT...
alex@alexcartoon.com
AS A RESULT NONE OF HIS CLIENTS HAVE SHARED IN THE BONANZA ENJOYED BY OTHER INVESTORS OF LATE. BUT HE'S GONE NOW AND I'M HERE TO GIVE YOU THE BENEFIT OF MY INSIGHT AND EXPERIENCE...
SO WHAT WILL YOUR STRATEGY BE?
ER, THE SAME... WHEN THE ULTRA-CYNICS START GETTING FIRED IT'S USUALLY A SIGN THAT THE MARKET HAS TURNED AND THEY'RE ABOUT TO BE PROVED RIGHT.
SO YOU'LL CONTINUE TO KEEP ALL MY MONEY IN GOLD?
TAP
YES. LET'S HOPE WILLIAM NEVER FINDS OUT, EH?

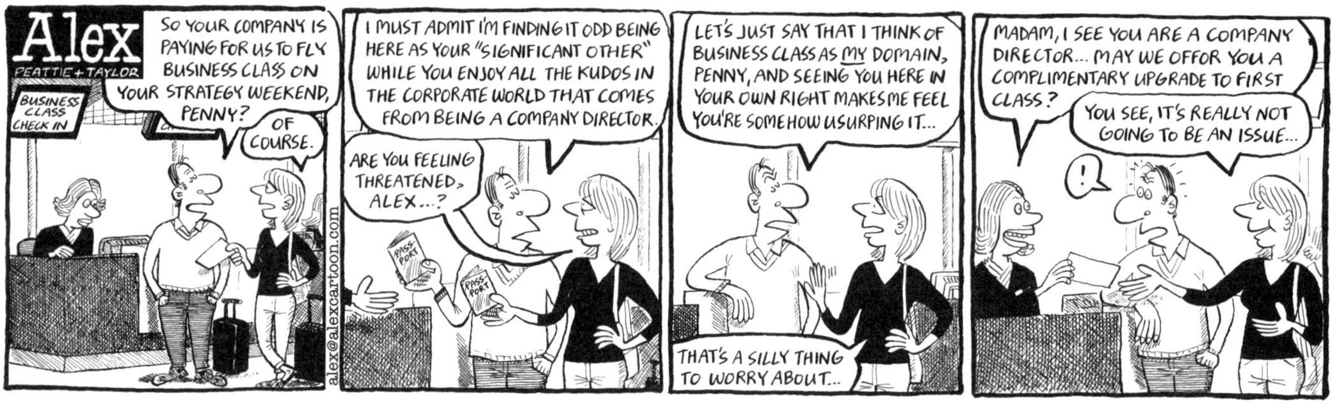
Alex
PEATTIE + TAYLOR
SO YOUR COMPANY IS PAYING FOR US TO FLY BUSINESS CLASS ON YOUR STRATEGY WEEKEND, PENNY?
OF COURSE.
BUSINESS CLASS CHECK IN
I MUST ADMIT I'M FINDING IT ODD BEING HERE AS YOUR "SIGNIFICANT OTHER" WHILE YOU ENJOY ALL THE KUDOS IN THE CORPORATE WORLD THAT COMES FROM BEING A COMPANY DIRECTOR.
ARE YOU FEELING THREATENED, ALEX...?
alex@alexcartoon.com
LET'S JUST SAY THAT I THINK OF BUSINESS CLASS AS MY DOMAIN, PENNY, AND SEEING YOU HERE IN YOUR OWN RIGHT MAKES ME FEEL YOU'RE SOMEHOW USURPING IT...
THAT'S A SILLY THING TO WORRY ABOUT...
MADAM, I SEE YOU ARE A COMPANY DIRECTOR... MAY WE OFFER YOU A COMPLIMENTARY UPGRADE TO FIRST CLASS?
YOU SEE, IT'S REALLY NOT GOING TO BE AN ISSUE...
!

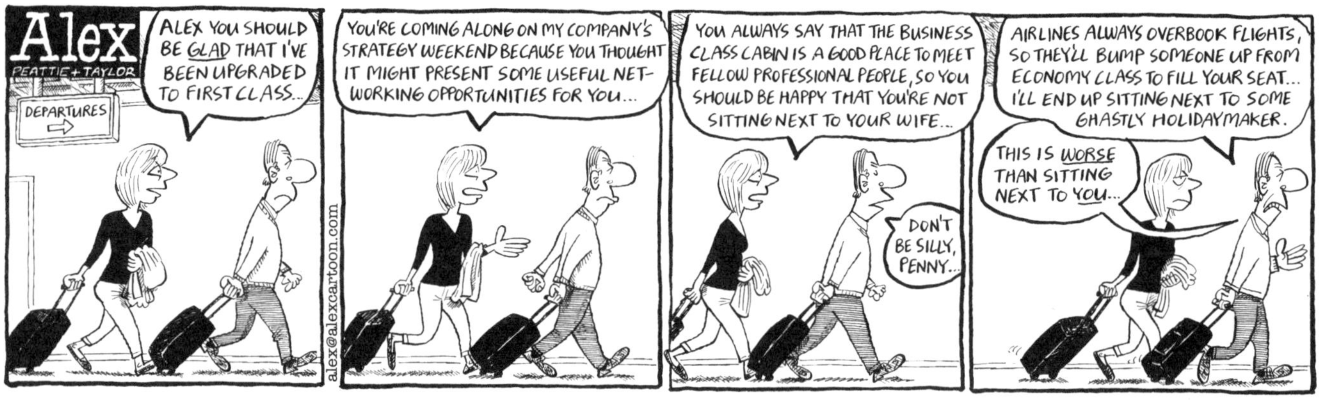
Alex
PEATTIE + TAYLOR
ALEX YOU SHOULD BE GLAD THAT I'VE BEEN UPGRADED TO FIRST CLASS...
DEPARTURES
YOU'RE COMING ALONG ON MY COMPANY'S STRATEGY WEEKEND BECAUSE YOU THOUGHT IT MIGHT PRESENT SOME USEFUL NETWORKING OPPORTUNITIES FOR YOU...
alex@alexcartoon.com
YOU ALWAYS SAY THAT THE BUSINESS CLASS CABIN IS A GOOD PLACE TO MEET FELLOW PROFESSIONAL PEOPLE, SO YOU SHOULD BE HAPPY THAT YOU'RE NOT SITTING NEXT TO YOUR WIFE...
DON'T BE SILLY, PENNY...
AIRLINES ALWAYS OVERBOOK FLIGHTS, SO THEY'LL BUMP SOMEONE UP FROM ECONOMY CLASS TO FILL YOUR SEAT... I'LL END UP SITTING NEXT TO SOME GHASTLY HOLIDAYMAKER.
THIS IS WORSE THAN SITTING NEXT TO YOU...

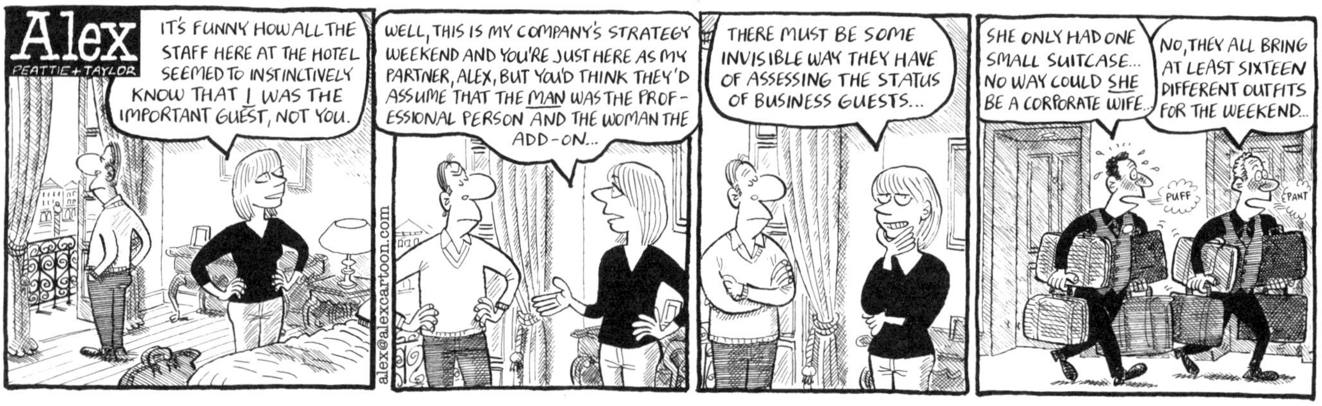
Alex
PEATTIE + TAYLOR
IT'S FUNNY HOW ALL THE STAFF HERE AT THE HOTEL SEEMED TO INSTINCTIVELY KNOW THAT I WAS THE IMPORTANT GUEST, NOT YOU.
WELL, THIS IS MY COMPANY'S STRATEGY WEEKEND AND YOU'RE JUST HERE AS MY PARTNER, ALEX, BUT YOU'D THINK THEY'D ASSUME THAT THE MAN WAS THE PROFESSIONAL PERSON AND THE WOMAN THE ADD-ON...
alex@alexcartoon.com
THERE MUST BE SOME INVISIBLE WAY THEY HAVE OF ASSESSING THE STATUS OF BUSINESS GUESTS...
SHE ONLY HAD ONE SMALL SUITCASE... NO WAY COULD SHE BE A CORPORATE WIFE...
NO, THEY ALL BRING AT LEAST SIXTEEN DIFFERENT OUTFITS FOR THE WEEKEND...
PUFF
PANT

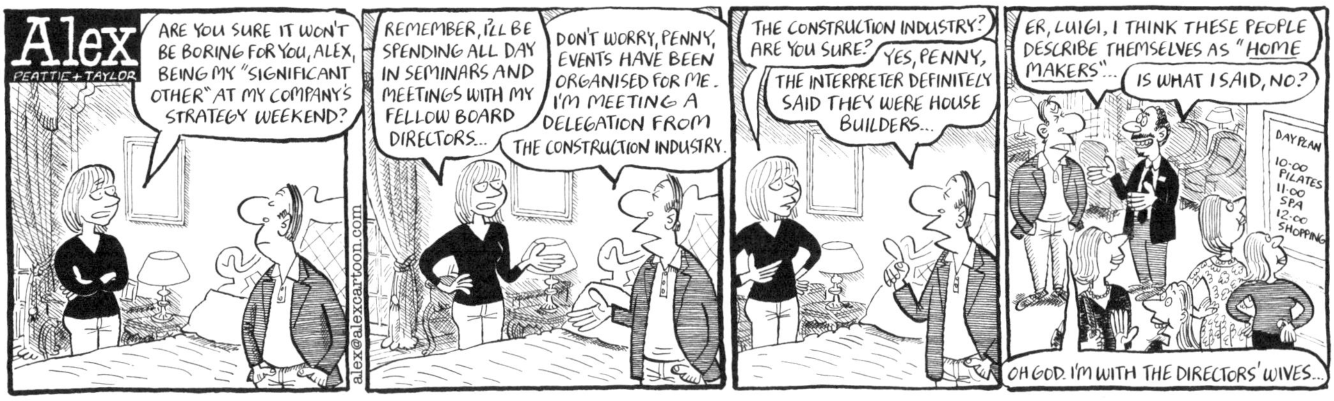
Alex
PEATTIE + TAYLOR
ARE YOU SURE IT WON'T BE BORING FOR YOU, ALEX, BEING MY "SIGNIFICANT OTHER" AT MY COMPANY'S STRATEGY WEEKEND?
alex@alexcartoon.com
REMEMBER, I'LL BE SPENDING ALL DAY IN SEMINARS AND MEETINGS WITH MY FELLOW BOARD DIRECTORS...
DON'T WORRY, PENNY, EVENTS HAVE BEEN ORGANISED FOR ME. I'M MEETING A DELEGATION FROM THE CONSTRUCTION INDUSTRY.
THE CONSTRUCTION INDUSTRY? ARE YOU SURE?
YES, PENNY, THE INTERPRETER DEFINITELY SAID THEY WERE HOUSE BUILDERS...
ER, LUIGI, I THINK THESE PEOPLE DESCRIBE THEMSELVES AS "HOME MAKERS"...
IS WHAT I SAID, NO?
DAY PLAN 10·00 PILATES 11·00 SPA 12·00 SHOPPING
OH GOD. I'M WITH THE DIRECTORS' WIVES...

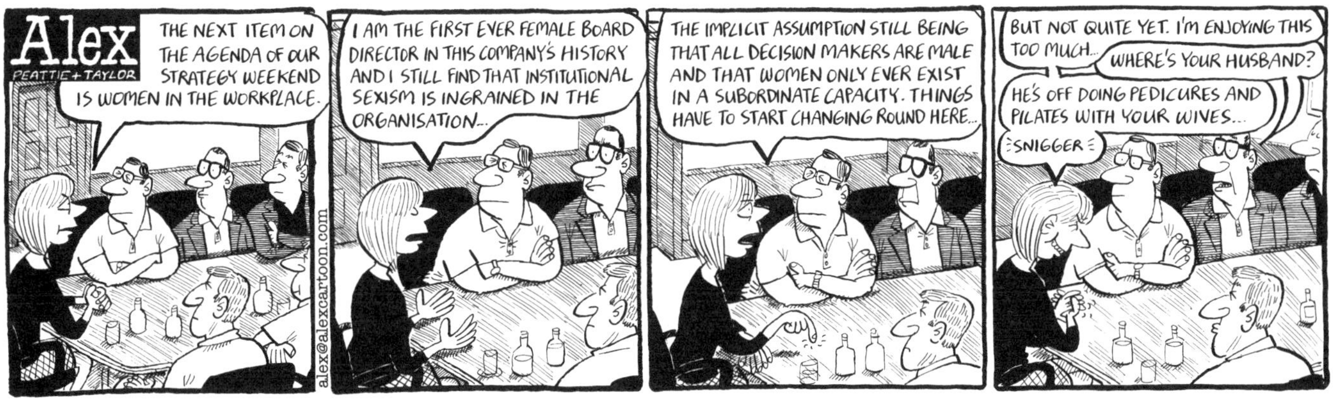
Alex
PEATTIE + TAYLOR
THE NEXT ITEM ON THE AGENDA OF OUR STRATEGY WEEKEND IS WOMEN IN THE WORKPLACE.
alex@alexcartoon.com
I AM THE FIRST EVER FEMALE BOARD DIRECTOR IN THIS COMPANY'S HISTORY AND I STILL FIND THAT INSTITUTIONAL SEXISM IS INGRAINED IN THE ORGANISATION...
THE IMPLICIT ASSUMPTION STILL BEING THAT ALL DECISION MAKERS ARE MALE AND THAT WOMEN ONLY EVER EXIST IN A SUBORDINATE CAPACITY. THINGS HAVE TO START CHANGING ROUND HERE...
BUT NOT QUITE YET. I'M ENJOYING THIS TOO MUCH...
WHERE'S YOUR HUSBAND?
HE'S OFF DOING PEDICURES AND PILATES WITH YOUR WIVES...
SNIGGER

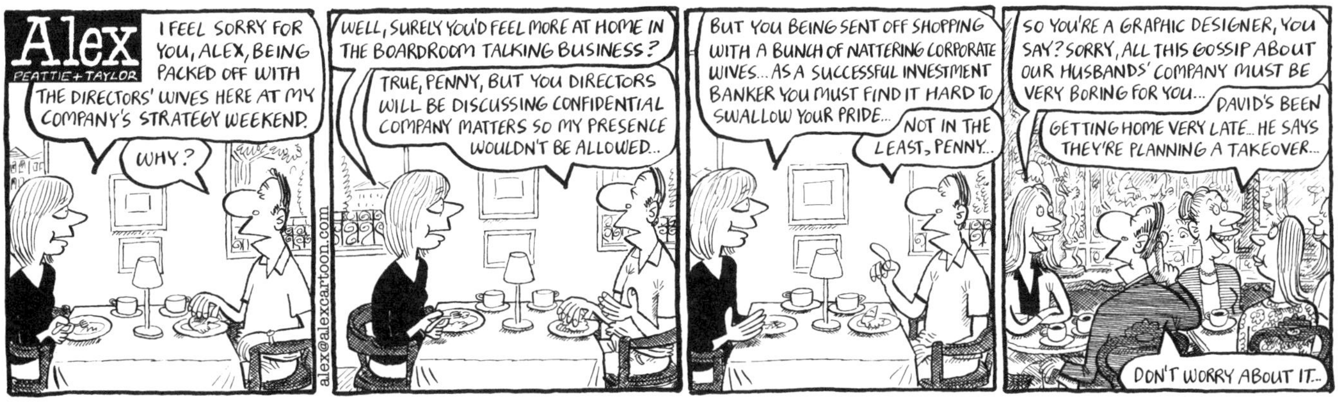
Alex
PEATTIE + TAYLOR
I FEEL SORRY FOR YOU, ALEX, BEING PACKED OFF WITH THE DIRECTORS' WIVES HERE AT MY COMPANY'S STRATEGY WEEKEND.
WHY?
alex@alexcartoon.com
WELL, SURELY YOU'D FEEL MORE AT HOME IN THE BOARDROOM TALKING BUSINESS?
TRUE, PENNY, BUT YOU DIRECTORS WILL BE DISCUSSING CONFIDENTIAL COMPANY MATTERS SO MY PRESENCE WOULDN'T BE ALLOWED...
BUT YOU BEING SENT OFF SHOPPING WITH A BUNCH OF NATTERING CORPORATE WIVES... AS A SUCCESSFUL INVESTMENT BANKER YOU MUST FIND IT HARD TO SWALLOW YOUR PRIDE...
NOT IN THE LEAST, PENNY...
SO YOU'RE A GRAPHIC DESIGNER, YOU SAY? SORRY, ALL THIS GOSSIP ABOUT OUR HUSBANDS' COMPANY MUST BE VERY BORING FOR YOU...
DAVID'S BEEN GETTING HOME VERY LATE... HE SAYS THEY'RE PLANNING A TAKEOVER...
DON'T WORRY ABOUT IT...

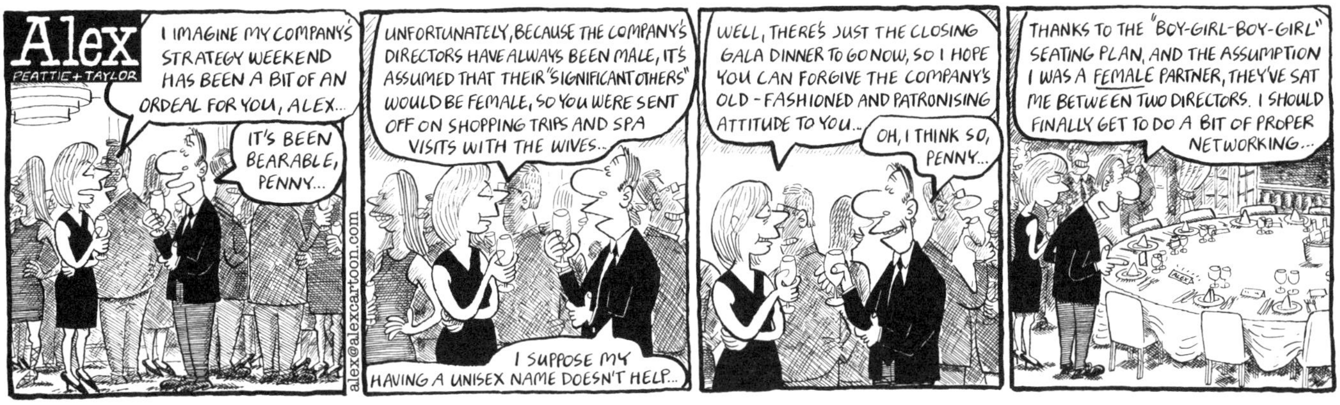
Alex
PEATTIE + TAYLOR
I IMAGINE MY COMPANY'S STRATEGY WEEKEND HAS BEEN A BIT OF AN ORDEAL FOR YOU, ALEX...
IT'S BEEN BEARABLE, PENNY...
alex@alexcartoon.com
UNFORTUNATELY, BECAUSE THE COMPANY'S DIRECTORS HAVE ALWAYS BEEN MALE, IT'S ASSUMED THAT THEIR "SIGNIFICANT OTHERS" WOULD BE FEMALE, SO YOU WERE SENT OFF ON SHOPPING TRIPS AND SPA VISITS WITH THE WIVES...
I SUPPOSE MY HAVING A UNISEX NAME DOESN'T HELP...
WELL, THERE'S JUST THE CLOSING GALA DINNER TO GO NOW, SO I HOPE YOU CAN FORGIVE THE COMPANY'S OLD-FASHIONED AND PATRONISING ATTITUDE TO YOU...
OH, I THINK SO, PENNY...
THANKS TO THE "BOY-GIRL-BOY-GIRL" SEATING PLAN, AND THE ASSUMPTION I WAS A FEMALE PARTNER, THEY'VE SAT ME BETWEEN TWO DIRECTORS. I SHOULD FINALLY GET TO DO A BIT OF PROPER NETWORKING...

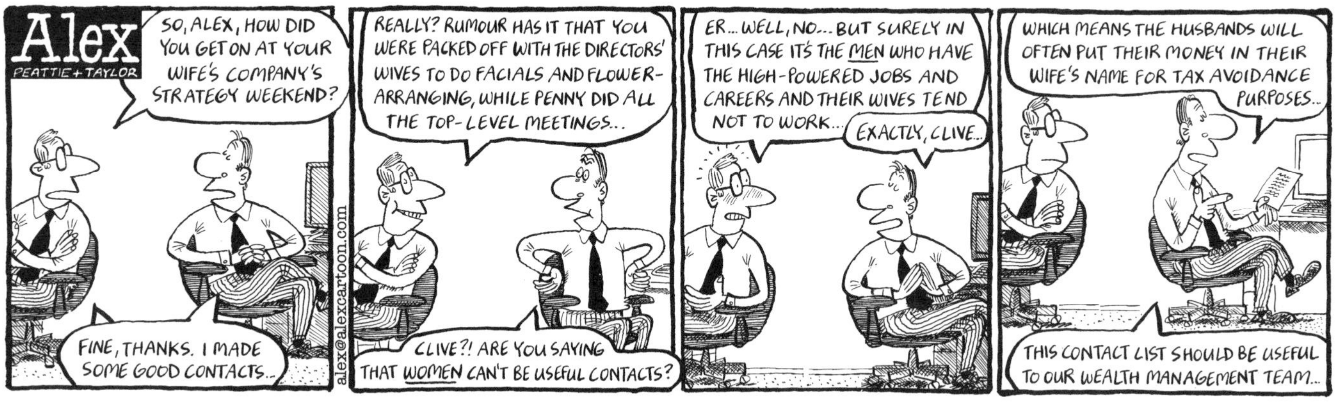
Alex
PEATTIE+TAYLOR
SO, ALEX, HOW DID YOU GET ON AT YOUR WIFE'S COMPANY'S STRATEGY WEEKEND?
FINE, THANKS. I MADE SOME GOOD CONTACTS...
alex@alexcartoon.com
REALLY? RUMOUR HAS IT THAT YOU WERE PACKED OFF WITH THE DIRECTORS' WIVES TO DO FACIALS AND FLOWER-ARRANGING, WHILE PENNY DID ALL THE TOP-LEVEL MEETINGS...
CLIVE?! ARE YOU SAYING THAT WOMEN CAN'T BE USEFUL CONTACTS?
ER... WELL, NO... BUT SURELY IN THIS CASE IT'S THE MEN WHO HAVE THE HIGH-POWERED JOBS AND CAREERS AND THEIR WIVES TEND NOT TO WORK...
EXACTLY, CLIVE...
WHICH MEANS THE HUSBANDS WILL OFTEN PUT THEIR MONEY IN THEIR WIFE'S NAME FOR TAX AVOIDANCE PURPOSES...
THIS CONTACT LIST SHOULD BE USEFUL TO OUR WEALTH MANAGEMENT TEAM...

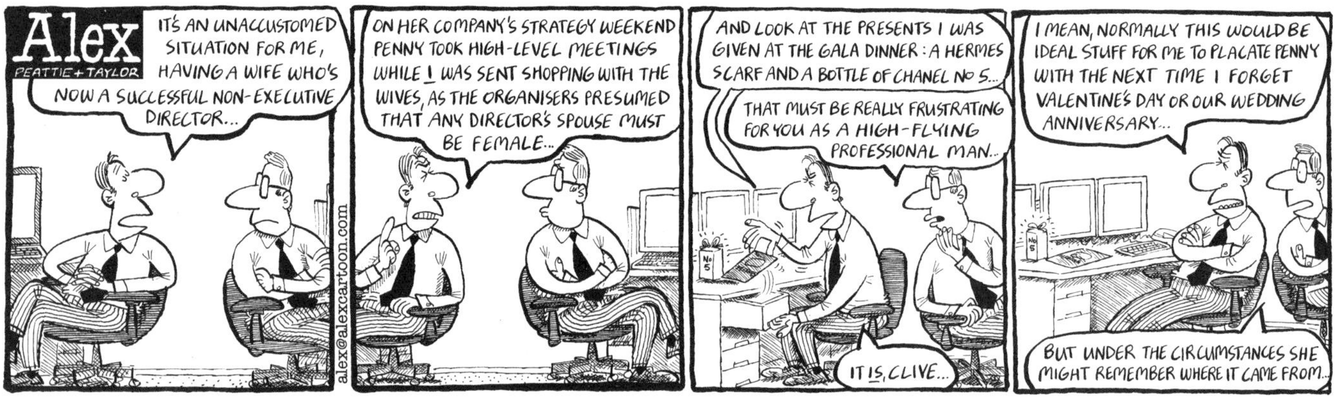
Alex
PEATTIE+TAYLOR
IT'S AN UNACCUSTOMED SITUATION FOR ME, HAVING A WIFE WHO'S NOW A SUCCESSFUL NON-EXECUTIVE DIRECTOR...
alex@alexcartoon.com
ON HER COMPANY'S STRATEGY WEEKEND PENNY TOOK HIGH-LEVEL MEETINGS WHILE I WAS SENT SHOPPING WITH THE WIVES, AS THE ORGANISERS PRESUMED THAT ANY DIRECTOR'S SPOUSE MUST BE FEMALE...
AND LOOK AT THE PRESENTS I WAS GIVEN AT THE GALA DINNER: A HERMES SCARF AND A BOTTLE OF CHANEL No 5...
THAT MUST BE REALLY FRUSTRATING FOR YOU AS A HIGH-FLYING PROFESSIONAL MAN...
IT IS, CLIVE...
I MEAN, NORMALLY THIS WOULD BE IDEAL STUFF FOR ME TO PLACATE PENNY WITH THE NEXT TIME I FORGET VALENTINE'S DAY OR OUR WEDDING ANNIVERSARY...
BUT UNDER THE CIRCUMSTANCES SHE MIGHT REMEMBER WHERE IT CAME FROM...

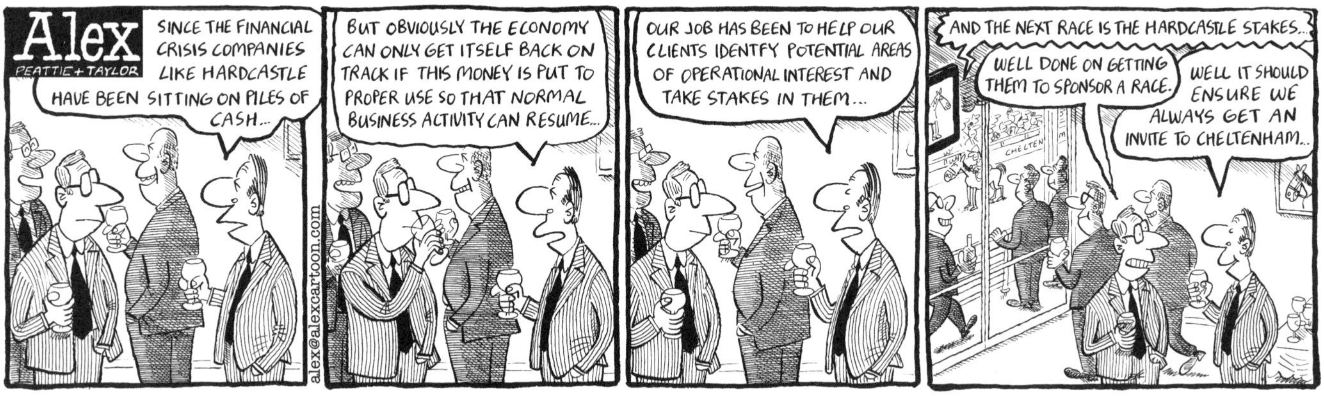
Alex
PEATTIE+TAYLOR
SINCE THE FINANCIAL CRISIS COMPANIES LIKE HARDCASTLE HAVE BEEN SITTING ON PILES OF CASH...
alex@alexcartoon.com
BUT OBVIOUSLY THE ECONOMY CAN ONLY GET ITSELF BACK ON TRACK IF THIS MONEY IS PUT TO PROPER USE SO THAT NORMAL BUSINESS ACTIVITY CAN RESUME...
OUR JOB HAS BEEN TO HELP OUR CLIENTS IDENTFY POTENTIAL AREAS OF OPERATIONAL INTEREST AND TAKE STAKES IN THEM...
AND THE NEXT RACE IS THE HARDCASTLE STAKES...
WELL DONE ON GETTING THEM TO SPONSOR A RACE.
WELL IT SHOULD ENSURE WE ALWAYS GET AN INVITE TO CHELTENHAM...

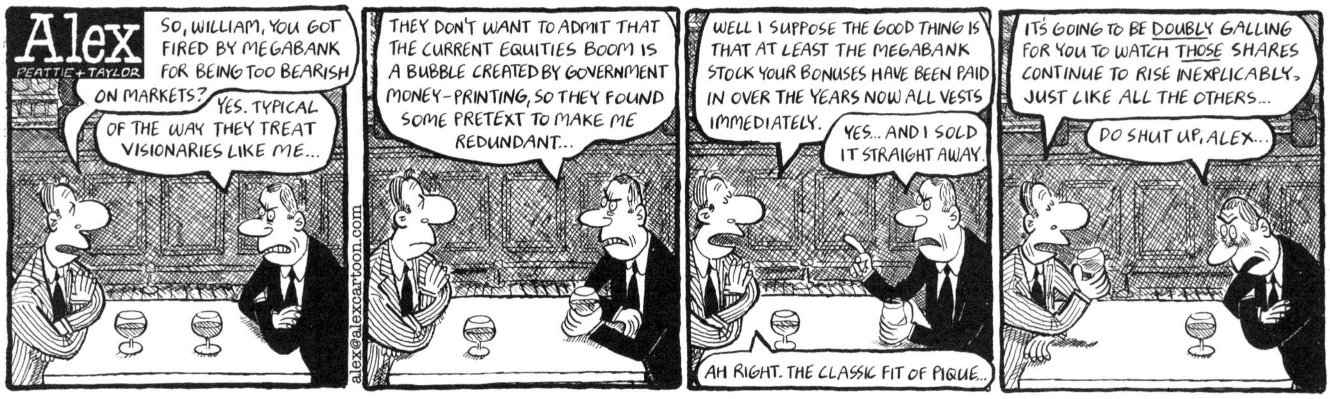
Alex
PEATTIE+TAYLOR
SO, WILLIAM, YOU GOT FIRED BY MEGABANK FOR BEING TOO BEARISH ON MARKETS?
YES. TYPICAL OF THE WAY THEY TREAT VISIONARIES LIKE ME...
alex@alexcartoon.com
THEY DON'T WANT TO ADMIT THAT THE CURRENT EQUITIES BOOM IS A BUBBLE CREATED BY GOVERNMENT MONEY-PRINTING, SO THEY FOUND SOME PRETEXT TO MAKE ME REDUNDANT...
WELL I SUPPOSE THE GOOD THING IS THAT AT LEAST THE MEGABANK STOCK YOUR BONUSES HAVE BEEN PAID IN OVER THE YEARS NOW ALL VESTS IMMEDIATELY.
YES... AND I SOLD IT STRAIGHT AWAY.
AH RIGHT. THE CLASSIC FIT OF PIQUE...
IT'S GOING TO BE DOUBLY GALLING FOR YOU TO WATCH THOSE SHARES CONTINUE TO RISE INEXPLICABLY, JUST LIKE ALL THE OTHERS...
DO SHUT UP, ALEX...

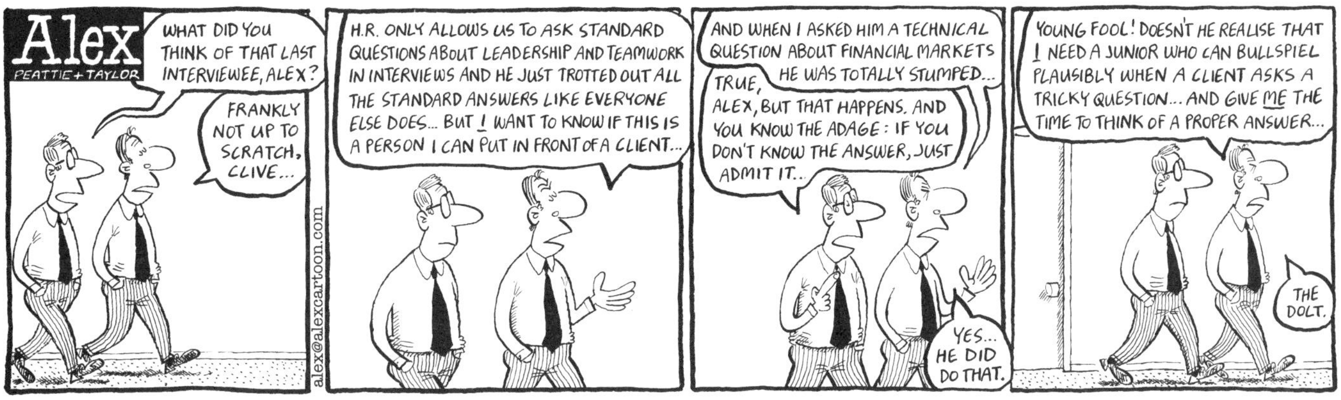
Alex
PEATTIE + TAYLOR
WHAT DID YOU THINK OF THAT LAST INTERVIEWEE, ALEX?
FRANKLY NOT UP TO SCRATCH, CLIVE...
alex@alexcartoon.com
H.R. ONLY ALLOWS US TO ASK STANDARD QUESTIONS ABOUT LEADERSHIP AND TEAMWORK IN INTERVIEWS AND HE JUST TROTTED OUT ALL THE STANDARD ANSWERS LIKE EVERYONE ELSE DOES... BUT I WANT TO KNOW IF THIS IS A PERSON I CAN PUT IN FRONT OF A CLIENT...
AND WHEN I ASKED HIM A TECHNICAL QUESTION ABOUT FINANCIAL MARKETS HE WAS TOTALLY STUMPED...
TRUE, ALEX, BUT THAT HAPPENS. AND YOU KNOW THE ADAGE: IF YOU DON'T KNOW THE ANSWER, JUST ADMIT IT...
YES... HE DID DO THAT.
YOUNG FOOL! DOESN'T HE REALISE THAT I NEED A JUNIOR WHO CAN BULLSPIEL PLAUSIBLY WHEN A CLIENT ASKS A TRICKY QUESTION... AND GIVE ME THE TIME TO THINK OF A PROPER ANSWER...
THE DOLT.

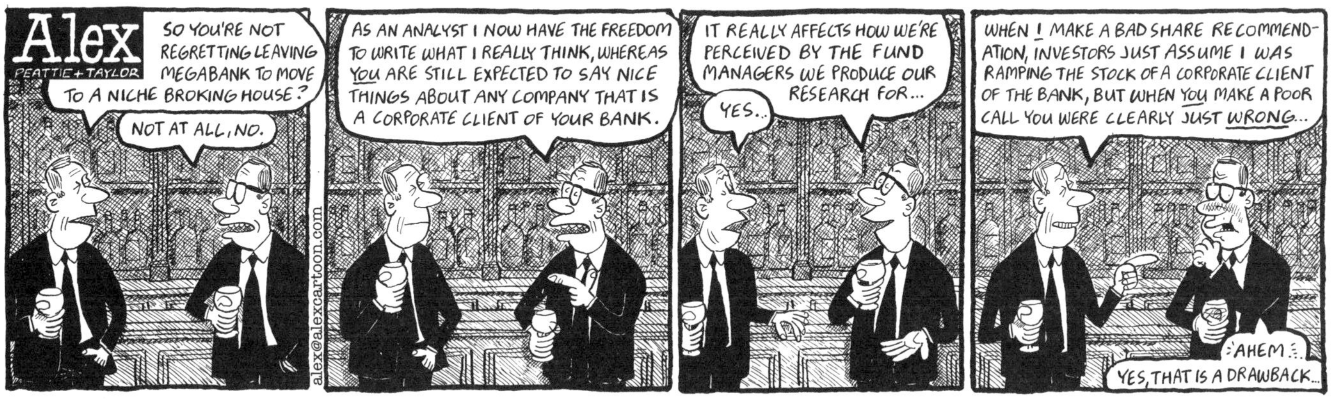
Alex
PEATTIE + TAYLOR
SO YOU'RE NOT REGRETTING LEAVING MEGABANK TO MOVE TO A NICHE BROKING HOUSE?
NOT AT ALL, NO.
alex@alexcartoon.com
AS AN ANALYST I NOW HAVE THE FREEDOM TO WRITE WHAT I REALLY THINK, WHEREAS YOU ARE STILL EXPECTED TO SAY NICE THINGS ABOUT ANY COMPANY THAT IS A CORPORATE CLIENT OF YOUR BANK.
IT REALLY AFFECTS HOW WE'RE PERCEIVED BY THE FUND MANAGERS WE PRODUCE OUR RESEARCH FOR...
YES...
WHEN I MAKE A BAD SHARE RECOMMENDATION, INVESTORS JUST ASSUME I WAS RAMPING THE STOCK OF A CORPORATE CLIENT OF THE BANK, BUT WHEN YOU MAKE A POOR CALL YOU WERE CLEARLY JUST WRONG...
AHEM
YES, THAT IS A DRAWBACK...

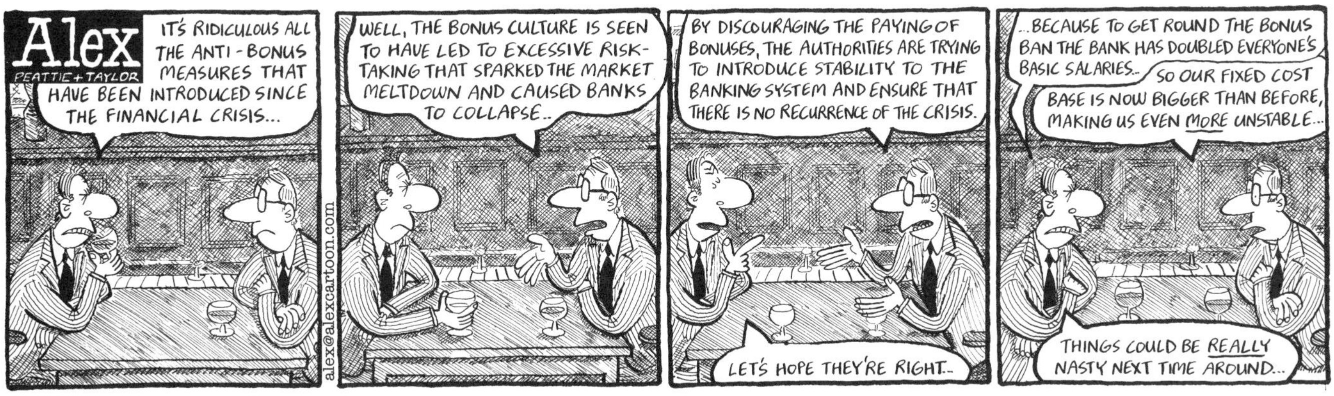
Alex
PEATTIE + TAYLOR
IT'S RIDICULOUS ALL THE ANTI-BONUS MEASURES THAT HAVE BEEN INTRODUCED SINCE THE FINANCIAL CRISIS...
alex@alexcartoon.com
WELL, THE BONUS CULTURE IS SEEN TO HAVE LED TO EXCESSIVE RISK-TAKING THAT SPARKED THE MARKET MELTDOWN AND CAUSED BANKS TO COLLAPSE...
BY DISCOURAGING THE PAYING OF BONUSES, THE AUTHORITIES ARE TRYING TO INTRODUCE STABILITY TO THE BANKING SYSTEM AND ENSURE THAT THERE IS NO RECURRENCE OF THE CRISIS.
LET'S HOPE THEY'RE RIGHT...
...BECAUSE TO GET ROUND THE BONUS BAN THE BANK HAS DOUBLED EVERYONE'S BASIC SALARIES...
SO OUR FIXED COST BASE IS NOW BIGGER THAN BEFORE, MAKING US EVEN MORE UNSTABLE...
THINGS COULD BE REALLY NASTY NEXT TIME AROUND...

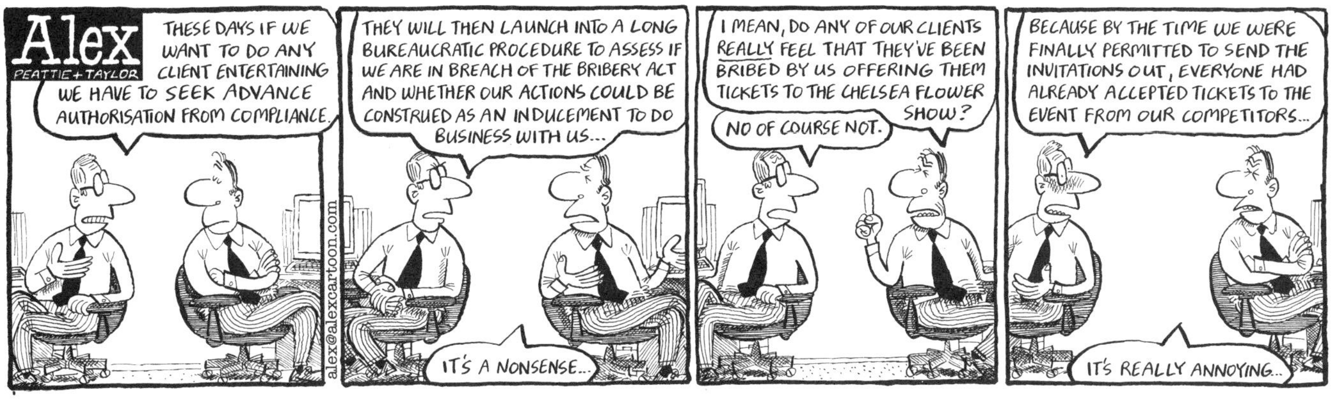
Alex
PEATTIE + TAYLOR
THESE DAYS IF WE WANT TO DO ANY CLIENT ENTERTAINING WE HAVE TO SEEK ADVANCE AUTHORISATION FROM COMPLIANCE.
alex@alexcartoon.com
THEY WILL THEN LAUNCH INTO A LONG BUREAUCRATIC PROCEDURE TO ASSESS IF WE ARE IN BREACH OF THE BRIBERY ACT AND WHETHER OUR ACTIONS COULD BE CONSTRUED AS AN INDUCEMENT TO DO BUSINESS WITH US...
IT'S A NONSENSE...
I MEAN, DO ANY OF OUR CLIENTS REALLY FEEL THAT THEY'VE BEEN BRIBED BY US OFFERING THEM TICKETS TO THE CHELSEA FLOWER SHOW?
NO OF COURSE NOT.
BECAUSE BY THE TIME WE WERE FINALLY PERMITTED TO SEND THE INVITATIONS OUT, EVERYONE HAD ALREADY ACCEPTED TICKETS TO THE EVENT FROM OUR COMPETITORS...
IT'S REALLY ANNOYING...

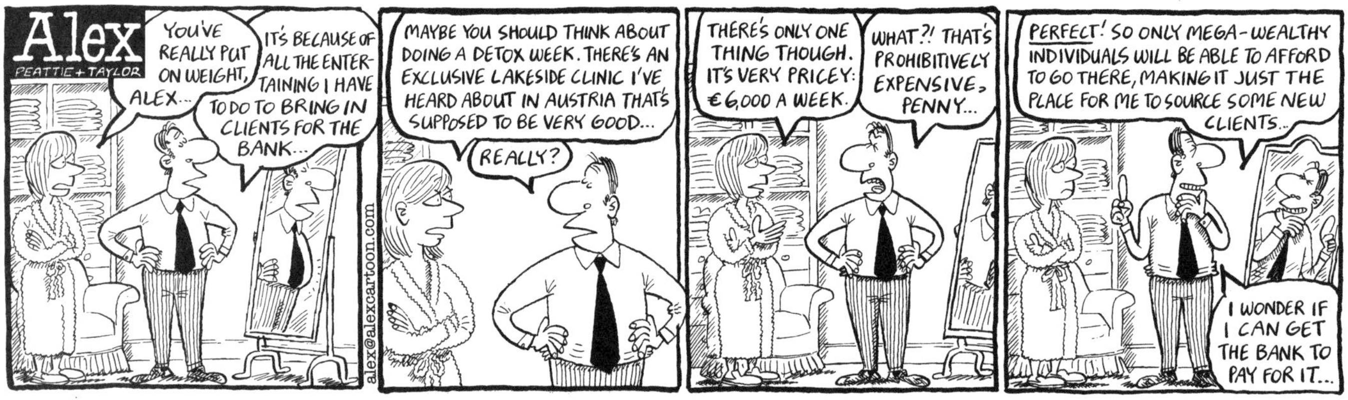
Alex
PEATTIE + TAYLOR
YOU'VE REALLY PUT ON WEIGHT, ALEX...
IT'S BECAUSE OF ALL THE ENTERTAINING I HAVE TO DO TO BRING IN CLIENTS FOR THE BANK...
alex@alexcartoon.com
MAYBE YOU SHOULD THINK ABOUT DOING A DETOX WEEK. THERE'S AN EXCLUSIVE LAKESIDE CLINIC I'VE HEARD ABOUT IN AUSTRIA THAT'S SUPPOSED TO BE VERY GOOD...
REALLY?
THERE'S ONLY ONE THING THOUGH. IT'S VERY PRICEY: €6,000 A WEEK.
WHAT?! THAT'S PROHIBITIVELY EXPENSIVE, PENNY...
PERFECT! SO ONLY MEGA-WEALTHY INDIVIDUALS WILL BE ABLE TO AFFORD TO GO THERE, MAKING IT JUST THE PLACE FOR ME TO SOURCE SOME NEW CLIENTS...
I WONDER IF I CAN GET THE BANK TO PAY FOR IT...

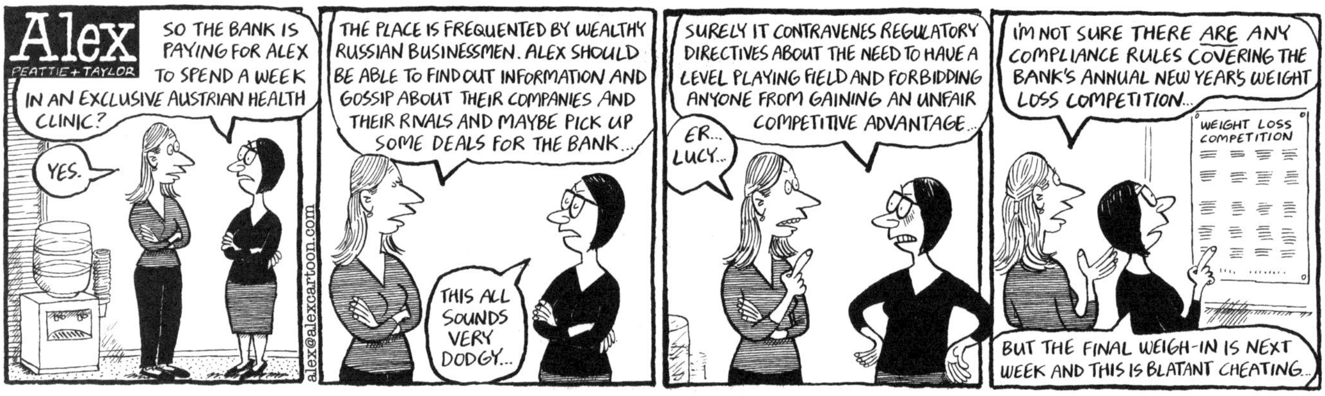
Alex
PEATTIE + TAYLOR
SO THE BANK IS PAYING FOR ALEX TO SPEND A WEEK IN AN EXCLUSIVE AUSTRIAN HEALTH CLINIC?
YES.
alex@alexcartoon.com
THE PLACE IS FREQUENTED BY WEALTHY RUSSIAN BUSINESSMEN. ALEX SHOULD BE ABLE TO FIND OUT INFORMATION AND GOSSIP ABOUT THEIR COMPANIES AND THEIR RIVALS AND MAYBE PICK UP SOME DEALS FOR THE BANK...
THIS ALL SOUNDS VERY DODGY...
SURELY IT CONTRAVENES REGULATORY DIRECTIVES ABOUT THE NEED TO HAVE A LEVEL PLAYING FIELD AND FORBIDDING ANYONE FROM GAINING AN UNFAIR COMPETITIVE ADVANTAGE...
ER... LUCY...
I'M NOT SURE THERE ARE ANY COMPLIANCE RULES COVERING THE BANK'S ANNUAL NEW YEAR'S WEIGHT LOSS COMPETITION...
WEIGHT LOSS COMPETITION
BUT THE FINAL WEIGH-IN IS NEXT WEEK AND THIS IS BLATANT CHEATING...

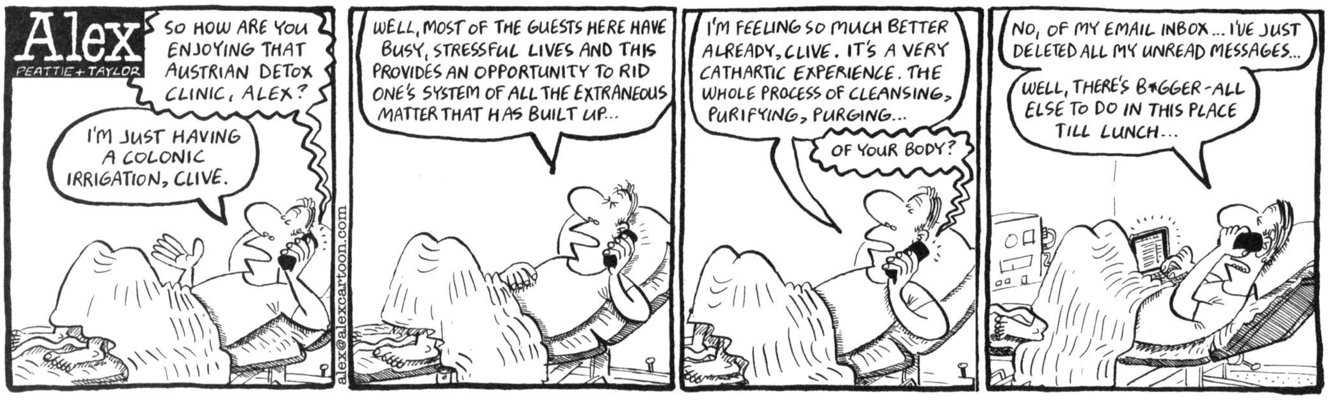
Alex
PEATTIE + TAYLOR
SO HOW ARE YOU ENJOYING THAT AUSTRIAN DETOX CLINIC, ALEX?
I'M JUST HAVING A COLONIC IRRIGATION, CLIVE.
alex@alexcartoon.com
WELL, MOST OF THE GUESTS HERE HAVE BUSY, STRESSFUL LIVES AND THIS PROVIDES AN OPPORTUNITY TO RID ONE'S SYSTEM OF ALL THE EXTRANEOUS MATTER THAT HAS BUILT UP...
I'M FEELING SO MUCH BETTER ALREADY, CLIVE. IT'S A VERY CATHARTIC EXPERIENCE. THE WHOLE PROCESS OF CLEANSING, PURIFYING, PURGING...
OF YOUR BODY?
NO, OF MY EMAIL INBOX... I'VE JUST DELETED ALL MY UNREAD MESSAGES...
WELL, THERE'S B*GGER-ALL ELSE TO DO IN THIS PLACE TILL LUNCH...

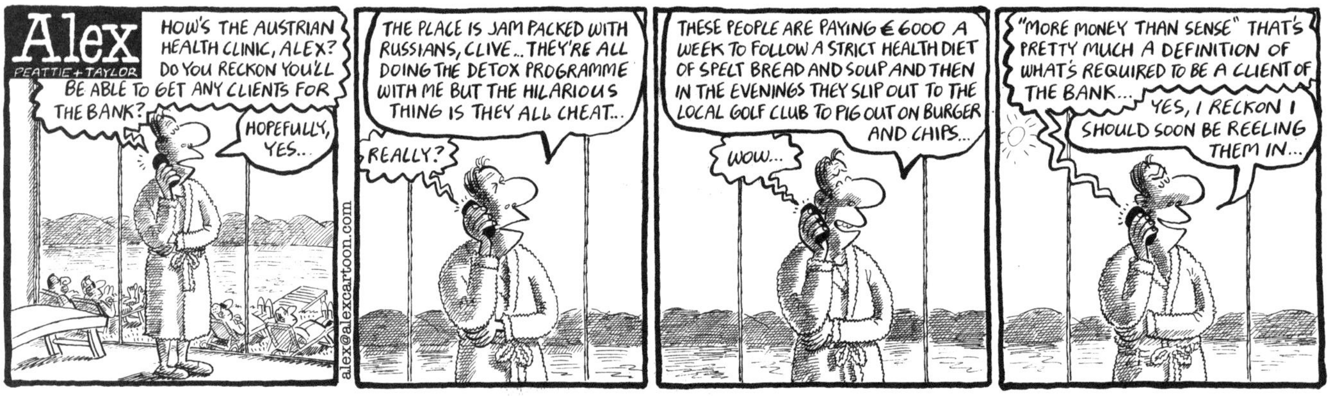
Alex
PEATTIE + TAYLOR
HOW'S THE AUSTRIAN HEALTH CLINIC, ALEX? DO YOU RECKON YOU'LL BE ABLE TO GET ANY CLIENTS FOR THE BANK?
HOPEFULLY, YES...
alex@alexcartoon.com
THE PLACE IS JAM PACKED WITH RUSSIANS, CLIVE... THEY'RE ALL DOING THE DETOX PROGRAMME WITH ME BUT THE HILARIOUS THING IS THEY ALL CHEAT...
REALLY?
THESE PEOPLE ARE PAYING €6000 A WEEK TO FOLLOW A STRICT HEALTH DIET OF SPELT BREAD AND SOUP AND THEN IN THE EVENINGS THEY SLIP OUT TO THE LOCAL GOLF CLUB TO PIG OUT ON BURGER AND CHIPS...
WOW...
"MORE MONEY THAN SENSE" THAT'S PRETTY MUCH A DEFINITION OF WHAT'S REQUIRED TO BE A CLIENT OF THE BANK...
YES, I RECKON I SHOULD SOON BE REELING THEM IN...

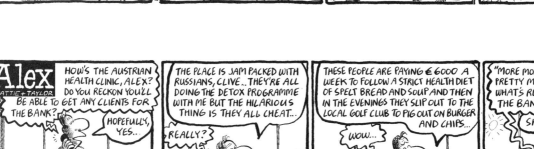

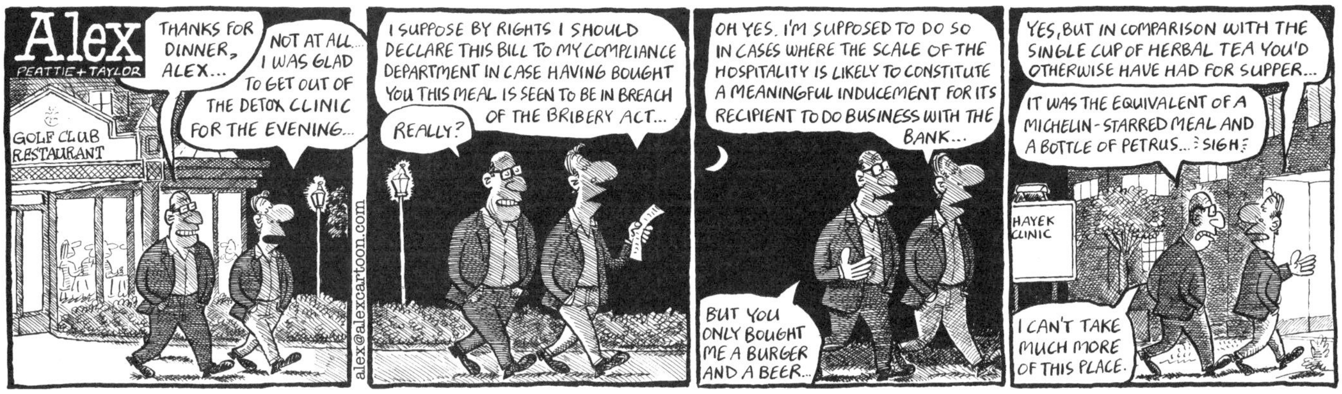
Alex
PEATTIE + TAYLOR
THANKS FOR DINNER, ALEX...
NOT AT ALL... I WAS GLAD TO GET OUT OF THE DETOX CLINIC FOR THE EVENING...
GOLF CLUB RESTAURANT
alex@alexcartoon.com
I SUPPOSE BY RIGHTS I SHOULD DECLARE THIS BILL TO MY COMPLIANCE DEPARTMENT IN CASE HAVING BOUGHT YOU THIS MEAL IS SEEN TO BE IN BREACH OF THE BRIBERY ACT...
REALLY?
OH YES. I'M SUPPOSED TO DO SO IN CASES WHERE THE SCALE OF THE HOSPITALITY IS LIKELY TO CONSTITUTE A MEANINGFUL INDUCEMENT FOR ITS RECIPIENT TO DO BUSINESS WITH THE BANK...
BUT YOU ONLY BOUGHT ME A BURGER AND A BEER...
YES, BUT IN COMPARISON WITH THE SINGLE CUP OF HERBAL TEA YOU'D OTHERWISE HAVE HAD FOR SUPPER...
IT WAS THE EQUIVALENT OF A MICHELIN-STARRED MEAL AND A BOTTLE OF PETRUS... SIGH
HAYEK CLINIC
I CAN'T TAKE MUCH MORE OF THIS PLACE.

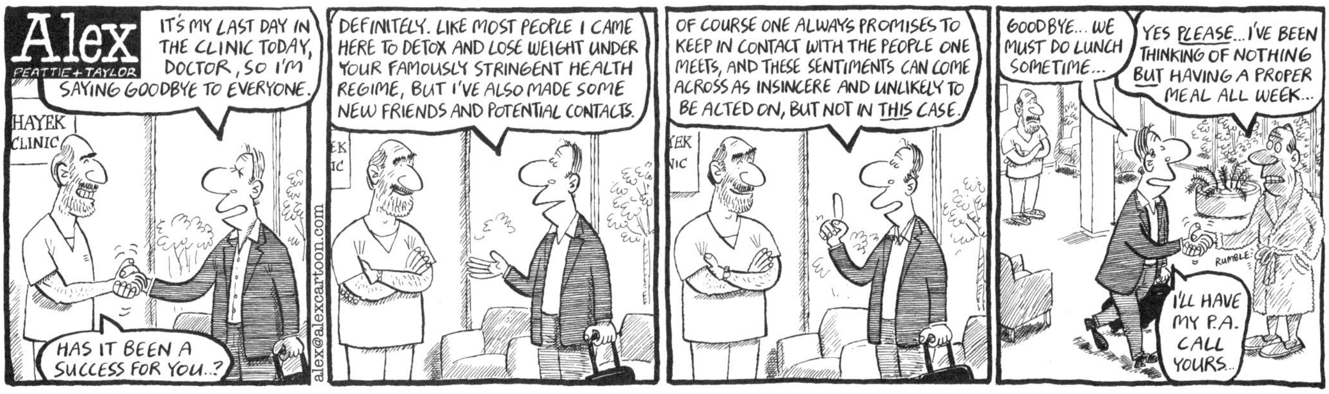
Alex
PEATTIE + TAYLOR
IT'S MY LAST DAY IN THE CLINIC TODAY, DOCTOR, SO I'M SAYING GOODBYE TO EVERYONE.
HAYEK CLINIC
HAS IT BEEN A SUCCESS FOR YOU..?
alex@alexcartoon.com
DEFINITELY. LIKE MOST PEOPLE I CAME HERE TO DETOX AND LOSE WEIGHT UNDER YOUR FAMOUSLY STRINGENT HEALTH REGIME, BUT I'VE ALSO MADE SOME NEW FRIENDS AND POTENTIAL CONTACTS.
OF COURSE ONE ALWAYS PROMISES TO KEEP IN CONTACT WITH THE PEOPLE ONE MEETS, AND THESE SENTIMENTS CAN COME ACROSS AS INSINCERE AND UNLIKELY TO BE ACTED ON, BUT NOT IN THIS CASE.
GOODBYE... WE MUST DO LUNCH SOMETIME...
YES PLEASE... I'VE BEEN THINKING OF NOTHING BUT HAVING A PROPER MEAL ALL WEEK...
RUMBLE
I'LL HAVE MY P.A. CALL YOURS...

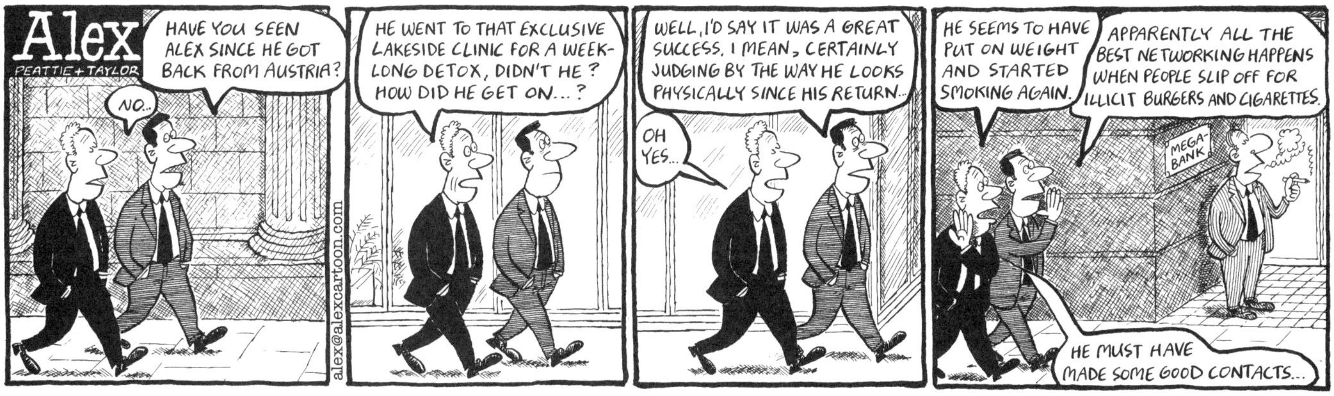
Alex
PEATTIE + TAYLOR
HAVE YOU SEEN ALEX SINCE HE GOT BACK FROM AUSTRIA?
NO..
alex@alexcartoon.com
HE WENT TO THAT EXCLUSIVE LAKESIDE CLINIC FOR A WEEK-LONG DETOX, DIDN'T HE? HOW DID HE GET ON...?
WELL, I'D SAY IT WAS A GREAT SUCCESS. I MEAN, CERTAINLY JUDGING BY THE WAY HE LOOKS PHYSICALLY SINCE HIS RETURN...
OH YES...
HE SEEMS TO HAVE PUT ON WEIGHT AND STARTED SMOKING AGAIN.
APPARENTLY ALL THE BEST NETWORKING HAPPENS WHEN PEOPLE SLIP OFF FOR ILLICIT BURGERS AND CIGARETTES.
MEGA-BANK
HE MUST HAVE MADE SOME GOOD CONTACTS...

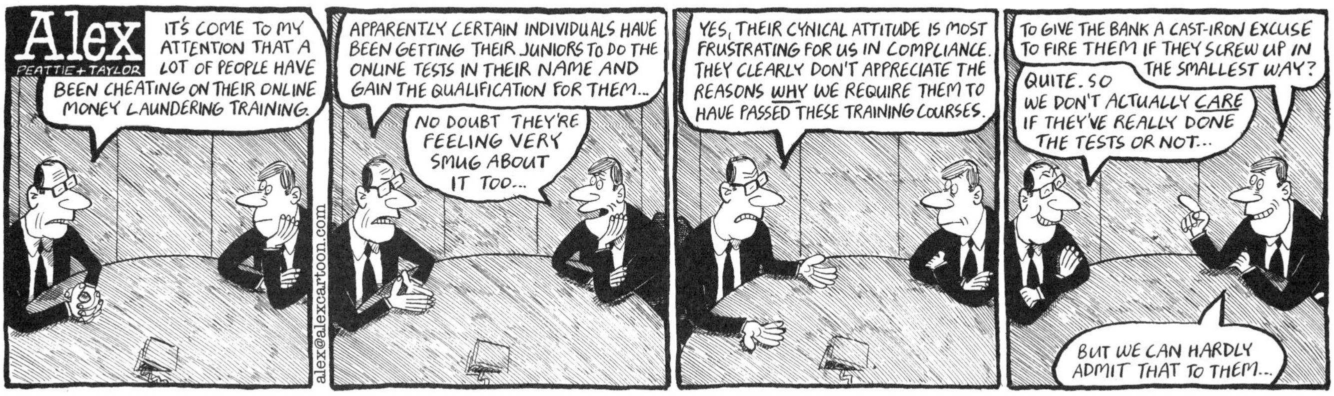
Alex
PEATTIE + TAYLOR
IT'S COME TO MY ATTENTION THAT A LOT OF PEOPLE HAVE BEEN CHEATING ON THEIR ONLINE MONEY LAUNDERING TRAINING.
alex@alexcartoon.com
APPARENTLY CERTAIN INDIVIDUALS HAVE BEEN GETTING THEIR JUNIORS TO DO THE ONLINE TESTS IN THEIR NAME AND GAIN THE QUALIFICATION FOR THEM...
NO DOUBT THEY'RE FEELING VERY SMUG ABOUT IT TOO...
YES, THEIR CYNICAL ATTITUDE IS MOST FRUSTRATING FOR US IN COMPLIANCE. THEY CLEARLY DON'T APPRECIATE THE REASONS WHY WE REQUIRE THEM TO HAVE PASSED THESE TRAINING COURSES.
TO GIVE THE BANK A CAST-IRON EXCUSE TO FIRE THEM IF THEY SCREW UP IN THE SMALLEST WAY?
QUITE. SO WE DON'T ACTUALLY CARE IF THEY'VE REALLY DONE THE TESTS OR NOT...
BUT WE CAN HARDLY ADMIT THAT TO THEM...

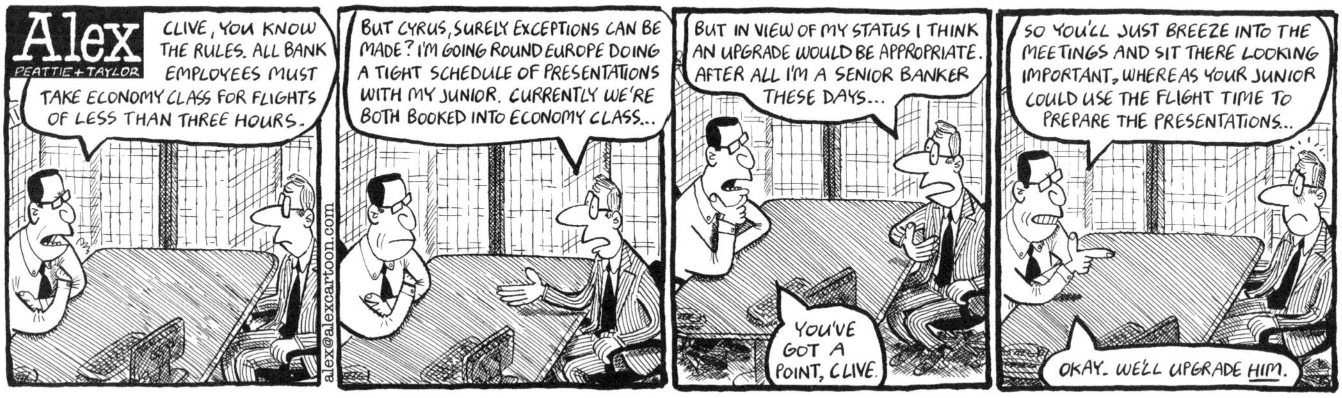
Alex
PEATTIE + TAYLOR
CLIVE, YOU KNOW THE RULES. ALL BANK EMPLOYEES MUST TAKE ECONOMY CLASS FOR FLIGHTS OF LESS THAN THREE HOURS.
BUT CYRUS, SURELY EXCEPTIONS CAN BE MADE? I'M GOING ROUND EUROPE DOING A TIGHT SCHEDULE OF PRESENTATIONS WITH MY JUNIOR. CURRENTLY WE'RE BOTH BOOKED INTO ECONOMY CLASS...
alex@alexcartoon.com
BUT IN VIEW OF MY STATUS I THINK AN UPGRADE WOULD BE APPROPRIATE. AFTER ALL I'M A SENIOR BANKER THESE DAYS...
YOU'VE GOT A POINT, CLIVE.
SO YOU'LL JUST BREEZE INTO THE MEETINGS AND SIT THERE LOOKING IMPORTANT, WHEREAS YOUR JUNIOR COULD USE THE FLIGHT TIME TO PREPARE THE PRESENTATIONS...
OKAY. WE'LL UPGRADE HIM.

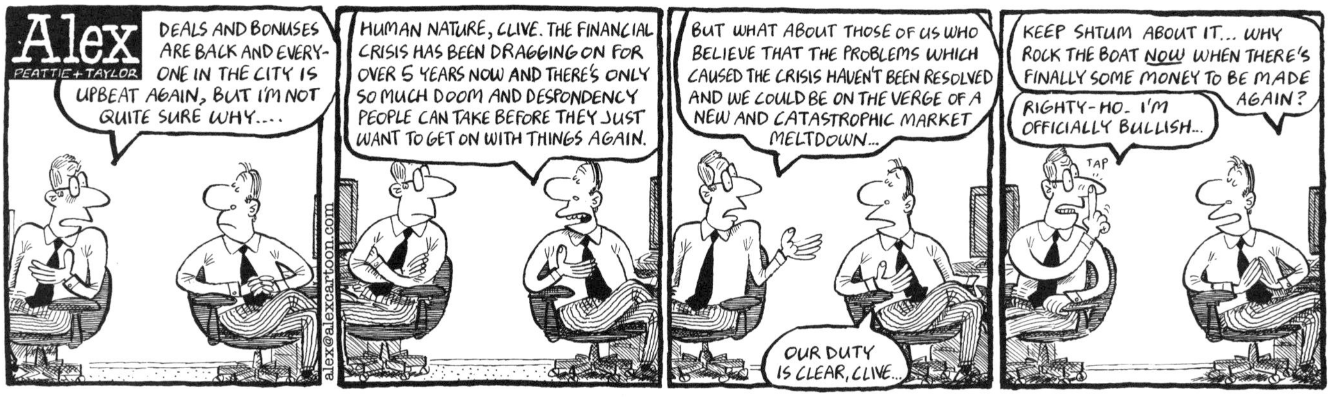
Alex
PEATTIE + TAYLOR
DEALS AND BONUSES ARE BACK AND EVERYONE IN THE CITY IS UPBEAT AGAIN, BUT I'M NOT QUITE SURE WHY....
alex@alexcartoon.com
HUMAN NATURE, CLIVE. THE FINANCIAL CRISIS HAS BEEN DRAGGING ON FOR OVER 5 YEARS NOW AND THERE'S ONLY SO MUCH DOOM AND DESPONDENCY PEOPLE CAN TAKE BEFORE THEY JUST WANT TO GET ON WITH THINGS AGAIN.
BUT WHAT ABOUT THOSE OF US WHO BELIEVE THAT THE PROBLEMS WHICH CAUSED THE CRISIS HAVEN'T BEEN RESOLVED AND WE COULD BE ON THE VERGE OF A NEW AND CATASTROPHIC MARKET MELTDOWN...
OUR DUTY IS CLEAR, CLIVE...
KEEP SHTUM ABOUT IT... WHY ROCK THE BOAT NOW WHEN THERE'S FINALLY SOME MONEY TO BE MADE AGAIN?
RIGHTY-HO. I'M OFFICIALLY BULLISH...
TAP

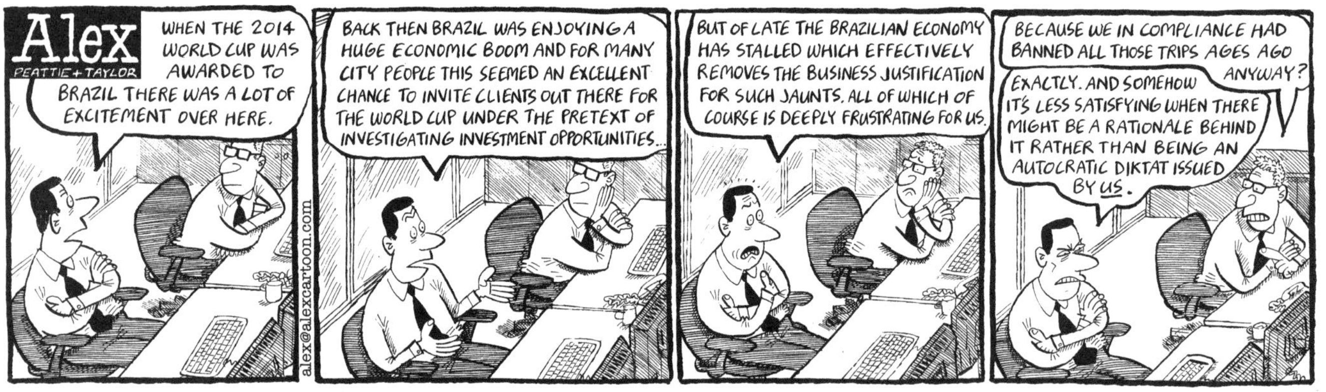
Alex
PEATTIE + TAYLOR
WHEN THE 2014 WORLD CUP WAS AWARDED TO BRAZIL THERE WAS A LOT OF EXCITEMENT OVER HERE.
alex@alexcartoon.com
BACK THEN BRAZIL WAS ENJOYING A HUGE ECONOMIC BOOM AND FOR MANY CITY PEOPLE THIS SEEMED AN EXCELLENT CHANCE TO INVITE CLIENTS OUT THERE FOR THE WORLD CUP UNDER THE PRETEXT OF INVESTIGATING INVESTMENT OPPORTUNITIES...
BUT OF LATE THE BRAZILIAN ECONOMY HAS STALLED WHICH EFFECTIVELY REMOVES THE BUSINESS JUSTIFICATION FOR SUCH JAUNTS. ALL OF WHICH OF COURSE IS DEEPLY FRUSTRATING FOR US.
BECAUSE WE IN COMPLIANCE HAD BANNED ALL THOSE TRIPS AGES AGO ANYWAY?
EXACTLY. AND SOMEHOW IT'S LESS SATISFYING WHEN THERE MIGHT BE A RATIONALE BEHIND IT RATHER THAN BEING AN AUTOCRATIC DIKTAT ISSUED BY US.

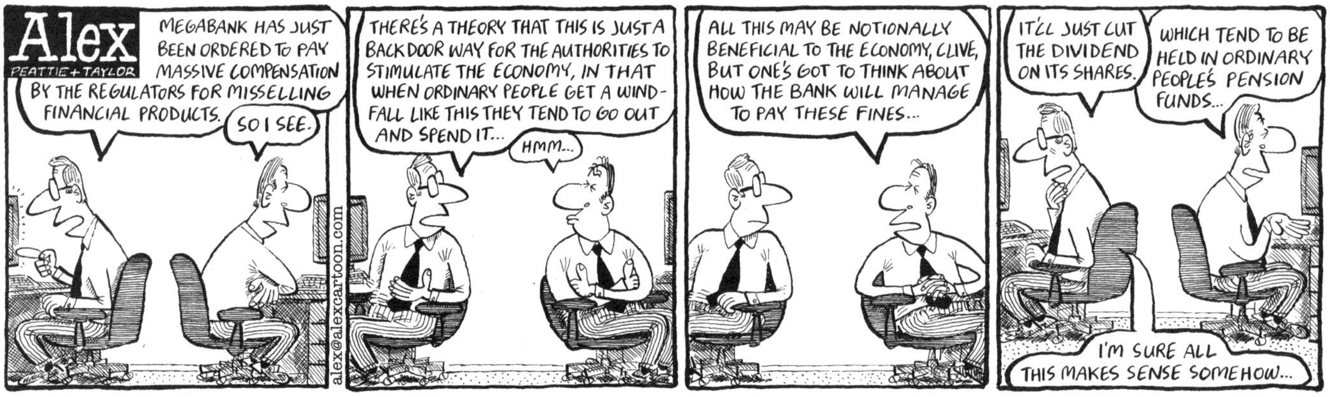
Alex
PEATTIE + TAYLOR
MEGABANK HAS JUST BEEN ORDERED TO PAY MASSIVE COMPENSATION BY THE REGULATORS FOR MISSELLING FINANCIAL PRODUCTS.
SO I SEE.
alex@alexcartoon.com
THERE'S A THEORY THAT THIS IS JUST A BACK DOOR WAY FOR THE AUTHORITIES TO STIMULATE THE ECONOMY, IN THAT WHEN ORDINARY PEOPLE GET A WINDFALL LIKE THIS THEY TEND TO GO OUT AND SPEND IT...
HMM...
ALL THIS MAY BE NOTIONALLY BENEFICIAL TO THE ECONOMY, CLIVE, BUT ONE'S GOT TO THINK ABOUT HOW THE BANK WILL MANAGE TO PAY THESE FINES...
IT'LL JUST CUT THE DIVIDEND ON ITS SHARES.
WHICH TEND TO BE HELD IN ORDINARY PEOPLE'S PENSION FUNDS...
I'M SURE ALL THIS MAKES SENSE SOMEHOW...

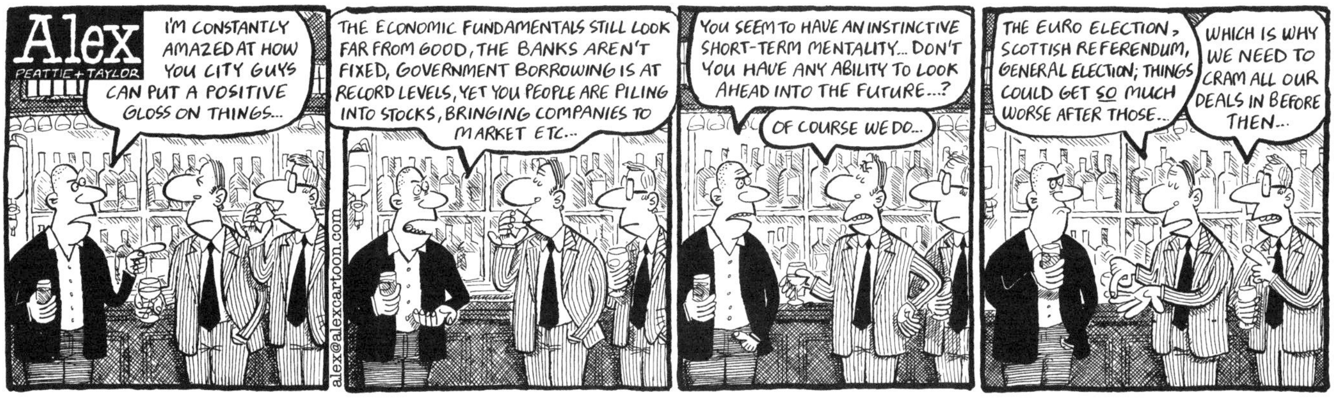
Alex
PEATTIE + TAYLOR
I'M CONSTANTLY AMAZED AT HOW YOU CITY GUYS CAN PUT A POSITIVE GLOSS ON THINGS...
THE ECONOMIC FUNDAMENTALS STILL LOOK FAR FROM GOOD, THE BANKS AREN'T FIXED, GOVERNMENT BORROWING IS AT RECORD LEVELS, YET YOU PEOPLE ARE PILING INTO STOCKS, BRINGING COMPANIES TO MARKET ETC...
alex@alexcartoon.com
YOU SEEM TO HAVE AN INSTINCTIVE SHORT-TERM MENTALITY... DON'T YOU HAVE ANY ABILITY TO LOOK AHEAD INTO THE FUTURE...?
OF COURSE WE DO...
THE EURO ELECTION, SCOTTISH REFERENDUM, GENERAL ELECTION; THINGS COULD GET SO MUCH WORSE AFTER THOSE...
WHICH IS WHY WE NEED TO CRAM ALL OUR DEALS IN BEFORE THEN...

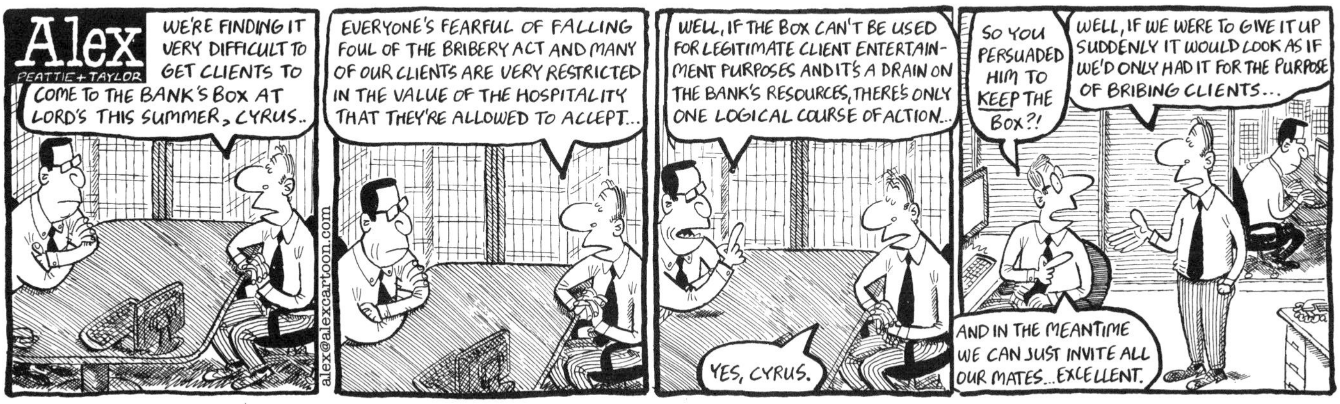
Alex
PEATTIE + TAYLOR
WE'RE FINDING IT VERY DIFFICULT TO GET CLIENTS TO COME TO THE BANK'S BOX AT LORD'S THIS SUMMER, CYRUS..
EVERYONE'S FEARFUL OF FALLING FOUL OF THE BRIBERY ACT AND MANY OF OUR CLIENTS ARE VERY RESTRICTED IN THE VALUE OF THE HOSPITALITY THAT THEY'RE ALLOWED TO ACCEPT...
alex@alexcartoon.com
WELL, IF THE BOX CAN'T BE USED FOR LEGITIMATE CLIENT ENTERTAINMENT PURPOSES AND IT'S A DRAIN ON THE BANK'S RESOURCES, THERE'S ONLY ONE LOGICAL COURSE OF ACTION...
YES, CYRUS.
SO YOU PERSUADED HIM TO KEEP THE BOX?!
WELL, IF WE WERE TO GIVE IT UP SUDDENLY IT WOULD LOOK AS IF WE'D ONLY HAD IT FOR THE PURPOSE OF BRIBING CLIENTS...
AND IN THE MEANTIME WE CAN JUST INVITE ALL OUR MATES... EXCELLENT.

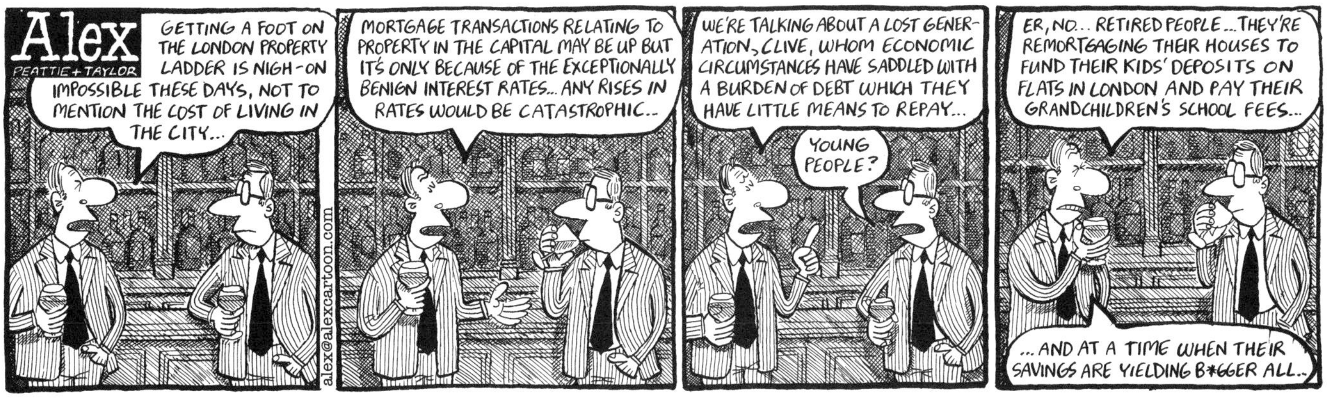
Alex
PEATTIE + TAYLOR
GETTING A FOOT ON THE LONDON PROPERTY LADDER IS NIGH-ON IMPOSSIBLE THESE DAYS, NOT TO MENTION THE COST OF LIVING IN THE CITY...
MORTGAGE TRANSACTIONS RELATING TO PROPERTY IN THE CAPITAL MAY BE UP BUT IT'S ONLY BECAUSE OF THE EXCEPTIONALLY BENIGN INTEREST RATES... ANY RISES IN RATES WOULD BE CATASTROPHIC...
alex@alexcartoon.com
WE'RE TALKING ABOUT A LOST GENERATION, CLIVE, WHOM ECONOMIC CIRCUMSTANCES HAVE SADDLED WITH A BURDEN OF DEBT WHICH THEY HAVE LITTLE MEANS TO REPAY...
YOUNG PEOPLE?
ER, NO... RETIRED PEOPLE... THEY'RE REMORTGAGING THEIR HOUSES TO FUND THEIR KIDS' DEPOSITS ON FLATS IN LONDON AND PAY THEIR GRANDCHILDREN'S SCHOOL FEES...
... AND AT A TIME WHEN THEIR SAVINGS ARE YIELDING B*GGER ALL...

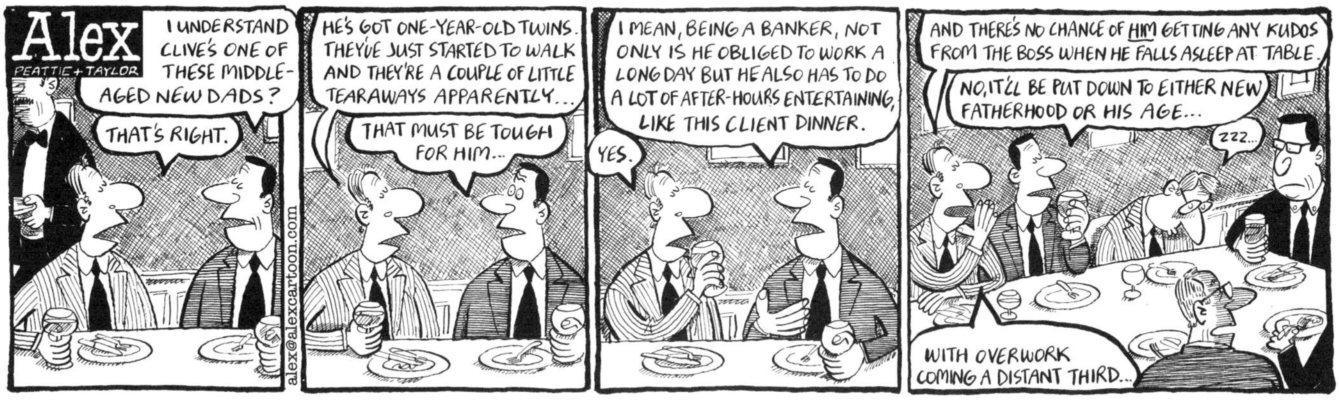
Alex
PEATTIE + TAYLOR
I UNDERSTAND CLIVE'S ONE OF THESE MIDDLE-AGED NEW DADS?
THAT'S RIGHT.
HE'S GOT ONE-YEAR-OLD TWINS. THEY'VE JUST STARTED TO WALK AND THEY'RE A COUPLE OF LITTLE TEARAWAYS APPARENTLY...
THAT MUST BE TOUGH FOR HIM...
alex@alexcartoon.com
I MEAN, BEING A BANKER, NOT ONLY IS HE OBLIGED TO WORK A LONG DAY BUT HE ALSO HAS TO DO A LOT OF AFTER-HOURS ENTERTAINING, LIKE THIS CLIENT DINNER.
YES.
AND THERE'S NO CHANCE OF HIM GETTING ANY KUDOS FROM THE BOSS WHEN HE FALLS ASLEEP AT TABLE.
NO, IT'LL BE PUT DOWN TO EITHER NEW FATHERHOOD OR HIS AGE...
ZZZ...
WITH OVERWORK COMING A DISTANT THIRD...

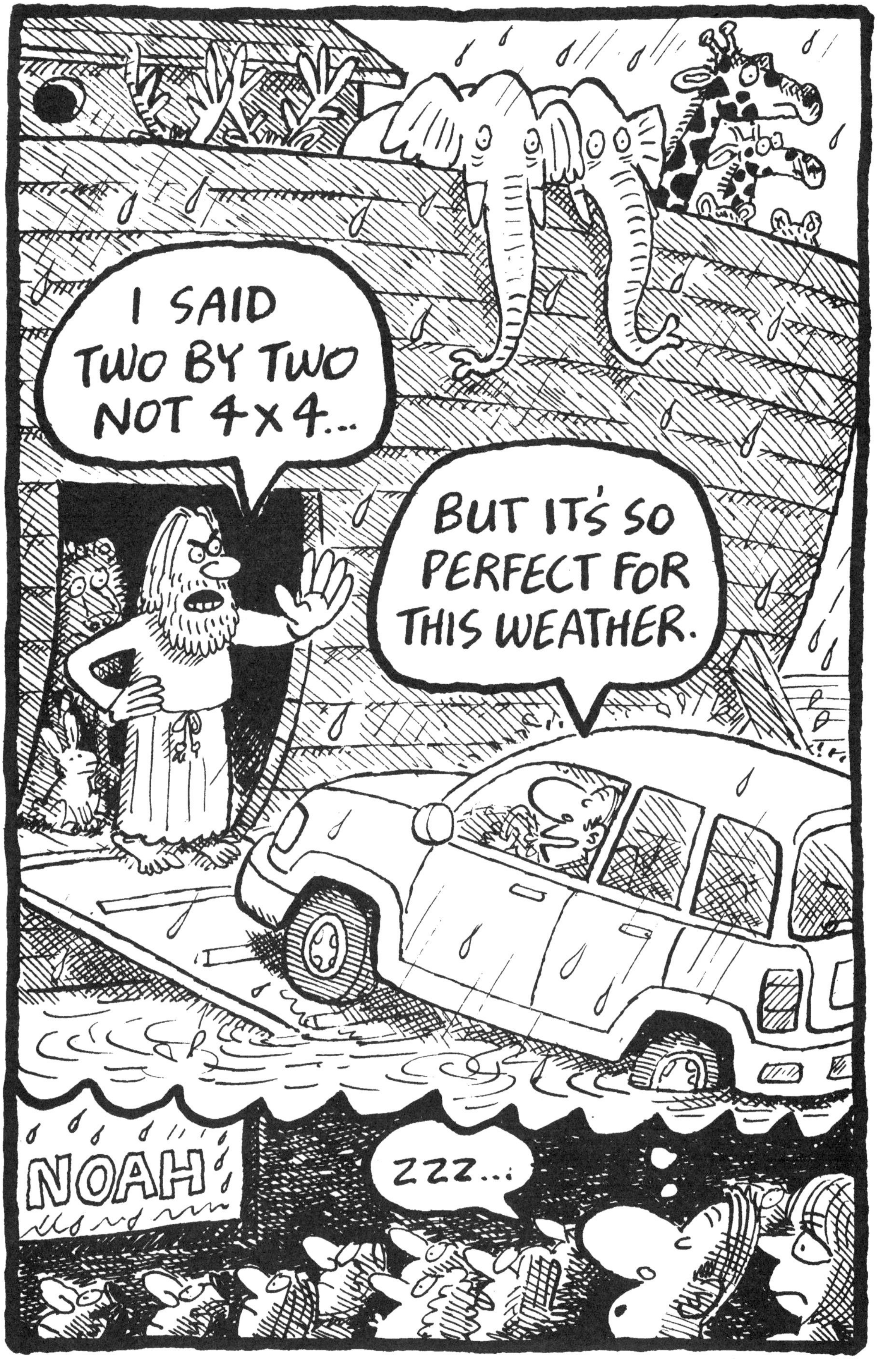
I SAID TWO BY TWO NOT 4 x 4...
BUT IT'S SO PERFECT FOR THIS WEATHER.
NOAH
ZZZ...

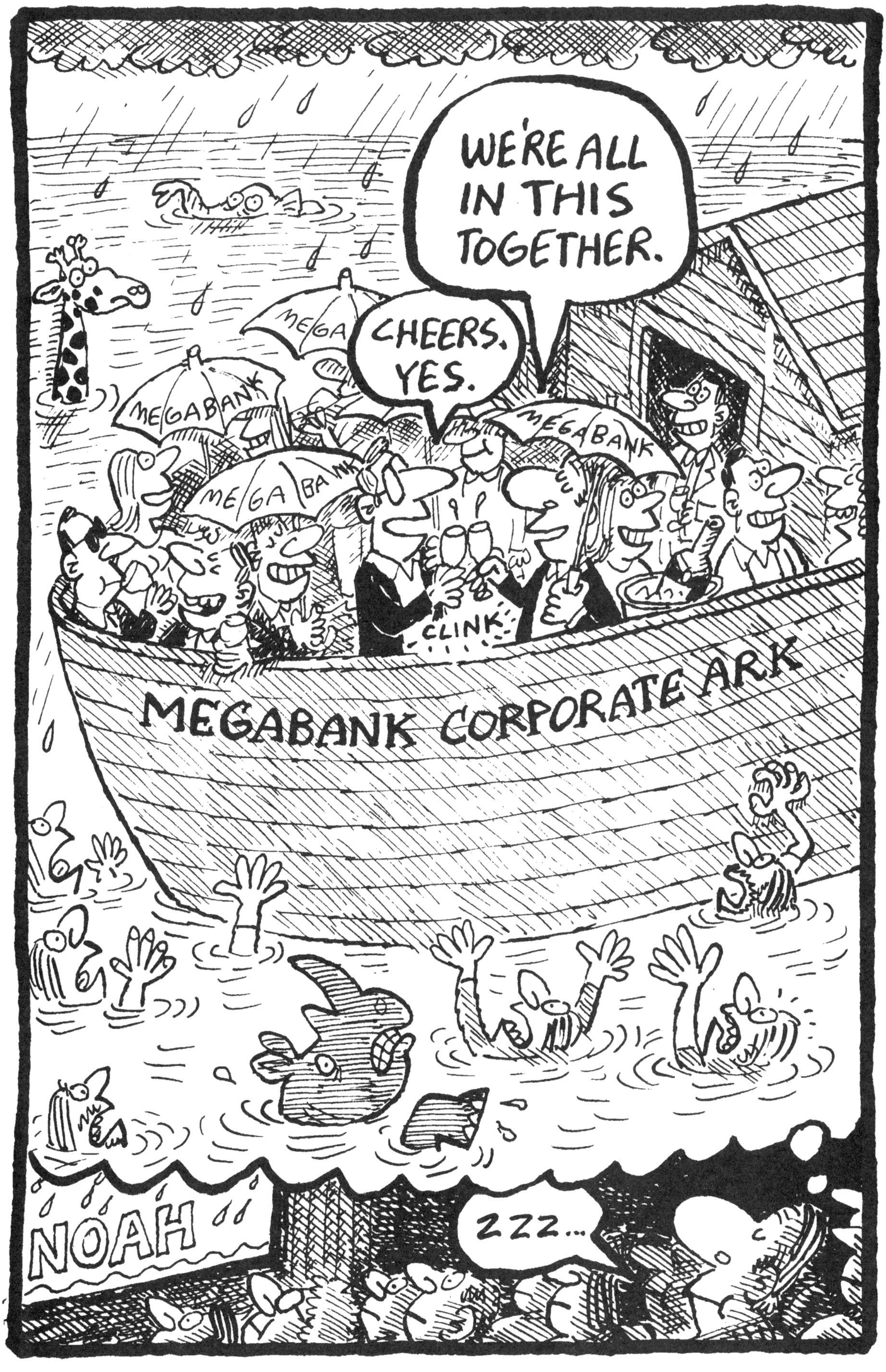
WE'RE ALL IN THIS TOGETHER.
CHEERS. YES.
MEGABANK
MEGABANK
MEGABANK
MEGABANK
CLINK
MEGABANK CORPORATE ARK
NOAH
ZZZ...

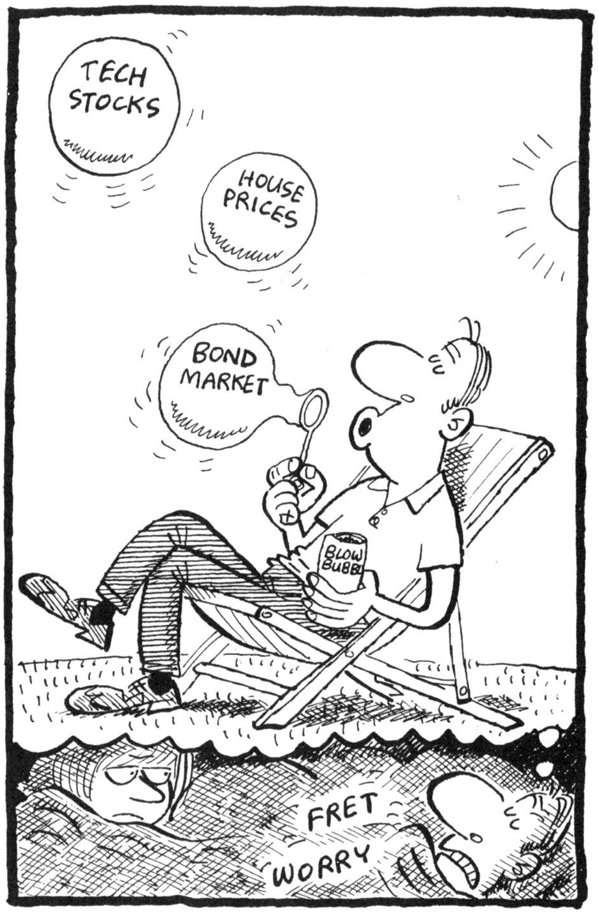
TECH STOCKS
HOUSE PRICES
BOND MARKET
FRET
WORRY

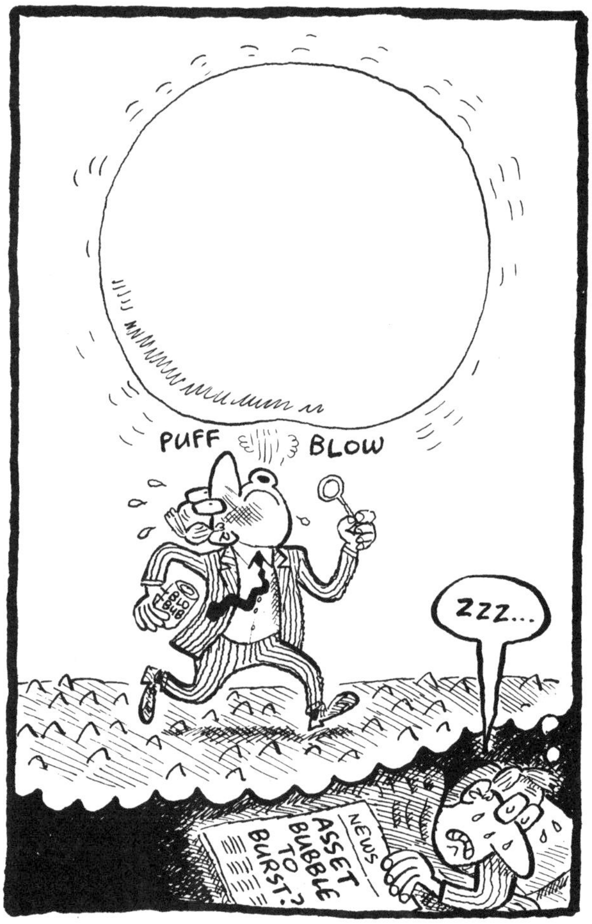
PUFF
BLOW
ZZZ...
NEWS
ASSET BUBBLE TO BURST?

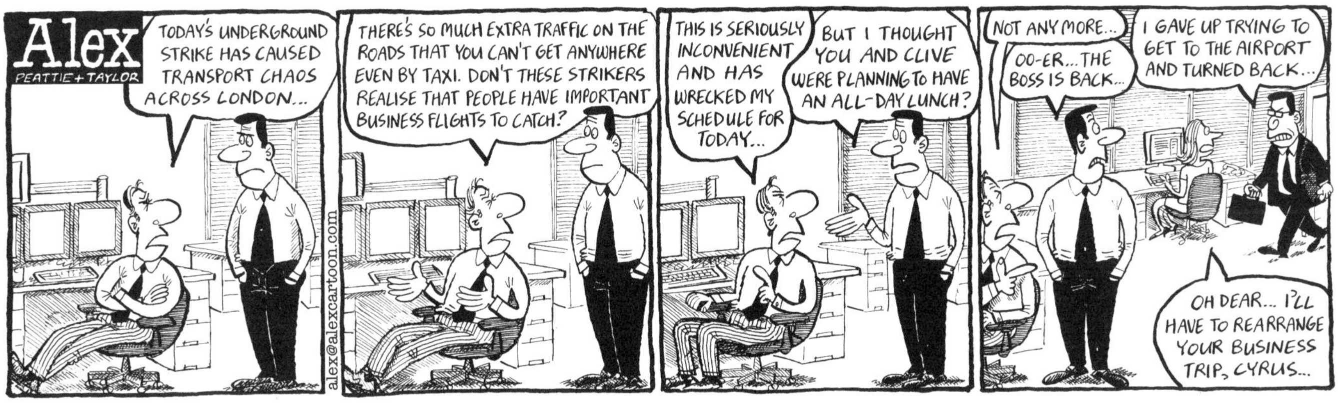
Alex
PEATTIE+TAYLOR
TODAY'S UNDERGROUND STRIKE HAS CAUSED TRANSPORT CHAOS ACROSS LONDON...
THERE'S SO MUCH EXTRA TRAFFIC ON THE ROADS THAT YOU CAN'T GET ANYWHERE EVEN BY TAXI. DON'T THESE STRIKERS REALISE THAT PEOPLE HAVE IMPORTANT BUSINESS FLIGHTS TO CATCH?
alex@alexcartoon.com
THIS IS SERIOUSLY INCONVENIENT AND HAS WRECKED MY SCHEDULE FOR TODAY...
BUT I THOUGHT YOU AND CLIVE WERE PLANNING TO HAVE AN ALL-DAY LUNCH?
NOT ANY MORE...
OO-ER... THE BOSS IS BACK...
I GAVE UP TRYING TO GET TO THE AIRPORT AND TURNED BACK...
OH DEAR... I'LL HAVE TO REARRANGE YOUR BUSINESS TRIP, CYRUS...

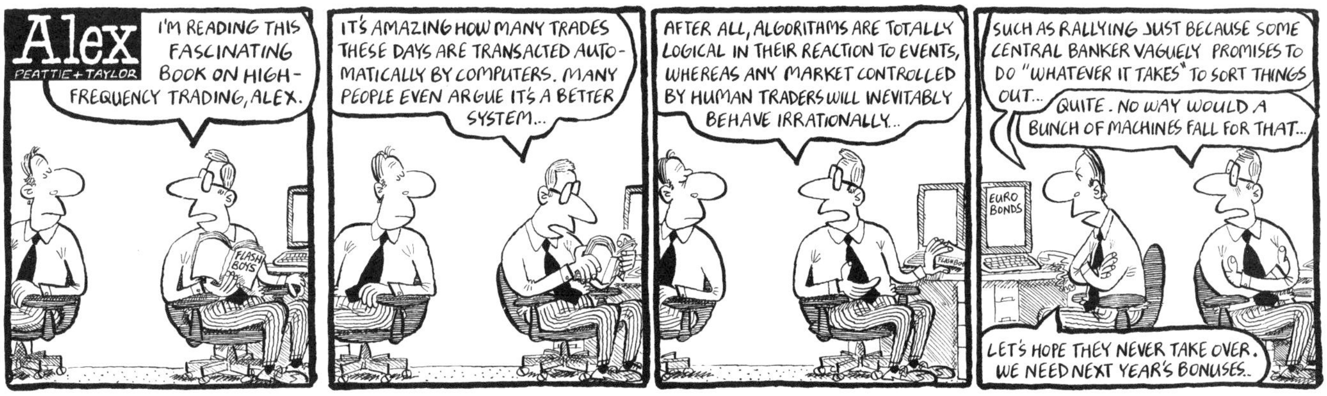
Alex
PEATTIE+TAYLOR
I'M READING THIS FASCINATING BOOK ON HIGH-FREQUENCY TRADING, ALEX.
FLASH BOYS
IT'S AMAZING HOW MANY TRADES THESE DAYS ARE TRANSACTED AUTOMATICALLY BY COMPUTERS. MANY PEOPLE EVEN ARGUE IT'S A BETTER SYSTEM...
AFTER ALL, ALGORITHMS ARE TOTALLY LOGICAL IN THEIR REACTION TO EVENTS, WHEREAS ANY MARKET CONTROLLED BY HUMAN TRADERS WILL INEVITABLY BEHAVE IRRATIONALLY...
SUCH AS RALLYING JUST BECAUSE SOME CENTRAL BANKER VAGUELY PROMISES TO DO "WHATEVER IT TAKES" TO SORT THINGS OUT...
QUITE. NO WAY WOULD A BUNCH OF MACHINES FALL FOR THAT...
EURO BONDS
LET'S HOPE THEY NEVER TAKE OVER. WE NEED NEXT YEAR'S BONUSES..

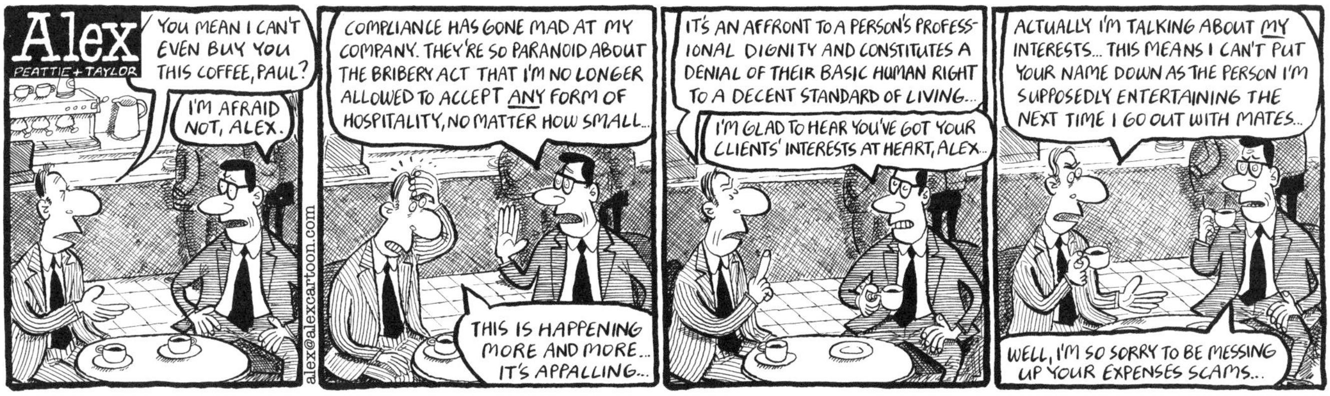
Alex
PEATTIE+TAYLOR
YOU MEAN I CAN'T EVEN BUY YOU THIS COFFEE, PAUL?
I'M AFRAID NOT, ALEX.
alex@alexcartoon.com
COMPLIANCE HAS GONE MAD AT MY COMPANY. THEY'RE SO PARANOID ABOUT THE BRIBERY ACT THAT I'M NO LONGER ALLOWED TO ACCEPT ANY FORM OF HOSPITALITY, NO MATTER HOW SMALL...
THIS IS HAPPENING MORE AND MORE... IT'S APPALLING...
IT'S AN AFFRONT TO A PERSON'S PROFESSIONAL DIGNITY AND CONSTITUTES A DENIAL OF THEIR BASIC HUMAN RIGHT TO A DECENT STANDARD OF LIVING...
I'M GLAD TO HEAR YOU'VE GOT YOUR CLIENTS' INTERESTS AT HEART, ALEX...
ACTUALLY I'M TALKING ABOUT MY INTERESTS... THIS MEANS I CAN'T PUT YOUR NAME DOWN AS THE PERSON I'M SUPPOSEDLY ENTERTAINING THE NEXT TIME I GO OUT WITH MATES...
WELL, I'M SO SORRY TO BE MESSING UP YOUR EXPENSES SCAMS...

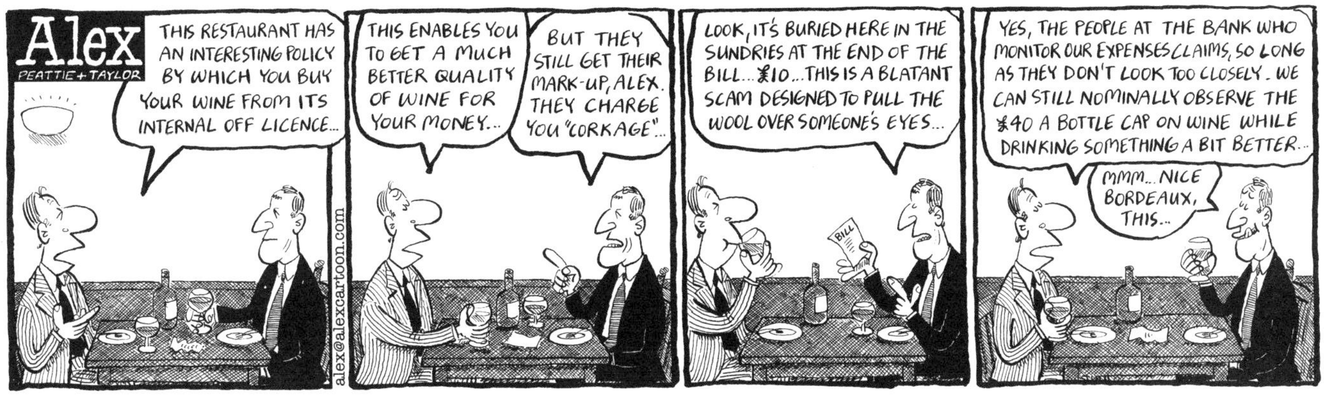
Alex
PEATTIE+TAYLOR
THIS RESTAURANT HAS AN INTERESTING POLICY BY WHICH YOU BUY YOUR WINE FROM ITS INTERNAL OFF LICENCE...
alex@alexcartoon.com
THIS ENABLES YOU TO GET A MUCH BETTER QUALITY OF WINE FOR YOUR MONEY...
BUT THEY STILL GET THEIR MARK-UP, ALEX. THEY CHARGE YOU "CORKAGE"...
LOOK, IT'S BURIED HERE IN THE SUNDRIES AT THE END OF THE BILL... ¥10... THIS IS A BLATANT SCAM DESIGNED TO PULL THE WOOL OVER SOMEONE'S EYES...
BILL
YES, THE PEOPLE AT THE BANK WHO MONITOR OUR EXPENSES CLAIMS, SO LONG AS THEY DON'T LOOK TOO CLOSELY. WE CAN STILL NOMINALLY OBSERVE THE ¥40 A BOTTLE CAP ON WINE WHILE DRINKING SOMETHING A BIT BETTER...
MMM... NICE BORDEAUX, THIS...

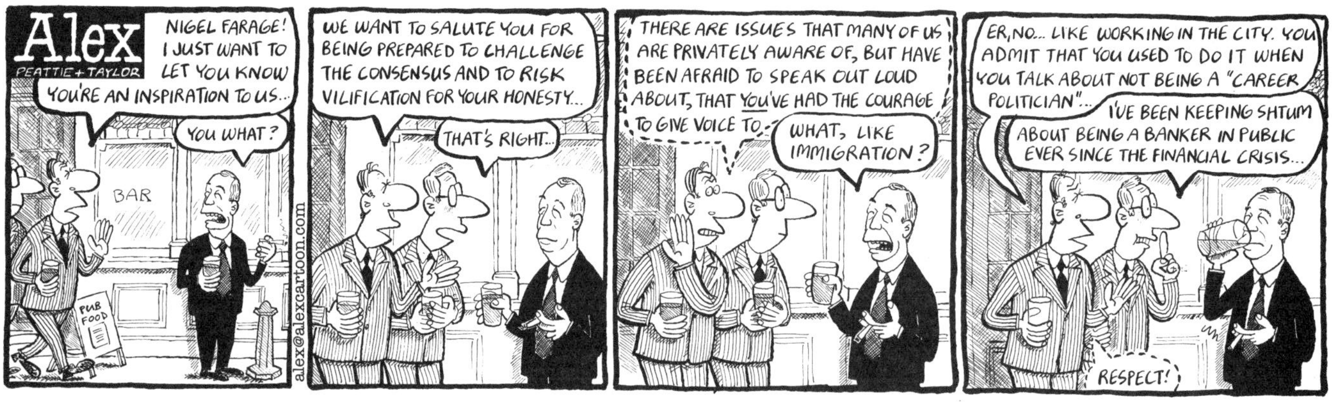
Alex
PEATTIE + TAYLOR
NIGEL FARAGE! I JUST WANT TO LET YOU KNOW YOU'RE AN INSPIRATION TO US...
YOU WHAT?
BAR
PUB FOOD
alex@alexcartoon.com
WE WANT TO SALUTE YOU FOR BEING PREPARED TO CHALLENGE THE CONSENSUS AND TO RISK VILIFICATION FOR YOUR HONESTY...
THAT'S RIGHT...
THERE ARE ISSUES THAT MANY OF US ARE PRIVATELY AWARE OF, BUT HAVE BEEN AFRAID TO SPEAK OUT LOUD ABOUT, THAT YOU'VE HAD THE COURAGE TO GIVE VOICE TO...
WHAT, LIKE IMMIGRATION?
ER, NO... LIKE WORKING IN THE CITY. YOU ADMIT THAT YOU USED TO DO IT WHEN YOU TALK ABOUT NOT BEING A "CAREER POLITICIAN"...
I'VE BEEN KEEPING SHTUM ABOUT BEING A BANKER IN PUBLIC EVER SINCE THE FINANCIAL CRISIS...
RESPECT!

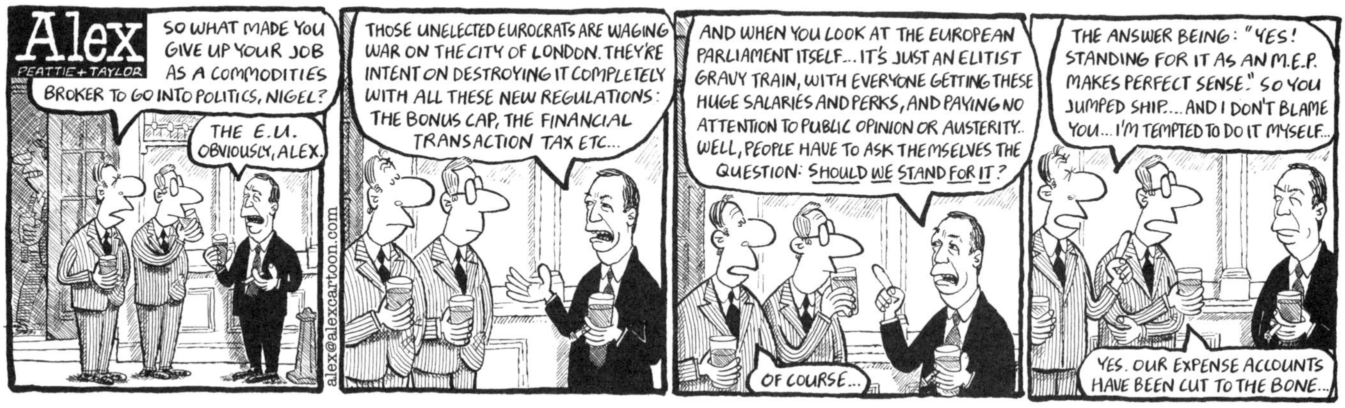
Alex
PEATTIE + TAYLOR
SO WHAT MADE YOU GIVE UP YOUR JOB AS A COMMODITIES BROKER TO GO INTO POLITICS, NIGEL?
THE E.U. OBVIOUSLY, ALEX.
alex@alexcartoon.com
THOSE UNELECTED EUROCRATS ARE WAGING WAR ON THE CITY OF LONDON. THEY'RE INTENT ON DESTROYING IT COMPLETELY WITH ALL THESE NEW REGULATIONS: THE BONUS CAP, THE FINANCIAL TRANSACTION TAX ETC...
AND WHEN YOU LOOK AT THE EUROPEAN PARLIAMENT ITSELF... IT'S JUST AN ELITIST GRAVY TRAIN, WITH EVERYONE GETTING THESE HUGE SALARIES AND PERKS, AND PAYING NO ATTENTION TO PUBLIC OPINION OR AUSTERITY.. WELL, PEOPLE HAVE TO ASK THEMSELVES THE QUESTION: SHOULD WE STAND FOR IT?
OF COURSE...
THE ANSWER BEING: "YES! STANDING FOR IT AS AN M.E.P. MAKES PERFECT SENSE." SO YOU JUMPED SHIP... AND I DON'T BLAME YOU... I'M TEMPTED TO DO IT MYSELF...
YES. OUR EXPENSE ACCOUNTS HAVE BEEN CUT TO THE BONE...

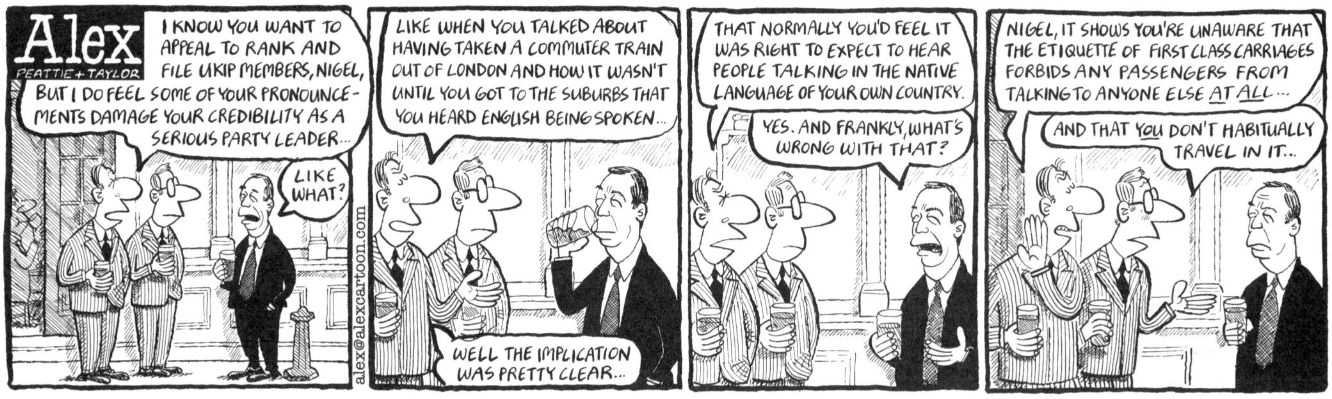
Alex
PEATTIE + TAYLOR
I KNOW YOU WANT TO APPEAL TO RANK AND FILE UKIP MEMBERS, NIGEL,
BUT I DO FEEL SOME OF YOUR PRONOUNCEMENTS DAMAGE YOUR CREDIBILITY AS A SERIOUS PARTY LEADER...
LIKE WHAT?
alex@alexcartoon.com
LIKE WHEN YOU TALKED ABOUT HAVING TAKEN A COMMUTER TRAIN OUT OF LONDON AND HOW IT WASN'T UNTIL YOU GOT TO THE SUBURBS THAT YOU HEARD ENGLISH BEING SPOKEN...
WELL THE IMPLICATION WAS PRETTY CLEAR...
THAT NORMALLY YOU'D FEEL IT WAS RIGHT TO EXPECT TO HEAR PEOPLE TALKING IN THE NATIVE LANGUAGE OF YOUR OWN COUNTRY.
YES. AND FRANKLY, WHAT'S WRONG WITH THAT?
NIGEL, IT SHOWS YOU'RE UNAWARE THAT THE ETIQUETTE OF FIRST CLASS CARRIAGES FORBIDS ANY PASSENGERS FROM TALKING TO ANYONE ELSE AT ALL...
AND THAT YOU DON'T HABITUALLY TRAVEL IN IT...

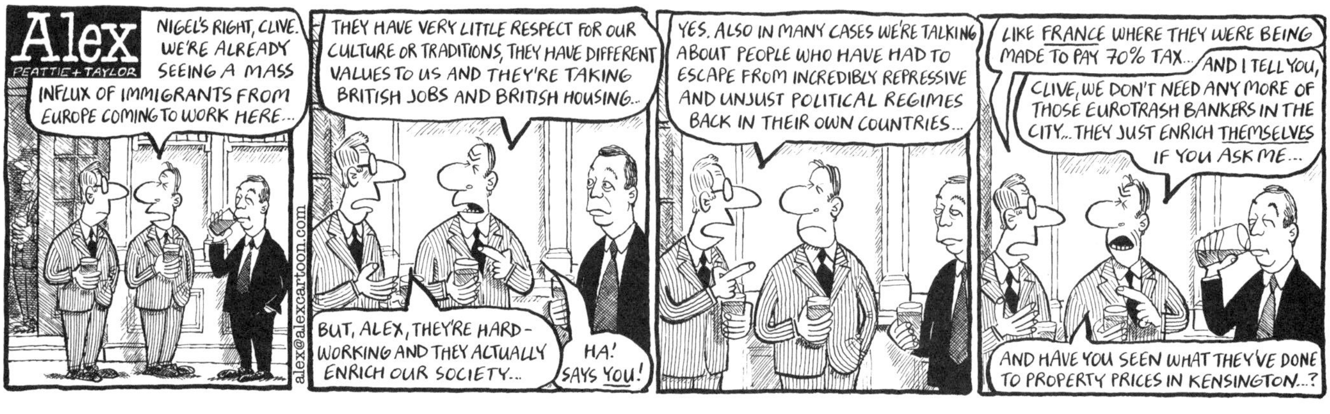
Alex
PEATTIE + TAYLOR
NIGEL'S RIGHT, CLIVE. WE'RE ALREADY SEEING A MASS INFLUX OF IMMIGRANTS FROM EUROPE COMING TO WORK HERE...
alex@alexcartoon.com
THEY HAVE VERY LITTLE RESPECT FOR OUR CULTURE OR TRADITIONS, THEY HAVE DIFFERENT VALUES TO US AND THEY'RE TAKING BRITISH JOBS AND BRITISH HOUSING...
BUT, ALEX, THEY'RE HARD-WORKING AND THEY ACTUALLY ENRICH OUR SOCIETY...
HA! SAYS YOU!
YES. ALSO IN MANY CASES WE'RE TALKING ABOUT PEOPLE WHO HAVE HAD TO ESCAPE FROM INCREDIBLY REPRESSIVE AND UNJUST POLITICAL REGIMES BACK IN THEIR OWN COUNTRIES...
LIKE FRANCE WHERE THEY WERE BEING MADE TO PAY 70% TAX...
AND I TELL YOU, CLIVE, WE DON'T NEED ANY MORE OF THOSE EUROTRASH BANKERS IN THE CITY... THEY JUST ENRICH THEMSELVES IF YOU ASK ME...
AND HAVE YOU SEEN WHAT THEY'VE DONE TO PROPERTY PRICES IN KENSINGTON...?

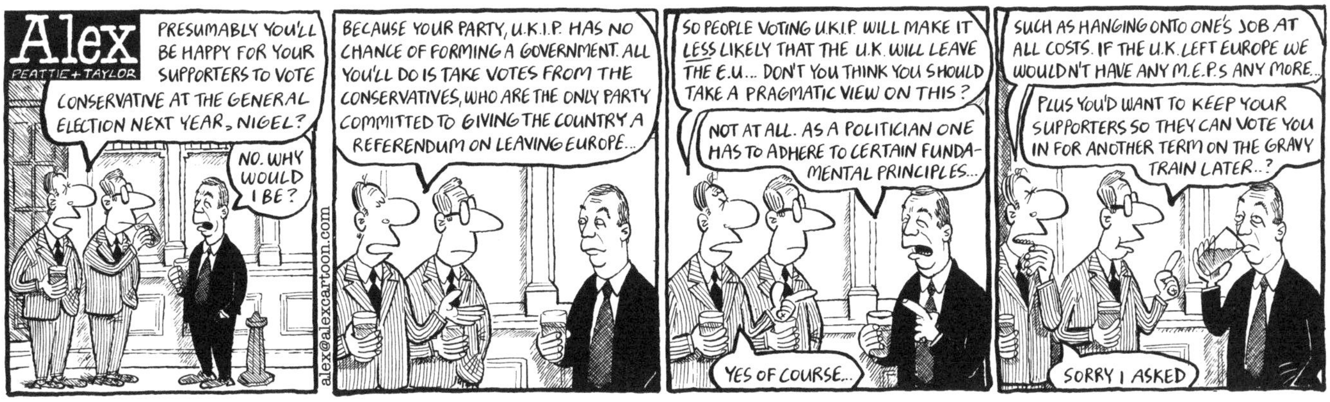
Alex
PEATTIE+TAYLOR
PRESUMABLY YOU'LL BE HAPPY FOR YOUR SUPPORTERS TO VOTE CONSERVATIVE AT THE GENERAL ELECTION NEXT YEAR, NIGEL?
NO. WHY WOULD I BE?
alex@alexcartoon.com
BECAUSE YOUR PARTY, U.K.I.P. HAS NO CHANCE OF FORMING A GOVERNMENT. ALL YOU'LL DO IS TAKE VOTES FROM THE CONSERVATIVES, WHO ARE THE ONLY PARTY COMMITTED TO GIVING THE COUNTRY A REFERENDUM ON LEAVING EUROPE...
SO PEOPLE VOTING U.K.I.P. WILL MAKE IT LESS LIKELY THAT THE U.K. WILL LEAVE THE E.U... DON'T YOU THINK YOU SHOULD TAKE A PRAGMATIC VIEW ON THIS?
NOT AT ALL. AS A POLITICIAN ONE HAS TO ADHERE TO CERTAIN FUNDAMENTAL PRINCIPLES...
YES OF COURSE...
SUCH AS HANGING ONTO ONE'S JOB AT ALL COSTS. IF THE U.K. LEFT EUROPE WE WOULDN'T HAVE ANY M.E.P.S ANY MORE...
PLUS YOU'D WANT TO KEEP YOUR SUPPORTERS SO THEY CAN VOTE YOU IN FOR ANOTHER TERM ON THE GRAVY TRAIN LATER...?
SORRY I ASKED

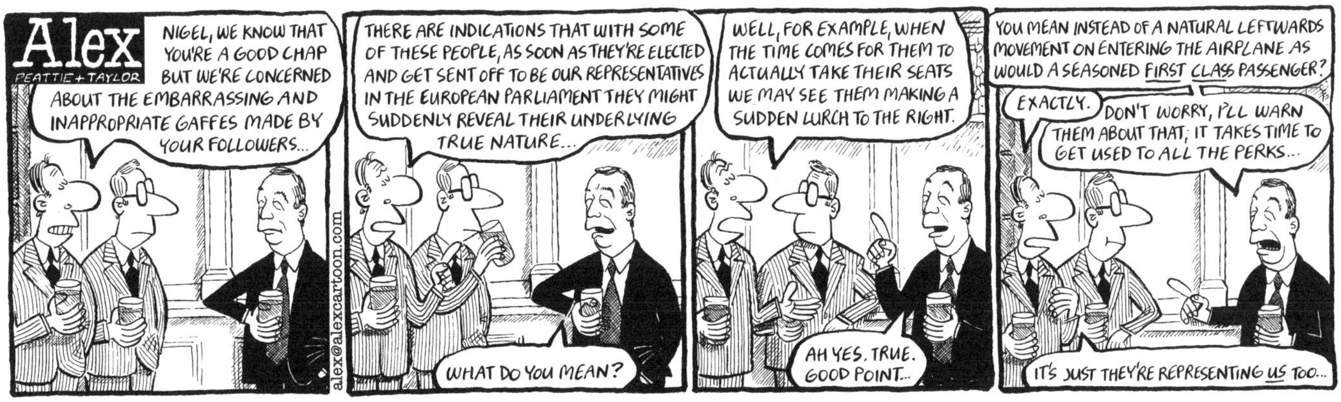
Alex
PEATTIE+TAYLOR
NIGEL, WE KNOW THAT YOU'RE A GOOD CHAP BUT WE'RE CONCERNED ABOUT THE EMBARRASSING AND INAPPROPRIATE GAFFES MADE BY YOUR FOLLOWERS...
alex@alexcartoon.com
THERE ARE INDICATIONS THAT WITH SOME OF THESE PEOPLE, AS SOON AS THEY'RE ELECTED AND GET SENT OFF TO BE OUR REPRESENTATIVES IN THE EUROPEAN PARLIAMENT THEY MIGHT SUDDENLY REVEAL THEIR UNDERLYING TRUE NATURE...
WHAT DO YOU MEAN?
WELL, FOR EXAMPLE, WHEN THE TIME COMES FOR THEM TO ACTUALLY TAKE THEIR SEATS WE MAY SEE THEM MAKING A SUDDEN LURCH TO THE RIGHT.
AH YES. TRUE. GOOD POINT...
YOU MEAN INSTEAD OF A NATURAL LEFTWARDS MOVEMENT ON ENTERING THE AIRPLANE AS WOULD A SEASONED FIRST CLASS PASSENGER?
EXACTLY.
DON'T WORRY, I'LL WARN THEM ABOUT THAT; IT TAKES TIME TO GET USED TO ALL THE PERKS...
IT'S JUST THEY'RE REPRESENTING US TOO...

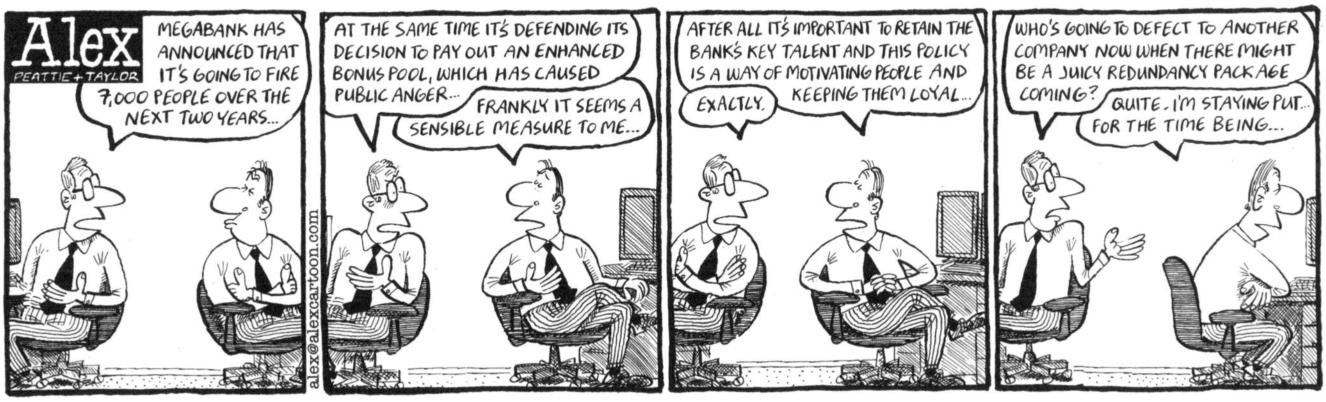
Alex
PEATTIE+TAYLOR
MEGABANK HAS ANNOUNCED THAT IT'S GOING TO FIRE 7,000 PEOPLE OVER THE NEXT TWO YEARS...
alex@alexcartoon.com
AT THE SAME TIME IT'S DEFENDING ITS DECISION TO PAY OUT AN ENHANCED BONUS POOL, WHICH HAS CAUSED PUBLIC ANGER...
FRANKLY IT SEEMS A SENSIBLE MEASURE TO ME...
AFTER ALL IT'S IMPORTANT TO RETAIN THE BANK'S KEY TALENT AND THIS POLICY IS A WAY OF MOTIVATING PEOPLE AND KEEPING THEM LOYAL...
EXACTLY.
WHO'S GOING TO DEFECT TO ANOTHER COMPANY NOW WHEN THERE MIGHT BE A JUICY REDUNDANCY PACKAGE COMING?
QUITE. I'M STAYING PUT... FOR THE TIME BEING...

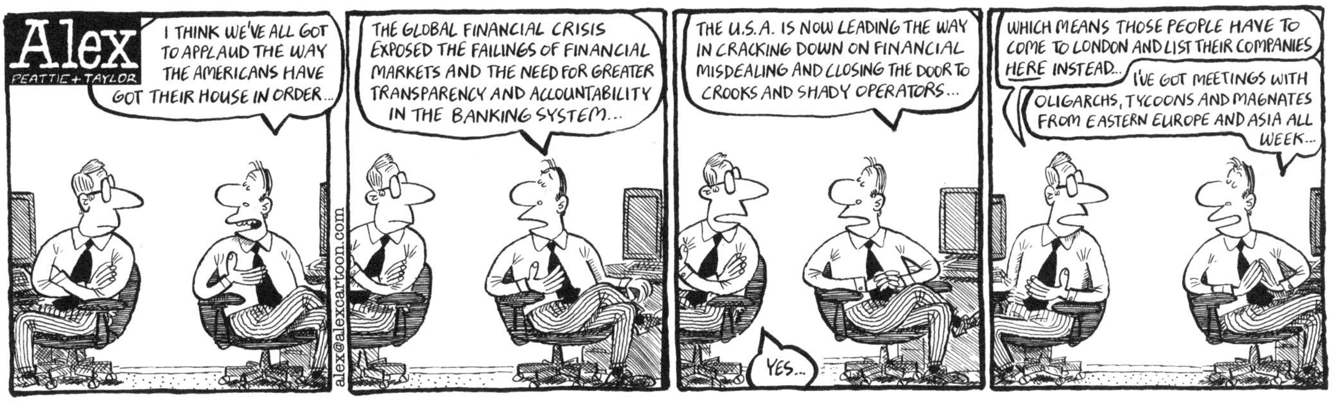
Alex
PEATTIE+TAYLOR
I THINK WE'VE ALL GOT TO APPLAUD THE WAY THE AMERICANS HAVE GOT THEIR HOUSE IN ORDER...
alex@alexcartoon.com
THE GLOBAL FINANCIAL CRISIS EXPOSED THE FAILINGS OF FINANCIAL MARKETS AND THE NEED FOR GREATER TRANSPARENCY AND ACCOUNTABILITY IN THE BANKING SYSTEM...
THE U.S.A. IS NOW LEADING THE WAY IN CRACKING DOWN ON FINANCIAL MISDEALING AND CLOSING THE DOOR TO CROOKS AND SHADY OPERATORS...
YES...
WHICH MEANS THOSE PEOPLE HAVE TO COME TO LONDON AND LIST THEIR COMPANIES HERE INSTEAD...
I'VE GOT MEETINGS WITH OLIGARCHS, TYCOONS AND MAGNATES FROM EASTERN EUROPE AND ASIA ALL WEEK...

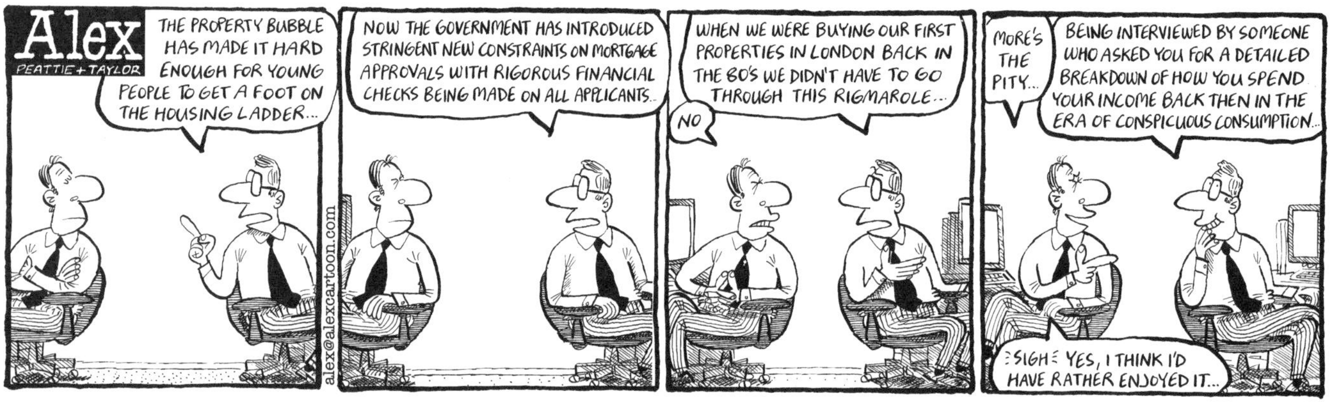
Alex
PEATTIE + TAYLOR
THE PROPERTY BUBBLE HAS MADE IT HARD ENOUGH FOR YOUNG PEOPLE TO GET A FOOT ON THE HOUSING LADDER...
alex@alexcartoon.com
NOW THE GOVERNMENT HAS INTRODUCED STRINGENT NEW CONSTRAINTS ON MORTGAGE APPROVALS WITH RIGOROUS FINANCIAL CHECKS BEING MADE ON ALL APPLICANTS...
WHEN WE WERE BUYING OUR FIRST PROPERTIES IN LONDON BACK IN THE 80'S WE DIDN'T HAVE TO GO THROUGH THIS RIGMAROLE...
NO
MORE'S THE PITY...
BEING INTERVIEWED BY SOMEONE WHO ASKED YOU FOR A DETAILED BREAKDOWN OF HOW YOU SPEND YOUR INCOME BACK THEN IN THE ERA OF CONSPICUOUS CONSUMPTION...
SIGH YES, I THINK I'D HAVE RATHER ENJOYED IT...

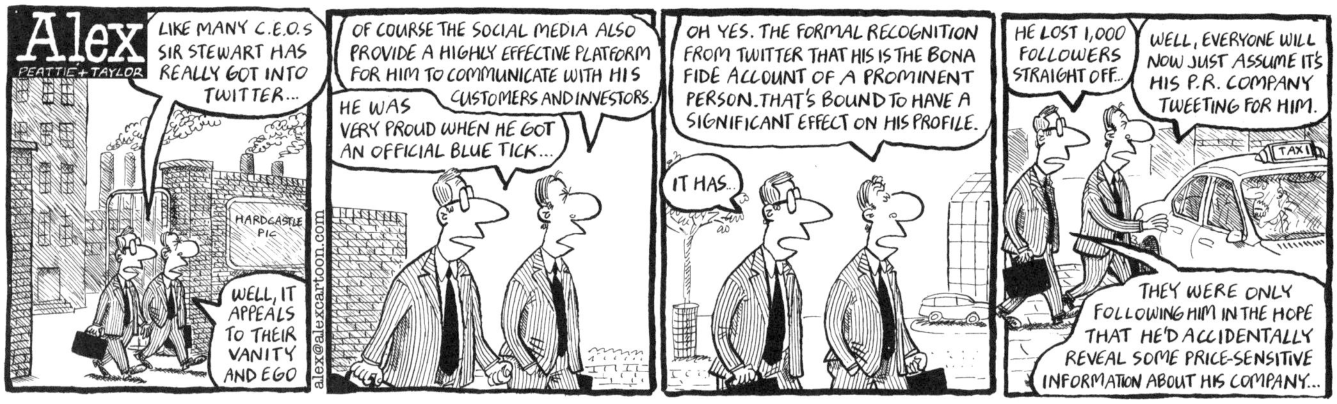
Alex
PEATTIE + TAYLOR
LIKE MANY C.E.O.s SIR STEWART HAS REALLY GOT INTO TWITTER...
HARDCASTLE PLC
WELL, IT APPEALS TO THEIR VANITY AND EGO
alex@alexcartoon.com
OF COURSE THE SOCIAL MEDIA ALSO PROVIDE A HIGHLY EFFECTIVE PLATFORM FOR HIM TO COMMUNICATE WITH HIS CUSTOMERS AND INVESTORS.
HE WAS VERY PROUD WHEN HE GOT AN OFFICIAL BLUE TICK...
OH YES. THE FORMAL RECOGNITION FROM TWITTER THAT HIS IS THE BONA FIDE ACCOUNT OF A PROMINENT PERSON. THAT'S BOUND TO HAVE A SIGNIFICANT EFFECT ON HIS PROFILE.
IT HAS...
HE LOST 1,000 FOLLOWERS STRAIGHT OFF...
WELL, EVERYONE WILL NOW JUST ASSUME IT'S HIS P.R. COMPANY TWEETING FOR HIM.
TAXI
THEY WERE ONLY FOLLOWING HIM IN THE HOPE THAT HE'D ACCIDENTALLY REVEAL SOME PRICE-SENSITIVE INFORMATION ABOUT HIS COMPANY...

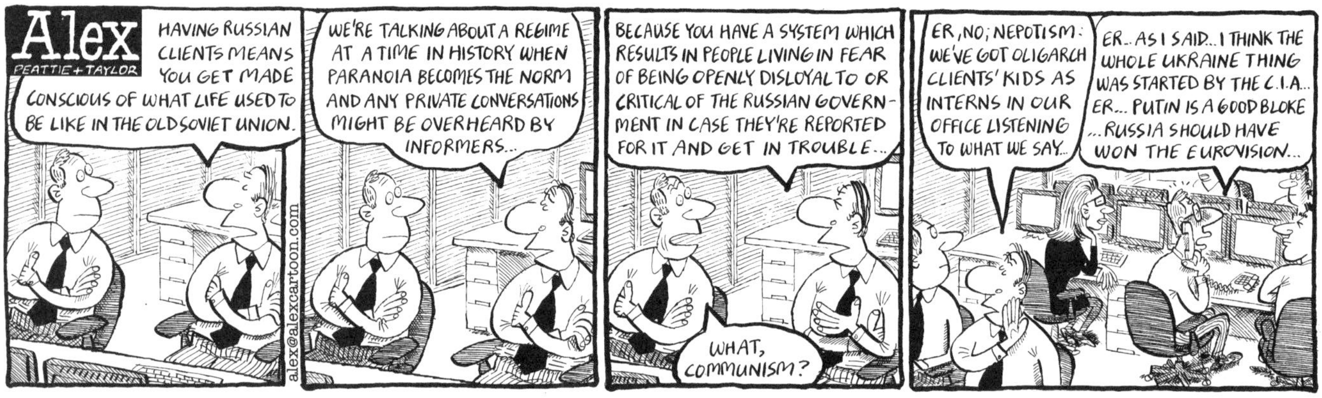
Alex
PEATTIE + TAYLOR
HAVING RUSSIAN CLIENTS MEANS YOU GET MADE CONSCIOUS OF WHAT LIFE USED TO BE LIKE IN THE OLD SOVIET UNION.
alex@alexcartoon.com
WE'RE TALKING ABOUT A REGIME AT A TIME IN HISTORY WHEN PARANOIA BECOMES THE NORM AND ANY PRIVATE CONVERSATIONS MIGHT BE OVERHEARD BY INFORMERS...
BECAUSE YOU HAVE A SYSTEM WHICH RESULTS IN PEOPLE LIVING IN FEAR OF BEING OPENLY DISLOYAL TO OR CRITICAL OF THE RUSSIAN GOVERNMENT IN CASE THEY'RE REPORTED FOR IT AND GET IN TROUBLE...
WHAT, COMMUNISM?
ER, NO; NEPOTISM: WE'VE GOT OLIGARCH CLIENTS' KIDS AS INTERNS IN OUR OFFICE LISTENING TO WHAT WE SAY...
ER... AS I SAID... I THINK THE WHOLE UKRAINE THING WAS STARTED BY THE C.I.A... ER... PUTIN IS A GOOD BLOKE ...RUSSIA SHOULD HAVE WON THE EUROVISION...

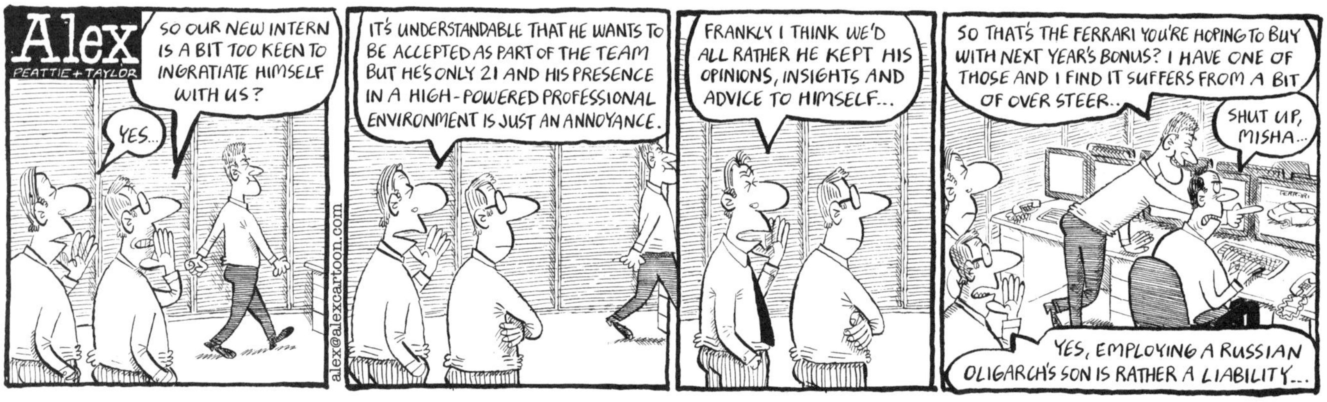
Alex
PEATTIE + TAYLOR
SO OUR NEW INTERN IS A BIT TOO KEEN TO INGRATIATE HIMSELF WITH US?
YES...
alex@alexcartoon.com
IT'S UNDERSTANDABLE THAT HE WANTS TO BE ACCEPTED AS PART OF THE TEAM BUT HE'S ONLY 21 AND HIS PRESENCE IN A HIGH-POWERED PROFESSIONAL ENVIRONMENT IS JUST AN ANNOYANCE.
FRANKLY I THINK WE'D ALL RATHER HE KEPT HIS OPINIONS, INSIGHTS AND ADVICE TO HIMSELF...
SO THAT'S THE FERRARI YOU'RE HOPING TO BUY WITH NEXT YEAR'S BONUS? I HAVE ONE OF THOSE AND I FIND IT SUFFERS FROM A BIT OF OVER STEER...
SHUT UP, MISHA...
YES, EMPLOYING A RUSSIAN OLIGARCH'S SON IS RATHER A LIABILITY...

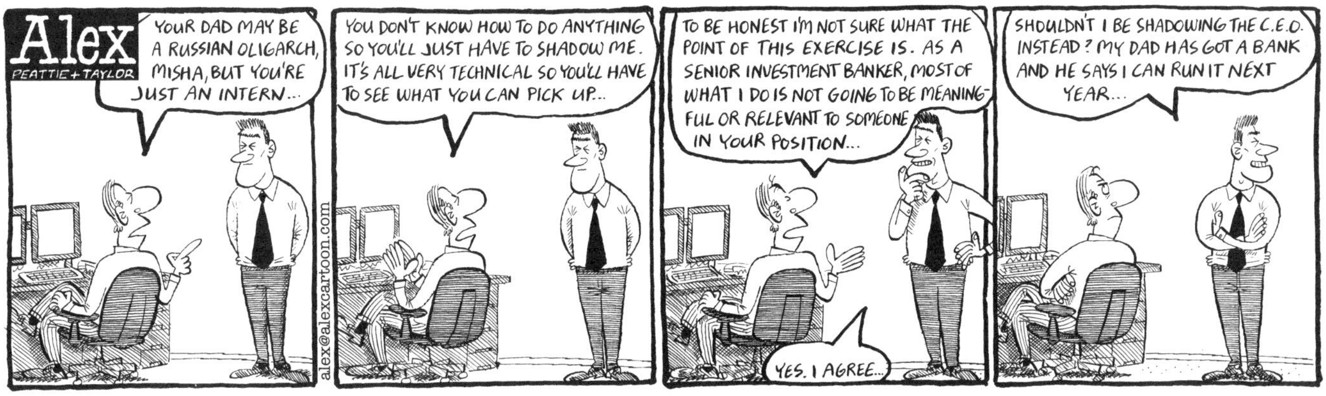
Alex
PEATTIE + TAYLOR
YOUR DAD MAY BE A RUSSIAN OLIGARCH, MISHA, BUT YOU'RE JUST AN INTERN...
alex@alexcartoon.com
YOU DON'T KNOW HOW TO DO ANYTHING SO YOU'LL JUST HAVE TO SHADOW ME. IT'S ALL VERY TECHNICAL SO YOU'LL HAVE TO SEE WHAT YOU CAN PICK UP...
TO BE HONEST I'M NOT SURE WHAT THE POINT OF THIS EXERCISE IS. AS A SENIOR INVESTMENT BANKER, MOST OF WHAT I DO IS NOT GOING TO BE MEANINGFUL OR RELEVANT TO SOMEONE IN YOUR POSITION...
YES. I AGREE...
SHOULDN'T I BE SHADOWING THE C.E.O. INSTEAD? MY DAD HAS GOT A BANK AND HE SAYS I CAN RUN IT NEXT YEAR...

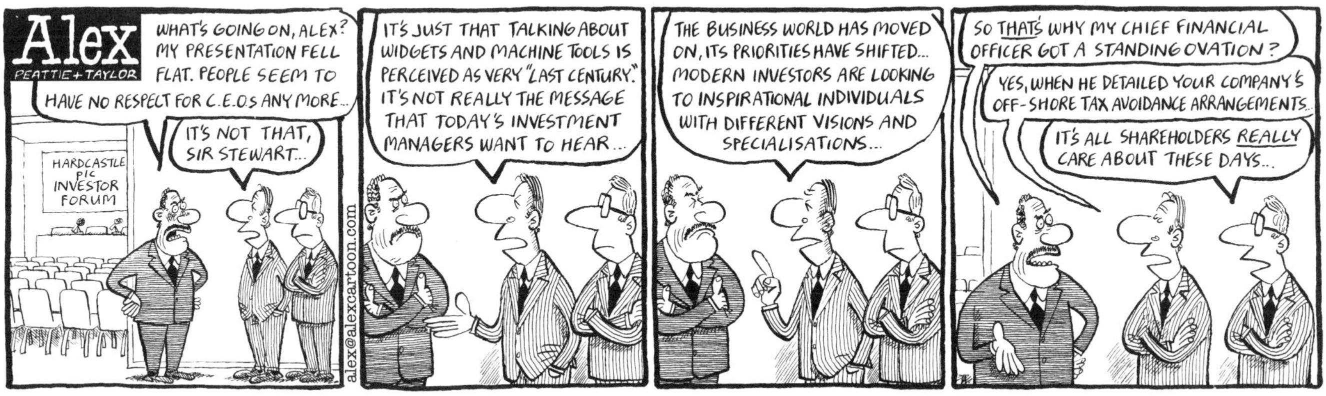
Alex
PEATTIE + TAYLOR
WHAT'S GOING ON, ALEX? MY PRESENTATION FELL FLAT. PEOPLE SEEM TO HAVE NO RESPECT FOR C.E.O.S ANY MORE...
IT'S NOT THAT, SIR STEWART...
HARDCASTLE PLC INVESTOR FORUM
alex@alexcartoon.com
IT'S JUST THAT TALKING ABOUT WIDGETS AND MACHINE TOOLS IS PERCEIVED AS VERY "LAST CENTURY." IT'S NOT REALLY THE MESSAGE THAT TODAY'S INVESTMENT MANAGERS WANT TO HEAR...
THE BUSINESS WORLD HAS MOVED ON, ITS PRIORITIES HAVE SHIFTED... MODERN INVESTORS ARE LOOKING TO INSPIRATIONAL INDIVIDUALS WITH DIFFERENT VISIONS AND SPECIALISATIONS...
SO THAT'S WHY MY CHIEF FINANCIAL OFFICER GOT A STANDING OVATION?
YES, WHEN HE DETAILED YOUR COMPANY'S OFF-SHORE TAX AVOIDANCE ARRANGEMENTS.
IT'S ALL SHAREHOLDERS REALLY CARE ABOUT THESE DAYS...

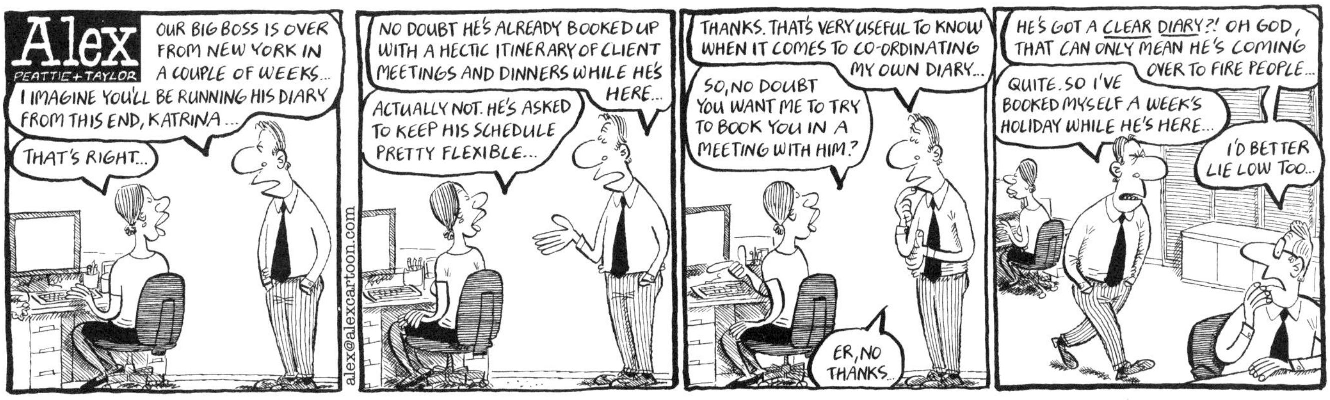
Alex
PEATTIE + TAYLOR
OUR BIG BOSS IS OVER FROM NEW YORK IN A COUPLE OF WEEKS... I IMAGINE YOU'LL BE RUNNING HIS DIARY FROM THIS END, KATRINA...
THAT'S RIGHT...
alex@alexcartoon.com
NO DOUBT HE'S ALREADY BOOKED UP WITH A HECTIC ITINERARY OF CLIENT MEETINGS AND DINNERS WHILE HE'S HERE...
ACTUALLY NOT. HE'S ASKED TO KEEP HIS SCHEDULE PRETTY FLEXIBLE...
THANKS. THAT'S VERY USEFUL TO KNOW WHEN IT COMES TO CO-ORDINATING MY OWN DIARY...
SO, NO DOUBT YOU WANT ME TO TRY TO BOOK YOU IN A MEETING WITH HIM?
ER, NO THANKS...
HE'S GOT A CLEAR DIARY?! OH GOD, THAT CAN ONLY MEAN HE'S COMING OVER TO FIRE PEOPLE...
QUITE. SO I'VE BOOKED MYSELF A WEEK'S HOLIDAY WHILE HE'S HERE...
I'D BETTER LIE LOW TOO...

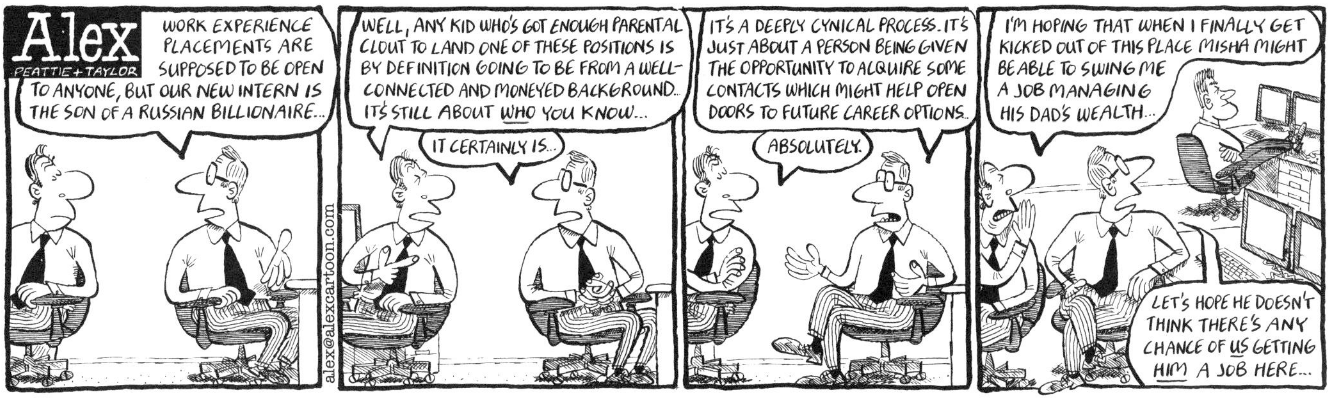
Alex
PEATTIE + TAYLOR
WORK EXPERIENCE PLACEMENTS ARE SUPPOSED TO BE OPEN TO ANYONE, BUT OUR NEW INTERN IS THE SON OF A RUSSIAN BILLIONAIRE...
alex@alexcartoon.com
WELL, ANY KID WHO'S GOT ENOUGH PARENTAL CLOUT TO LAND ONE OF THESE POSITIONS IS BY DEFINITION GOING TO BE FROM A WELL-CONNECTED AND MONEYED BACKGROUND... IT'S STILL ABOUT WHO YOU KNOW...
IT CERTAINLY IS...
IT'S A DEEPLY CYNICAL PROCESS. IT'S JUST ABOUT A PERSON BEING GIVEN THE OPPORTUNITY TO ACQUIRE SOME CONTACTS WHICH MIGHT HELP OPEN DOORS TO FUTURE CAREER OPTIONS...
ABSOLUTELY.
I'M HOPING THAT WHEN I FINALLY GET KICKED OUT OF THIS PLACE MISHA MIGHT BE ABLE TO SWING ME A JOB MANAGING HIS DAD'S WEALTH...
LET'S HOPE HE DOESN'T THINK THERE'S ANY CHANCE OF US GETTING HIM A JOB HERE...

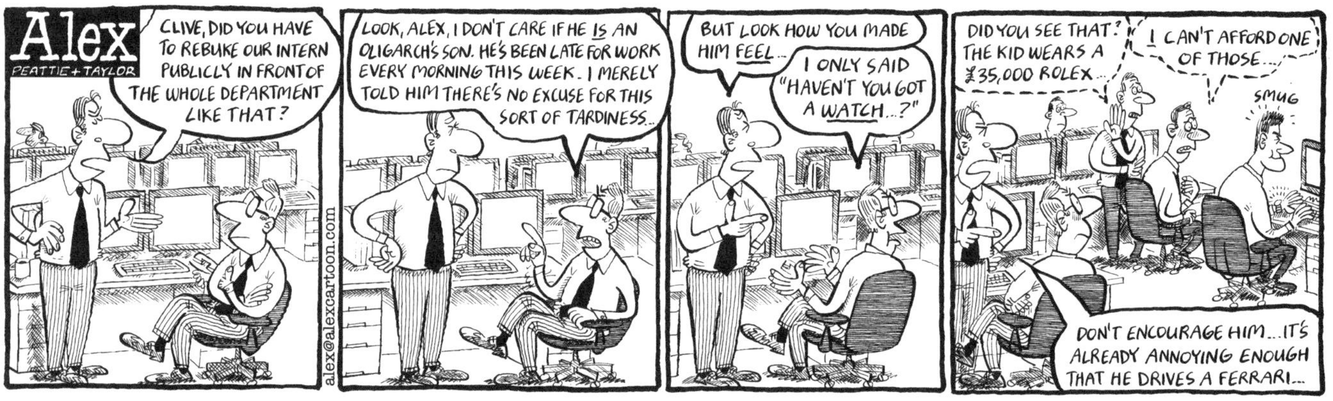
Alex
PEATTIE+TAYLOR
CLIVE, DID YOU HAVE TO REBUKE OUR INTERN PUBLICLY IN FRONT OF THE WHOLE DEPARTMENT LIKE THAT?
LOOK, ALEX, I DON'T CARE IF HE IS AN OLIGARCH'S SON. HE'S BEEN LATE FOR WORK EVERY MORNING THIS WEEK. I MERELY TOLD HIM THERE'S NO EXCUSE FOR THIS SORT OF TARDINESS...
alex@alexcartoon.com
BUT LOOK HOW YOU MADE HIM FEEL...
I ONLY SAID "HAVEN'T YOU GOT A WATCH...?"
DID YOU SEE THAT? THE KID WEARS A ¥35,000 ROLEX...
I CAN'T AFFORD ONE OF THOSE...
SMUG
DON'T ENCOURAGE HIM...IT'S ALREADY ANNOYING ENOUGH THAT HE DRIVES A FERRARI...

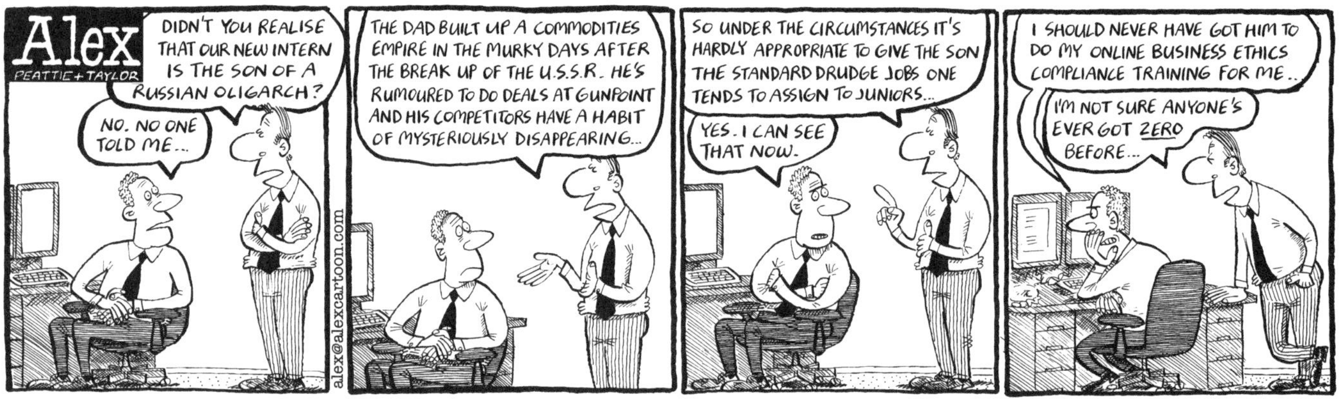
Alex
PEATTIE+TAYLOR
DIDN'T YOU REALISE THAT OUR NEW INTERN IS THE SON OF A RUSSIAN OLIGARCH?
NO. NO ONE TOLD ME...
THE DAD BUILT UP A COMMODITIES EMPIRE IN THE MURKY DAYS AFTER THE BREAK UP OF THE U.S.S.R. HE'S RUMOURED TO DO DEALS AT GUNPOINT AND HIS COMPETITORS HAVE A HABIT OF MYSTERIOUSLY DISAPPEARING...
alex@alexcartoon.com
SO UNDER THE CIRCUMSTANCES IT'S HARDLY APPROPRIATE TO GIVE THE SON THE STANDARD DRUDGE JOBS ONE TENDS TO ASSIGN TO JUNIORS...
YES. I CAN SEE THAT NOW.
I SHOULD NEVER HAVE GOT HIM TO DO MY ONLINE BUSINESS ETHICS COMPLIANCE TRAINING FOR ME...
I'M NOT SURE ANYONE'S EVER GOT ZERO BEFORE...

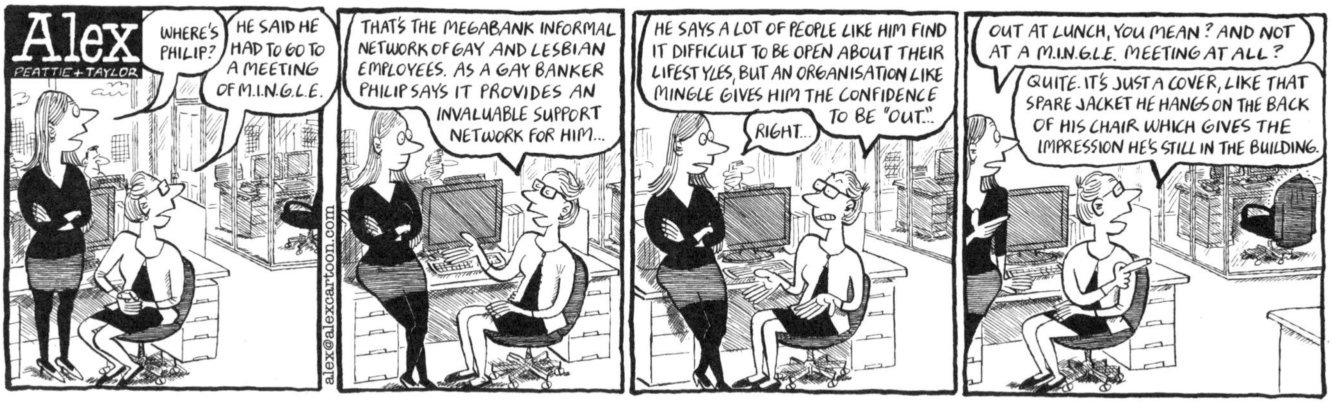
Alex
PEATTIE+TAYLOR
WHERE'S PHILIP?
HE SAID HE HAD TO GO TO A MEETING OF M.I.N.G.L.E.
THAT'S THE MEGABANK INFORMAL NETWORK OF GAY AND LESBIAN EMPLOYEES. AS A GAY BANKER PHILIP SAYS IT PROVIDES AN INVALUABLE SUPPORT NETWORK FOR HIM...
alex@alexcartoon.com
HE SAYS A LOT OF PEOPLE LIKE HIM FIND IT DIFFICULT TO BE OPEN ABOUT THEIR LIFESTYLES, BUT AN ORGANISATION LIKE MINGLE GIVES HIM THE CONFIDENCE TO BE "OUT."
RIGHT...
OUT AT LUNCH, YOU MEAN? AND NOT AT A M.I.N.G.L.E. MEETING AT ALL?
QUITE. IT'S JUST A COVER, LIKE THAT SPARE JACKET HE HANGS ON THE BACK OF HIS CHAIR WHICH GIVES THE IMPRESSION HE'S STILL IN THE BUILDING.

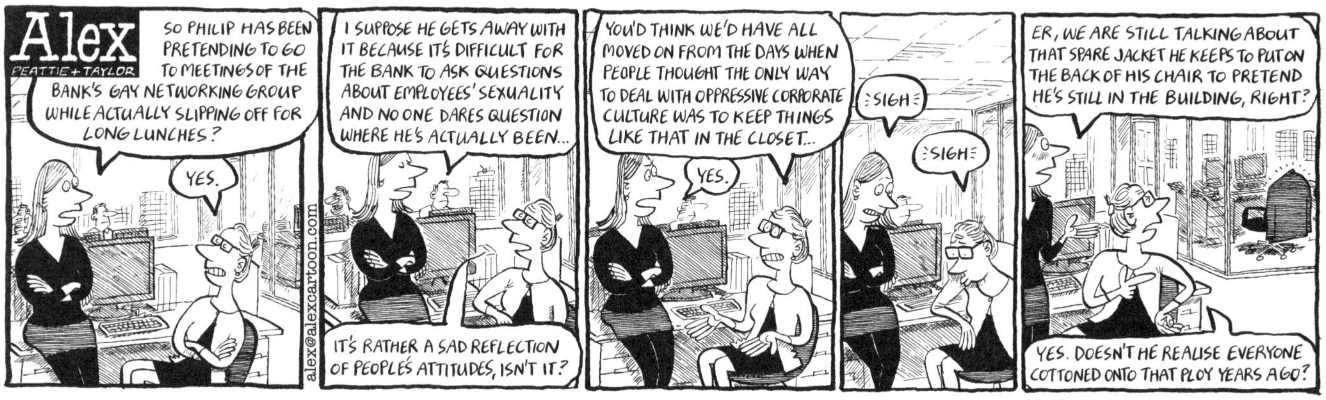
Alex
PEATTIE+TAYLOR
SO PHILIP HAS BEEN PRETENDING TO GO TO MEETINGS OF THE BANK'S GAY NETWORKING GROUP WHILE ACTUALLY SLIPPING OFF FOR LONG LUNCHES?
YES.
I SUPPOSE HE GETS AWAY WITH IT BECAUSE IT'S DIFFICULT FOR THE BANK TO ASK QUESTIONS ABOUT EMPLOYEES' SEXUALITY AND NO ONE DARES QUESTION WHERE HE'S ACTUALLY BEEN...
IT'S RATHER A SAD REFLECTION OF PEOPLE'S ATTITUDES, ISN'T IT?
alex@alexcartoon.com
YOU'D THINK WE'D HAVE ALL MOVED ON FROM THE DAYS WHEN PEOPLE THOUGHT THE ONLY WAY TO DEAL WITH OPPRESSIVE CORPORATE CULTURE WAS TO KEEP THINGS LIKE THAT IN THE CLOSET...
YES.
SIGH
SIGH
ER, WE ARE STILL TALKING ABOUT THAT SPARE JACKET HE KEEPS TO PUT ON THE BACK OF HIS CHAIR TO PRETEND HE'S STILL IN THE BUILDING, RIGHT?
YES. DOESN'T HE REALISE EVERYONE COTTONED ONTO THAT PLOY YEARS AGO?

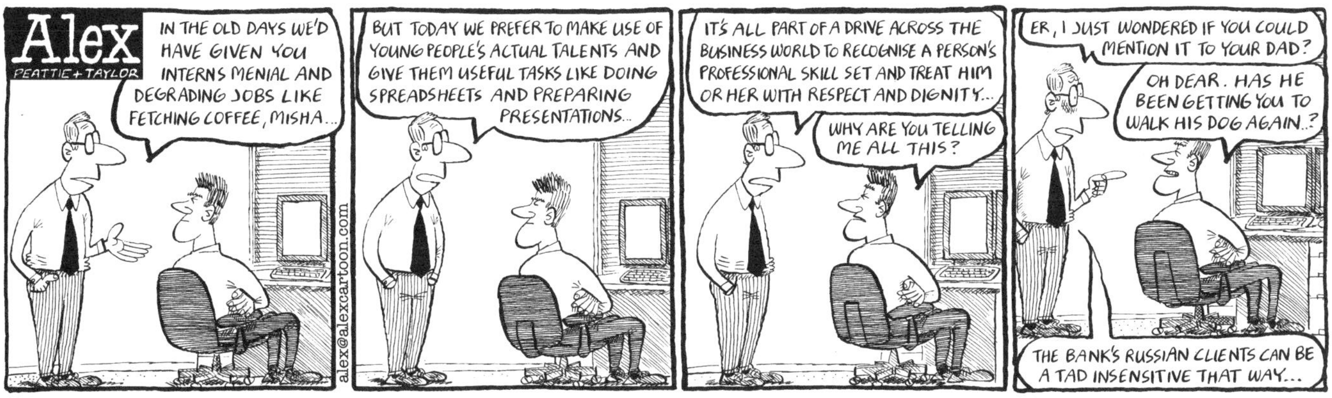
Alex
PEATTIE+TAYLOR
IN THE OLD DAYS WE'D HAVE GIVEN YOU INTERNS MENIAL AND DEGRADING JOBS LIKE FETCHING COFFEE, MISHA...
alex@alexcartoon.com
BUT TODAY WE PREFER TO MAKE USE OF YOUNG PEOPLE'S ACTUAL TALENTS AND GIVE THEM USEFUL TASKS LIKE DOING SPREADSHEETS AND PREPARING PRESENTATIONS...
IT'S ALL PART OF A DRIVE ACROSS THE BUSINESS WORLD TO RECOGNISE A PERSON'S PROFESSIONAL SKILL SET AND TREAT HIM OR HER WITH RESPECT AND DIGNITY...
WHY ARE YOU TELLING ME ALL THIS?
ER, I JUST WONDERED IF YOU COULD MENTION IT TO YOUR DAD?
OH DEAR. HAS HE BEEN GETTING YOU TO WALK HIS DOG AGAIN..?
THE BANK'S RUSSIAN CLIENTS CAN BE A TAD INSENSITIVE THAT WAY...

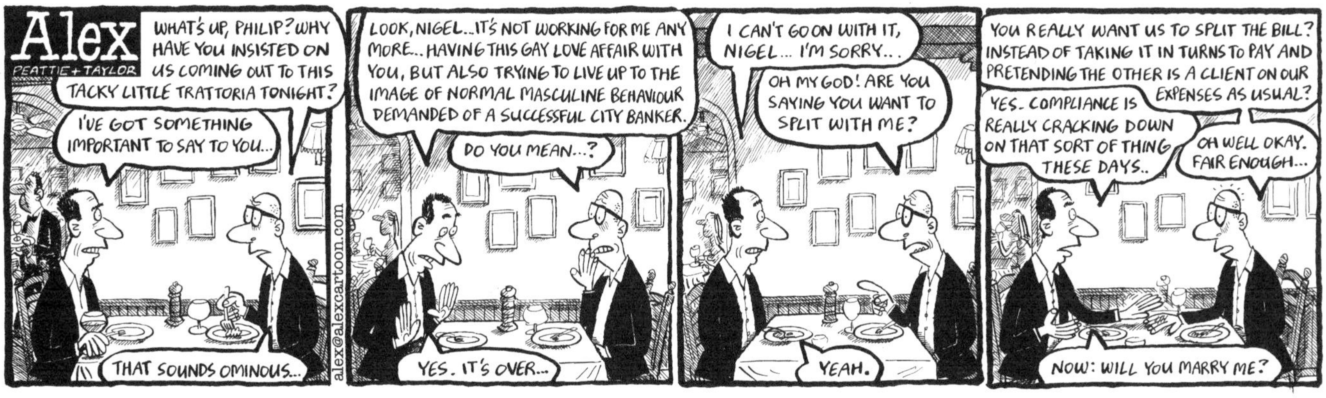
Alex
PEATTIE+TAYLOR
WHAT'S UP, PHILIP? WHY HAVE YOU INSISTED ON US COMING OUT TO THIS TACKY LITTLE TRATTORIA TONIGHT?
I'VE GOT SOMETHING IMPORTANT TO SAY TO YOU...
THAT SOUNDS OMINOUS...
alex@alexcartoon.com
LOOK, NIGEL...IT'S NOT WORKING FOR ME ANY MORE... HAVING THIS GAY LOVE AFFAIR WITH YOU, BUT ALSO TRYING TO LIVE UP TO THE IMAGE OF NORMAL MASCULINE BEHAVIOUR DEMANDED OF A SUCCESSFUL CITY BANKER.
DO YOU MEAN...?
YES. IT'S OVER...
I CAN'T GO ON WITH IT, NIGEL... I'M SORRY...
OH MY GOD! ARE YOU SAYING YOU WANT TO SPLIT WITH ME?
YEAH.
YOU REALLY WANT US TO SPLIT THE BILL? INSTEAD OF TAKING IT IN TURNS TO PAY AND PRETENDING THE OTHER IS A CLIENT ON OUR EXPENSES AS USUAL?
YES. COMPLIANCE IS REALLY CRACKING DOWN ON THAT SORT OF THING THESE DAYS..
OH WELL OKAY. FAIR ENOUGH...
NOW: WILL YOU MARRY ME?

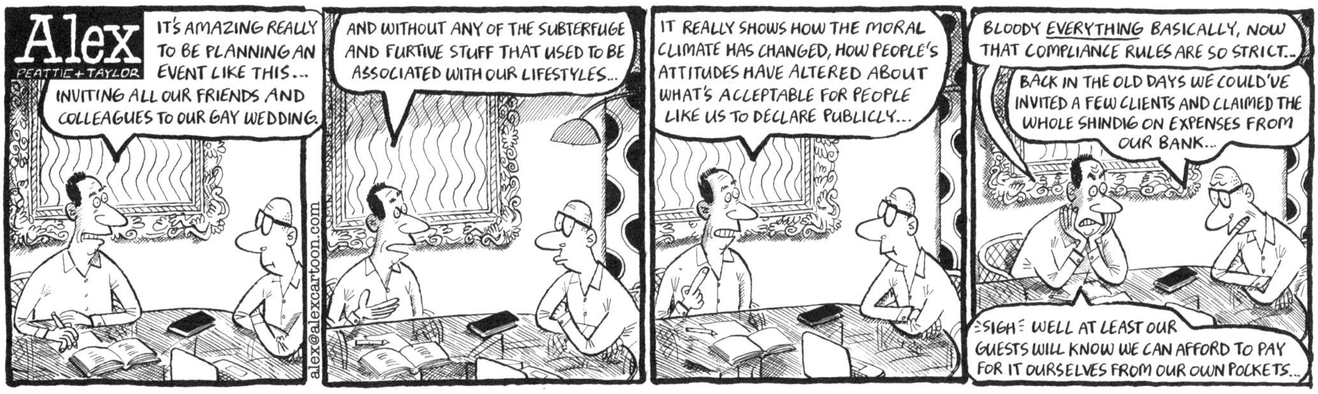
Alex
PEATTIE+TAYLOR
IT'S AMAZING REALLY TO BE PLANNING AN EVENT LIKE THIS... INVITING ALL OUR FRIENDS AND COLLEAGUES TO OUR GAY WEDDING.
alex@alexcartoon.com
AND WITHOUT ANY OF THE SUBTERFUGE AND FURTIVE STUFF THAT USED TO BE ASSOCIATED WITH OUR LIFESTYLES...
IT REALLY SHOWS HOW THE MORAL CLIMATE HAS CHANGED, HOW PEOPLE'S ATTITUDES HAVE ALTERED ABOUT WHAT'S ACCEPTABLE FOR PEOPLE LIKE US TO DECLARE PUBLICLY...
BLOODY EVERYTHING BASICALLY, NOW THAT COMPLIANCE RULES ARE SO STRICT..
BACK IN THE OLD DAYS WE COULD'VE INVITED A FEW CLIENTS AND CLAIMED THE WHOLE SHINDIG ON EXPENSES FROM OUR BANK...
SIGH WELL AT LEAST OUR GUESTS WILL KNOW WE CAN AFFORD TO PAY FOR IT OURSELVES FROM OUR OWN POCKETS...

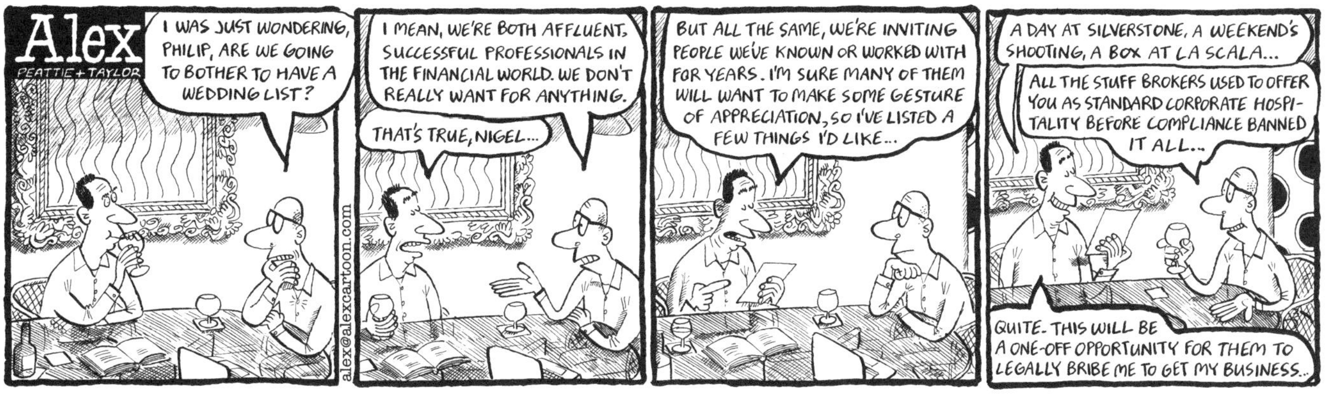
Alex
PEATTIE+TAYLOR
I WAS JUST WONDERING, PHILIP, ARE WE GOING TO BOTHER TO HAVE A WEDDING LIST?
alex@alexcartoon.com
I MEAN, WE'RE BOTH AFFLUENT, SUCCESSFUL PROFESSIONALS IN THE FINANCIAL WORLD. WE DON'T REALLY WANT FOR ANYTHING.
THAT'S TRUE, NIGEL...
BUT ALL THE SAME, WE'RE INVITING PEOPLE WE'VE KNOWN OR WORKED WITH FOR YEARS. I'M SURE MANY OF THEM WILL WANT TO MAKE SOME GESTURE OF APPRECIATION, SO I'VE LISTED A FEW THINGS I'D LIKE...
A DAY AT SILVERSTONE, A WEEKEND'S SHOOTING, A BOX AT LA SCALA...
ALL THE STUFF BROKERS USED TO OFFER YOU AS STANDARD CORPORATE HOSPITALITY BEFORE COMPLIANCE BANNED IT ALL...
QUITE. THIS WILL BE A ONE-OFF OPPORTUNITY FOR THEM TO LEGALLY BRIBE ME TO GET MY BUSINESS...

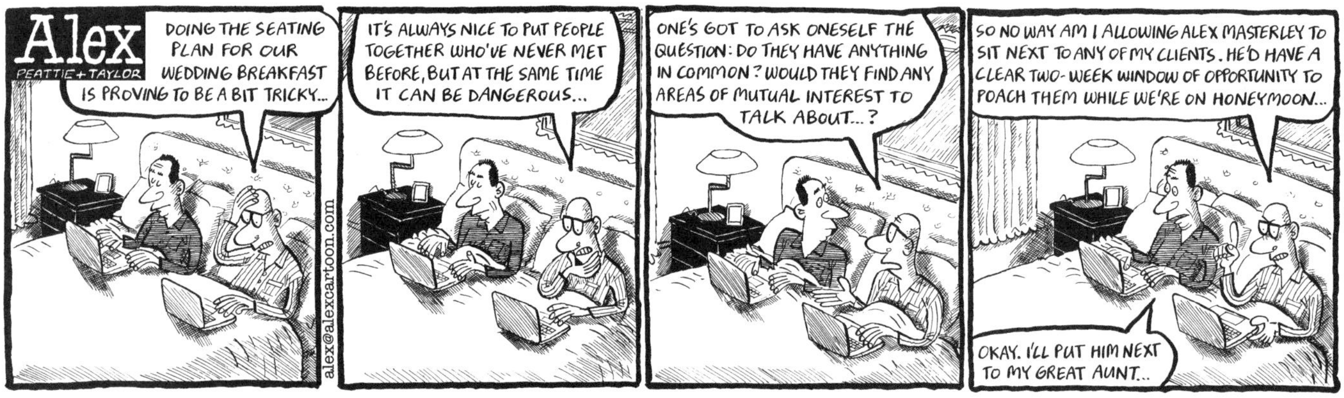
Alex
PEATTIE + TAYLOR
DOING THE SEATING PLAN FOR OUR WEDDING BREAKFAST IS PROVING TO BE A BIT TRICKY...
IT'S ALWAYS NICE TO PUT PEOPLE TOGETHER WHO'VE NEVER MET BEFORE, BUT AT THE SAME TIME IT CAN BE DANGEROUS...
alex@alexcartoon.com
ONE'S GOT TO ASK ONESELF THE QUESTION: DO THEY HAVE ANYTHING IN COMMON? WOULD THEY FIND ANY AREAS OF MUTUAL INTEREST TO TALK ABOUT...?
SO NO WAY AM I ALLOWING ALEX MASTERLEY TO SIT NEXT TO ANY OF MY CLIENTS. HE'D HAVE A CLEAR TWO-WEEK WINDOW OF OPPORTUNITY TO POACH THEM WHILE WE'RE ON HONEYMOON...
OKAY. I'LL PUT HIM NEXT TO MY GREAT AUNT...

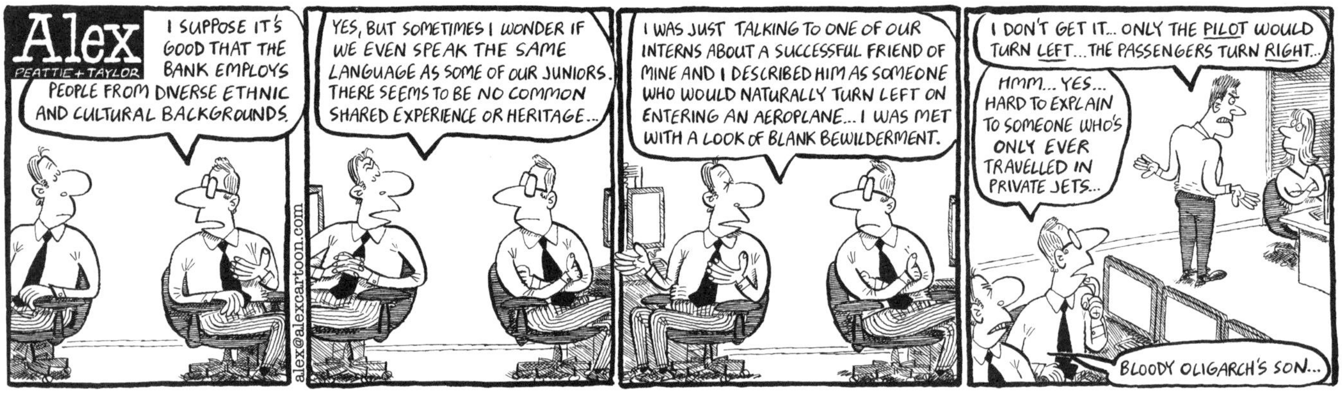
Alex
PEATTIE + TAYLOR
I SUPPOSE IT'S GOOD THAT THE BANK EMPLOYS PEOPLE FROM DIVERSE ETHNIC AND CULTURAL BACKGROUNDS.
alex@alexcartoon.com
YES, BUT SOMETIMES I WONDER IF WE EVEN SPEAK THE SAME LANGUAGE AS SOME OF OUR JUNIORS. THERE SEEMS TO BE NO COMMON SHARED EXPERIENCE OR HERITAGE...
I WAS JUST TALKING TO ONE OF OUR INTERNS ABOUT A SUCCESSFUL FRIEND OF MINE AND I DESCRIBED HIM AS SOMEONE WHO WOULD NATURALLY TURN LEFT ON ENTERING AN AEROPLANE... I WAS MET WITH A LOOK OF BLANK BEWILDERMENT.
I DON'T GET IT... ONLY THE PILOT WOULD TURN LEFT... THE PASSENGERS TURN RIGHT...
HMM... YES... HARD TO EXPLAIN TO SOMEONE WHO'S ONLY EVER TRAVELLED IN PRIVATE JETS...
BLOODY OLIGARCH'S SON...

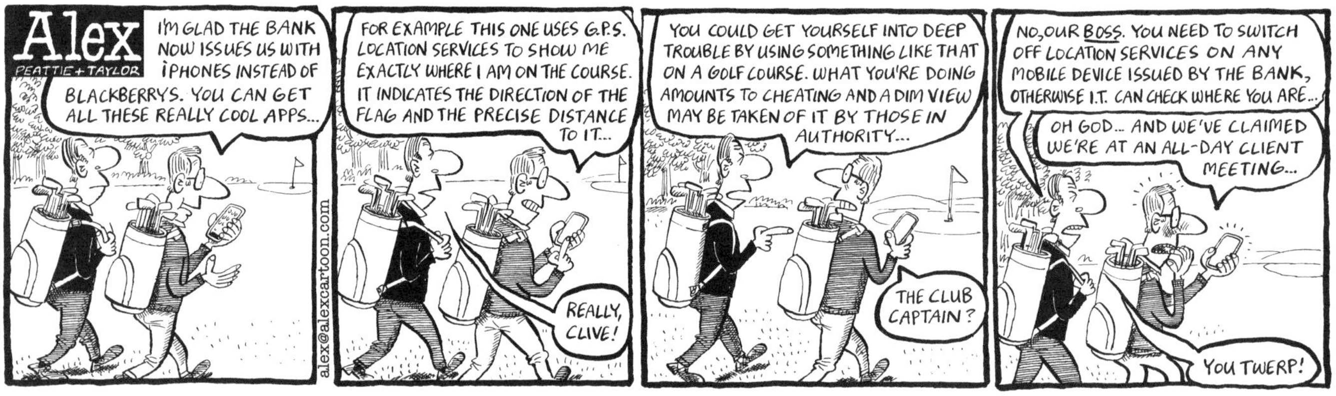
Alex
PEATTIE + TAYLOR
I'M GLAD THE BANK NOW ISSUES US WITH iPHONES INSTEAD OF BLACKBERRYS. YOU CAN GET ALL THESE REALLY COOL APPS...
FOR EXAMPLE THIS ONE USES G.P.S. LOCATION SERVICES TO SHOW ME EXACTLY WHERE I AM ON THE COURSE. IT INDICATES THE DIRECTION OF THE FLAG AND THE PRECISE DISTANCE TO IT...
alex@alexcartoon.com
REALLY, CLIVE!
YOU COULD GET YOURSELF INTO DEEP TROUBLE BY USING SOMETHING LIKE THAT ON A GOLF COURSE. WHAT YOU'RE DOING AMOUNTS TO CHEATING AND A DIM VIEW MAY BE TAKEN OF IT BY THOSE IN AUTHORITY...
THE CLUB CAPTAIN?
NO, OUR BOSS. YOU NEED TO SWITCH OFF LOCATION SERVICES ON ANY MOBILE DEVICE ISSUED BY THE BANK, OTHERWISE I.T. CAN CHECK WHERE YOU ARE...
OH GOD... AND WE'VE CLAIMED WE'RE AT AN ALL-DAY CLIENT MEETING...
YOU TWERP!

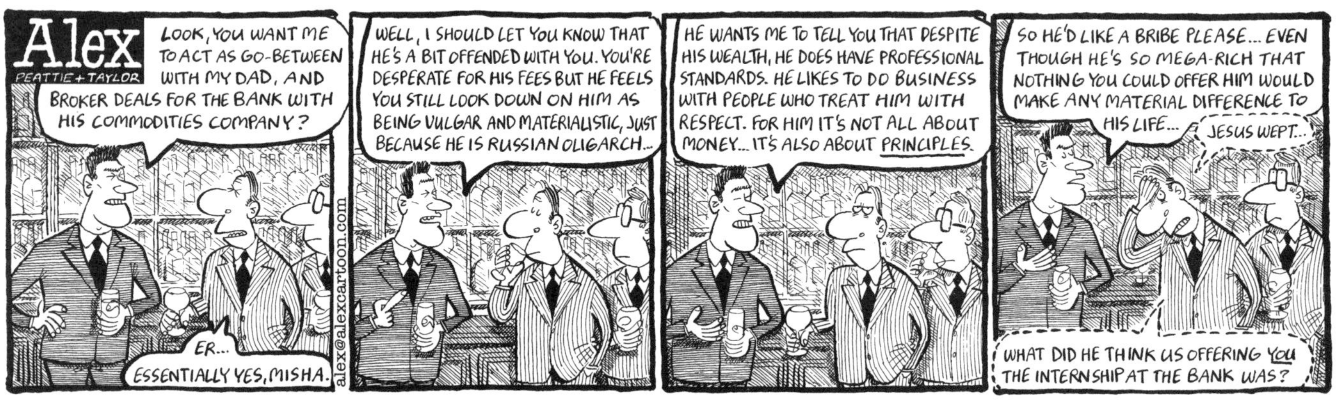
Alex
PEATTIE + TAYLOR
LOOK, YOU WANT ME TO ACT AS GO-BETWEEN WITH MY DAD, AND BROKER DEALS FOR THE BANK WITH HIS COMMODITIES COMPANY?
ER... ESSENTIALLY YES, MISHA.
alex@alexcartoon.com
WELL, I SHOULD LET YOU KNOW THAT HE'S A BIT OFFENDED WITH YOU. YOU'RE DESPERATE FOR HIS FEES BUT HE FEELS YOU STILL LOOK DOWN ON HIM AS BEING VULGAR AND MATERIALISTIC, JUST BECAUSE HE IS RUSSIAN OLIGARCH...
HE WANTS ME TO TELL YOU THAT DESPITE HIS WEALTH, HE DOES HAVE PROFESSIONAL STANDARDS. HE LIKES TO DO BUSINESS WITH PEOPLE WHO TREAT HIM WITH RESPECT. FOR HIM IT'S NOT ALL ABOUT MONEY... IT'S ALSO ABOUT PRINCIPLES.
SO HE'D LIKE A BRIBE PLEASE... EVEN THOUGH HE'S SO MEGA-RICH THAT NOTHING YOU COULD OFFER HIM WOULD MAKE ANY MATERIAL DIFFERENCE TO HIS LIFE...
JESUS WEPT...
WHAT DID HE THINK US OFFERING YOU THE INTERNSHIP AT THE BANK WAS?

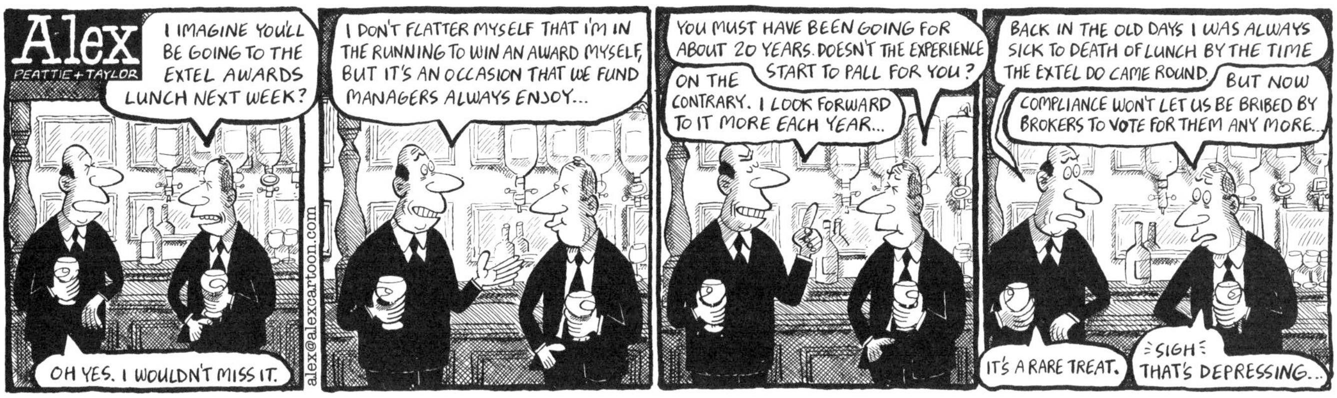
Alex
PEATTIE + TAYLOR
I IMAGINE YOU'LL BE GOING TO THE EXTEL AWARDS LUNCH NEXT WEEK?
OH YES. I WOULDN'T MISS IT.
alex@alexcartoon.com
I DON'T FLATTER MYSELF THAT I'M IN THE RUNNING TO WIN AN AWARD MYSELF, BUT IT'S AN OCCASION THAT WE FUND MANAGERS ALWAYS ENJOY...
YOU MUST HAVE BEEN GOING FOR ABOUT 20 YEARS. DOESN'T THE EXPERIENCE START TO PALL FOR YOU?
ON THE CONTRARY. I LOOK FORWARD TO IT MORE EACH YEAR...
BACK IN THE OLD DAYS I WAS ALWAYS SICK TO DEATH OF LUNCH BY THE TIME THE EXTEL DO CAME ROUND.
BUT NOW COMPLIANCE WON'T LET US BE BRIBED BY BROKERS TO VOTE FOR THEM ANY MORE...
IT'S A RARE TREAT.
SIGH
THAT'S DEPRESSING...

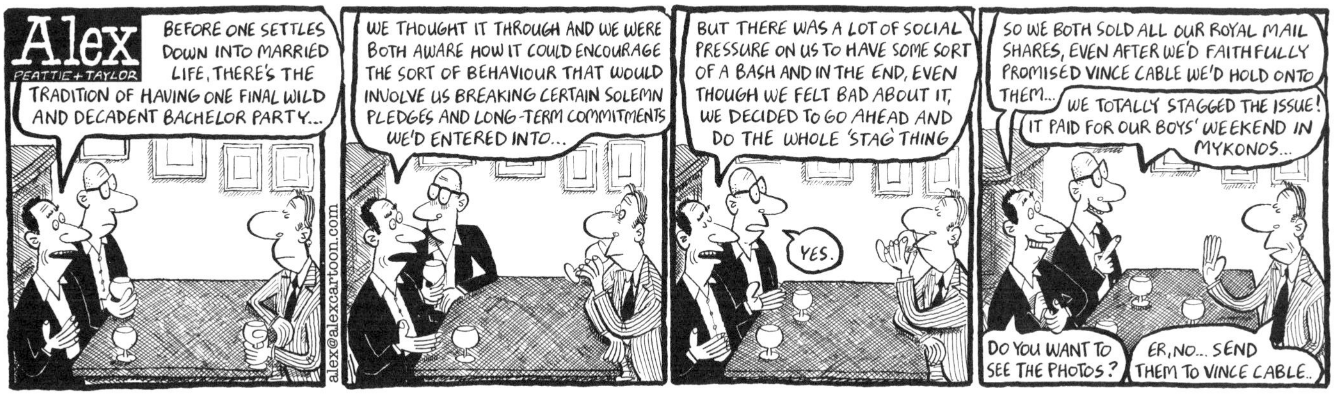
Alex
PEATTIE + TAYLOR
BEFORE ONE SETTLES DOWN INTO MARRIED LIFE, THERE'S THE TRADITION OF HAVING ONE FINAL WILD AND DECADENT BACHELOR PARTY...
alex@alexcartoon.com
WE THOUGHT IT THROUGH AND WE WERE BOTH AWARE HOW IT COULD ENCOURAGE THE SORT OF BEHAVIOUR THAT WOULD INVOLVE US BREAKING CERTAIN SOLEMN PLEDGES AND LONG-TERM COMMITMENTS WE'D ENTERED INTO...
BUT THERE WAS A LOT OF SOCIAL PRESSURE ON US TO HAVE SOME SORT OF A BASH AND IN THE END, EVEN THOUGH WE FELT BAD ABOUT IT, WE DECIDED TO GO AHEAD AND DO THE WHOLE 'STAG' THING
YES.
SO WE BOTH SOLD ALL OUR ROYAL MAIL SHARES, EVEN AFTER WE'D FAITHFULLY PROMISED VINCE CABLE WE'D HOLD ONTO THEM...
WE TOTALLY STAGGED THE ISSUE! IT PAID FOR OUR BOYS' WEEKEND IN MYKONOS...
DO YOU WANT TO SEE THE PHOTOS?
ER, NO... SEND THEM TO VINCE CABLE...

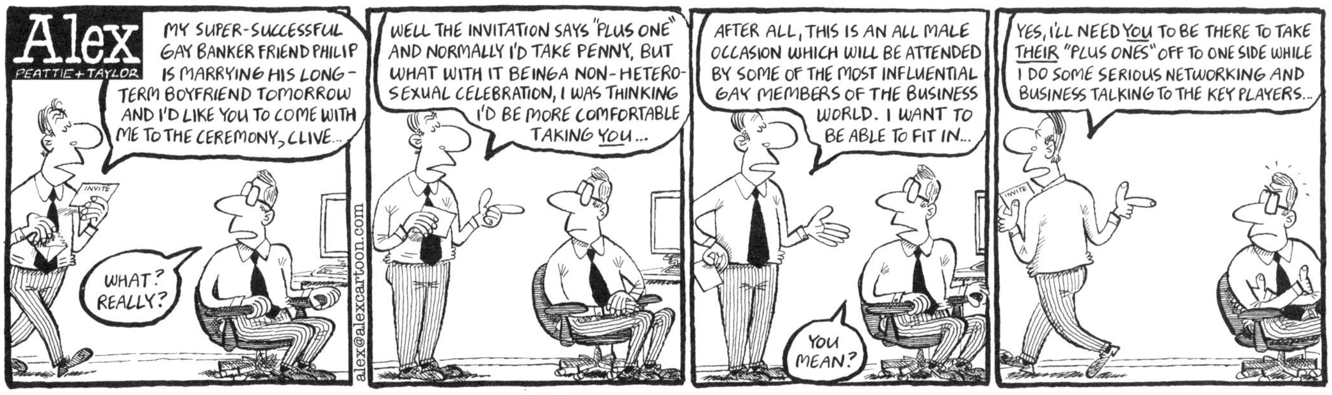
Alex
PEATTIE + TAYLOR
MY SUPER-SUCCESSFUL GAY BANKER FRIEND PHILIP IS MARRYING HIS LONG-TERM BOYFRIEND TOMORROW AND I'D LIKE YOU TO COME WITH ME TO THE CEREMONY, CLIVE...
INVITE
WHAT? REALLY?
alex@alexcartoon.com
WELL THE INVITATION SAYS "PLUS ONE" AND NORMALLY I'D TAKE PENNY, BUT WHAT WITH IT BEING A NON-HETERO-SEXUAL CELEBRATION, I WAS THINKING I'D BE MORE COMFORTABLE TAKING YOU...
AFTER ALL, THIS IS AN ALL MALE OCCASION WHICH WILL BE ATTENDED BY SOME OF THE MOST INFLUENTIAL GAY MEMBERS OF THE BUSINESS WORLD. I WANT TO BE ABLE TO FIT IN...
YOU MEAN?
YES, I'LL NEED YOU TO BE THERE TO TAKE THEIR "PLUS ONES" OFF TO ONE SIDE WHILE I DO SOME SERIOUS NETWORKING AND BUSINESS TALKING TO THE KEY PLAYERS...
INVITE

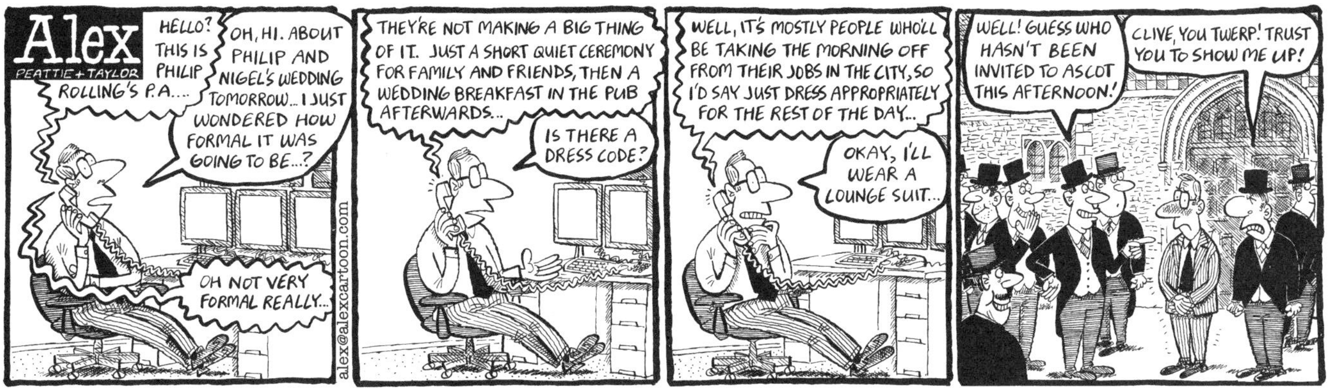
Alex
PEATTIE + TAYLOR
HELLO? THIS IS PHILIP ROLLING'S P.A....
OH, HI. ABOUT PHILIP AND NIGEL'S WEDDING TOMORROW... I JUST WONDERED HOW FORMAL IT WAS GOING TO BE...?
OH NOT VERY FORMAL REALLY...
alex@alexcartoon.com
THEY'RE NOT MAKING A BIG THING OF IT. JUST A SHORT QUIET CEREMONY FOR FAMILY AND FRIENDS, THEN A WEDDING BREAKFAST IN THE PUB AFTERWARDS...
IS THERE A DRESS CODE?
WELL, IT'S MOSTLY PEOPLE WHO'LL BE TAKING THE MORNING OFF FROM THEIR JOBS IN THE CITY, SO I'D SAY JUST DRESS APPROPRIATELY FOR THE REST OF THE DAY...
OKAY, I'LL WEAR A LOUNGE SUIT...
WELL! GUESS WHO HASN'T BEEN INVITED TO ASCOT THIS AFTERNOON!
CLIVE, YOU TWERP! TRUST YOU TO SHOW ME UP!

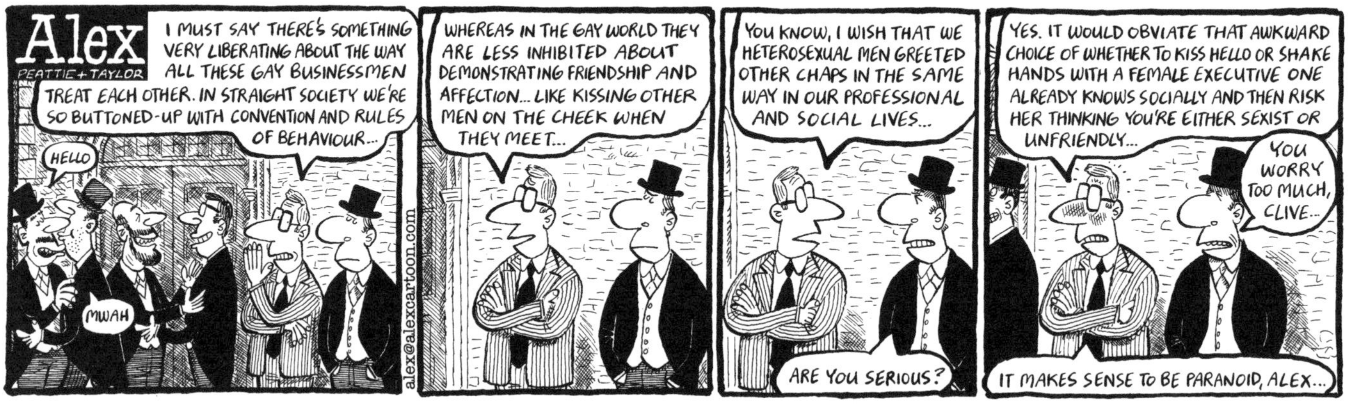
Alex
PEATTIE + TAYLOR
I MUST SAY THERE'S SOMETHING VERY LIBERATING ABOUT THE WAY ALL THESE GAY BUSINESSMEN TREAT EACH OTHER. IN STRAIGHT SOCIETY WE'RE SO BUTTONED-UP WITH CONVENTION AND RULES OF BEHAVIOUR...
HELLO
MWAH
alex@alexcartoon.com
WHEREAS IN THE GAY WORLD THEY ARE LESS INHIBITED ABOUT DEMONSTRATING FRIENDSHIP AND AFFECTION... LIKE KISSING OTHER MEN ON THE CHEEK WHEN THEY MEET...
YOU KNOW, I WISH THAT WE HETEROSEXUAL MEN GREETED OTHER CHAPS IN THE SAME WAY IN OUR PROFESSIONAL AND SOCIAL LIVES...
ARE YOU SERIOUS?
YES. IT WOULD OBVIATE THAT AWKWARD CHOICE OF WHETHER TO KISS HELLO OR SHAKE HANDS WITH A FEMALE EXECUTIVE ONE ALREADY KNOWS SOCIALLY AND THEN RISK HER THINKING YOU'RE EITHER SEXIST OR UNFRIENDLY...
YOU WORRY TOO MUCH, CLIVE...
IT MAKES SENSE TO BE PARANOID, ALEX...

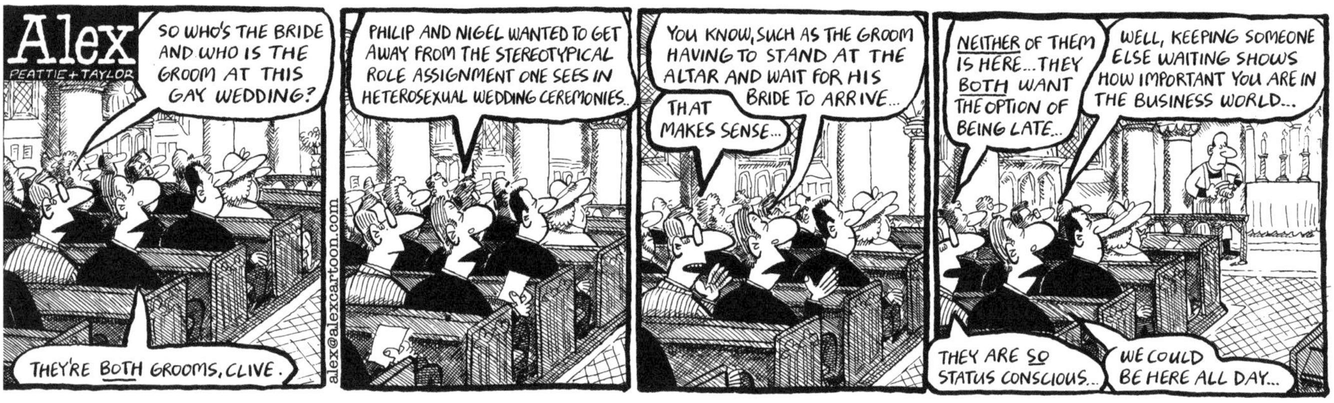
Alex
PEATTIE + TAYLOR
SO WHO'S THE BRIDE AND WHO IS THE GROOM AT THIS GAY WEDDING?
THEY'RE BOTH GROOMS, CLIVE.
alex@alexcartoon.com
PHILIP AND NIGEL WANTED TO GET AWAY FROM THE STEREOTYPICAL ROLE ASSIGNMENT ONE SEES IN HETEROSEXUAL WEDDING CEREMONIES...
YOU KNOW, SUCH AS THE GROOM HAVING TO STAND AT THE ALTAR AND WAIT FOR HIS BRIDE TO ARRIVE...
THAT MAKES SENSE...
NEITHER OF THEM IS HERE...THEY BOTH WANT THE OPTION OF BEING LATE...
WELL, KEEPING SOMEONE ELSE WAITING SHOWS HOW IMPORTANT YOU ARE IN THE BUSINESS WORLD...
THEY ARE SO STATUS CONSCIOUS...
WE COULD BE HERE ALL DAY...

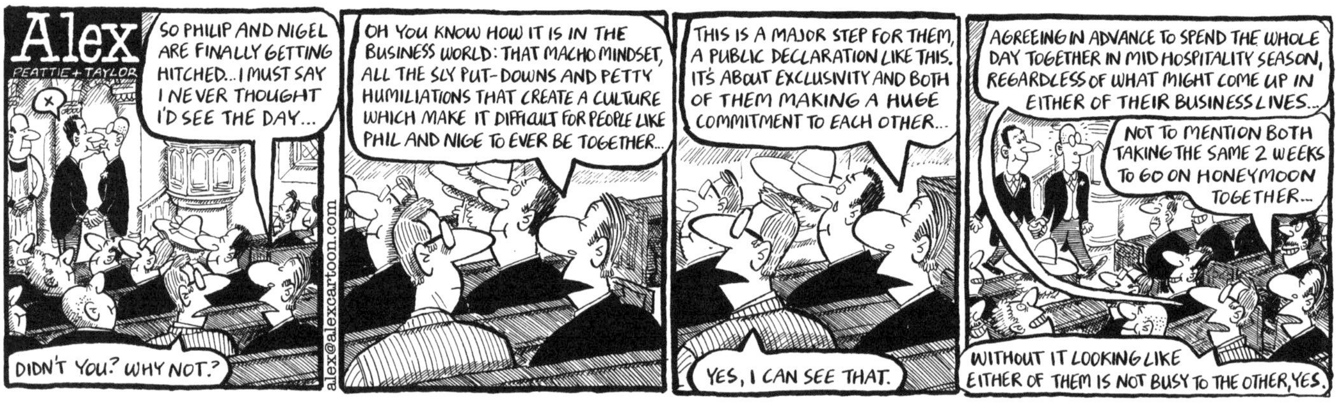
Alex
PEATTIE + TAYLOR
SO PHILIP AND NIGEL ARE FINALLY GETTING HITCHED... I MUST SAY I NEVER THOUGHT I'D SEE THE DAY...
DIDN'T YOU? WHY NOT?
alex@alexcartoon.com
OH YOU KNOW HOW IT IS IN THE BUSINESS WORLD: THAT MACHO MINDSET, ALL THE SLY PUT-DOWNS AND PETTY HUMILIATIONS THAT CREATE A CULTURE WHICH MAKE IT DIFFICULT FOR PEOPLE LIKE PHIL AND NIGE TO EVER BE TOGETHER...
THIS IS A MAJOR STEP FOR THEM, A PUBLIC DECLARATION LIKE THIS. IT'S ABOUT EXCLUSIVITY AND BOTH OF THEM MAKING A HUGE COMMITMENT TO EACH OTHER...
YES, I CAN SEE THAT.
AGREEING IN ADVANCE TO SPEND THE WHOLE DAY TOGETHER IN MID HOSPITALITY SEASON, REGARDLESS OF WHAT MIGHT COME UP IN EITHER OF THEIR BUSINESS LIVES...
NOT TO MENTION BOTH TAKING THE SAME 2 WEEKS TO GO ON HONEYMOON TOGETHER...
WITHOUT IT LOOKING LIKE EITHER OF THEM IS NOT BUSY TO THE OTHER, YES.

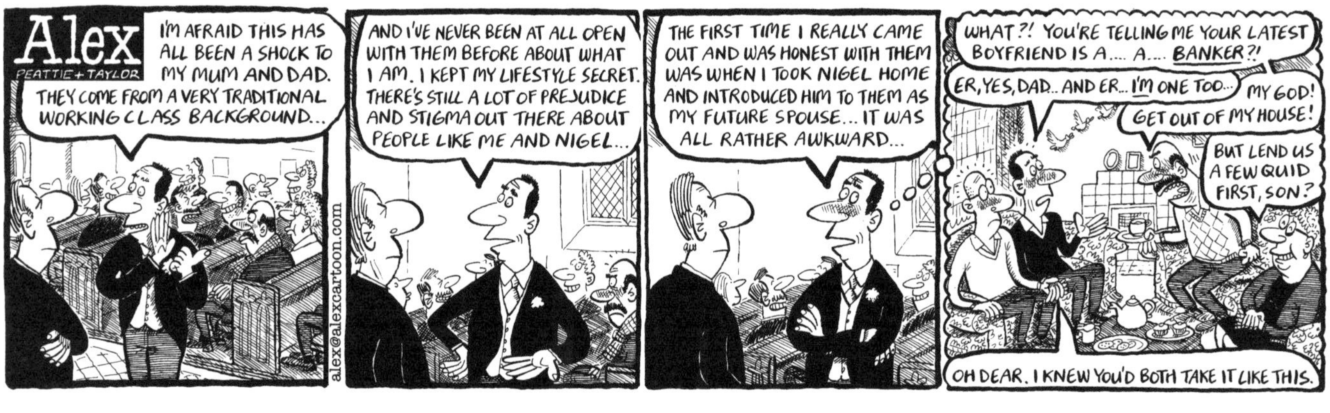
Alex
PEATTIE + TAYLOR
I'M AFRAID THIS HAS ALL BEEN A SHOCK TO MY MUM AND DAD. THEY COME FROM A VERY TRADITIONAL WORKING CLASS BACKGROUND...
alex@alexcartoon.com
AND I'VE NEVER BEEN AT ALL OPEN WITH THEM BEFORE ABOUT WHAT I AM. I KEPT MY LIFESTYLE SECRET. THERE'S STILL A LOT OF PREJUDICE AND STIGMA OUT THERE ABOUT PEOPLE LIKE ME AND NIGEL...
THE FIRST TIME I REALLY CAME OUT AND WAS HONEST WITH THEM WAS WHEN I TOOK NIGEL HOME AND INTRODUCED HIM TO THEM AS MY FUTURE SPOUSE... IT WAS ALL RATHER AWKWARD...
WHAT?! YOU'RE TELLING ME YOUR LATEST BOYFRIEND IS A.... A.... BANKER?!
ER, YES, DAD... AND ER... I'M ONE TOO...
MY GOD! GET OUT OF MY HOUSE!
BUT LEND US A FEW QUID FIRST, SON?
OH DEAR. I KNEW YOU'D BOTH TAKE IT LIKE THIS.

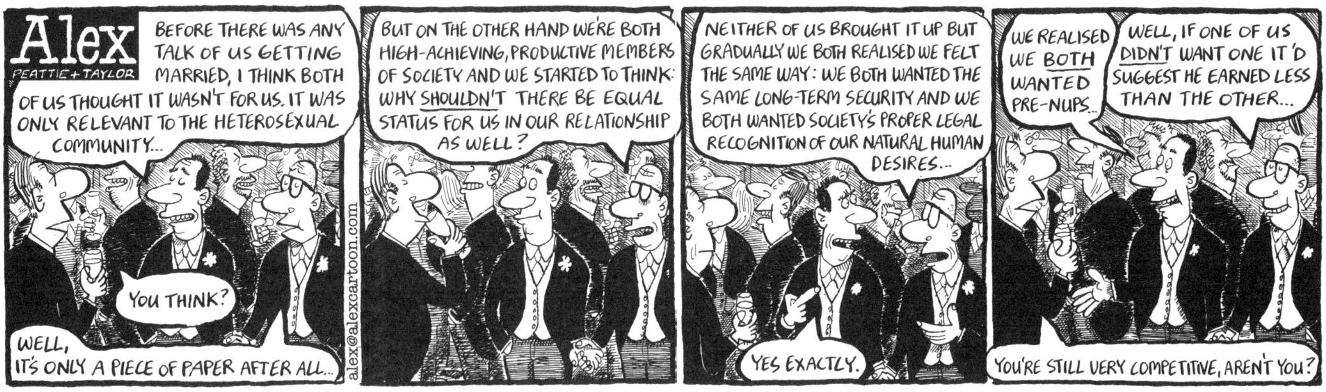
Alex
PEATTIE+TAYLOR
BEFORE THERE WAS ANY TALK OF US GETTING MARRIED, I THINK BOTH OF US THOUGHT IT WASN'T FOR US. IT WAS ONLY RELEVANT TO THE HETEROSEXUAL COMMUNITY...
YOU THINK?
WELL, IT'S ONLY A PIECE OF PAPER AFTER ALL...
alex@alexcartoon.com
BUT ON THE OTHER HAND WE'RE BOTH HIGH-ACHIEVING, PRODUCTIVE MEMBERS OF SOCIETY AND WE STARTED TO THINK: WHY SHOULDN'T THERE BE EQUAL STATUS FOR US IN OUR RELATIONSHIP AS WELL?
NEITHER OF US BROUGHT IT UP BUT GRADUALLY WE BOTH REALISED WE FELT THE SAME WAY: WE BOTH WANTED THE SAME LONG-TERM SECURITY AND WE BOTH WANTED SOCIETY'S PROPER LEGAL RECOGNITION OF OUR NATURAL HUMAN DESIRES...
YES EXACTLY.
WE REALISED WE BOTH WANTED PRE-NUPS...
WELL, IF ONE OF US DIDN'T WANT ONE IT'D SUGGEST HE EARNED LESS THAN THE OTHER...
YOU'RE STILL VERY COMPETITIVE, AREN'T YOU?

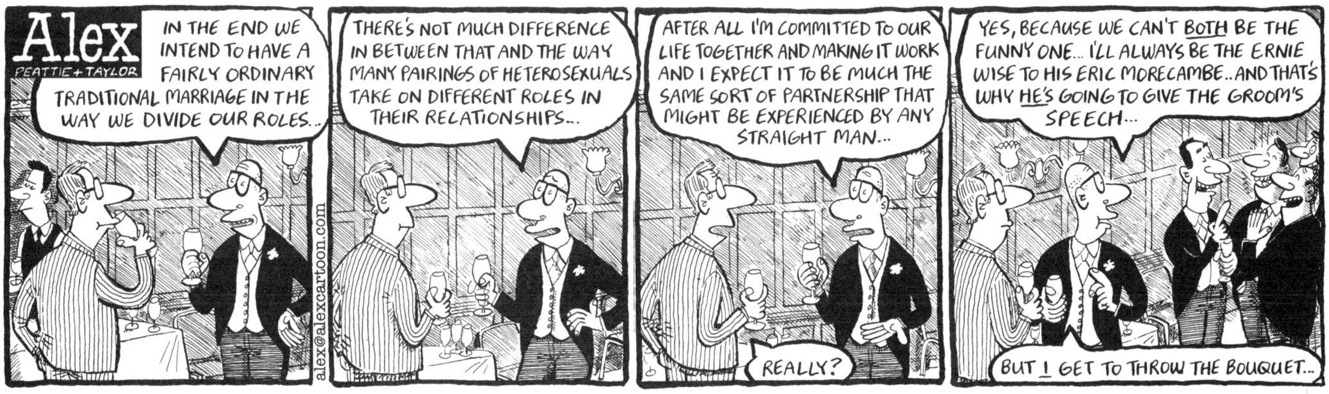
Alex
PEATTIE+TAYLOR
IN THE END WE INTEND TO HAVE A FAIRLY ORDINARY TRADITIONAL MARRIAGE IN THE WAY WE DIVIDE OUR ROLES...
alex@alexcartoon.com
THERE'S NOT MUCH DIFFERENCE IN BETWEEN THAT AND THE WAY MANY PAIRINGS OF HETEROSEXUALS TAKE ON DIFFERENT ROLES IN THEIR RELATIONSHIPS...
AFTER ALL I'M COMMITTED TO OUR LIFE TOGETHER AND MAKING IT WORK AND I EXPECT IT TO BE MUCH THE SAME SORT OF PARTNERSHIP THAT MIGHT BE EXPERIENCED BY ANY STRAIGHT MAN...
REALLY?
YES, BECAUSE WE CAN'T BOTH BE THE FUNNY ONE... I'LL ALWAYS BE THE ERNIE WISE TO HIS ERIC MORECAMBE... AND THAT'S WHY HE'S GOING TO GIVE THE GROOM'S SPEECH...
BUT I GET TO THROW THE BOUQUET...

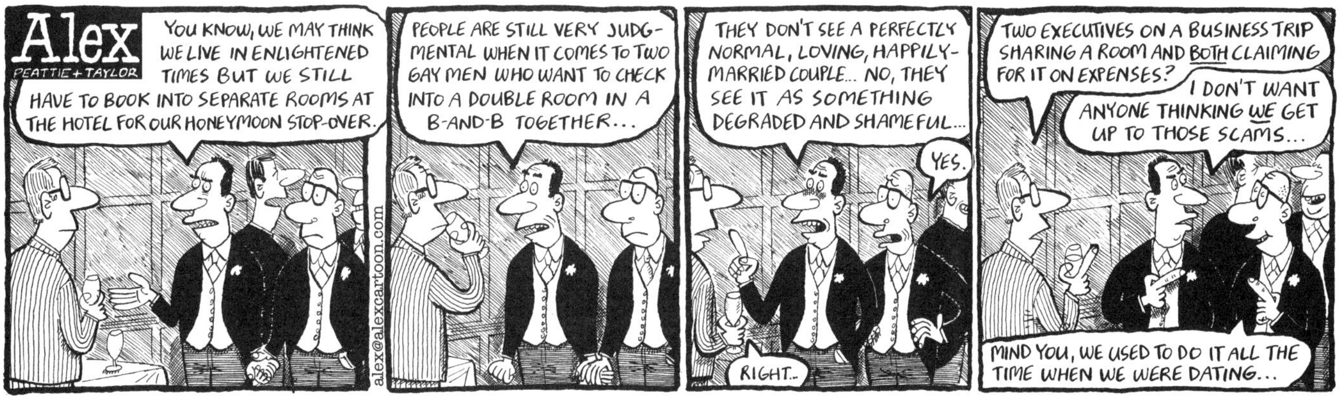
Alex
PEATTIE+TAYLOR
YOU KNOW, WE MAY THINK WE LIVE IN ENLIGHTENED TIMES BUT WE STILL HAVE TO BOOK INTO SEPARATE ROOMS AT THE HOTEL FOR OUR HONEYMOON STOP-OVER.
alex@alexcartoon.com
PEOPLE ARE STILL VERY JUDGMENTAL WHEN IT COMES TO TWO GAY MEN WHO WANT TO CHECK INTO A DOUBLE ROOM IN A B-AND-B TOGETHER...
THEY DON'T SEE A PERFECTLY NORMAL, LOVING, HAPPILY-MARRIED COUPLE... NO, THEY SEE IT AS SOMETHING DEGRADED AND SHAMEFUL...
YES.
RIGHT...
TWO EXECUTIVES ON A BUSINESS TRIP SHARING A ROOM AND BOTH CLAIMING FOR IT ON EXPENSES?
I DON'T WANT ANYONE THINKING WE GET UP TO THOSE SCAMS...
MIND YOU, WE USED TO DO IT ALL THE TIME WHEN WE WERE DATING...

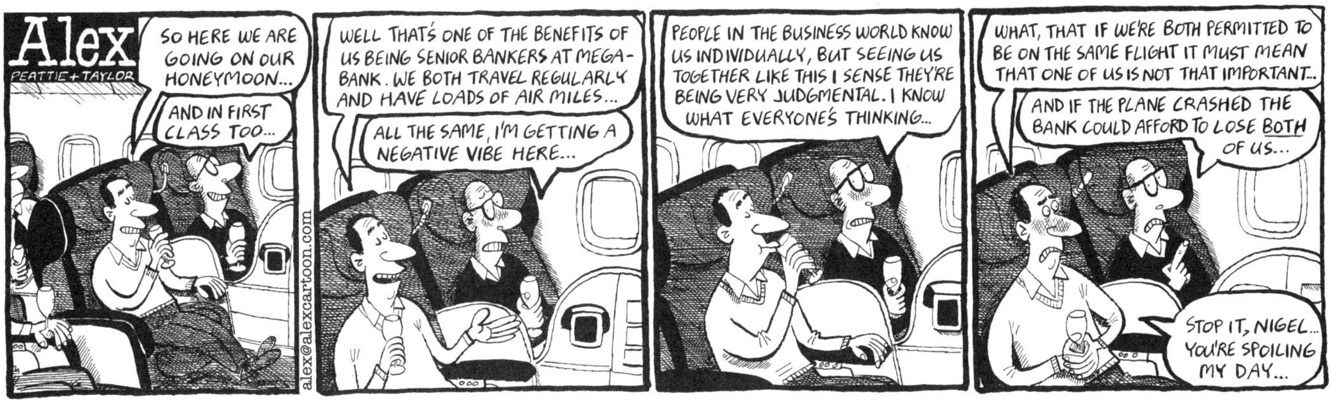
Alex
PEATTIE+TAYLOR
SO HERE WE ARE GOING ON OUR HONEYMOON...
AND IN FIRST CLASS TOO...
alex@alexcartoon.com
WELL THAT'S ONE OF THE BENEFITS OF US BEING SENIOR BANKERS AT MEGA-BANK. WE BOTH TRAVEL REGULARLY AND HAVE LOADS OF AIR MILES...
ALL THE SAME, I'M GETTING A NEGATIVE VIBE HERE...
PEOPLE IN THE BUSINESS WORLD KNOW US INDIVIDUALLY, BUT SEEING US TOGETHER LIKE THIS I SENSE THEY'RE BEING VERY JUDGMENTAL. I KNOW WHAT EVERYONE'S THINKING...
WHAT, THAT IF WE'RE BOTH PERMITTED TO BE ON THE SAME FLIGHT IT MUST MEAN THAT ONE OF US IS NOT THAT IMPORTANT...
AND IF THE PLANE CRASHED THE BANK COULD AFFORD TO LOSE BOTH OF US...
STOP IT, NIGEL... YOU'RE SPOILING MY DAY...

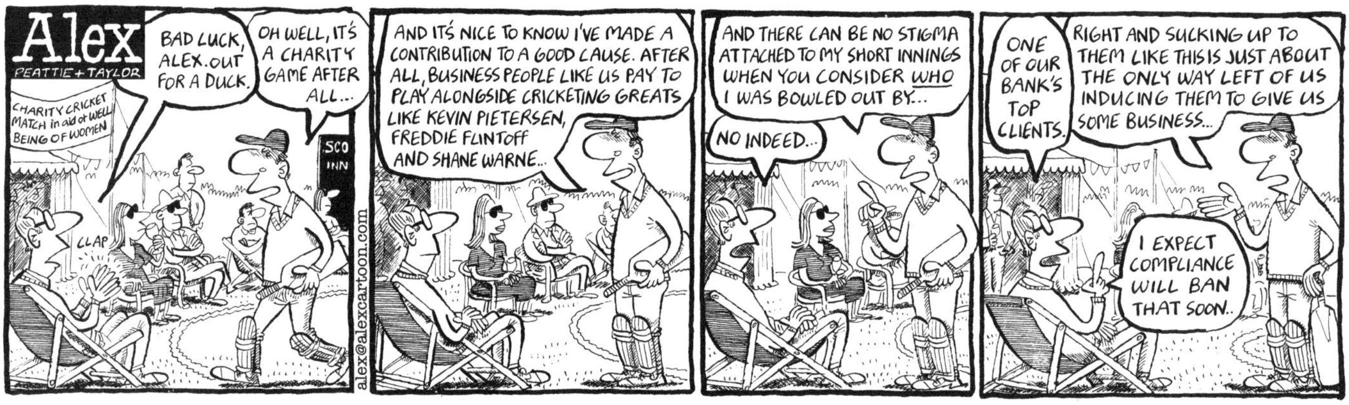
Alex
PEATTIE + TAYLOR
BAD LUCK, ALEX..OUT FOR A DUCK.
OH WELL, IT'S A CHARITY GAME AFTER ALL...
CHARITY CRICKET MATCH in aid of WELL BEING OF WOMEN
CLAP
AND IT'S NICE TO KNOW I'VE MADE A CONTRIBUTION TO A GOOD CAUSE. AFTER ALL, BUSINESS PEOPLE LIKE US PAY TO PLAY ALONGSIDE CRICKETING GREATS LIKE KEVIN PIETERSEN, FREDDIE FLINTOFF AND SHANE WARNE...
alex@alexcartoon.com
AND THERE CAN BE NO STIGMA ATTACHED TO MY SHORT INNINGS WHEN YOU CONSIDER WHO I WAS BOWLED OUT BY...
NO INDEED...
ONE OF OUR BANK'S TOP CLIENTS.
RIGHT AND SUCKING UP TO THEM LIKE THIS IS JUST ABOUT THE ONLY WAY LEFT OF US INDUCING THEM TO GIVE US SOME BUSINESS...
I EXPECT COMPLIANCE WILL BAN THAT SOON..

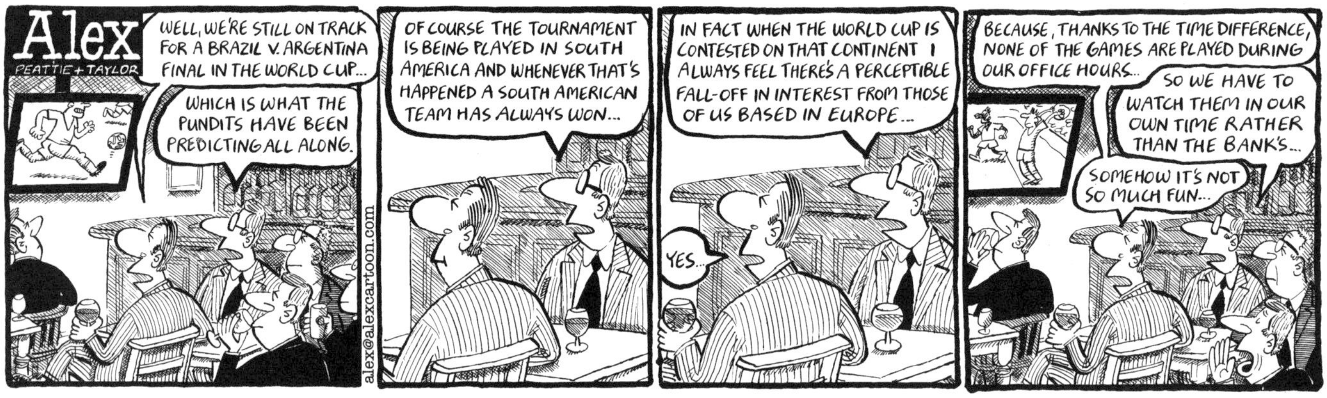
Alex
PEATTIE + TAYLOR
WELL, WE'RE STILL ON TRACK FOR A BRAZIL V. ARGENTINA FINAL IN THE WORLD CUP...
WHICH IS WHAT THE PUNDITS HAVE BEEN PREDICTING ALL ALONG.
alex@alexcartoon.com
OF COURSE THE TOURNAMENT IS BEING PLAYED IN SOUTH AMERICA AND WHENEVER THAT'S HAPPENED A SOUTH AMERICAN TEAM HAS ALWAYS WON...
IN FACT WHEN THE WORLD CUP IS CONTESTED ON THAT CONTINENT I ALWAYS FEEL THERE'S A PERCEPTIBLE FALL-OFF IN INTEREST FROM THOSE OF US BASED IN EUROPE...
YES...
BECAUSE, THANKS TO THE TIME DIFFERENCE, NONE OF THE GAMES ARE PLAYED DURING OUR OFFICE HOURS...
SO WE HAVE TO WATCH THEM IN OUR OWN TIME RATHER THAN THE BANK'S...
SOMEHOW IT'S NOT SO MUCH FUN...

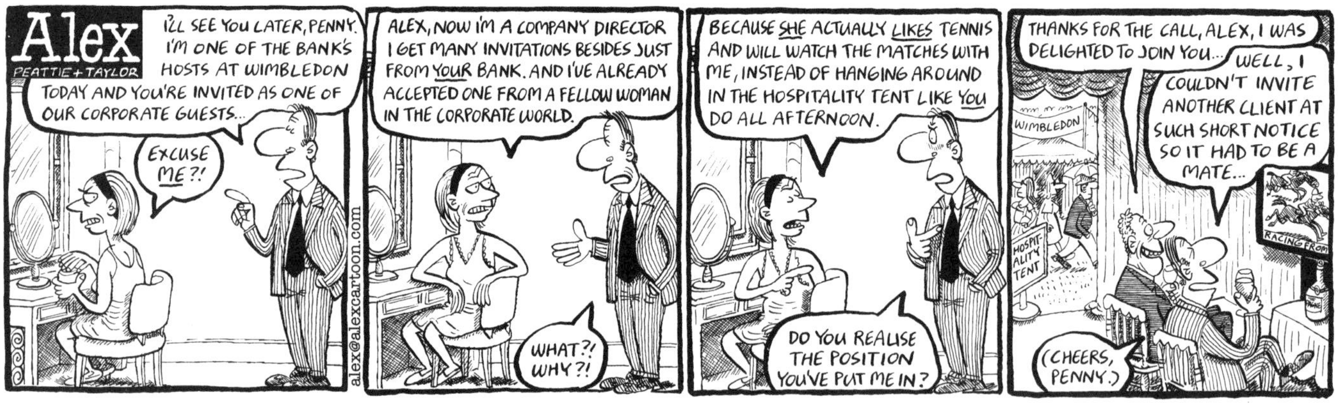
Alex
PEATTIE + TAYLOR
I'LL SEE YOU LATER, PENNY. I'M ONE OF THE BANK'S HOSTS AT WIMBLEDON TODAY AND YOU'RE INVITED AS ONE OF OUR CORPORATE GUESTS...
EXCUSE ME?!
alex@alexcartoon.com
ALEX, NOW I'M A COMPANY DIRECTOR I GET MANY INVITATIONS BESIDES JUST FROM YOUR BANK. AND I'VE ALREADY ACCEPTED ONE FROM A FELLOW WOMAN IN THE CORPORATE WORLD.
WHAT?! WHY?!
BECAUSE SHE ACTUALLY LIKES TENNIS AND WILL WATCH THE MATCHES WITH ME, INSTEAD OF HANGING AROUND IN THE HOSPITALITY TENT LIKE YOU DO ALL AFTERNOON.
DO YOU REALISE THE POSITION YOU'VE PUT ME IN?
THANKS FOR THE CALL, ALEX, I WAS DELIGHTED TO JOIN YOU...
WELL, I COULDN'T INVITE ANOTHER CLIENT AT SUCH SHORT NOTICE SO IT HAD TO BE A MATE...
WIMBLEDON
HOSPITALITY TENT
RACING FROM
(CHEERS, PENNY.)

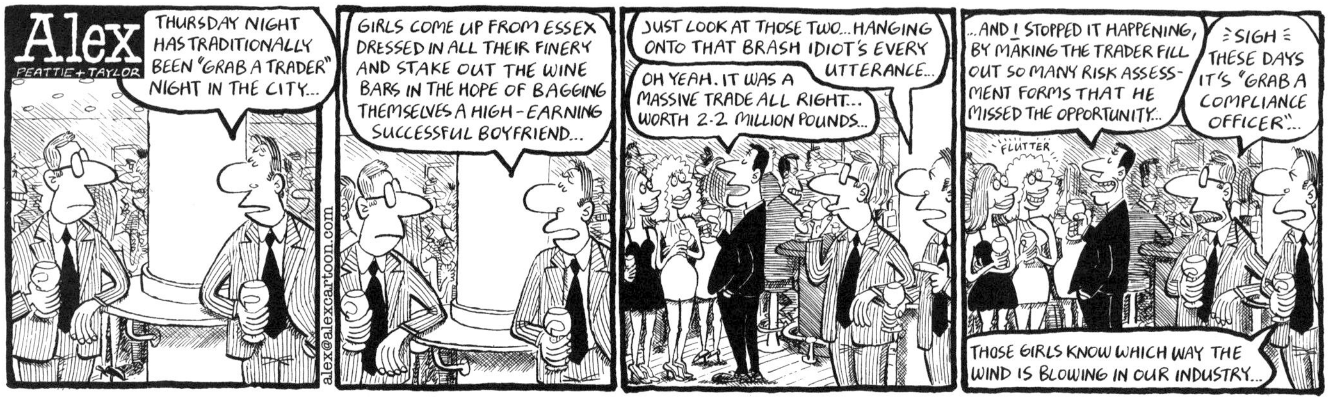
Alex
PEATTIE + TAYLOR
THURSDAY NIGHT HAS TRADITIONALLY BEEN "GRAB A TRADER" NIGHT IN THE CITY...
alex@alexcartoon.com
GIRLS COME UP FROM ESSEX DRESSED IN ALL THEIR FINERY AND STAKE OUT THE WINE BARS IN THE HOPE OF BAGGING THEMSELVES A HIGH-EARNING SUCCESSFUL BOYFRIEND...
JUST LOOK AT THOSE TWO... HANGING ONTO THAT BRASH IDIOT'S EVERY UTTERANCE...
OH YEAH. IT WAS A MASSIVE TRADE ALL RIGHT... WORTH 2.2 MILLION POUNDS...
...AND I STOPPED IT HAPPENING, BY MAKING THE TRADER FILL OUT SO MANY RISK ASSESSMENT FORMS THAT HE MISSED THE OPPORTUNITY...
SIGH THESE DAYS IT'S "GRAB A COMPLIANCE OFFICER"...
FLUTTER
THOSE GIRLS KNOW WHICH WAY THE WIND IS BLOWING IN OUR INDUSTRY...

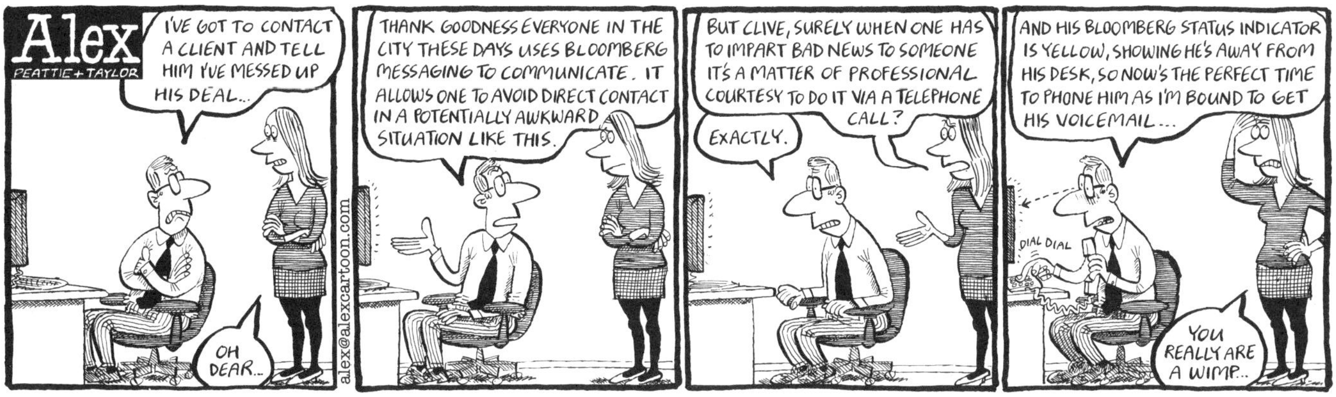
Alex
PEATTIE + TAYLOR
I'VE GOT TO CONTACT A CLIENT AND TELL HIM I'VE MESSED UP HIS DEAL...
OH DEAR...
alex@alexcartoon.com
THANK GOODNESS EVERYONE IN THE CITY THESE DAYS USES BLOOMBERG MESSAGING TO COMMUNICATE. IT ALLOWS ONE TO AVOID DIRECT CONTACT IN A POTENTIALLY AWKWARD SITUATION LIKE THIS.
BUT CLIVE, SURELY WHEN ONE HAS TO IMPART BAD NEWS TO SOMEONE IT'S A MATTER OF PROFESSIONAL COURTESY TO DO IT VIA A TELEPHONE CALL?
EXACTLY.
AND HIS BLOOMBERG STATUS INDICATOR IS YELLOW, SHOWING HE'S AWAY FROM HIS DESK, SO NOW'S THE PERFECT TIME TO PHONE HIM AS I'M BOUND TO GET HIS VOICEMAIL...
DIAL DIAL
YOU REALLY ARE A WIMP...

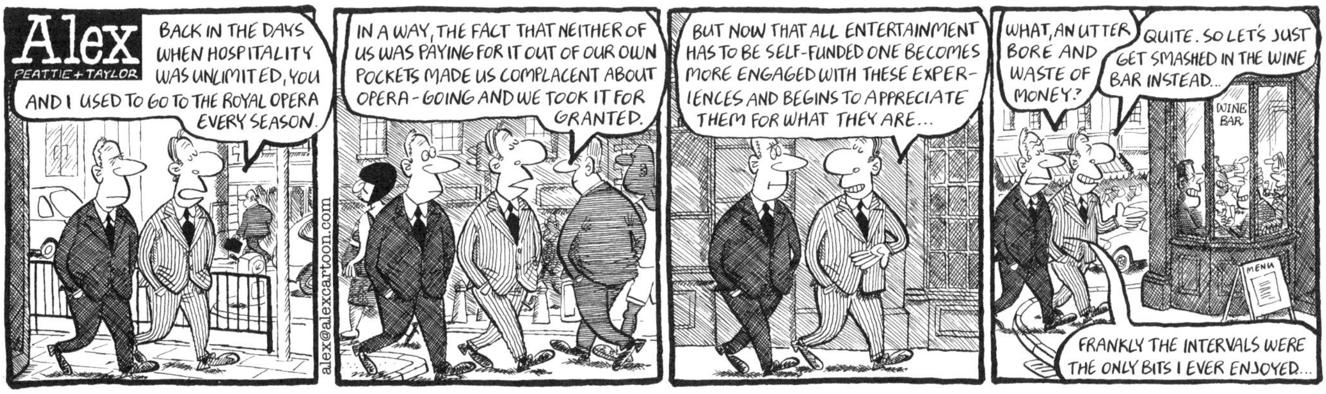
Alex
PEATTIE + TAYLOR
BACK IN THE DAYS WHEN HOSPITALITY WAS UNLIMITED, YOU AND I USED TO GO TO THE ROYAL OPERA EVERY SEASON.
alex@alexcartoon.com
IN A WAY, THE FACT THAT NEITHER OF US WAS PAYING FOR IT OUT OF OUR OWN POCKETS MADE US COMPLACENT ABOUT OPERA-GOING AND WE TOOK IT FOR GRANTED.
BUT NOW THAT ALL ENTERTAINMENT HAS TO BE SELF-FUNDED ONE BECOMES MORE ENGAGED WITH THESE EXPERIENCES AND BEGINS TO APPRECIATE THEM FOR WHAT THEY ARE...
WHAT, AN UTTER BORE AND WASTE OF MONEY?
QUITE. SO LET'S JUST GET SMASHED IN THE WINE BAR INSTEAD...
WINE BAR
MENU
FRANKLY THE INTERVALS WERE THE ONLY BITS I EVER ENJOYED...

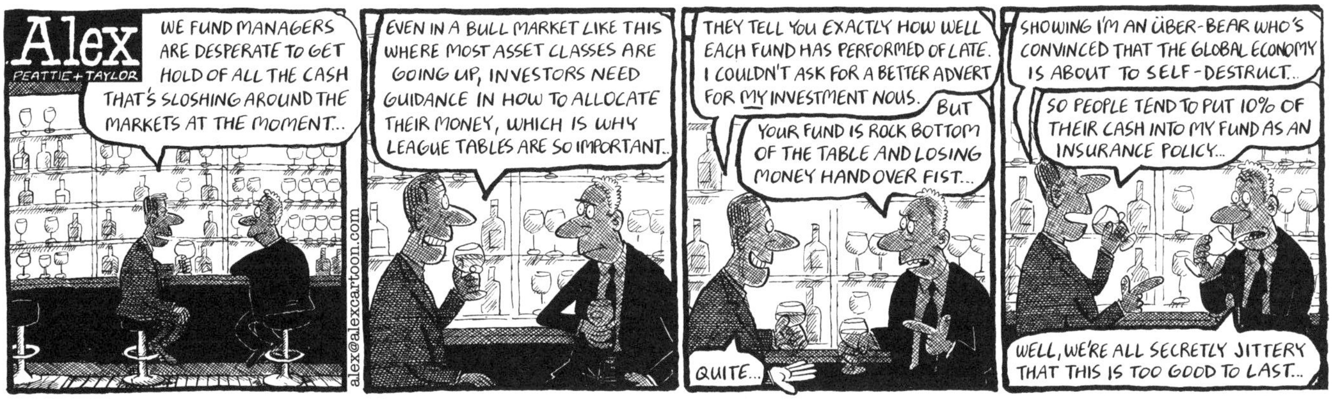
Alex
PEATTIE + TAYLOR
WE FUND MANAGERS ARE DESPERATE TO GET HOLD OF ALL THE CASH THAT'S SLOSHING AROUND THE MARKETS AT THE MOMENT...
alex@alexcartoon.com
EVEN IN A BULL MARKET LIKE THIS WHERE MOST ASSET CLASSES ARE GOING UP, INVESTORS NEED GUIDANCE IN HOW TO ALLOCATE THEIR MONEY, WHICH IS WHY LEAGUE TABLES ARE SO IMPORTANT...
THEY TELL YOU EXACTLY HOW WELL EACH FUND HAS PERFORMED OF LATE. I COULDN'T ASK FOR A BETTER ADVERT FOR MY INVESTMENT NOUS.
BUT YOUR FUND IS ROCK BOTTOM OF THE TABLE AND LOSING MONEY HAND OVER FIST...
QUITE...
SHOWING I'M AN ÜBER-BEAR WHO'S CONVINCED THAT THE GLOBAL ECONOMY IS ABOUT TO SELF-DESTRUCT...
SO PEOPLE TEND TO PUT 10% OF THEIR CASH INTO MY FUND AS AN INSURANCE POLICY...
WELL, WE'RE ALL SECRETLY JITTERY THAT THIS IS TOO GOOD TO LAST...

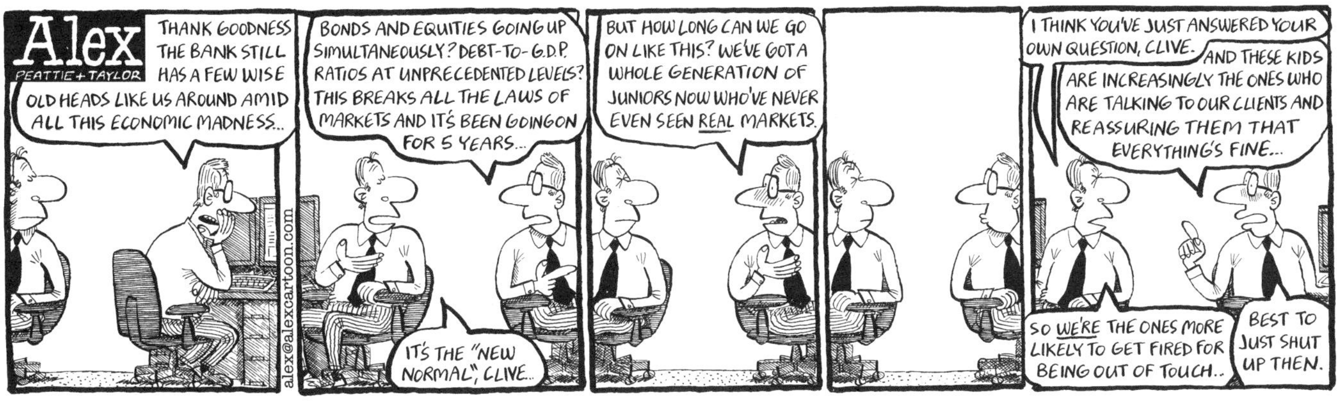
Alex
PEATTIE + TAYLOR
THANK GOODNESS THE BANK STILL HAS A FEW WISE OLD HEADS LIKE US AROUND AMID ALL THIS ECONOMIC MADNESS...
alex@alexcartoon.com
BONDS AND EQUITIES GOING UP SIMULTANEOUSLY? DEBT-TO-G.D.P. RATIOS AT UNPRECEDENTED LEVELS? THIS BREAKS ALL THE LAWS OF MARKETS AND IT'S BEEN GOING ON FOR 5 YEARS...
IT'S THE "NEW NORMAL", CLIVE...
BUT HOW LONG CAN WE GO ON LIKE THIS? WE'VE GOT A WHOLE GENERATION OF JUNIORS NOW WHO'VE NEVER EVEN SEEN REAL MARKETS.
I THINK YOU'VE JUST ANSWERED YOUR OWN QUESTION, CLIVE.
AND THESE KIDS ARE INCREASINGLY THE ONES WHO ARE TALKING TO OUR CLIENTS AND REASSURING THEM THAT EVERYTHING'S FINE...
SO WE'RE THE ONES MORE LIKELY TO GET FIRED FOR BEING OUT OF TOUCH...
BEST TO JUST SHUT UP THEN.

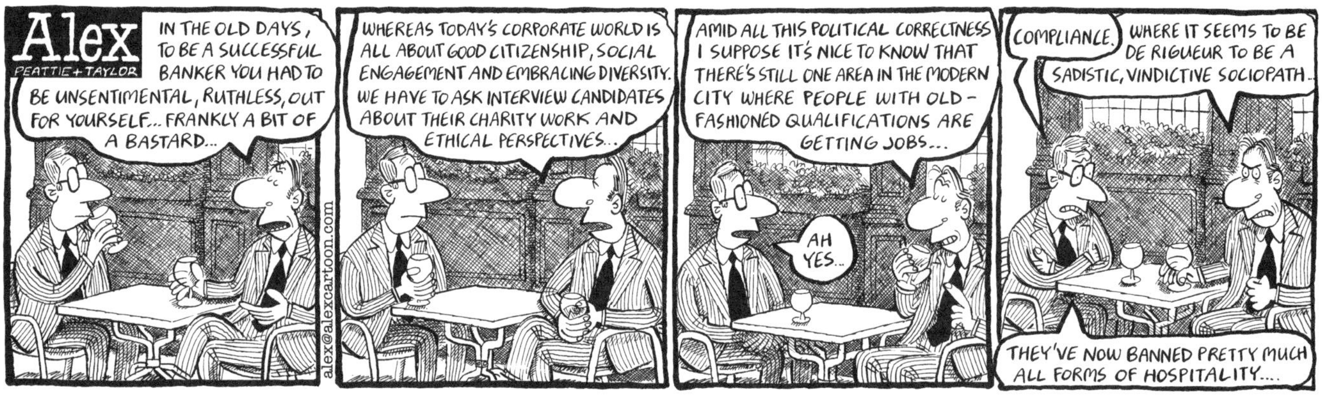
Alex
PEATTIE + TAYLOR
IN THE OLD DAYS, TO BE A SUCCESSFUL BANKER YOU HAD TO BE UNSENTIMENTAL, RUTHLESS, OUT FOR YOURSELF... FRANKLY A BIT OF A BASTARD...
alex@alexcartoon.com
WHEREAS TODAY'S CORPORATE WORLD IS ALL ABOUT GOOD CITIZENSHIP, SOCIAL ENGAGEMENT AND EMBRACING DIVERSITY. WE HAVE TO ASK INTERVIEW CANDIDATES ABOUT THEIR CHARITY WORK AND ETHICAL PERSPECTIVES...
AMID ALL THIS POLITICAL CORRECTNESS I SUPPOSE IT'S NICE TO KNOW THAT THERE'S STILL ONE AREA IN THE MODERN CITY WHERE PEOPLE WITH OLD-FASHIONED QUALIFICATIONS ARE GETTING JOBS...
AH YES...
COMPLIANCE.
WHERE IT SEEMS TO BE DE RIGUEUR TO BE A SADISTIC, VINDICTIVE SOCIOPATH...
THEY'VE NOW BANNED PRETTY MUCH ALL FORMS OF HOSPITALITY....

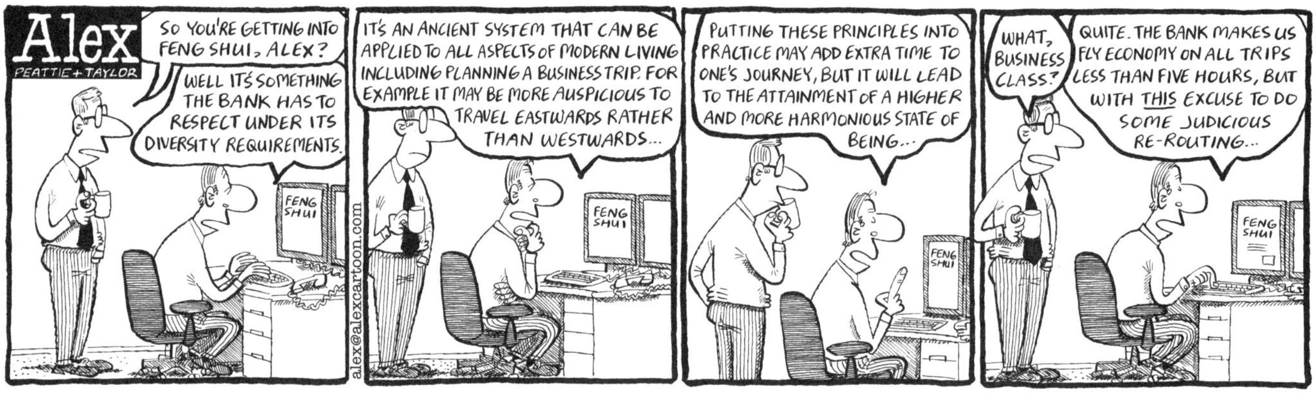
Alex
PEATTIE + TAYLOR
SO YOU'RE GETTING INTO FENG SHUI, ALEX?
WELL IT'S SOMETHING THE BANK HAS TO RESPECT UNDER ITS DIVERSITY REQUIREMENTS.
FENG SHUI
alex@alexcartoon.com
IT'S AN ANCIENT SYSTEM THAT CAN BE APPLIED TO ALL ASPECTS OF MODERN LIVING INCLUDING PLANNING A BUSINESS TRIP. FOR EXAMPLE IT MAY BE MORE AUSPICIOUS TO TRAVEL EASTWARDS RATHER THAN WESTWARDS...
FENG SHUI
PUTTING THESE PRINCIPLES INTO PRACTICE MAY ADD EXTRA TIME TO ONE'S JOURNEY, BUT IT WILL LEAD TO THE ATTAINMENT OF A HIGHER AND MORE HARMONIOUS STATE OF BEING...
FENG SHUI
WHAT, BUSINESS CLASS?
QUITE. THE BANK MAKES US FLY ECONOMY ON ALL TRIPS LESS THAN FIVE HOURS, BUT WITH THIS EXCUSE TO DO SOME JUDICIOUS RE-ROUTING...
FENG SHUI

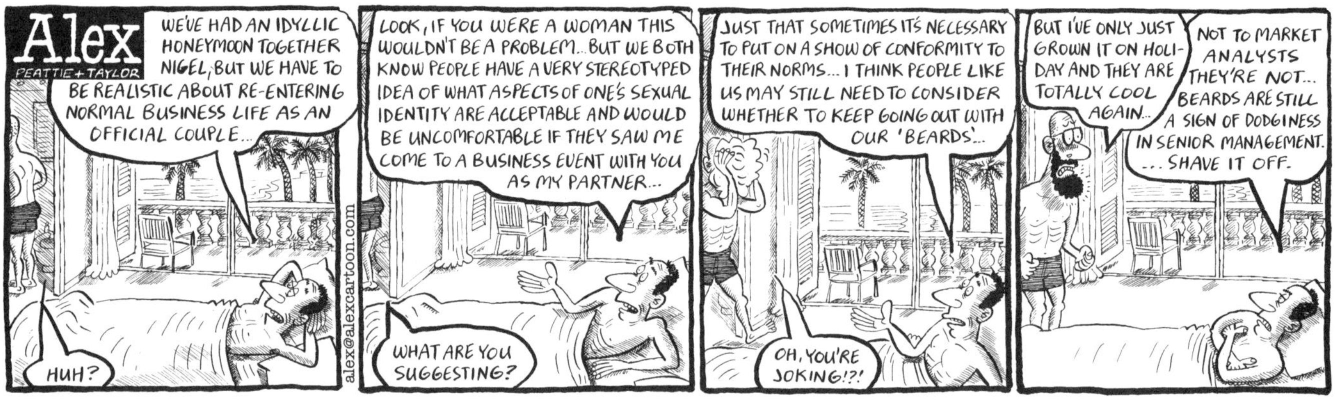
Alex
PEATTIE + TAYLOR
WE'VE HAD AN IDYLLIC HONEYMOON TOGETHER NIGEL, BUT WE HAVE TO BE REALISTIC ABOUT RE-ENTERING NORMAL BUSINESS LIFE AS AN OFFICIAL COUPLE...
HUH?
alex@alexcartoon.com
LOOK, IF YOU WERE A WOMAN THIS WOULDN'T BE A PROBLEM... BUT WE BOTH KNOW PEOPLE HAVE A VERY STEREOTYPED IDEA OF WHAT ASPECTS OF ONE'S SEXUAL IDENTITY ARE ACCEPTABLE AND WOULD BE UNCOMFORTABLE IF THEY SAW ME COME TO A BUSINESS EVENT WITH YOU AS MY PARTNER...
WHAT ARE YOU SUGGESTING?
JUST THAT SOMETIMES IT'S NECESSARY TO PUT ON A SHOW OF CONFORMITY TO THEIR NORMS... I THINK PEOPLE LIKE US MAY STILL NEED TO CONSIDER WHETHER TO KEEP GOING OUT WITH OUR 'BEARDS'...
OH, YOU'RE JOKING!?!
BUT I'VE ONLY JUST GROWN IT ON HOLIDAY AND THEY ARE TOTALLY COOL AGAIN...
NOT TO MARKET ANALYSTS THEY'RE NOT... BEARDS ARE STILL A SIGN OF DODGINESS IN SENIOR MANAGEMENT. ...SHAVE IT OFF.

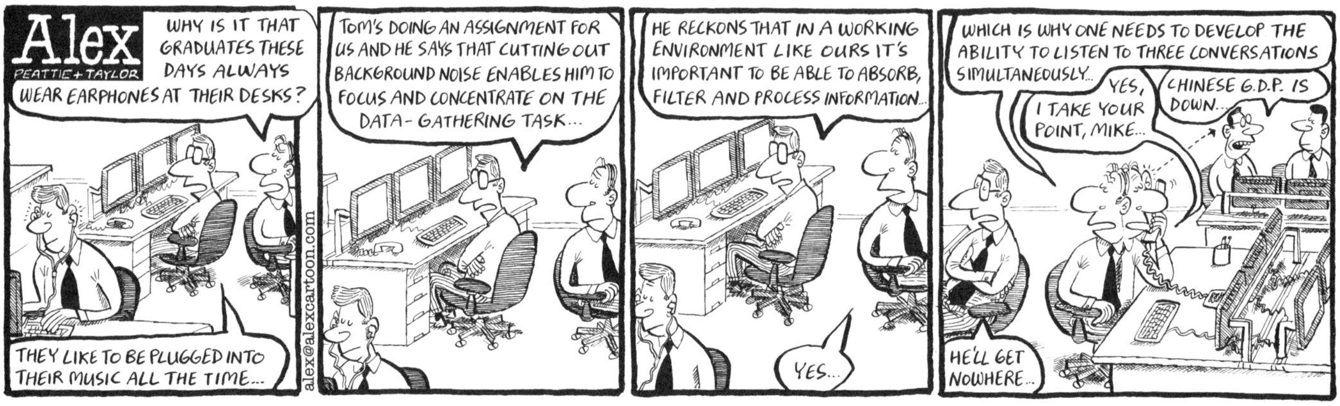
Alex
PEATTIE + TAYLOR
WHY IS IT THAT GRADUATES THESE DAYS ALWAYS WEAR EARPHONES AT THEIR DESKS?
THEY LIKE TO BE PLUGGED INTO THEIR MUSIC ALL THE TIME...
alex@alexcartoon.com
TOM'S DOING AN ASSIGNMENT FOR US AND HE SAYS THAT CUTTING OUT BACKGROUND NOISE ENABLES HIM TO FOCUS AND CONCENTRATE ON THE DATA-GATHERING TASK...
HE RECKONS THAT IN A WORKING ENVIRONMENT LIKE OURS IT'S IMPORTANT TO BE ABLE TO ABSORB, FILTER AND PROCESS INFORMATION...
YES...
WHICH IS WHY ONE NEEDS TO DEVELOP THE ABILITY TO LISTEN TO THREE CONVERSATIONS SIMULTANEOUSLY...
YES, I TAKE YOUR POINT, MIKE...
CHINESE G.D.P. IS DOWN...
HE'LL GET NOWHERE...

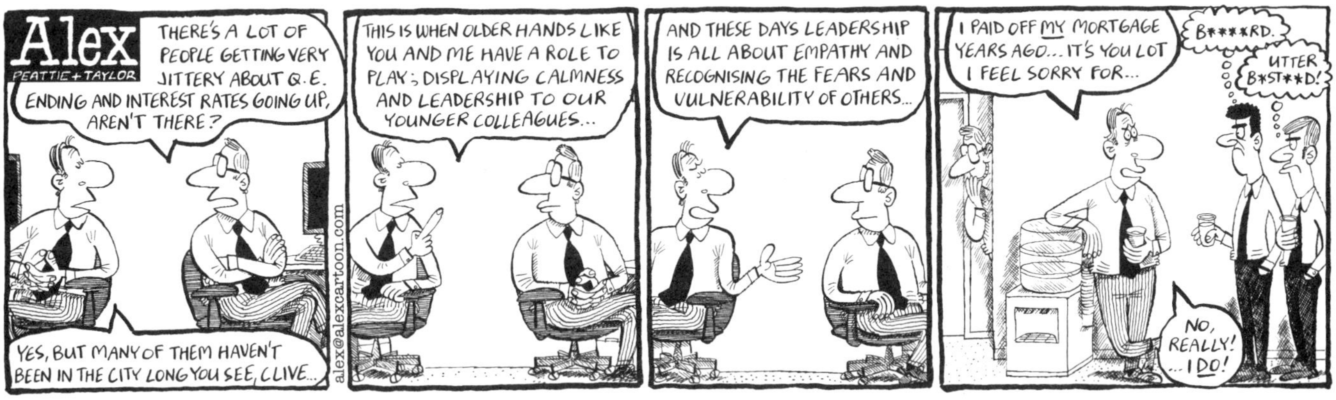
Alex
PEATTIE+TAYLOR
THERE'S A LOT OF PEOPLE GETTING VERY JITTERY ABOUT Q.E. ENDING AND INTEREST RATES GOING UP, AREN'T THERE?
YES, BUT MANY OF THEM HAVEN'T BEEN IN THE CITY LONG YOU SEE, CLIVE...
alex@alexcartoon.com
THIS IS WHEN OLDER HANDS LIKE YOU AND ME HAVE A ROLE TO PLAY; DISPLAYING CALMNESS AND LEADERSHIP TO OUR YOUNGER COLLEAGUES...
AND THESE DAYS LEADERSHIP IS ALL ABOUT EMPATHY AND RECOGNISING THE FEARS AND VULNERABILITY OF OTHERS...
I PAID OFF MY MORTGAGE YEARS AGO... IT'S YOU LOT I FEEL SORRY FOR...
B****RD.
UTTER B*ST**D!
NO, REALLY! ...I DO!

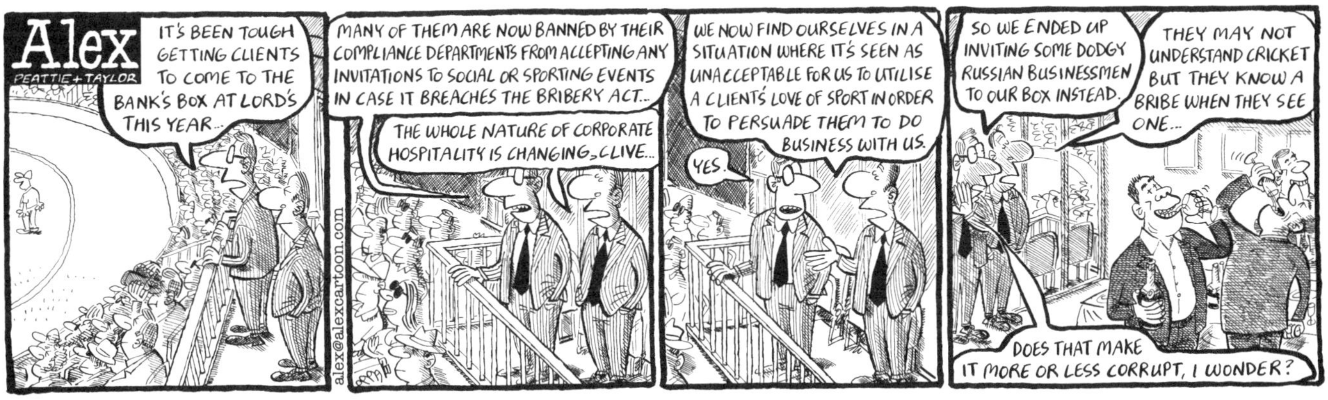
Alex
PEATTIE+TAYLOR
IT'S BEEN TOUGH GETTING CLIENTS TO COME TO THE BANK'S BOX AT LORD'S THIS YEAR...
alex@alexcartoon.com
MANY OF THEM ARE NOW BANNED BY THEIR COMPLIANCE DEPARTMENTS FROM ACCEPTING ANY INVITATIONS TO SOCIAL OR SPORTING EVENTS IN CASE IT BREACHES THE BRIBERY ACT...
THE WHOLE NATURE OF CORPORATE HOSPITALITY IS CHANGING, CLIVE...
WE NOW FIND OURSELVES IN A SITUATION WHERE IT'S SEEN AS UNACCEPTABLE FOR US TO UTILISE A CLIENTS' LOVE OF SPORT IN ORDER TO PERSUADE THEM TO DO BUSINESS WITH US.
YES.
SO WE ENDED UP INVITING SOME DODGY RUSSIAN BUSINESSMEN TO OUR BOX INSTEAD.
THEY MAY NOT UNDERSTAND CRICKET BUT THEY KNOW A BRIBE WHEN THEY SEE ONE...
DOES THAT MAKE IT MORE OR LESS CORRUPT, I WONDER?

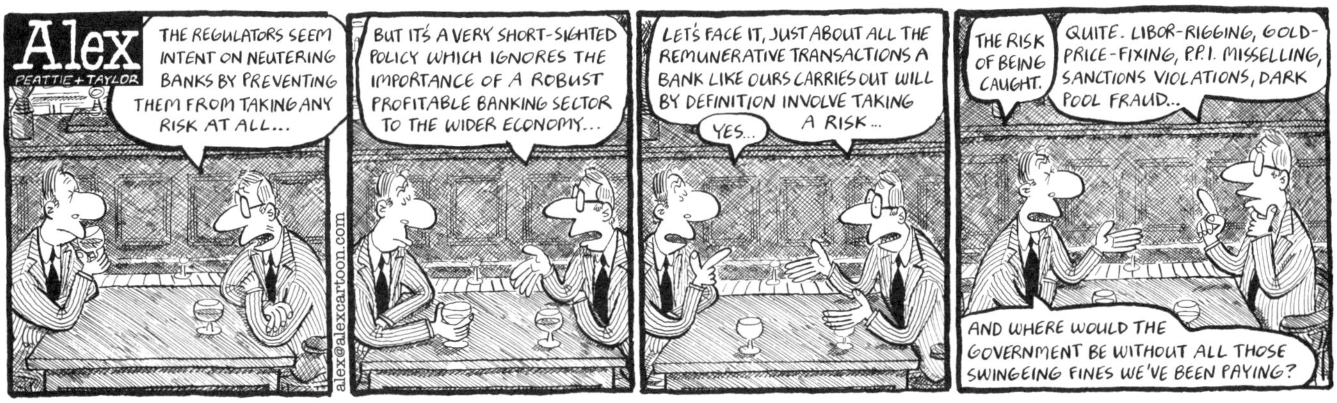
Alex
PEATTIE+TAYLOR
THE REGULATORS SEEM INTENT ON NEUTERING BANKS BY PREVENTING THEM FROM TAKING ANY RISK AT ALL...
alex@alexcartoon.com
BUT IT'S A VERY SHORT-SIGHTED POLICY WHICH IGNORES THE IMPORTANCE OF A ROBUST PROFITABLE BANKING SECTOR TO THE WIDER ECONOMY...
LET'S FACE IT, JUST ABOUT ALL THE REMUNERATIVE TRANSACTIONS A BANK LIKE OURS CARRIES OUT WILL BY DEFINITION INVOLVE TAKING A RISK...
YES...
THE RISK OF BEING CAUGHT.
QUITE. LIBOR-RIGGING, GOLD-PRICE-FIXING, P.P.I. MISSELLING, SANCTIONS VIOLATIONS, DARK POOL FRAUD...
AND WHERE WOULD THE GOVERNMENT BE WITHOUT ALL THOSE SWINGEING FINES WE'VE BEEN PAYING?

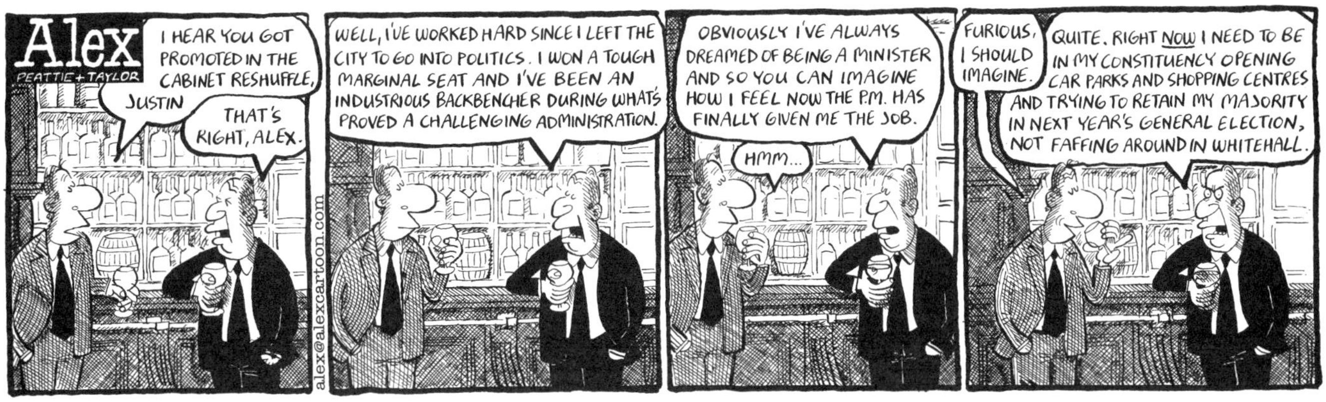
Alex
PEATTIE+TAYLOR
I HEAR YOU GOT PROMOTED IN THE CABINET RESHUFFLE, JUSTIN
THAT'S RIGHT, ALEX.
alex@alexcartoon.com
WELL, I'VE WORKED HARD SINCE I LEFT THE CITY TO GO INTO POLITICS. I WON A TOUGH MARGINAL SEAT AND I'VE BEEN AN INDUSTRIOUS BACKBENCHER DURING WHAT'S PROVED A CHALLENGING ADMINISTRATION.
OBVIOUSLY I'VE ALWAYS DREAMED OF BEING A MINISTER AND SO YOU CAN IMAGINE HOW I FEEL NOW THE P.M. HAS FINALLY GIVEN ME THE JOB.
HMM...
FURIOUS, I SHOULD IMAGINE.
QUITE. RIGHT NOW I NEED TO BE IN MY CONSTITUENCY OPENING CAR PARKS AND SHOPPING CENTRES AND TRYING TO RETAIN MY MAJORITY IN NEXT YEAR'S GENERAL ELECTION, NOT FAFFING AROUND IN WHITEHALL.

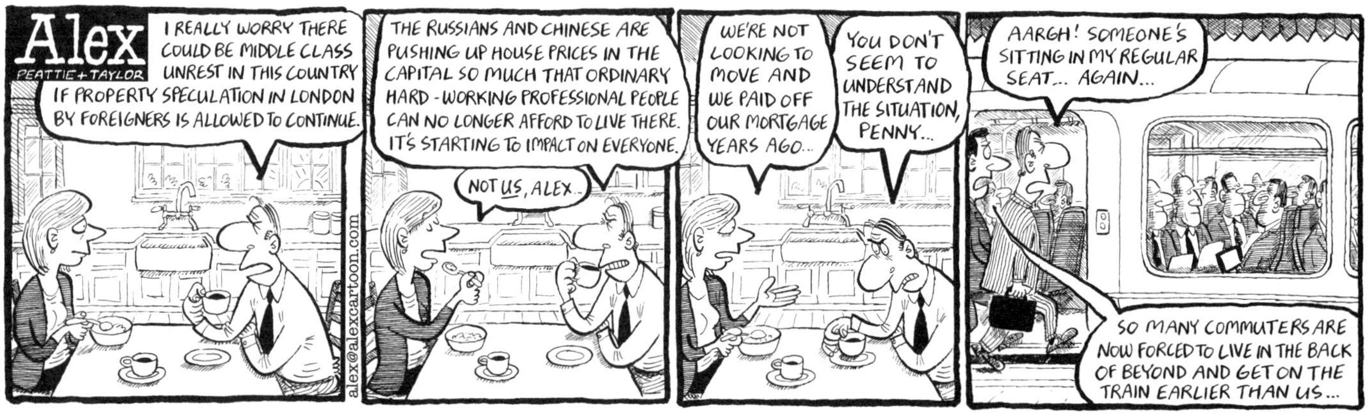
Alex
PEATTIE + TAYLOR
I REALLY WORRY THERE COULD BE MIDDLE CLASS UNREST IN THIS COUNTRY IF PROPERTY SPECULATION IN LONDON BY FOREIGNERS IS ALLOWED TO CONTINUE.
THE RUSSIANS AND CHINESE ARE PUSHING UP HOUSE PRICES IN THE CAPITAL SO MUCH THAT ORDINARY HARD-WORKING PROFESSIONAL PEOPLE CAN NO LONGER AFFORD TO LIVE THERE. IT'S STARTING TO IMPACT ON EVERYONE.
NOT US, ALEX.
alex@alexcartoon.com
WE'RE NOT LOOKING TO MOVE AND WE PAID OFF OUR MORTGAGE YEARS AGO...
YOU DON'T SEEM TO UNDERSTAND THE SITUATION, PENNY...
AARGH! SOMEONE'S SITTING IN MY REGULAR SEAT... AGAIN...
SO MANY COMMUTERS ARE NOW FORCED TO LIVE IN THE BACK OF BEYOND AND GET ON THE TRAIN EARLIER THAN US...

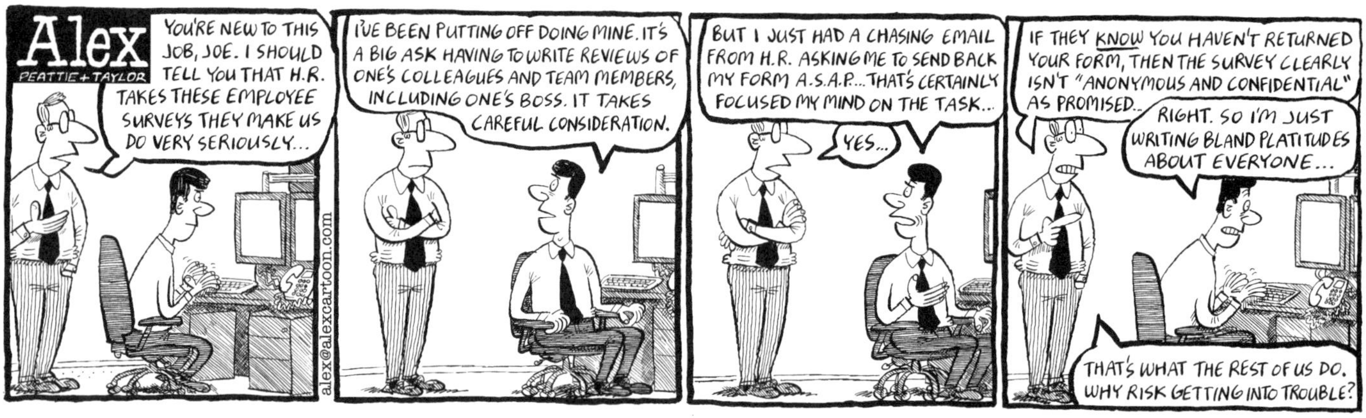
Alex
PEATTIE + TAYLOR
YOU'RE NEW TO THIS JOB, JOE. I SHOULD TELL YOU THAT H.R. TAKES THESE EMPLOYEE SURVEYS THEY MAKE US DO VERY SERIOUSLY...
alex@alexcartoon.com
I'VE BEEN PUTTING OFF DOING MINE. IT'S A BIG ASK HAVING TO WRITE REVIEWS OF ONE'S COLLEAGUES AND TEAM MEMBERS, INCLUDING ONE'S BOSS. IT TAKES CAREFUL CONSIDERATION.
BUT I JUST HAD A CHASING EMAIL FROM H.R. ASKING ME TO SEND BACK MY FORM A.S.A.P... THAT'S CERTAINLY FOCUSED MY MIND ON THE TASK...
YES...
IF THEY KNOW YOU HAVEN'T RETURNED YOUR FORM, THEN THE SURVEY CLEARLY ISN'T "ANONYMOUS AND CONFIDENTIAL" AS PROMISED...
RIGHT. SO I'M JUST WRITING BLAND PLATITUDES ABOUT EVERYONE...
THAT'S WHAT THE REST OF US DO. WHY RISK GETTING INTO TROUBLE?

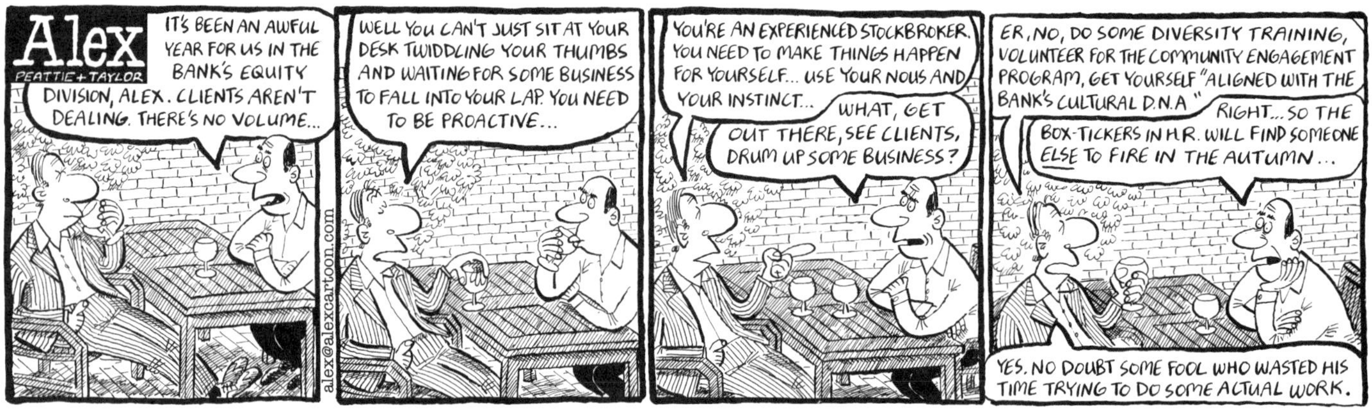
Alex
PEATTIE + TAYLOR
IT'S BEEN AN AWFUL YEAR FOR US IN THE BANK'S EQUITY DIVISION, ALEX. CLIENTS AREN'T DEALING. THERE'S NO VOLUME...
alex@alexcartoon.com
WELL YOU CAN'T JUST SIT AT YOUR DESK TWIDDLING YOUR THUMBS AND WAITING FOR SOME BUSINESS TO FALL INTO YOUR LAP. YOU NEED TO BE PROACTIVE...
YOU'RE AN EXPERIENCED STOCKBROKER. YOU NEED TO MAKE THINGS HAPPEN FOR YOURSELF... USE YOUR NOUS AND YOUR INSTINCT...
WHAT, GET OUT THERE, SEE CLIENTS, DRUM UP SOME BUSINESS?
ER, NO, DO SOME DIVERSITY TRAINING, VOLUNTEER FOR THE COMMUNITY ENGAGEMENT PROGRAM, GET YOURSELF "ALIGNED WITH THE BANK'S CULTURAL D.N.A"
RIGHT... SO THE BOX-TICKERS IN H.R. WILL FIND SOMEONE ELSE TO FIRE IN THE AUTUMN...
YES. NO DOUBT SOME FOOL WHO WASTED HIS TIME TRYING TO DO SOME ACTUAL WORK.

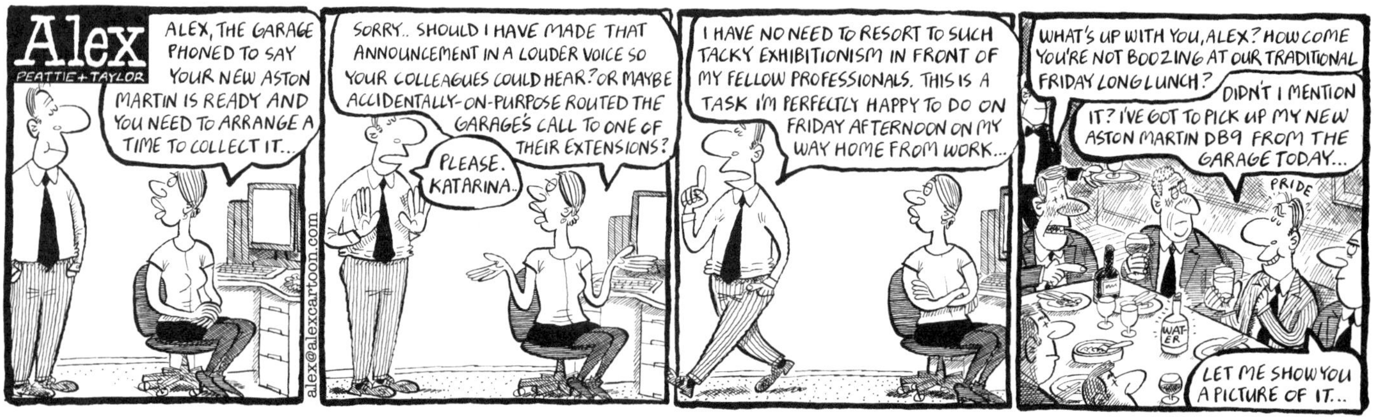
Alex
PEATTIE + TAYLOR
ALEX, THE GARAGE PHONED TO SAY YOUR NEW ASTON MARTIN IS READY AND YOU NEED TO ARRANGE A TIME TO COLLECT IT...
alex@alexcartoon.com
SORRY.. SHOULD I HAVE MADE THAT ANNOUNCEMENT IN A LOUDER VOICE SO YOUR COLLEAGUES COULD HEAR? OR MAYBE ACCIDENTALLY-ON-PURPOSE ROUTED THE GARAGE'S CALL TO ONE OF THEIR EXTENSIONS?
PLEASE. KATARINA.
I HAVE NO NEED TO RESORT TO SUCH TACKY EXHIBITIONISM IN FRONT OF MY FELLOW PROFESSIONALS. THIS IS A TASK I'M PERFECTLY HAPPY TO DO ON FRIDAY AFTERNOON ON MY WAY HOME FROM WORK...
WHAT'S UP WITH YOU, ALEX? HOW COME YOU'RE NOT BOOZING AT OUR TRADITIONAL FRIDAY LONG LUNCH?
DIDN'T I MENTION IT? I'VE GOT TO PICK UP MY NEW ASTON MARTIN DB9 FROM THE GARAGE TODAY...
PRIDE
WATER
LET ME SHOW YOU A PICTURE OF IT...

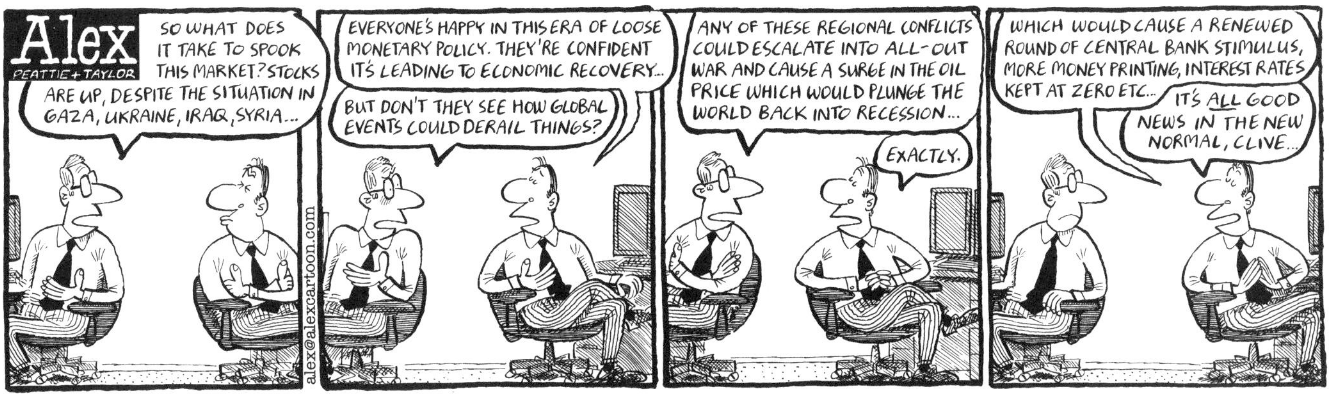
Alex
PEATTIE + TAYLOR
SO WHAT DOES IT TAKE TO SPOOK THIS MARKET? STOCKS ARE UP, DESPITE THE SITUATION IN GAZA, UKRAINE, IRAQ, SYRIA...
alex@alexcartoon.com
EVERYONE'S HAPPY IN THIS ERA OF LOOSE MONETARY POLICY. THEY'RE CONFIDENT IT'S LEADING TO ECONOMIC RECOVERY...
BUT DON'T THEY SEE HOW GLOBAL EVENTS COULD DERAIL THINGS?
ANY OF THESE REGIONAL CONFLICTS COULD ESCALATE INTO ALL-OUT WAR AND CAUSE A SURGE IN THE OIL PRICE WHICH WOULD PLUNGE THE WORLD BACK INTO RECESSION...
EXACTLY.
WHICH WOULD CAUSE A RENEWED ROUND OF CENTRAL BANK STIMULUS, MORE MONEY PRINTING, INTEREST RATES KEPT AT ZERO ETC...
IT'S ALL GOOD NEWS IN THE NEW NORMAL, CLIVE...

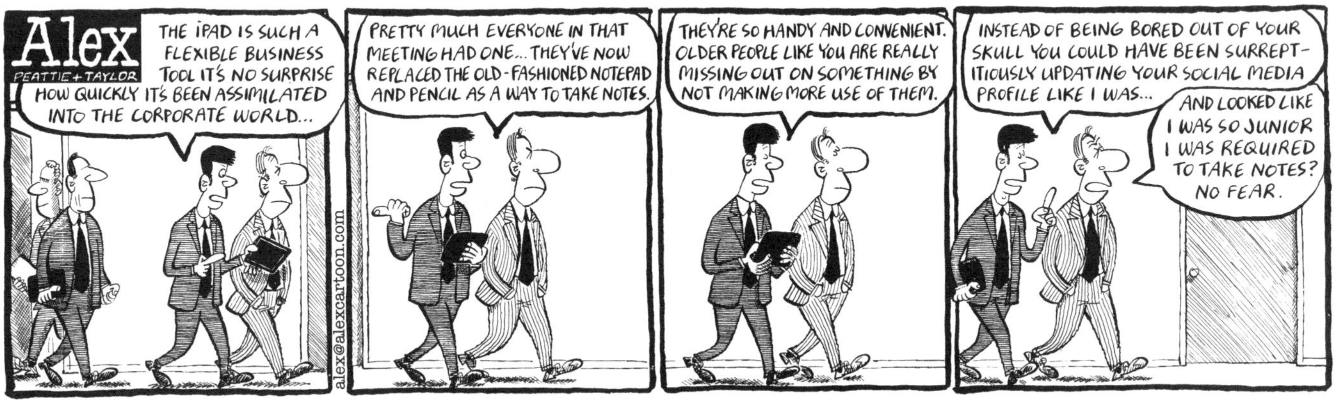
Alex
PEATTIE + TAYLOR
THE iPAD IS SUCH A FLEXIBLE BUSINESS TOOL IT'S NO SURPRISE HOW QUICKLY IT'S BEEN ASSIMILATED INTO THE CORPORATE WORLD...
alex@alexcartoon.com
PRETTY MUCH EVERYONE IN THAT MEETING HAD ONE... THEY'VE NOW REPLACED THE OLD-FASHIONED NOTEPAD AND PENCIL AS A WAY TO TAKE NOTES.
THEY'RE SO HANDY AND CONVENIENT. OLDER PEOPLE LIKE YOU ARE REALLY MISSING OUT ON SOMETHING BY NOT MAKING MORE USE OF THEM.
INSTEAD OF BEING BORED OUT OF YOUR SKULL YOU COULD HAVE BEEN SURREPTITIOUSLY UPDATING YOUR SOCIAL MEDIA PROFILE LIKE I WAS...
AND LOOKED LIKE I WAS SO JUNIOR I WAS REQUIRED TO TAKE NOTES? NO FEAR.

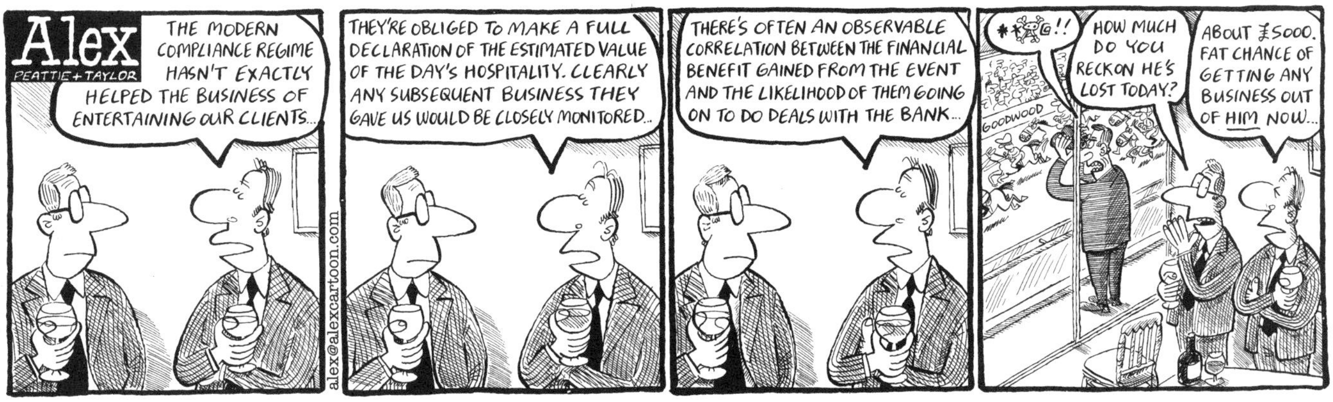
Alex
PEATTIE + TAYLOR
THE MODERN COMPLIANCE REGIME HASN'T EXACTLY HELPED THE BUSINESS OF ENTERTAINING OUR CLIENTS...
alex@alexcartoon.com
THEY'RE OBLIGED TO MAKE A FULL DECLARATION OF THE ESTIMATED VALUE OF THE DAY'S HOSPITALITY. CLEARLY ANY SUBSEQUENT BUSINESS THEY GAVE US WOULD BE CLOSELY MONITORED...
THERE'S OFTEN AN OBSERVABLE CORRELATION BETWEEN THE FINANCIAL BENEFIT GAINED FROM THE EVENT AND THE LIKELIHOOD OF THEM GOING ON TO DO DEALS WITH THE BANK...
GOODWOOD
HOW MUCH DO YOU RECKON HE'S LOST TODAY?
ABOUT £5000. FAT CHANCE OF GETTING ANY BUSINESS OUT OF HIM NOW...

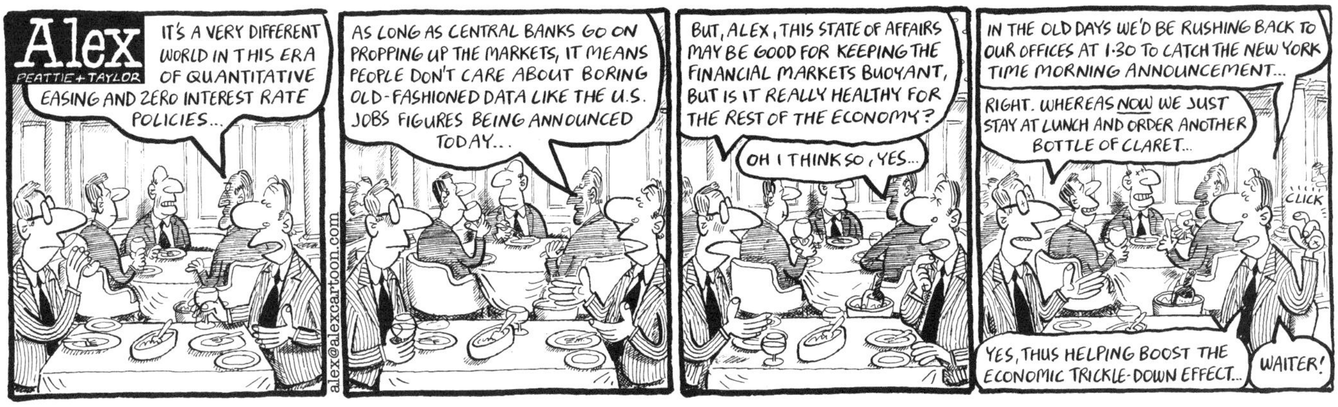
Alex
PEATTIE + TAYLOR
IT'S A VERY DIFFERENT WORLD IN THIS ERA OF QUANTITATIVE EASING AND ZERO INTEREST RATE POLICIES...
alex@alexcartoon.com
AS LONG AS CENTRAL BANKS GO ON PROPPING UP THE MARKETS, IT MEANS PEOPLE DON'T CARE ABOUT BORING OLD-FASHIONED DATA LIKE THE U.S. JOBS FIGURES BEING ANNOUNCED TODAY...
BUT, ALEX, THIS STATE OF AFFAIRS MAY BE GOOD FOR KEEPING THE FINANCIAL MARKETS BUOYANT, BUT IS IT REALLY HEALTHY FOR THE REST OF THE ECONOMY?
OH I THINK SO, YES...
IN THE OLD DAYS WE'D BE RUSHING BACK TO OUR OFFICES AT 1.30 TO CATCH THE NEW YORK TIME MORNING ANNOUNCEMENT...
RIGHT. WHEREAS NOW WE JUST STAY AT LUNCH AND ORDER ANOTHER BOTTLE OF CLARET...
CLICK
YES, THUS HELPING BOOST THE ECONOMIC TRICKLE-DOWN EFFECT...
WAITER!

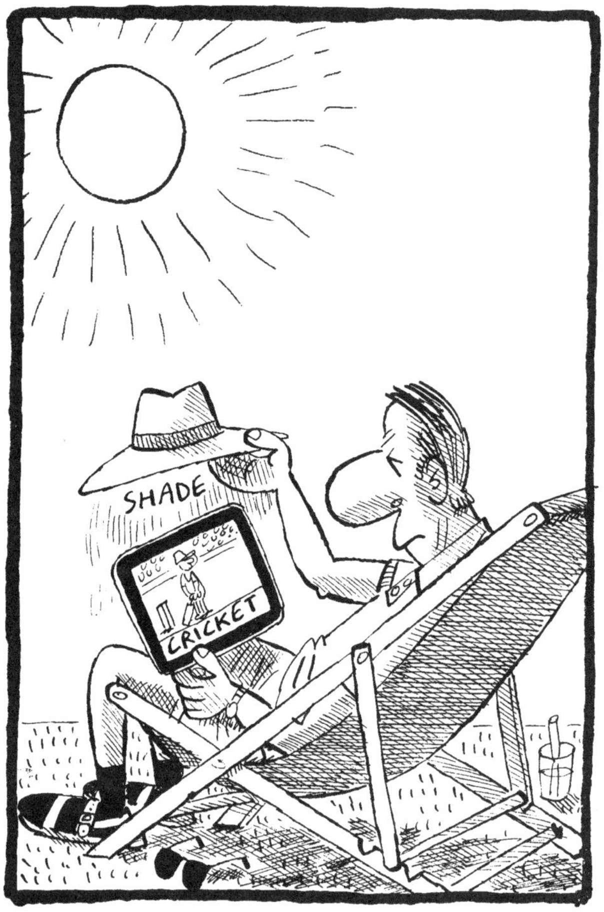
SHADE
CRICKET

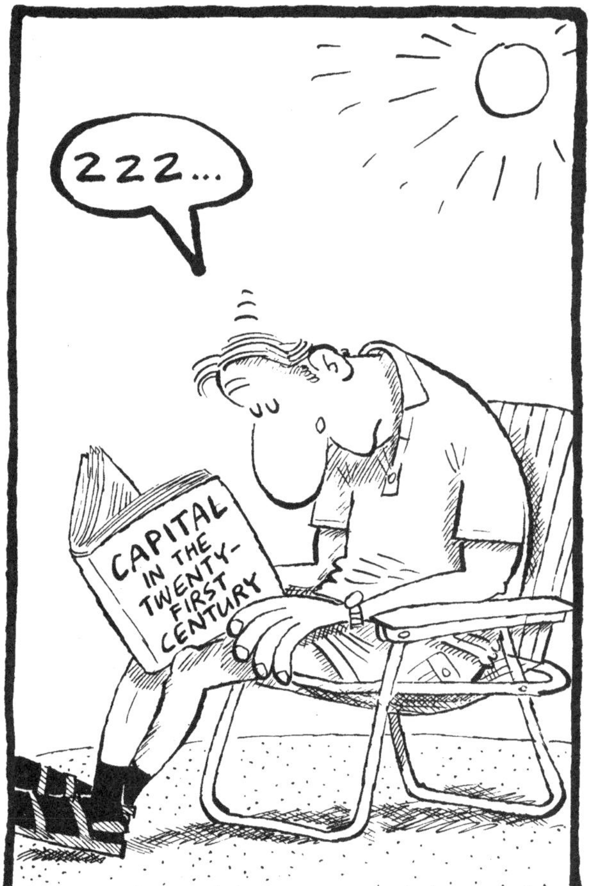
ZZZ...
CAPITAL IN THE TWENTY-FIRST CENTURY

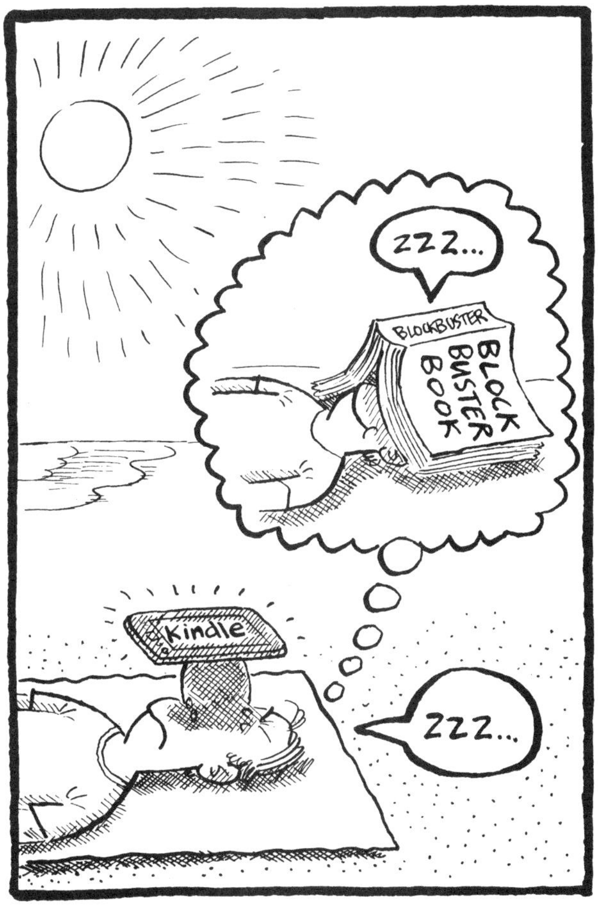
ZZZ...
BLOCKBUSTER
BLOCK BUSTER BOOK
Kindle
ZZZ...

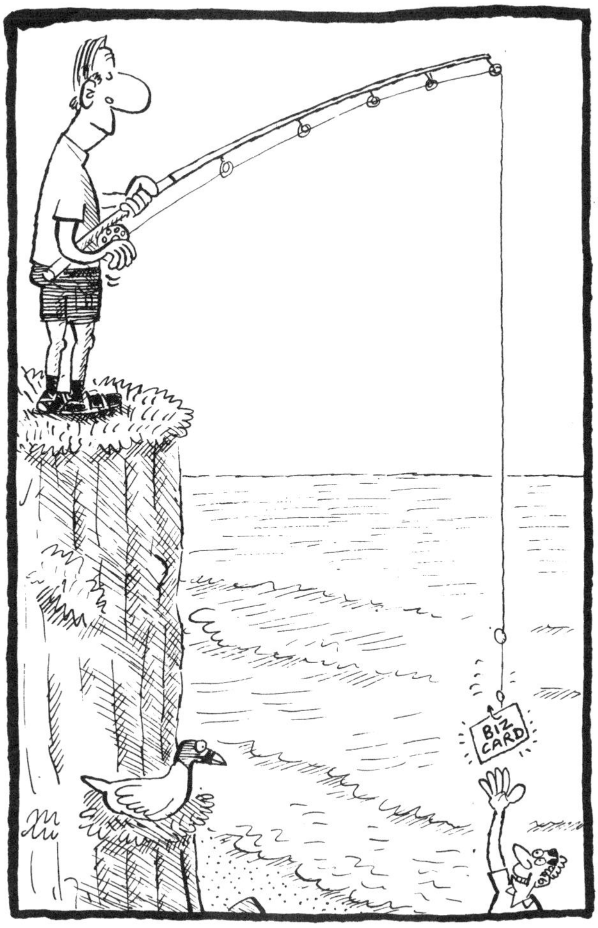
BIZ CARD

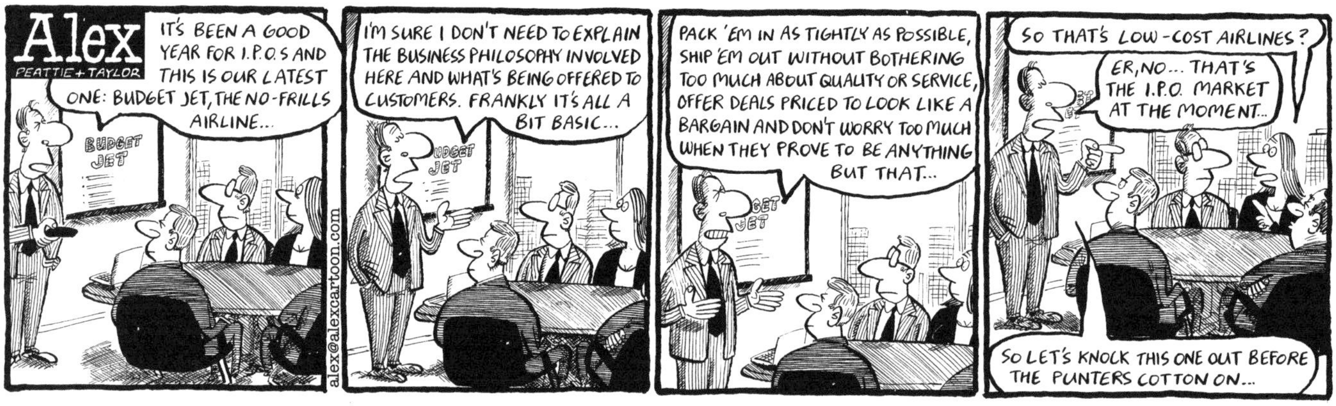
Alex
PEATTIE + TAYLOR
IT'S BEEN A GOOD YEAR FOR I.P.O.S AND THIS IS OUR LATEST ONE: BUDGET JET, THE NO-FRILLS AIRLINE...
BUDGET JET
I'M SURE I DON'T NEED TO EXPLAIN THE BUSINESS PHILOSOPHY INVOLVED HERE AND WHAT'S BEING OFFERED TO CUSTOMERS. FRANKLY IT'S ALL A BIT BASIC...
PACK 'EM IN AS TIGHTLY AS POSSIBLE, SHIP 'EM OUT WITHOUT BOTHERING TOO MUCH ABOUT QUALITY OR SERVICE, OFFER DEALS PRICED TO LOOK LIKE A BARGAIN AND DON'T WORRY TOO MUCH WHEN THEY PROVE TO BE ANYTHING BUT THAT...
SO THAT'S LOW-COST AIRLINES?
ER, NO... THAT'S THE I.P.O. MARKET AT THE MOMENT...
SO LET'S KNOCK THIS ONE OUT BEFORE THE PUNTERS COTTON ON...
alex@alexcartoon.com

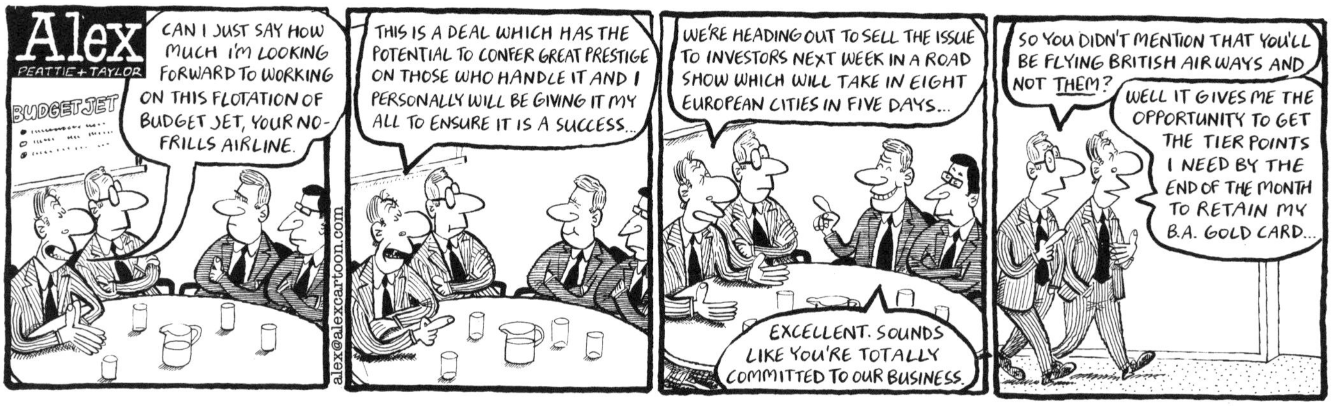
Alex
PEATTIE + TAYLOR
CAN I JUST SAY HOW MUCH I'M LOOKING FORWARD TO WORKING ON THIS FLOTATION OF BUDGET JET, YOUR NO-FRILLS AIRLINE.
BUDGET JET
THIS IS A DEAL WHICH HAS THE POTENTIAL TO CONFER GREAT PRESTIGE ON THOSE WHO HANDLE IT AND I PERSONALLY WILL BE GIVING IT MY ALL TO ENSURE IT IS A SUCCESS...
WE'RE HEADING OUT TO SELL THE ISSUE TO INVESTORS NEXT WEEK IN A ROAD SHOW WHICH WILL TAKE IN EIGHT EUROPEAN CITIES IN FIVE DAYS...
EXCELLENT. SOUNDS LIKE YOU'RE TOTALLY COMMITTED TO OUR BUSINESS.
SO YOU DIDN'T MENTION THAT YOU'LL BE FLYING BRITISH AIRWAYS AND NOT THEM?
WELL IT GIVES ME THE OPPORTUNITY TO GET THE TIER POINTS I NEED BY THE END OF THE MONTH TO RETAIN MY B.A. GOLD CARD...
alex@alexcartoon.com

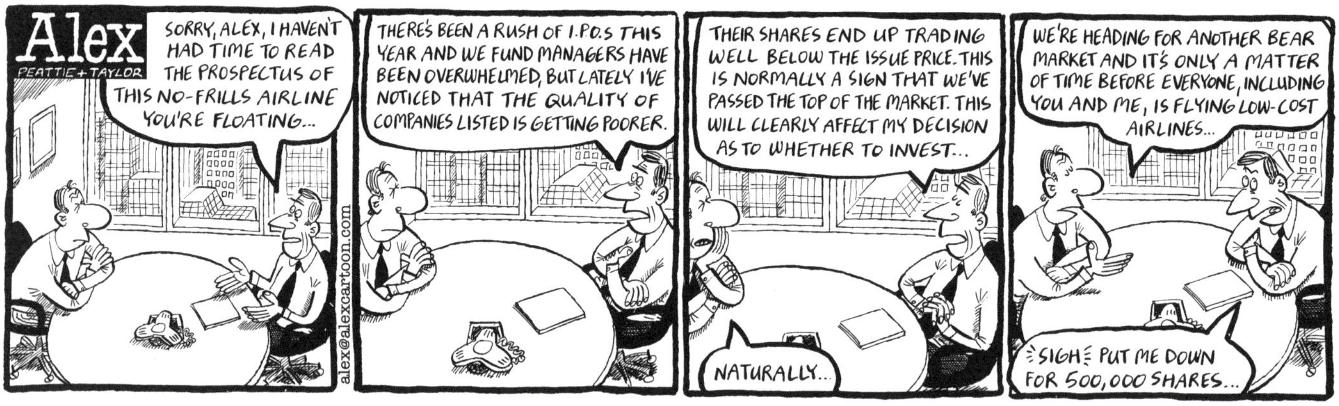
Alex
PEATTIE + TAYLOR
SORRY, ALEX, I HAVEN'T HAD TIME TO READ THE PROSPECTUS OF THIS NO-FRILLS AIRLINE YOU'RE FLOATING...
THERE'S BEEN A RUSH OF I.P.O.S THIS YEAR AND WE FUND MANAGERS HAVE BEEN OVERWHELMED, BUT LATELY I'VE NOTICED THAT THE QUALITY OF COMPANIES LISTED IS GETTING POORER.
THEIR SHARES END UP TRADING WELL BELOW THE ISSUE PRICE. THIS IS NORMALLY A SIGN THAT WE'VE PASSED THE TOP OF THE MARKET. THIS WILL CLEARLY AFFECT MY DECISION AS TO WHETHER TO INVEST...
NATURALLY...
WE'RE HEADING FOR ANOTHER BEAR MARKET AND IT'S ONLY A MATTER OF TIME BEFORE EVERYONE, INCLUDING YOU AND ME, IS FLYING LOW-COST AIRLINES...
SIGH PUT ME DOWN FOR 500,000 SHARES...
alex@alexcartoon.com

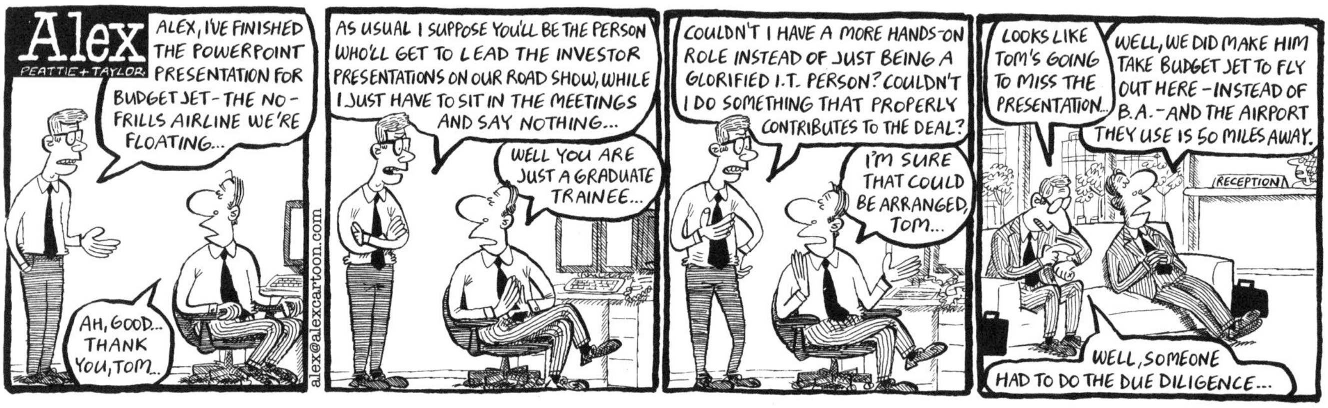
Alex
PEATTIE + TAYLOR
ALEX, I'VE FINISHED THE POWERPOINT PRESENTATION FOR BUDGET JET - THE NO-FRILLS AIRLINE WE'RE FLOATING...
AH, GOOD... THANK YOU, TOM...
AS USUAL I SUPPOSE YOU'LL BE THE PERSON WHO'LL GET TO LEAD THE INVESTOR PRESENTATIONS ON OUR ROAD SHOW, WHILE I JUST HAVE TO SIT IN THE MEETINGS AND SAY NOTHING...
WELL YOU ARE JUST A GRADUATE TRAINEE...
COULDN'T I HAVE A MORE HANDS-ON ROLE INSTEAD OF JUST BEING A GLORIFIED I.T. PERSON? COULDN'T I DO SOMETHING THAT PROPERLY CONTRIBUTES TO THE DEAL?
I'M SURE THAT COULD BE ARRANGED, TOM...
LOOKS LIKE TOM'S GOING TO MISS THE PRESENTATION...
WELL, WE DID MAKE HIM TAKE BUDGET JET TO FLY OUT HERE - INSTEAD OF B.A. - AND THE AIRPORT THEY USE IS 50 MILES AWAY.
RECEPTION
WELL, SOMEONE HAD TO DO THE DUE DILIGENCE...
alex@alexcartoon.com

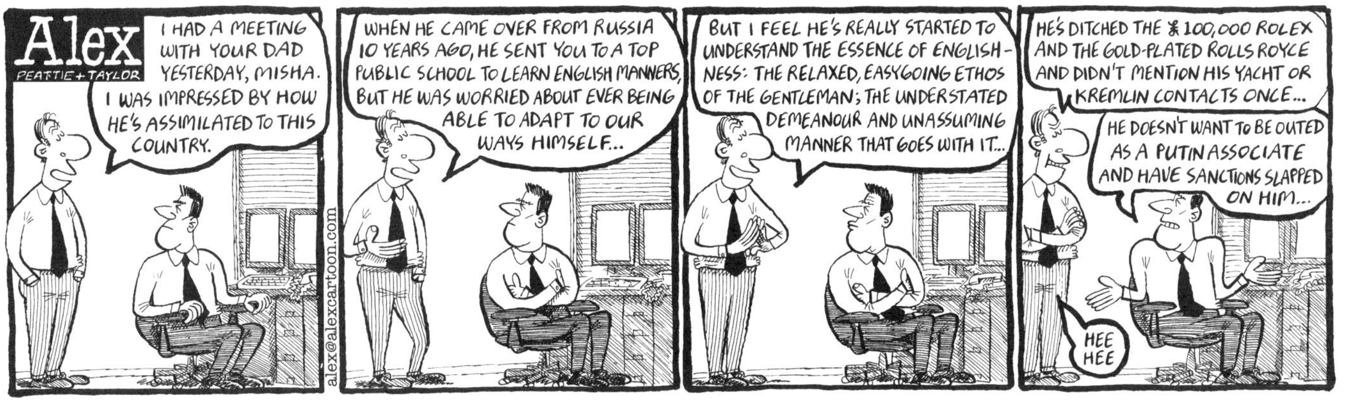
Alex
PEATTIE + TAYLOR
I HAD A MEETING WITH YOUR DAD YESTERDAY, MISHA. I WAS IMPRESSED BY HOW HE'S ASSIMILATED TO THIS COUNTRY.
WHEN HE CAME OVER FROM RUSSIA 10 YEARS AGO, HE SENT YOU TO A TOP PUBLIC SCHOOL TO LEARN ENGLISH MANNERS, BUT HE WAS WORRIED ABOUT EVER BEING ABLE TO ADAPT TO OUR WAYS HIMSELF...
BUT I FEEL HE'S REALLY STARTED TO UNDERSTAND THE ESSENCE OF ENGLISH-NESS: THE RELAXED, EASYGOING ETHOS OF THE GENTLEMAN; THE UNDERSTATED DEMEANOUR AND UNASSUMING MANNER THAT GOES WITH IT...
HE'S DITCHED THE £100,000 ROLEX AND THE GOLD-PLATED ROLLS ROYCE AND DIDN'T MENTION HIS YACHT OR KREMLIN CONTACTS ONCE...
HE DOESN'T WANT TO BE OUTED AS A PUTIN ASSOCIATE AND HAVE SANCTIONS SLAPPED ON HIM...
HEE HEE
alex@alexcartoon.com

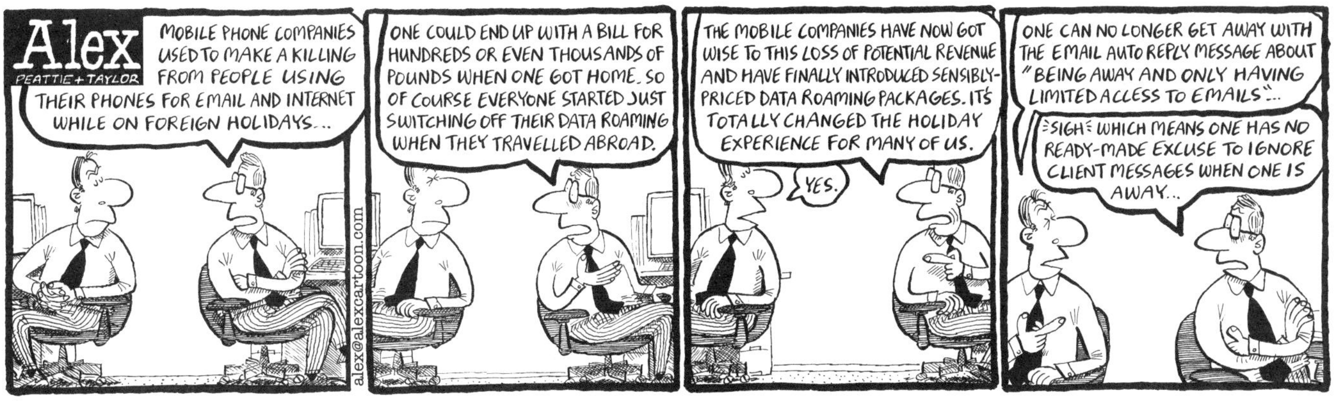
Alex
PEATTIE + TAYLOR
MOBILE PHONE COMPANIES USED TO MAKE A KILLING FROM PEOPLE USING THEIR PHONES FOR EMAIL AND INTERNET WHILE ON FOREIGN HOLIDAYS...
ONE COULD END UP WITH A BILL FOR HUNDREDS OR EVEN THOUSANDS OF POUNDS WHEN ONE GOT HOME. SO OF COURSE EVERYONE STARTED JUST SWITCHING OFF THEIR DATA ROAMING WHEN THEY TRAVELLED ABROAD.
THE MOBILE COMPANIES HAVE NOW GOT WISE TO THIS LOSS OF POTENTIAL REVENUE AND HAVE FINALLY INTRODUCED SENSIBLY-PRICED DATA ROAMING PACKAGES. IT'S TOTALLY CHANGED THE HOLIDAY EXPERIENCE FOR MANY OF US.
YES.
ONE CAN NO LONGER GET AWAY WITH THE EMAIL AUTO REPLY MESSAGE ABOUT "BEING AWAY AND ONLY HAVING LIMITED ACCESS TO EMAILS"...
SIGH WHICH MEANS ONE HAS NO READY-MADE EXCUSE TO IGNORE CLIENT MESSAGES WHEN ONE IS AWAY...
alex@alexcartoon.com

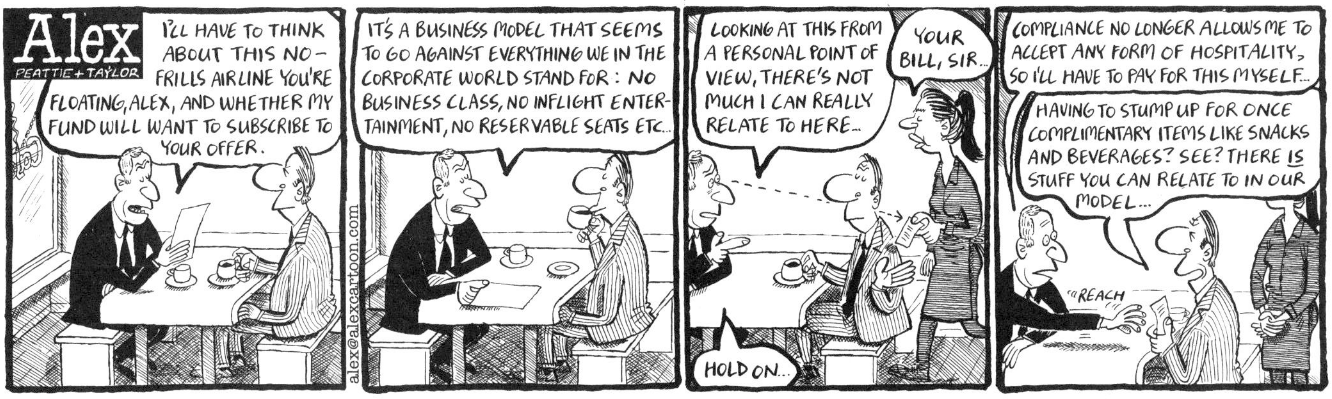
Alex
PEATTIE + TAYLOR
I'LL HAVE TO THINK ABOUT THIS NO-FRILLS AIRLINE YOU'RE FLOATING, ALEX, AND WHETHER MY FUND WILL WANT TO SUBSCRIBE TO YOUR OFFER.
IT'S A BUSINESS MODEL THAT SEEMS TO GO AGAINST EVERYTHING WE IN THE CORPORATE WORLD STAND FOR: NO BUSINESS CLASS, NO INFLIGHT ENTER-TAINMENT, NO RESERVABLE SEATS ETC...
LOOKING AT THIS FROM A PERSONAL POINT OF VIEW, THERE'S NOT MUCH I CAN REALLY RELATE TO HERE...
YOUR BILL, SIR...
HOLD ON...
COMPLIANCE NO LONGER ALLOWS ME TO ACCEPT ANY FORM OF HOSPITALITY, SO I'LL HAVE TO PAY FOR THIS MYSELF...
HAVING TO STUMP UP FOR ONCE COMPLIMENTARY ITEMS LIKE SNACKS AND BEVERAGES? SEE? THERE IS STUFF YOU CAN RELATE TO IN OUR MODEL...
REACH
alex@alexcartoon.com

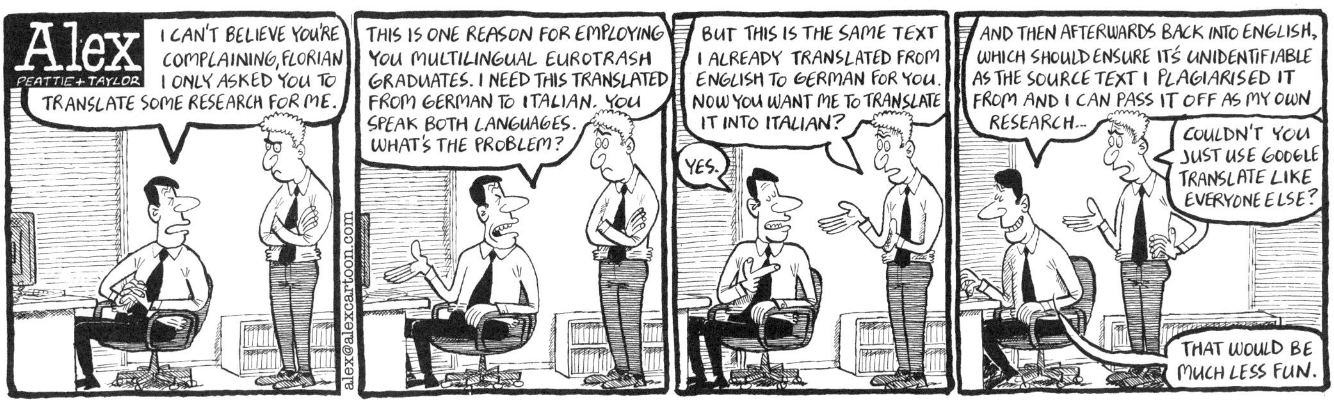
Alex
PEATTIE + TAYLOR
I CAN'T BELIEVE YOU'RE COMPLAINING, FLORIAN I ONLY ASKED YOU TO TRANSLATE SOME RESEARCH FOR ME.
THIS IS ONE REASON FOR EMPLOYING YOU MULTILINGUAL EUROTRASH GRADUATES. I NEED THIS TRANSLATED FROM GERMAN TO ITALIAN. YOU SPEAK BOTH LANGUAGES. WHAT'S THE PROBLEM?
BUT THIS IS THE SAME TEXT I ALREADY TRANSLATED FROM ENGLISH TO GERMAN FOR YOU. NOW YOU WANT ME TO TRANSLATE IT INTO ITALIAN?
YES.
AND THEN AFTERWARDS BACK INTO ENGLISH, WHICH SHOULD ENSURE IT'S UNIDENTIFIABLE AS THE SOURCE TEXT I PLAGIARISED IT FROM AND I CAN PASS IT OFF AS MY OWN RESEARCH...
COULDN'T YOU JUST USE GOOGLE TRANSLATE LIKE EVERYONE ELSE?
THAT WOULD BE MUCH LESS FUN.
alex@alexcartoon.com

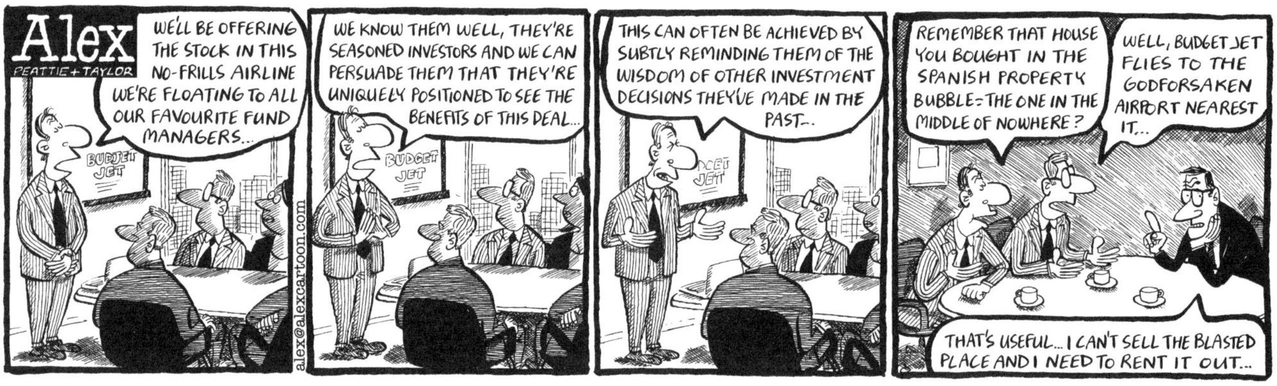
Alex
PEATTIE + TAYLOR
WE'LL BE OFFERING THE STOCK IN THIS NO-FRILLS AIRLINE WE'RE FLOATING TO ALL OUR FAVOURITE FUND MANAGERS...
BUDGET JET
alex@alexcartoon.com
WE KNOW THEM WELL, THEY'RE SEASONED INVESTORS AND WE CAN PERSUADE THEM THAT THEY'RE UNIQUELY POSITIONED TO SEE THE BENEFITS OF THIS DEAL...
BUDGET JET
THIS CAN OFTEN BE ACHIEVED BY SUBTLY REMINDING THEM OF THE WISDOM OF OTHER INVESTMENT DECISIONS THEY'VE MADE IN THE PAST...
REMEMBER THAT HOUSE YOU BOUGHT IN THE SPANISH PROPERTY BUBBLE - THE ONE IN THE MIDDLE OF NOWHERE?
WELL, BUDGET JET FLIES TO THE GODFORSAKEN AIRPORT NEAREST IT...
THAT'S USEFUL... I CAN'T SELL THE BLASTED PLACE AND I NEED TO RENT IT OUT...

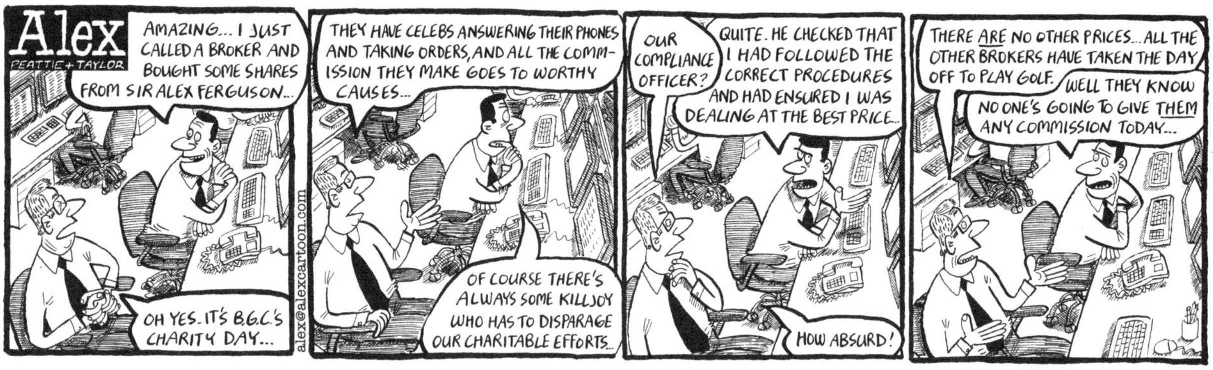
Alex
PEATTIE + TAYLOR
AMAZING... I JUST CALLED A BROKER AND BOUGHT SOME SHARES FROM SIR ALEX FERGUSON...
OH YES. IT'S B.G.C.'S CHARITY DAY...
alex@alexcartoon.com
THEY HAVE CELEBS ANSWERING THEIR PHONES AND TAKING ORDERS, AND ALL THE COMMISSION THEY MAKE GOES TO WORTHY CAUSES...
OF COURSE THERE'S ALWAYS SOME KILLJOY WHO HAS TO DISPARAGE OUR CHARITABLE EFFORTS...
OUR COMPLIANCE OFFICER?
QUITE. HE CHECKED THAT I HAD FOLLOWED THE CORRECT PROCEDURES AND HAD ENSURED I WAS DEALING AT THE BEST PRICE...
HOW ABSURD!
THERE ARE NO OTHER PRICES... ALL THE OTHER BROKERS HAVE TAKEN THE DAY OFF TO PLAY GOLF.
WELL THEY KNOW NO ONE'S GOING TO GIVE THEM ANY COMMISSION TODAY...

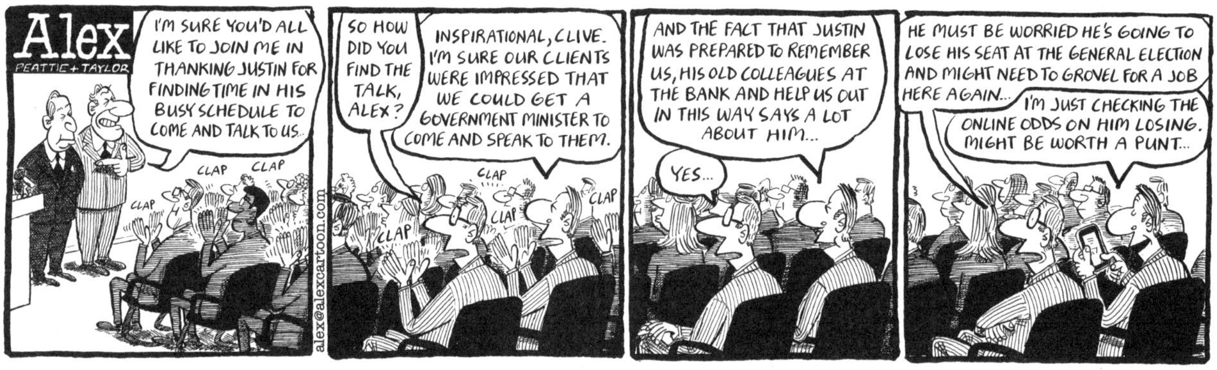
Alex
PEATTIE + TAYLOR
I'M SURE YOU'D ALL LIKE TO JOIN ME IN THANKING JUSTIN FOR FINDING TIME IN HIS BUSY SCHEDULE TO COME AND TALK TO US...
CLAP CLAP CLAP
alex@alexcartoon.com
SO HOW DID YOU FIND THE TALK, ALEX?
INSPIRATIONAL, CLIVE. I'M SURE OUR CLIENTS WERE IMPRESSED THAT WE COULD GET A GOVERNMENT MINISTER TO COME AND SPEAK TO THEM.
CLAP CLAP CLAP CLAP
AND THE FACT THAT JUSTIN WAS PREPARED TO REMEMBER US, HIS OLD COLLEAGUES AT THE BANK AND HELP US OUT IN THIS WAY SAYS A LOT ABOUT HIM...
YES...
HE MUST BE WORRIED HE'S GOING TO LOSE HIS SEAT AT THE GENERAL ELECTION AND MIGHT NEED TO GROVEL FOR A JOB HERE AGAIN...
I'M JUST CHECKING THE ONLINE ODDS ON HIM LOSING. MIGHT BE WORTH A PUNT...

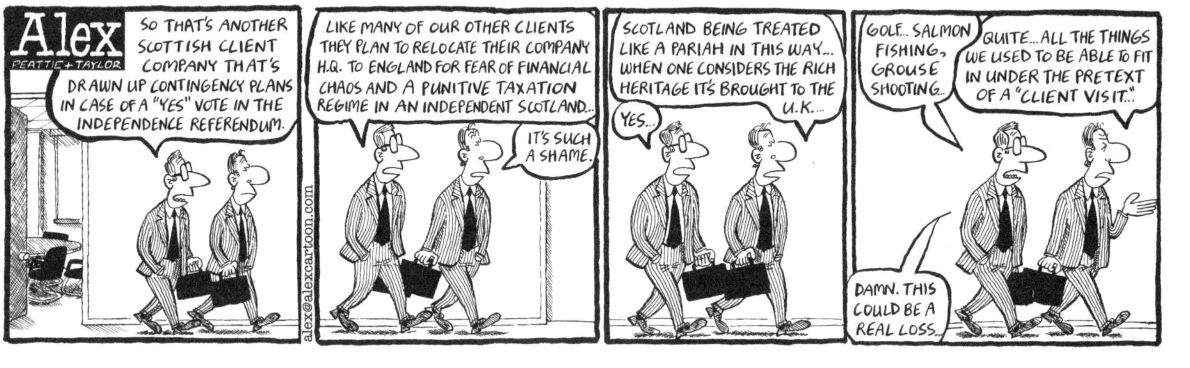
Alex
PEATTIE + TAYLOR
SO THAT'S ANOTHER SCOTTISH CLIENT COMPANY THAT'S DRAWN UP CONTINGENCY PLANS IN CASE OF A "YES" VOTE IN THE INDEPENDENCE REFERENDUM.
alex@alexcartoon.com
LIKE MANY OF OUR OTHER CLIENTS THEY PLAN TO RELOCATE THEIR COMPANY H.Q. TO ENGLAND FOR FEAR OF FINANCIAL CHAOS AND A PUNITIVE TAXATION REGIME IN AN INDEPENDENT SCOTLAND...
IT'S SUCH A SHAME.
SCOTLAND BEING TREATED LIKE A PARIAH IN THIS WAY... WHEN ONE CONSIDERS THE RICH HERITAGE IT'S BROUGHT TO THE U.K....
YES...
GOLF... SALMON FISHING, GROUSE SHOOTING...
QUITE... ALL THE THINGS WE USED TO BE ABLE TO FIT IN UNDER THE PRETEXT OF A "CLIENT VISIT."
DAMN. THIS COULD BE A REAL LOSS...

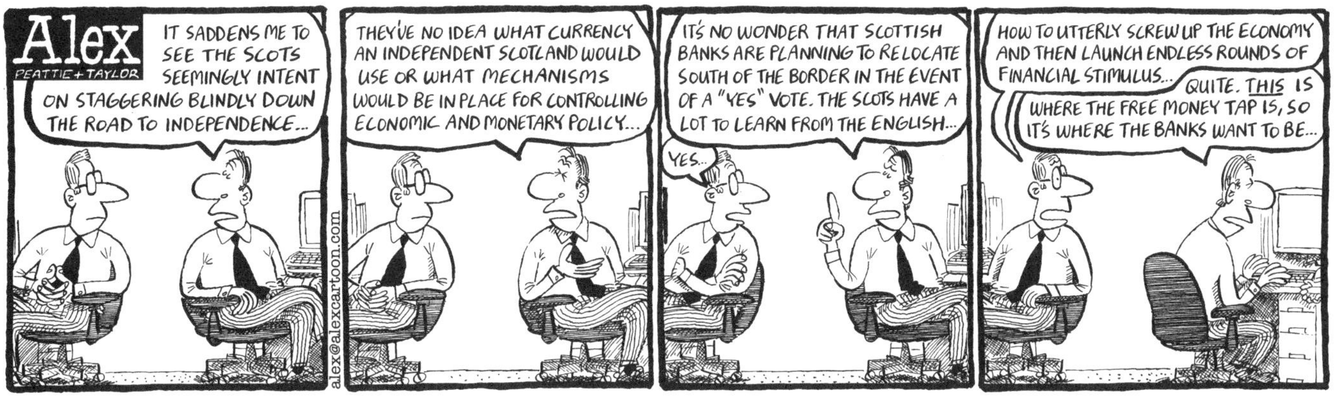
Alex
PEATTIE + TAYLOR
IT SADDENS ME TO SEE THE SCOTS SEEMINGLY INTENT ON STAGGERING BLINDLY DOWN THE ROAD TO INDEPENDENCE...
alex@alexcartoon.com
THEY'VE NO IDEA WHAT CURRENCY AN INDEPENDENT SCOTLAND WOULD USE OR WHAT MECHANISMS WOULD BE IN PLACE FOR CONTROLLING ECONOMIC AND MONETARY POLICY...
IT'S NO WONDER THAT SCOTTISH BANKS ARE PLANNING TO RELOCATE SOUTH OF THE BORDER IN THE EVENT OF A "YES" VOTE. THE SCOTS HAVE A LOT TO LEARN FROM THE ENGLISH...
YES...
HOW TO UTTERLY SCREW UP THE ECONOMY AND THEN LAUNCH ENDLESS ROUNDS OF FINANCIAL STIMULUS...
QUITE. THIS IS WHERE THE FREE MONEY TAP IS, SO IT'S WHERE THE BANKS WANT TO BE...

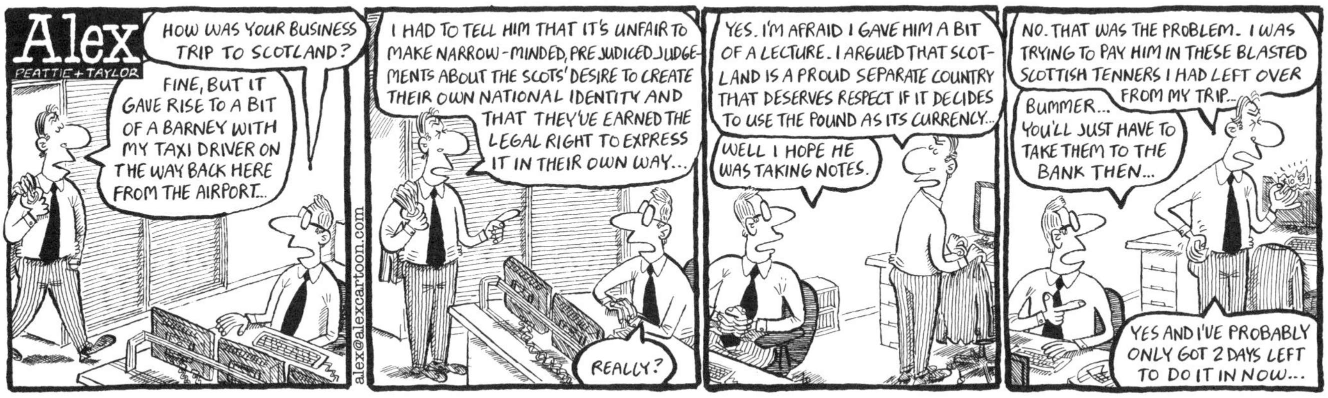
Alex
PEATTIE + TAYLOR
HOW WAS YOUR BUSINESS TRIP TO SCOTLAND?
FINE, BUT IT GAVE RISE TO A BIT OF A BARNEY WITH MY TAXI DRIVER ON THE WAY BACK HERE FROM THE AIRPORT...
alex@alexcartoon.com
I HAD TO TELL HIM THAT IT'S UNFAIR TO MAKE NARROW-MINDED, PREJUDICED JUDGEMENTS ABOUT THE SCOTS' DESIRE TO CREATE THEIR OWN NATIONAL IDENTITY AND THAT THEY'VE EARNED THE LEGAL RIGHT TO EXPRESS IT IN THEIR OWN WAY...
REALLY?
YES. I'M AFRAID I GAVE HIM A BIT OF A LECTURE. I ARGUED THAT SCOTLAND IS A PROUD SEPARATE COUNTRY THAT DESERVES RESPECT IF IT DECIDES TO USE THE POUND AS ITS CURRENCY...
WELL I HOPE HE WAS TAKING NOTES.
NO. THAT WAS THE PROBLEM. I WAS TRYING TO PAY HIM IN THESE BLASTED SCOTTISH TENNERS I HAD LEFT OVER FROM MY TRIP...
BUMMER... YOU'LL JUST HAVE TO TAKE THEM TO THE BANK THEN...
YES AND I'VE PROBABLY ONLY GOT 2 DAYS LEFT TO DO IT IN NOW...

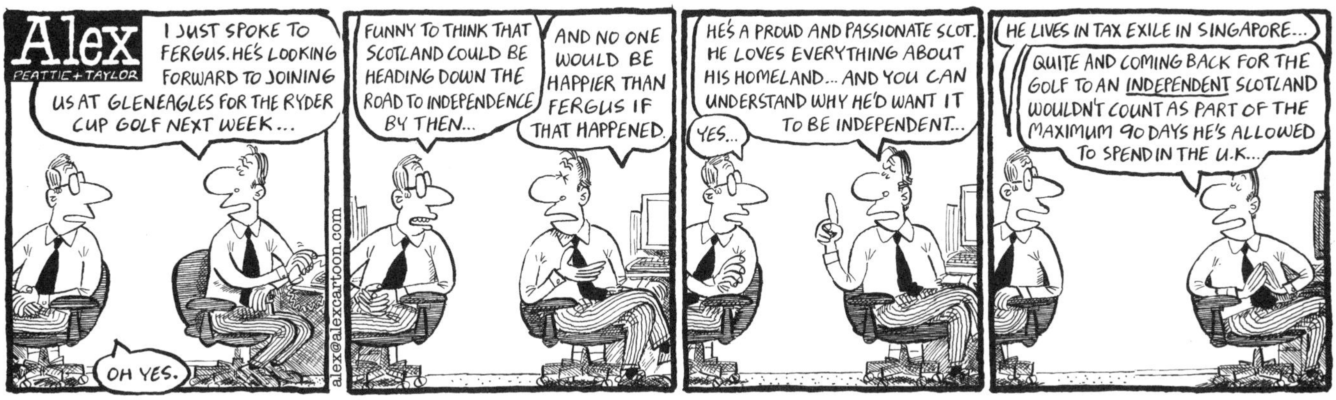
Alex
PEATTIE + TAYLOR
I JUST SPOKE TO FERGUS. HE'S LOOKING FORWARD TO JOINING US AT GLENEAGLES FOR THE RYDER CUP GOLF NEXT WEEK...
OH YES.
alex@alexcartoon.com
FUNNY TO THINK THAT SCOTLAND COULD BE HEADING DOWN THE ROAD TO INDEPENDENCE BY THEN...
AND NO ONE WOULD BE HAPPIER THAN FERGUS IF THAT HAPPENED.
HE'S A PROUD AND PASSIONATE SCOT. HE LOVES EVERYTHING ABOUT HIS HOMELAND... AND YOU CAN UNDERSTAND WHY HE'D WANT IT TO BE INDEPENDENT...
YES...
HE LIVES IN TAX EXILE IN SINGAPORE...
QUITE AND COMING BACK FOR THE GOLF TO AN INDEPENDENT SCOTLAND WOULDN'T COUNT AS PART OF THE MAXIMUM 90 DAYS HE'S ALLOWED TO SPEND IN THE U.K...

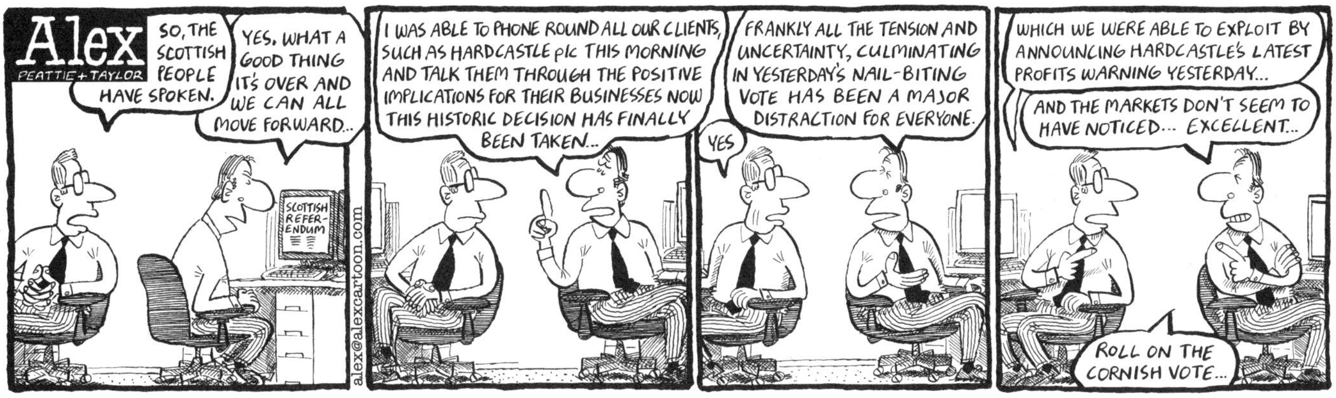
Alex
PEATTIE + TAYLOR
SO, THE SCOTTISH PEOPLE HAVE SPOKEN.
YES. WHAT A GOOD THING IT'S OVER AND WE CAN ALL MOVE FORWARD...
SCOTTISH REFERENDUM
alex@alexcartoon.com
I WAS ABLE TO PHONE ROUND ALL OUR CLIENTS, SUCH AS HARDCASTLE plc THIS MORNING AND TALK THEM THROUGH THE POSITIVE IMPLICATIONS FOR THEIR BUSINESSES NOW THIS HISTORIC DECISION HAS FINALLY BEEN TAKEN...
FRANKLY ALL THE TENSION AND UNCERTAINTY, CULMINATING IN YESTERDAY'S NAIL-BITING VOTE HAS BEEN A MAJOR DISTRACTION FOR EVERYONE.
YES
WHICH WE WERE ABLE TO EXPLOIT BY ANNOUNCING HARDCASTLE'S LATEST PROFITS WARNING YESTERDAY...
AND THE MARKETS DON'T SEEM TO HAVE NOTICED... EXCELLENT...
ROLL ON THE CORNISH VOTE...

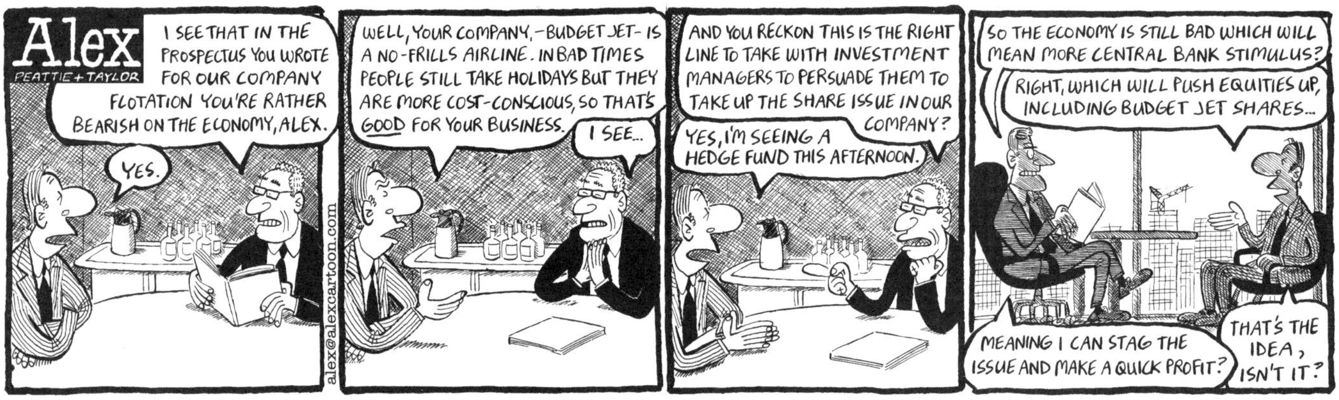
Alex
PEATTIE + TAYLOR
I SEE THAT IN THE PROSPECTUS YOU WROTE FOR OUR COMPANY FLOTATION YOU'RE RATHER BEARISH ON THE ECONOMY, ALEX.
YES.
alex@alexcartoon.com
WELL, YOUR COMPANY, - BUDGET JET - IS A NO-FRILLS AIRLINE. IN BAD TIMES PEOPLE STILL TAKE HOLIDAYS BUT THEY ARE MORE COST-CONSCIOUS, SO THAT'S GOOD FOR YOUR BUSINESS.
I SEE...
AND YOU RECKON THIS IS THE RIGHT LINE TO TAKE WITH INVESTMENT MANAGERS TO PERSUADE THEM TO TAKE UP THE SHARE ISSUE IN OUR COMPANY?
YES, I'M SEEING A HEDGE FUND THIS AFTERNOON.
SO THE ECONOMY IS STILL BAD WHICH WILL MEAN MORE CENTRAL BANK STIMULUS?
RIGHT, WHICH WILL PUSH EQUITIES UP, INCLUDING BUDGET JET SHARES...
MEANING I CAN STAG THE ISSUE AND MAKE A QUICK PROFIT?
THAT'S THE IDEA, ISN'T IT?

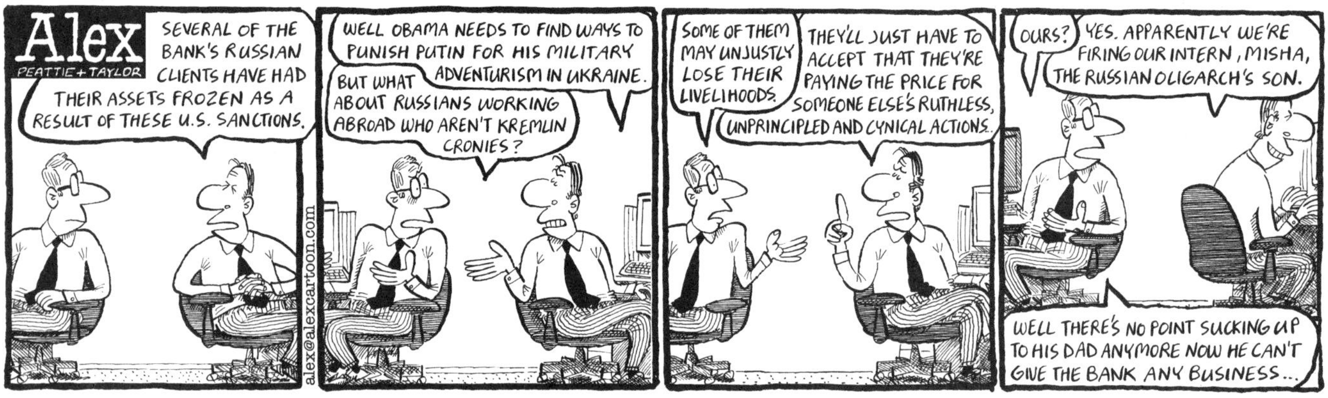
Alex
PEATTIE + TAYLOR
SEVERAL OF THE BANK'S RUSSIAN CLIENTS HAVE HAD THEIR ASSETS FROZEN AS A RESULT OF THESE U.S. SANCTIONS.
alex@alexcartoon.com
WELL OBAMA NEEDS TO FIND WAYS TO PUNISH PUTIN FOR HIS MILITARY ADVENTURISM IN UKRAINE.
BUT WHAT ABOUT RUSSIANS WORKING ABROAD WHO AREN'T KREMLIN CRONIES?
SOME OF THEM MAY UNJUSTLY LOSE THEIR LIVELIHOODS.
THEY'LL JUST HAVE TO ACCEPT THAT THEY'RE PAYING THE PRICE FOR SOMEONE ELSE'S RUTHLESS, UNPRINCIPLED AND CYNICAL ACTIONS.
OURS?
YES. APPARENTLY WE'RE FIRING OUR INTERN, MISHA, THE RUSSIAN OLIGARCH'S SON.
WELL THERE'S NO POINT SUCKING UP TO HIS DAD ANYMORE NOW HE CAN'T GIVE THE BANK ANY BUSINESS...

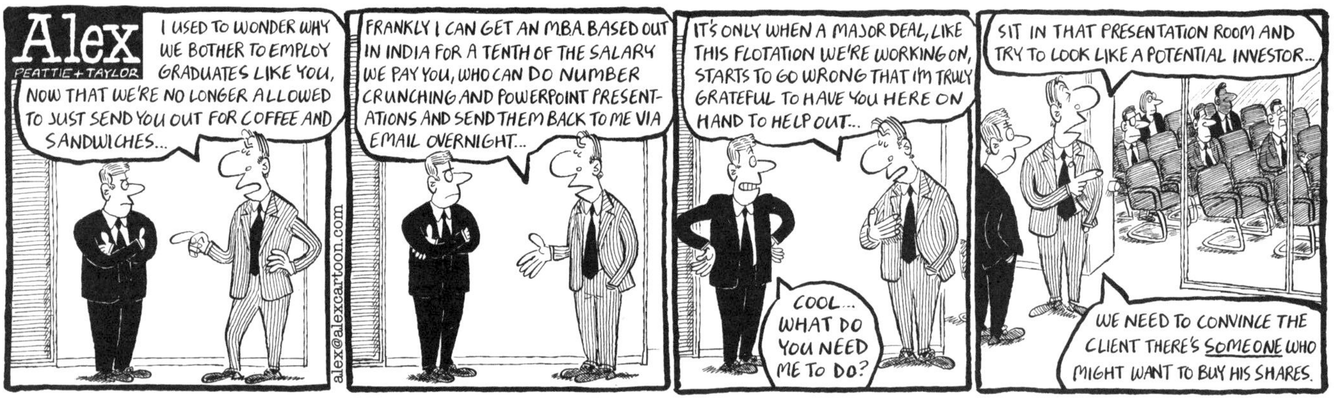
Alex
PEATTIE + TAYLOR
I USED TO WONDER WHY WE BOTHER TO EMPLOY GRADUATES LIKE YOU, NOW THAT WE'RE NO LONGER ALLOWED TO JUST SEND YOU OUT FOR COFFEE AND SANDWICHES...
alex@alexcartoon.com
FRANKLY I CAN GET AN M.B.A. BASED OUT IN INDIA FOR A TENTH OF THE SALARY WE PAY YOU, WHO CAN DO NUMBER CRUNCHING AND POWERPOINT PRESENTATIONS AND SEND THEM BACK TO ME VIA EMAIL OVERNIGHT...
IT'S ONLY WHEN A MAJOR DEAL, LIKE THIS FLOTATION WE'RE WORKING ON, STARTS TO GO WRONG THAT I'M TRULY GRATEFUL TO HAVE YOU HERE ON HAND TO HELP OUT...
COOL... WHAT DO YOU NEED ME TO DO?
SIT IN THAT PRESENTATION ROOM AND TRY TO LOOK LIKE A POTENTIAL INVESTOR...
WE NEED TO CONVINCE THE CLIENT THERE'S SOMEONE WHO MIGHT WANT TO BUY HIS SHARES.

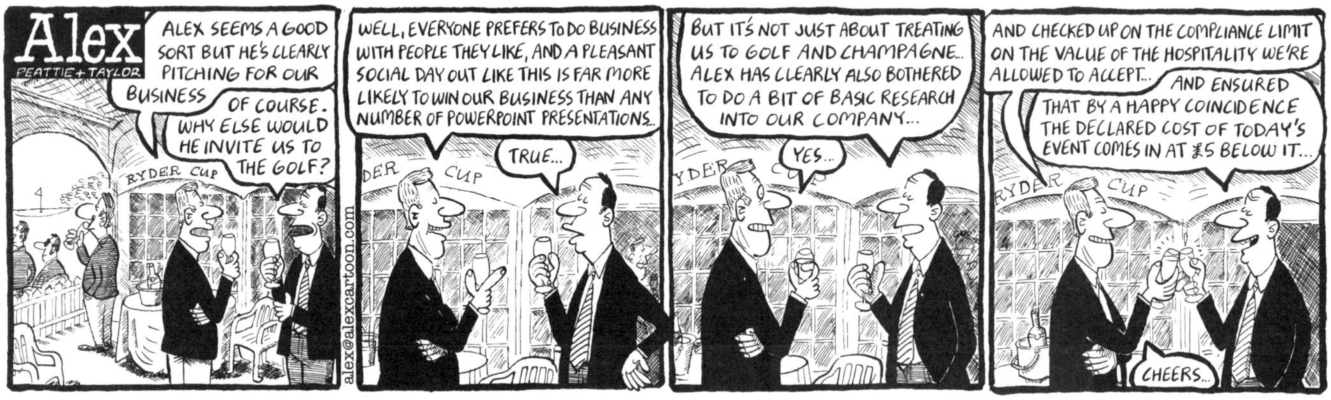
Alex
PEATTIE + TAYLOR
ALEX SEEMS A GOOD SORT BUT HE'S CLEARLY PITCHING FOR OUR BUSINESS
OF COURSE. WHY ELSE WOULD HE INVITE US TO THE GOLF?
RYDER CUP
alex@alexcartoon.com
WELL, EVERYONE PREFERS TO DO BUSINESS WITH PEOPLE THEY LIKE, AND A PLEASANT SOCIAL DAY OUT LIKE THIS IS FAR MORE LIKELY TO WIN OUR BUSINESS THAN ANY NUMBER OF POWERPOINT PRESENTATIONS...
TRUE...
BUT IT'S NOT JUST ABOUT TREATING US TO GOLF AND CHAMPAGNE... ALEX HAS CLEARLY ALSO BOTHERED TO DO A BIT OF BASIC RESEARCH INTO OUR COMPANY...
YES...
AND CHECKED UP ON THE COMPLIANCE LIMIT ON THE VALUE OF THE HOSPITALITY WE'RE ALLOWED TO ACCEPT...
AND ENSURED THAT BY A HAPPY COINCIDENCE THE DECLARED COST OF TODAY'S EVENT COMES IN AT £5 BELOW IT...
RYDER CUP
CHEERS...

Also available from Masterley Publishing

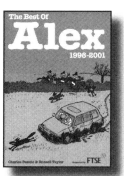

The Best Of
Alex
1998-2001

The Best of Alex 1998 - 2001
Boom to bust via the dotcom bubble.

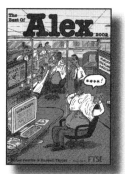

Alex

The Best of Alex 2002
Scandals rock the corporate world.

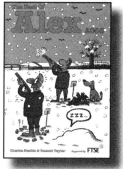

zzz..

The Best of Alex 2003
Alex gets made redundant.

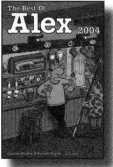

The Best Of
Alex
2004

The Best of Alex 2004
And gets his job back.

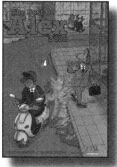

The Best of Alex 2005
Alex has problems with the French.

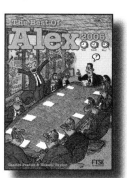

The Best Of
Alex

The Best of Alex 2006
Alex gets a new American boss.

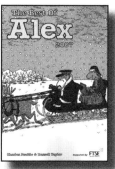

The Best Of
Alex

The Best of Alex 2007
Alex restructures Christmas.

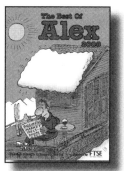

The Best Of
Alex

The Best of Alex 2008
The credit crunch bites.

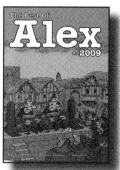

The Best Of
Alex
2009

The Best of Alex 2009
Global capitalism self-destructs.

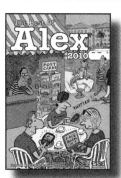

The Best Of
Alex
2010

The Best of Alex 2010
But somehow lurches on.

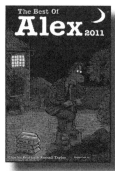

The Best Of
Alex
2011

The Best of Alex 2011
The financial crisis continues.

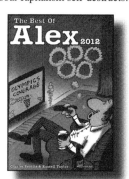

The Best Of
Alex
2012
OLYMPICS COVERAGE

The Best of Alex 2012
The Olympics come to London.

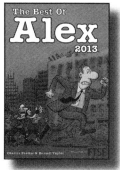

The Best Of
Alex
2013

The Best of Alex 2013
It's a wonderful crisis.

Celeb
The Original Gary Bloke From
PRIVATE EYE

Celeb
Wrinkly rockstar Gary Bloke.

All books are available from
www.alexcartoon.com
and are on Kindle.
Cartoon originals and prints are
also for sale.

tel: 020 8374 1225
email: alex@alexcartoon.com
twitter: @alexmasterley

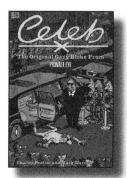